C000025357

# do-it-yourself
## essentials

# do-it-yourself
# essentials

**A complete step-by-step manual for every job around the home**

**painting • papering • tiling • flooring • woodwork • repairs • tools**

Consultant Editor
**John McGowan**

LORENZ BOOKS

This edition is published by Lorenz Books

Lorenz Books is an imprint of Anness Publishing Ltd
Hermes House, 88–89 Blackfriars Road, London SE1 8HA
tel. 020 7401 2077; fax 020 7633 9499; www.lorenzbooks.com; info@anness.com

© Anness Publishing Ltd 2004

UK agent: The Manning Partnership Ltd,
tel. 01225 478444; fax 01225 478440; sales@manning-partnership.co.uk
UK distributor: Grantham Book Services Ltd,
tel. 01476 541080; fax 01476 541061; orders@gbs.tbs-ltd.co.uk
North American agent/distributor: National Book Network,
tel. 301 459 3366; fax 301 429 5746; www.nbnbooks.com
Australian agent/distributor: Pan Macmillan Australia,
tel. 1300 135 113; fax 1300 135 103; customer.service@macmillan.com.au
New Zealand agent/distributor: David Bateman Ltd, tel. (09) 415 7664; fax (09) 415 8892

A CIP catalogue record for this book is available from the British Library.

Publisher: Joanna Lorenz
Managing Editor: Judith Simons
Project Editor: Felicity Forster
Text: Diane Carr, Sacha Cohen, Mike Collins,
Jonathan Edwards, David Holloway
and Mike Lawrence
Photographers: Peter Anderson, Colin Bowling,

Jonathan Buckley, Sarah Cuttle, Rodney Forte,
John Freeman, Andrea Jones, Debbie Patterson,
Lucinda Symons and Jo Whitworth
Illustrators: Peter Bull and Andrew Green
Editor: Ian Penberthy
Designer: Bill Mason
Production Controller: Darren Price

The author and publishers have made every effort to ensure that all instructions contained
within this book are accurate and safe, and cannot accept liability for any resulting injury,
damage or loss to persons or property, however it may arise. If in any doubt as to the correct
procedure to follow for any home improvements task, seek professional advice.

Previously published in 12 separate volumes, *Essential Tools*, *Painting Skills*, *Paint Finishes*,
*Papering Walls and Ceilings*, *Home Tiling*, *Laying Floors*, *Woodwork in the Home*, *Shelves and Storage*,
*Home Repairs*, *Home Insulation*, *Outdoor Projects* and *Outdoor Repairs*

1 3 5 7 9 10 8 6 4 2

# CONTENTS

# INTRODUCTION

I n recent years, the advent of the do-it-yourself superstore, the development of tools and materials aimed specifically at the amateur, and the proliferation of TV makeover shows have meant that when a job needs doing in or around the home, we no longer reach automatically for the telephone to call in a professional. First, we ask if we can do it ourselves, and more often than not, the answer is "yes". Today there are many home maintenance, repair and improvement tasks that can be done by anyone with a practical frame of mind. The major advantage, of course, is a saving in money, but that's not always the prime reason for tackling a job. There is an

ABOVE: Having the right tools will make any job go smoothly. As you learn new do-it-yourself skills, you can obtain the relevant special tools; look after them and they'll last a lifetime.

immense amount of satisfaction to be gained from learning a new skill and, most of all, being able to stamp your own personality on your home.

## SAFETY AND TOOLS

The most important requirements for any do-it-yourself job, even the simplest, are an understanding of the potential dangers involved and to take steps to protect not only yourself, but also others around you. Many tasks involve the use of sharp tools, electrical equipment or working from ladders, but there are other less obvious risks, such as injuries caused by lifting or dropping heavy objects, not to mention the mess caused by spilt paint. Always keep safety uppermost in your mind whatever you do.

ABOVE: Many do-it-yourself tasks require working at a height, and it is essential to create a safe working platform. An access tower such as this, which can be hired, is invaluable.

ABOVE: Paint is a versatile decorating material and need not always be applied in wide swathes of a single colour. Among the many decorative paint techniques is stencilling.

Ensuring you have the right tools for the job will be a big help in carrying out the task safely. Never scrimp when buying tools; get the best you can afford and look after them. They'll pay you back with a lifetime's service.

## PAINTING SKILLS

The most common of all do-it-yourself tasks is painting, and there is a wide range of paints and painting equipment available to suit the many different surfaces that can benefit from this decorative – and protective – treatment. Although modern materials and tools have made painting a simple procedure, it is still necessary to learn a variety of techniques to ensure the

best finish. By far the most crucial aspect is the correct and thorough preparation of the surface.

## PAINT FINISHES

One of the advantages of paint as a decorating material is that it can be used to create a wide variety of patterned effects on any surface, often with the simplest of techniques. Not only can you use ordinary paints in this way, but you can also buy special types that create unique finishes.

RIGHT: Decant paint into a paint pot rather than using it straight from the can. It will be easier to hold, and the paint in the can will not be exposed to air and form a skin.

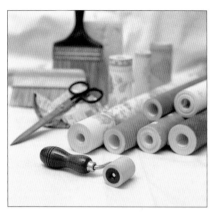

ABOVE: Papering walls and ceilings requires the minimum of special tools and is an effective way of producing a good-looking decorative finish. It's not as difficult as many think either.

### PAPERING WALLS AND CEILINGS

Applying patterned paper to walls and ceilings has been a popular decorative technique for centuries, and a common do-it-yourself task for decades. That said, many are put off by the thought of tripping over a bucket of paste, dealing

with long strips of sticky paper and hanging the paper so that it is free of wrinkles and bubbles and the pattern lines up. Consequently, papering has fallen out of favour a little in recent years. In truth, the job is not that difficult, provided you take care, and the results can be positively stunning.

There are so many patterned papers to choose from, ranging from the subtle to the flamboyant, with various degrees of wear resistance that they are suitable for every room in the house. They are definitely worth considering if you want to create a particular sense of luxury.

### HOME TILING

Ceramic tiles are a practical means of providing hard wearing, waterproof and easily cleaned surfaces on walls, floors and worktops, making them invaluable in kitchens and bathrooms. They can be decorative, too, offering many colours and patterns. Although tiling is a skilled job, there is no reason why

ABOVE: A freematch wallpaper or one with a continuous pattern, such as stripes, will not need an allowance for pattern matching.

ABOVE: A straight-match pattern has the same part of the pattern running down each side of the paper, making the cutting of drops simple.

ABOVE: An offset pattern has motifs staggered between drops, which must be taken into account when cutting and measuring the paper.

ABOVE: Ceramic tiles are ideal for creating waterproof splashbacks behind sinks and basins. The range of sizes, shapes, colours and patterns to choose from is huge.

ABOVE: Tiles need not always be used for practical purposes; they can make decorative features in their own right. Here, they have been used in place of a skirting (baseboard).

the amateur should not produce professional results, especially now that a variety of tiling tools have been designed with the do-it-yourselfer in mind.

## LAYING FLOORS

Of all the surfaces in the home, the floors offer the greatest variety of potential finishes and coverings. You can choose from wooden boards, blocks, panels and strips; sheet vinyl and linoleum; vinyl, linoleum and cork tiles; carpet and carpet tiles; and even rubber. Some of these materials are easier to lay than

others, but none is beyond the ability of anyone with a practical nature, and a few have actually been developed with the do-it-yourselfer in mind. As with so many do-it-yourself tasks, sound preparation is the key to success.

Another important consideration when selecting a floor covering is wear resistance – knowing what to use and where to use it is essential.

RIGHT: Wooden flooring comes in many forms and can make a really striking decorative feature. Here woodstrip flooring creates a sense of luxury.

## WOODWORK IN THE HOME

One of the commonest and most versatile materials found in the home is wood, which has many structural and decorative uses; in some cases, the entire house may be built on a wooden framework. Certainly, the doors and windows are likely to have wooden frames, and the rooms will have wooden skirtings (baseboards), architraves (trims) surrounding door openings and possibly wooden dado (chair) and picture rails. Then, of course, there is the furniture.

Wood has so many uses, that it won't be long before the do-it-yourselfer encounters a woodworking task. Fortunately, many jobs can be carried out with the minimum of skill and tools, and wood is a forgiving material to work with. As experience is gained, quite complex woodworking projects may be tackled with confidence.

ABOVE: As experience in working with wood grows, the do-it-yourselfer can take on simple projects such as this magazine rack.

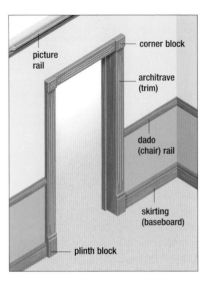

picture rail

corner block

architrave (trim)

dado (chair) rail

skirting (baseboard)

plinth block

ABOVE: The walls of a room can be finished off with a variety of wooden mouldings, which not only have a practical purpose (to protect vulnerable plaster), but also are decorative.

## SHELVES AND STORAGE

Without a variety of storage facilities, our homes would soon become cluttered with our belongings, but no two homes will have the same requirements for storage; it depends on individual circumstances. Consequently, tailoring storage to suit specific needs is essential to achieve the most efficient solution to the problem. Shelves, cupboards and drawers all have a role to play, and the combination of these must be determined in the light of what has to be stored.

In addition, storage can take the form of freestanding pieces of furniture or built-in structures that make the

ABOVE: Building your own storage allows you to tailor it exactly to your needs.

most of available space within the home. The latter can be made successfully by the do-it-yourselfer, as can pieces of furniture – normally purchased ready-made or in self-assembly form – provided care is taken.

ABOVE: If necessary, doors can be rehung to change the way they open, requiring the furniture to be repositioned.

## HOME REPAIRS

It makes sense to look after your home; it's likely to be the biggest investment you ever make. Regular maintenance will do much to keep it in good condition, but from time to time more ambitious repair work may be required. This may be necessary for a variety of reasons. For example, you may need to make good walls after removing old fittings, or cracks may have developed, internal woodwork may have become damaged, or floor boards or stairs may have become worn and loose. Moving items, such as doors and windows, also can suffer from wear and tear. All can be repaired effectively provided you have the correct tools and knowledge.

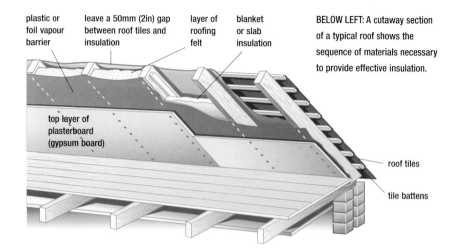

plastic or foil vapour barrier

leave a 50mm (2in) gap between roof tiles and insulation

layer of roofing felt

blanket or slab insulation

BELOW LEFT: A cutaway section of a typical roof shows the sequence of materials necessary to provide effective insulation.

top layer of plasterboard (gypsum board)

roof tiles

tile battens

## HOME INSULATION

These days, few can be unaware of the importance of keeping energy consumption in our homes to a minimum. Not only does this have a positive effect on our pockets, but also it prevents the wastage of fossil fuels, the burning of which contributes so much to global warming.

The efficient insulation of our homes is essential to prevent loss of heat, and a variety of techniques can be used to achieve this. The roof, walls, windows, doors and floors can all be protected. Fortunately, the methods are well within the scope of the do-it-yourselfer, providing even more savings.

Draughtproofing is essential as well, to prevent cold air from entering the house, but must be teamed with ventilation to allow moist air to escape, otherwise damage may be caused by condensation.

## OUTDOOR PROJECTS

One area where the do-it-yourselfer can make major savings by not having to employ professionals is in the garden. There's more to creating a beautiful garden than just filling it with plants; even the smallest will require a degree of structural work to give it form, which then is clothed and complemented by

ABOVE: A popular garden building task is to create a water feature, such as a pond. A preformed liner makes this simple, but requires accurate digging of the hole.

planting. You might need to erect fences, build walls, lay paving, construct decking and carry out a variety of other building tasks to achieve your ideal, but all are well within reach. Along the way you'll learn some useful new skills and gain a real sense of achievement.

ABOVE: Bricklaying is a useful skill, allowing the construction of attractive garden features.

## OUTDOOR REPAIRS

The biggest cause of maintenance and repair work around your home is the weather. Sun, rain, frost, snow and wind all combine to carry out a relentless attack on the exposed exterior structures. And once they begin to break down protective finishes or get into the raw materials, the rate of decay accelerates. Where the maintenance of your home's exterior is concerned, there is no room for complacency; immediate action is essential as soon as you notice a problem. Fortunately, much outdoor maintenance and repair work is well within the abilities of most do-it-yourselfers, although particular care is needed to ensure that the weather is kept at bay.

## IN THIS BOOK

In the following pages you'll find a comprehensive collection of do-it-yourself techniques that will allow you to tackle just about any job you come across in and around the home. If you study the step-by-step photography and follow the simple text, you'll soon learn the skills you need to give your home a personality that matches your own at a fraction of the cost of employing the professionals.

LEFT: Paving can be used to tie the various elements of a garden together and provide all-weather access to all parts. There are many types, including the traditional crazy paving.

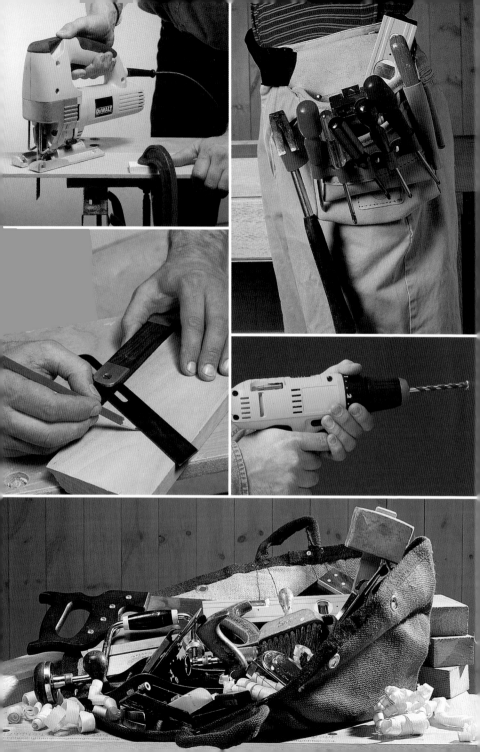

# SAFETY & TOOLS

- Safety & preparation
- Measuring, shaping & cutting tools
- Assembling tools
- Finishing tools

# INTRODUCTION

**M**ost people have a few basic tools in their home: a hammer, a screwdriver or two, perhaps a saw of some sort and a couple of paintbrushes – just about enough to tackle the occasional simple job or essential temporary repair. The more competent are likely to have a more comprehensive basic toolkit containing such items as a retractable tape measure, a craft knife, adjustable spanner, hand and tenon saws, a spirit (carpenter's) level, screwdrivers for different types of screw head, perhaps a chisel or two, pliers, pincers, an electric drill and a variety of decorating tools.

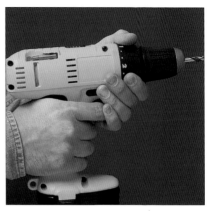

ABOVE: A power drill makes drilling easy. Buy one that offers a choice of speeds, has a chuck capacity of at least 12mm (½in), and a hammer facility if you intend drilling masonry.

ABOVE: Mounting your tools on a perforated tool board is a good idea. You will be able to find what you need quickly, and it will be obvious when a tool is missing. Buy one or make your own.

Some people, of course, are determined do-it-yourselfers who gain much pleasure and satisfaction from doing as many jobs as they can around the home. Others may even have a practical hobby, such as woodwork or model-making, that requires a dedicated home workshop containing a variety of complex and versatile machinery together with a range of specialized hand tools.

Whatever your level of interest in do-it-yourself, choosing the right tools for each job you tackle is essential. Attempting any task without the proper tools is a recipe for disaster.

ABOVE: Of all the do-it-yourself tasks, decorating is probably the most common. Painting requires brushes and rollers; papering requires tools such as scissors, a pasting brush and a seam roller.

Most toolkits grow organically as specific tools are added when the need arises. The tools featured in this chapter show a useful selection for starting your own projects.

LEFT: A belt sander is useful for heavy-duty shaping and sanding. As well as being hand-held, it can be inverted and secured in a woodworking vice.

When buying tools, always go for the best you can afford; the adage, "You get what you pay for," is particularly appropriate. Cheap tools may bend or break and are unlikely to last long; good-quality tools will last you a lifetime. If your budget is tight, it is best to buy several hand tools rather than one power tool. This has the benefit of improving your manual skills at an early stage, which will give encouraging results as well as increase the range of jobs you can undertake.

## USING PROFESSIONALS

As a do-it-yourself enthusiast, you have to be familiar with several trades, but it is often well worth employing a professional for structural work to save time and possibly money. There are many jobs, especially in plumbing and electrics, where professional help is welcome and indeed necessary. Professionals can also advise you in advance if your project is likely to fail for a reason you may not even have considered.

# SAFETY & PREPARATION

Even the simplest of do-it-yourself jobs carries with it some degree of risk, if only from the danger of upsetting a can of paint. Some tasks, however, have the potential to cause serious injury, so safety should be uppermost in your mind at all times. You must use the proper tools in the correct manner, wear appropriate clothing, ensure you have safe access to the job and take steps to protect others who may be at risk. Storing your tools correctly is important, too. Not only will they be ready for use when you need them, but they will also be protected from damage and from damaging other tools. Completing any do-it-yourself task can be immensely satisfying; the following pages show you how to do so in complete safety.

# AWARENESS AND CLOTHING

A complete book could be devoted to the subject of safety in the home, and there is a wide range of equipment designed to minimize our capacity for hurting ourselves. Nevertheless, there is one requirement that we cannot buy, without which all that equipment is virtually useless, namely concentration. This is particularly important when working alone.

ABOVE: Wear overalls to protect your clothes when painting, decorating or carrying out any dirty or dusty job. Disposable types are available for one-off jobs.

## AWARENESS

Concentration is essential when using any form of power tool, especially a saw, where one slip can mean the loss of a finger, or worse. The dangers of accidents involving electricity are well documented, as are those involving falls from ladders, spillages of toxic materials, and burns and injuries caused by contact with fire or abrasive surfaces. In almost every case, there is a loss of concentration, coupled with poor work practices and inadequate protective clothing or equipment. So, although the items shown here are all useful, concentrating on what you are doing is the best advice to prevent accidents from occurring.

## CLOTHING

Overalls are a good investment because they not only protect clothing, but are also designed to be close-fitting to prevent accidental contact with moving machinery. Industrial gloves provide protection against cuts and bruises when doing rough jobs, such as fencing and garden work. Safety boots should be worn when lifting heavy objects or when the use of machinery is involved.

Knee pads are necessary for comfort when carrying out any job that requires a lot of kneeling. They will also protect the wearer from injury if a nail or similar projection is knelt on accidentally. Finally, a bump cap will protect the head from minor injuries, but is not so cumbersome as the hard hat required on building sites.

ABOVE: A pair of thick gloves will be essential when handling rough materials such as sawn wood or sharp objects such as broken glass. Make sure they fit well.

ABOVE: If you have to do a job that involves a lot of kneeling, rubber knee pads will be invaluable. They provide comfort and protection from sharp projections such as nail heads.

ABOVE: Safety boots with steel toe caps will protect your feet from injury when working with heavy items such as large sections of wood, bricks and concrete blocks.

ABOVE: When working in situations where you may hit your head accidentally, the bump cap will provide protection without being as cumbersome as a conventional hard hat.

# SAFETY EQUIPMENT

Make sure you have the appropriate safety equipment to hand when carrying out do-it-yourself tasks, and always use it. Doing so can prevent nasty accidents and serious injury.

### AIRBORNE DANGERS

When you are working with wood, the most common airborne danger is dust, mainly from sawing and sanding. This can do long-term damage to the lungs. Many do-it-yourself enthusiasts do not do enough work to warrant a workshop dust extractor, but it would be worth considering if funds allowed. Such a

BELOW: Typical personal safety equipment – first aid kit, impact-resistant safety spectacles, ear protectors, two types of dust mask and sturdy industrial-type gloves.

### KEEPING IN TOUCH

Perhaps the most basic advice is never to work alone with machinery and, if it is possible, always have a friend or colleague nearby to help. If there is no telephone, having a mobile (cell) phone in the workshop is useful.

device can be wall-mounted or portable. In the latter case, it can be moved around the house or workshop to suit any tool in use.

A simple face mask, however, will offer adequate protection for occasional jobs. These can also be purchased for protection against fumes, such as from solvents, which can be very harmful. Dust, of course,

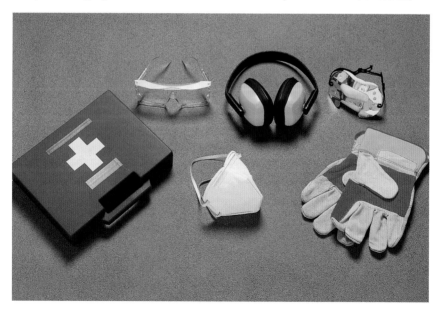

also affects the eyes, so it is worth investing in a pair of impact-resistant goggles, which will protect the wearer from both fine dust and flying debris. Full facial protection is available as a powered respirator for those working in dusty conditions over long periods.

Excessive noise is another airborne pollutant that can be dangerous over a long period. Power tools, particularly woodworking machinery such as planers and circular saws, are major culprits. Earplugs are the simplest solution and can be left in the ears over a long period. If you need to be able to hear between short bouts of working, ear protectors are the answer. These can be worn in conjunction with other facial protection quite easily.

## FIRST AID

Keeping a basic first aid kit is a common and wise precaution even before any do-it-yourself work is envisaged. It should always be prominently displayed for people unfamiliar with your workshop.

You can buy a home first aid kit that will contain all the necessary items to cope with minor injuries, or you can assemble your own, keeping it in a plastic sandwich box with an airtight lid, which should be clearly marked. You should include items such as bandages, plasters, wound dressings, antiseptic cream, eye pads, scissors, tweezers and safety pins. If you have cause to use the kit, replace the items you have removed as soon as possible.

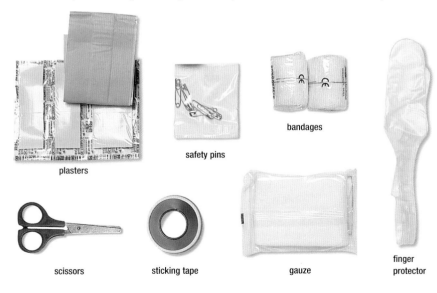

bandages

safety pins

plasters

scissors

sticking tape

gauze

finger protector

**ABOVE: Some of the basic items found in a first aid kit.**

# ELECTRICAL AND FIRE SAFETY

If used incorrectly, the dangers of electrical equipment can be life threatening, and the dangers of fire are obvious. Always treat the former with respect, and take sensible precautions against the latter.

## ELECTRICAL SAFETY

Some tools have removable switches that allow the user to immobilize them and prevent any unauthorized use. Provisions for the use of padlocks are also common on machinery, and it is wise to buy tools with such facilities.

To safeguard against electrocution, which can occur if the flex (power cord) is faulty or is cut accidentally, the ideal precaution is a residual current device (RCD). This is simply plugged into the main supply socket (electrical outlet) before the flex and will give complete protection to the user. Extension leads can be purchased with automatic safety cutouts and insulated sockets, and are ideal for outside and inside work.

The danger of electrocution or damage caused by accidentally drilling into an existing cable or pipe can be largely prevented by using an electronic pipe and cable detector, which will locate and differentiate between metal pipes, wooden studs and live wires through plaster and concrete to a depth of approximately 50mm (2in). These are not too expensive and will be very useful around the home.

## FIRE SAFETY

The danger of fire is ever-present in both the home and workshop, so a fire extinguisher (possibly two or three) is necessary for every do-it-yourself enthusiast. It should be wall-mounted in plain view and serviced regularly.

**LEFT: A simple circuit breaker can save a life by cutting off the power to faulty equipment.**

**ABOVE: A fire extinguisher is absolutely essential in the workshop or at home. Make sure the one you have is adequate for the size and type of your workshop, and the type of fire source.**

# LADDER SAFETY

Steps and ladders can be hazardous, so make sure they are in good condition. Accessories include a roof hook, which slips over the ridge for safety; a ladder stay, which spreads the weight of the ladder across a vertical surface, such as a wall, to prevent slippage; and a standing platform, which is used to provide a more comfortable and safer surface to stand on. The last often has a ribbed rubber surface and can be attached to the rungs of almost all ladders. Even more stable is a movable workstation or a board or staging slung between two pairs of steps or trestles. These can often be used with a safety rail, which prevents the operator from falling even if a slip occurs.

ABOVE: A ladder platform will provide a firm footing, especially if heavy footwear is worn.

ABOVE: A movable workstation simplifies the process of working at a height.

## TIPS

• Never overreach when working on steps or a ladder; climb down and reposition it.
• Never allow children or pets into areas where power tools or strong solvents are being used.
• Do not work when you are overtired. This causes lapses in concentration, which can lead to silly and/or dangerous mistakes being made.
• Keep the work environment tidy. Flexes (power cords) should not be walked on or coiled up tightly, because it damages them internally. Moreover, trailing flexes can be a trip hazard, and long extension leads can be prone to overheating.

ABOVE: Platforms supported by trestles offer a safe means of painting from a height.

# WORKBENCHES AND VICES

A solid and stable surface is essential for producing good work, and serious thought should be given to this by the enthusiast. A good bench need not be too expensive, nor too pretty; the prime requirements are sturdy construction, a flat-top surface and at least one good vice somewhere on the front of the bench. You can make your own or buy one, but beware of cheap benches that may not be up to the job. Suppliers and auctions of used industrial equipment are good sources.

## PORTABLE WORKBENCHES

By far the most popular form of portable support is the foldaway workbench. This is really convenient to use, both in the workshop, in the home and outdoors. It has the ingenious feature of a bench top constructed in two halves, which is capable of acting as a vice. It is handy for holding awkward shapes, such as pipes and large dowels.

## VICES

Your main workshop vice should be heavy and sturdy. It is normally screwed to the bench, close to one of the legs. If you intend doing a lot of woodworking, buy one with a quick-release action that allows you to open and close the jaws quickly, using the handle for final adjustments. You should certainly be able to fit false wooden jaws to prevent damage to the material you are working with.

ABOVE: Lightweight plastic sawhorses can be useful if you are undertaking small jobs.

ABOVE: A portable foldaway workbench with adjustable bench top.

ABOVE: Wooden sawhorses come in pairs and are often home-made.

Additional ways of protecting the work in the vice take the form of magnetic vice jaws faced with cork, rubber or aluminium, which fit inside the main jaws of the steel bench vice.

Another useful and portable addition to the bench is the swivelling bench-top vice. This can be fitted easily and removed very quickly, usually by means of a screw clamp. It is particularly handy for holding small pieces of work in awkward positions, when carving, for example. However, it is too light in construction to support work that is to be struck with any force.

The mitre clamp can also be considered as a bench vice of sorts and is useful for holding any assemblies that require clamping at 45 degrees, such as picture and mirror frames. Good quality examples are made from metal, since plastic will tend to flex when pressure is applied.

carpenter's vice

vice jaws faced with rubber

swivelling bench-top vice

mitre clamp

## TIPS

• Spend time adjusting your workbench to the exact height that suits you. An incorrect height can prove to be very tiring and is not good for your back. Never shorten the legs of a bench if it is too high; work off a duckboard if necessary.
• Always buy the best-quality vice you can afford; second-hand ones can be particularly good value.

# TOOL STORAGE

Tidy and effective storage of your tools pays off in many ways. Properly stored tools will be protected from the atmosphere and will not rust or discolour. The sharp cutting edges of saws and chisels will be protected from damage, as will the potential user's fingers. Moreover, tools will always be easily found near at hand when they are needed.

### STORAGE

Efficient storage saves bench and floor space for other uses, and tools will be more easily located, saving time and frustration. It is well worth taking the trouble to devise and even make your own storage facilities. There are plenty of benches, cabinets, racks, clips and tool rolls on the market so that you can equip your workshop with exactly what you need. Remember, too, that storage for tools often needs to be portable, so tool pouches and carrying bags also need to be part of the overall picture.

metal
toolbox

drill bit roll

### PORTABLE STORAGE

The traditional carpenter's tool bag can still be obtained. Made from heavy canvas, it has two carrying handles and brass eyelets for closing.

Compact, compartmentalized plastic or metal toolboxes with drawers, carrying handles and safety locks are another option for carrying tools from one job to another.

A leather tool pouch can be worn around the waist and has loops and pockets for tools as well as screws and nails. Various sizes and styles are available. They are ideal for use on projects that require you to keep moving about.

Drill bits and chisels should always be carried in a tool roll with their tips covered for protection. Some chisels are provided with individual plastic blade caps, and many saws are sold with a plastic blade guard to protect the teeth when not in use. Always make sure that these are fitted correctly.

ABOVE: A tool pouch worn around the waist is ideal for carrying tools when working in different parts of the home.

## STATIC STORAGE

The most important static storage space is that below the workbench top, and often this takes the form of cabinets or drawers. A useful device is a large tilting drawer, which can easily be made and is ideal for storing tools that are in frequent use.

Wall-mounted cabinets with sliding doors are really practical in the workshop. The sliding doors allow them to be sited in confined areas and make it impossible to hit your head on them when they are open, which is especially important above the bench.

Shelving units come in a variety of materials, shapes and sizes, and most can be added to as the need arises.

The tool board has the advantage of not only displaying the tools, but also making it obvious when a tool has not been replaced. To make one, arrange the tools on a flat board and draw around them with a marker pen. Then fit hooks, pegs or clips as necessary.

ABOVE: Specifically made in transparent plastics for easy identification of the contents, storage drawers for screws, nails, clips and a host of other small items are a must.

ABOVE: Use a length of wood to make your own storage block to keep your drill bits tidy.

### MAKING A TOOL BOARD

When making a tool board, remember to leave space around each tool so that it can be lifted clear when the board is on the wall. Draw around the tools with a felt-tipped pen to indicate their positions. Hammer in nails or hooks that will hold them in place. Wall hooks will hold larger items, such as saws. Alternatively, you can buy a tool board made from perforated plywood from a local builder's merchant.

# MEASURING, SHAPING & CUTTING TOOLS

One of the most crucial skills for do-it-yourself work is the ability to measure accurately. The quality of much of the work you undertake will rely on that skill, so it is worth taking time and care when measuring and marking out. Shaping wood is a task required for many projects, and knowing how to use a plane will pay dividends. Chisels are also used for this purpose, as well as making cut-outs. To be effective, both tools must be kept sharp. A good toolkit will also include a variety of saws and knives; make sure you know which to use and when. Drilling holes is something you will need to do on a regular basis, and there are many types of drill and drill bit to choose from.

# MEASURING TOOLS

Accurate measuring is a very basic, but essential, skill for the do-it-yourself enthusiast to master. Time spent on perfecting measuring is never wasted. The golden rule is to measure twice and cut once. Buy good-quality tools – poor measuring and marking devices can lose their accuracy very quickly and spoil your work.

## HOW TO MEASURE

There are dozens of types of flat, rigid rule for marking out, most of which are calibrated in both metric and imperial units. They may be wood or steel, although some cheaper varieties are plastic. Where curves are involved, greater accuracy will be achieved with a flexible steel rule or even a retractable steel tape, which can be bent around the work.

The T-square is useful for marking out large sheets of manufactured board such as plywood, MDF (medium-density fiberboard) and blockboard. Remember, however, that it must be used on a perfectly straight edge to produce a 90-degree line across the sheet. Any small discrepancy in the edge will be greatly magnified across the sheet width and even more so along the length.

The combination square incorporates a number of functions in one tool, and is used for both measuring and marking out. It comprises a graduated steel rule that slides within a shaped body. A clamping screw permits the rule to be secured at any point along its length, while the body itself has flat edges that allow guidelines to be marked at 90 and 45 degrees to a straight surface. Many combination squares also feature a spirit bubble, allowing the tool to be used for checking horizontals.

## FITTING PRE-MADE STRUCTURES

When fitting previously assembled cabinets or shelving to a wall, the most accurate method is to mark out the wall using a spirit (carpenter's) level. These are available in long and short lengths. Do not rely on existing lines, such as architraves (trims) around doors, picture rails or skirtings (baseboards), as these may not be truly horizontal.

Transferring measurements from one point to another can also be done with a straightedge, and although this is very similar to a heavy steel rule, the bevelled edge gives it the added advantage of being very easy to cut or mark against. Straightedges often have handles, making them easy to hold in place.

## CONVERTING MEASUREMENTS

On small work in particular, never be tempted to convert from metric to imperial or vice versa. Some quite large errors can occur with standard conversions. Always work in the unit specified.

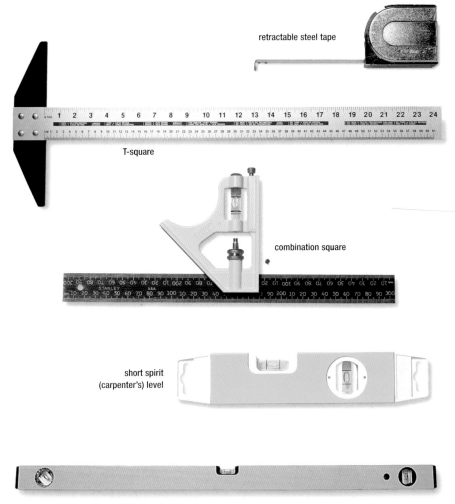

retractable steel tape

T-square

combination square

short spirit
(carpenter's) level

long spirit (carpenter's) level

straightedge

# MARKING-OUT TOOLS

Another essential do-it-yourself skill is marking out, which can make or mar many projects.

Where you need to mark off a series of equal spacings, simply set a pair of dividers or callipers to the correct distance, using a flat wooden or steel rule, and step off the divisions.

You can mark out your workpiece for cutting and/or shaping with a pencil or a marking knife. The latter is particularly useful for fine work. An ordinary pencil is quite acceptable, but a flat carpenter's pencil will have a chisel-shaped tip when sharpened, making for more accurate marking.

## MARKING JOINTS

Marking joints needs a fair degree of accuracy, so the first thing to ascertain is that your prepared wood is flat and square, which is done with a combination square or a try square. Either of these tools should be slid down the length of the wood to be cut, thus ensuring its uniformity and squareness.

For marking out a mortise, use a mortise gauge and set the points to the width of the chisel you intend to use to cut the mortise, not from a rule. This is far more accurate, as well as being much more convenient.

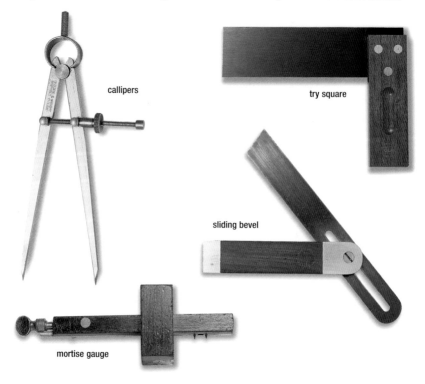

callipers

try square

sliding bevel

mortise gauge

A sliding bevel is a tool used for marking angles on to a square piece of wood. It can be adjusted to any angle, and is especially useful if the angles are to be repeated, such as when setting out treads for a staircase.

A good alternative for marking frequently repeated angles, such as on a staircase, is to make up a jig or template that can be laid on to the stringer (the long diagonal part of the staircase) and mark the treads accordingly. You should be able to buy such templates from most professional workshops. They are available in hardboard and Perspex.

ABOVE: Use a try square for marking right angles. Keep it clean and make sure the blade is not loose. It can be used with a pencil or a marking knife as required.

## THE RIGHT MARKER

Use a carpenter's pencil, ordinary pencil or chinagraph for setting out measurements. Never use a magic marker or a ballpoint pen, since the marks are virtually impossible to remove and will spoil your work. Whichever marking tool you choose, keep it sharp to ensure accuracy.

ABOVE: Use a mortise gauge to scribe directly on to the wood. The two steel pins of the tool are independently adjustable on accurate brass slides, while the sliding stock runs against the face of the work. There may be a single pin on the opposite side for marking a scribed line, used to gauge thickness.

# PLANES

The most commonly used varieties of plane are the jack plane for flattening the faces and edges of boards, and the smoothing plane for fine finishing. Good-quality examples are sufficiently weighty to avoid "chatter", which occurs when the plane skips over the surface of the wood without cutting properly. A block plane is often used for planing end grain because its blade is set at a low angle that severs the wood fibres cleanly.

block plane

smoothing plane

jack plane

### PLANING TECHNIQUE

Body weight plays a large part in planing technique. Position your body with your hips and shoulders in line with the plane, and your feet spaced apart.

At the beginning of the stroke, apply pressure to the front handle of the plane, switching to a general downward pressure during the middle of the stroke, and finish off by applying most of the pressure to the back of the plane at the end of the board.

### PLANING END GRAIN AND BOARDS

Plane end grain and boards using a block plane. To avoid splitting the ends of the wood, work from each side toward the middle. A useful technique for planing wide boards is to work diagonally, or even at right angles, across the grain. This method will remove material efficiently. To finish, it will be necessary to make fine cuts with the grain to obtain a smooth surface. Run your fingers lightly over the surface to identify any unevenness that needs removing.

## TIPS

• Cheap planes often serve to blunt enthusiasm by poor performance. Always buy the best you can afford and keep them sharp.
• Check for sharpness and adjustment each time a plane is used – and make sure the wood to be planed is held firmly.

## STARTING TO PLANE

**1** The correct body position helps to achieve the desired result. Keep your hips and shoulders parallel to the direction in which you are planing, with your weight balanced on both feet.

**2** Apply pressure to the front of the plane as you begin the stroke, equal pressure to front and back in the middle of the stroke, and pressure on the back of the plane at the end of the stroke.

**3** When planing a narrow edge, make sure you keep the plane centralized to ensure an even cut. To do this, you can tuck your fingers under the sole plate as a guide.

**4** If you have identical edges to plane, clamp them together and work on both at once. Check from time to time that you are planing them square with the aid of a try square.

# POWER PLANERS

If you need to remove large amounts of wood, a power planer is very useful. An electric planer should be handled with great care as it is extremely easy to remove too much wood and ruin the work. The depth of cut in one pass ranges from 1.5 to 5mm ($\frac{1}{16}$ to $\frac{3}{16}$in) on more powerful models; 3mm ($\frac{1}{8}$in) is quite adequate for most general purposes.

Look for a model that offers a dust bag to collect the copious shavings produced. Tungsten-carbide-tipped (TCT) disposable blades are best when working with manufactured boards such as MDF (medium-density fiberboard) and plywood.

**power planer**

The cutter block, in which the blades are mounted, rotates at very high speed and should be treated with great respect. Always hold the tool with both hands and keep it moving so that it does not cut for too long in one spot.

Although the power planer is very fast, the hand-held version rarely gives the quality of finish that can be achieved with a well-set and sharpened bench plane. Unless you intend doing a lot of work where a power planer will be needed, you may find it less expensive to hire one when you require it. Most tool hirers will have them.

ABOVE: Use two hands to plane end grain with a power planer to ensure complete control.

ABOVE: Plane across wide boards with a power planer to give quick results.

## POWER PLANING TECHNIQUES

It is very important to hold a power planer with both hands, as it can be a very aggressive tool. Make sure that the flex (power cord) is well out of the way so that it does not impede the work.

Keep your hands well away from the blades and wait for the cutter block to stop spinning before putting the tool down on the workbench.

Check for sharpness and adjustment each time you use a power planer, and make sure the wood to be planed is held firmly in a vice or clamped down.

As with the hand plane, an electric planer can also be used across the grain of wide boards for quick results, provided that final finishing is with the grain.

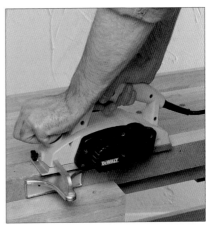

1 The depth of cut is controlled by the rotary knob at the front, which doubles as a handle. Push down firmly and evenly on the machine to remove a constant thickness of stock in one pass. The side fence keeps the sole plate square to the edge.

2 Most planers have a V-groove machined in the bottom of the sole plate to permit chamfering. Locate the groove on the square edge of the work to position the cutters at 45 degrees to each adjoining face. The work is in a jig to hold it in position.

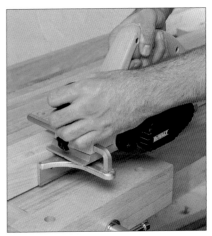

3 Some models allow you to form rebates (rabbets) up to 25mm (1in) deep, using the side fence to control the rebate width. The design of the planer body dictates the maximum rebate capacity, so always check that the tool you buy meets your needs.

# CHISELS

**E**ach with its own specific use, chisels come in a variety of shapes and sizes. For jobs around the home, only three basic types are required. Most commonly used is the firmer chisel, which is a compromise between a mortise chisel and a bevel-edged chisel. It can be regarded as a general-purpose tool, having a strong blade of rectangular section designed for medium/heavy work. Most home woodworkers will find blade widths of 6mm (¼in), 12mm (½in), 19mm (¾in) and 25mm (1in) sufficient for their needs.

### SPECIAL-PURPOSE CHISELS

Bevel-edged chisels have thinner blades than firmer chisels. The tops of the blades are bevelled along their length to allow better access into small recesses and corners, and to permit fine slicing cuts to be made in the wood.

The mortise chisel is a sturdy tool with a lot of steel just below the handle. It is used for chopping deep mortises across the grain, so it has to be able to withstand blows from a heavy mallet. For this reason, a wooden-handled mortise chisel may have a metal band around the top of the handle to prevent it from splitting. The thickness of the steel blade also allows it to be used as a lever for cleaning the waste from the mortise.

Many new chisels have shatter-resistant polypropylene handles that can be struck with a mallet, or even a hammer, without damage since the material is virtually unbreakable.

### TIPS

• Always make sure your chisels are sharp. A blunt tool needs more pressure to force it through the work and is more likely to slip, possibly causing an accident.
• Do not leave chisels lying where the blades can touch metal objects. Fit them with blade guards or keep them in a cloth.

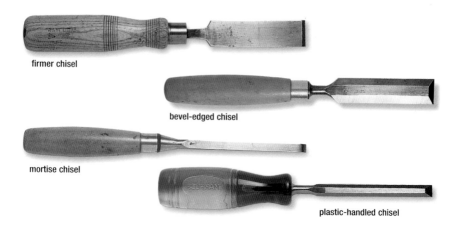

firmer chisel

bevel-edged chisel

mortise chisel

plastic-handled chisel

## CHISELLING TECHNIQUES

Always aim to remove as much waste wood as possible from the cut before using the chisel. For example, remove the waste with a saw before cleaning up with a chisel or, when cutting a mortise, drill out the waste and use the chisel to clean and square-up the sides.

When using a router to cut slots and rebates (rabbets), square the ends by hand with a chisel.

Remember to cut away from the marked line when chiselling so that any splitting will occur in the waste wood, and always cut away from yourself to avoid injury. Work patiently and never be tempted to make cuts that are too large. The chisel should be pushed or struck with one hand while being guided with the other.

## HORIZONTAL PARING

1 Horizontal paring, working from both sides to the middle, prevents "break out" and results in clean work using less pressure.

2 Chamfer an edge, first using the chisel with the bevel down to remove most of the waste. Then make the finishing cuts with the blade held bevel up, taking fine parings.

3 When making the finished cuts, use your thumb to control the cutting edge of the chisel, holding it close to the end of the blade. Make sure the chisel is sharp.

## VERTICAL PARING

ABOVE: When paring vertically by hand, guide the chisel blade with one hand while pushing down firmly on the handle with the other.

## REMOVING LARGE AMOUNTS

ABOVE: To remove larger amounts of waste wood, hold the chisel vertically and strike the handle firmly with a wooden mallet.

## MORTISING

ABOVE: You can form a mortise completely with a chisel, but it is much quicker to remove most of the waste by drilling it out, then use a chisel to clean up the sides and ends of the cutout.

## DOVETAILS

ABOVE: Dovetail joints are common in cabinet work. Begin by removing the bulk of the waste with a coping saw before using a narrow, bevel-edged chisel to finish off.

# SHARPENING EQUIPMENT

A good sharpening stone is a vital part of the toolkit. Without a sharp edge, a chisel will be not only difficult to work with, but also dangerous. The chisel will follow where the wood directs it, rather than where you want it to go, and can easily slip.

Chisels should be sharpened at the beginning and end of every session. If they are attended to regularly, just a few minutes' work will keep the honed edges in prime condition. Once in a while, a longer honing session might be necessary – if the bevel loses its original angle or if the edge is chipped.

Natural sharpening stones are quite expensive, and synthetic versions are commonly used. Japanese water stones are of natural stone and need water as a lubricant. They can produce a finely ground edge on the best-quality steel. For more general use, however, oilstones are sufficient.

A combination stone is the best buy, two stones of different grades being bonded together back to back.

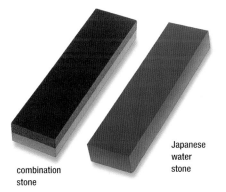

combination
stone

Japanese
water
stone

## SHARPENING PLANE IRONS

To sharpen a plane iron, apply a coat of thin oil to the oilstone, hold the blade at 35 degrees to the stone and maintain this angle while working it backward and forward. Honing jigs, which set the angle exactly, are readily available. Lay the back of the iron flat on the oilstone and rub off the burr formed by the sharpening process. Clean out the inside of the plane before reassembly, and apply a drop of oil to the adjustment mechanism.

**1** Hold the iron at a steady angle while rubbing it on the oilstone.

**2** Remove the burr from a sharpened blade by rubbing the back flat on the stone.

# SAWS

The most common saw used by the do-it-yourselfer is the hand saw. This is used for cross-cutting (across the grain) and ripping (along the grain), and the teeth of the saw are set accordingly, so you will need to ask your tool supplier for the correct one. There are also general-purpose hand saws that are reasonably suited to both tasks. These are quite often hardpoint saws, which cannot be sharpened, but their specially hardened teeth give them a long life.

The tenon saw, sometimes called a backsaw because of the solid strengthening bar along its top edge, is made specifically for cutting the tenons of mortise-and-tenon joints and other fine work. Really fine work is done with a dovetail saw, which is similar to a tenon saw, but has more teeth to the inch to give a finer cut.

The tenon saw is often used with a bench hook for making cross-cuts in small pieces, and one can be made quite easily as a do-it-yourself project. They usually measure about 300 x 150mm (12 x 6in). The mitre box is another handy aid for use with a tenon saw, allowing 90- and 45-degree angles to be cut accurately, but the beginner is best advised to buy one rather than attempt to make one.

A mitre saw makes short work of cutting accurate angles and offers fine adjustment. It is well worth the investment if working with delicate mouldings or making picture frames.

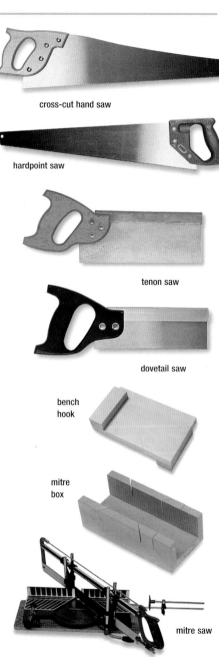

cross-cut hand saw

hardpoint saw

tenon saw

dovetail saw

bench hook

mitre box

mitre saw

## SAWING TECHNIQUES

When beginning a cut with a hand saw, draw the saw back toward your body to sever the wood fibres and produce a small kerf – the groove in which the saw blade will run. Always cut on the waste side of the marked line for perfect results.

When using a mitre box to make an angled cut, begin with the back of the saw raised slightly. This will make the cut easier to start.

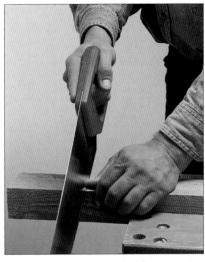

ABOVE: Draw the saw back a few times to start the cut, using your thumb to support the blade until a kerf has formed.

### TIP

Always find a comfortable position in which to saw. It will produce better results and reduce the risks of back strain or other injury.

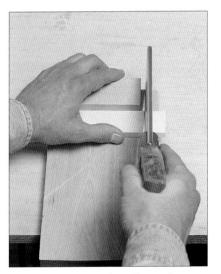

ABOVE: Use a tenon saw for cutting small components or sawing tenons and the like. A bench hook aids the cross-cutting.

ABOVE: A standard mitre box permits 90- and 45-degree angled cuts to be made with a tenon saw for a variety of applications.

# POWER SAWS

nvaluable for saving a lot of time and hard work, a power saw can also do a lot of damage if used incorrectly. Never force a saw through the work. If the blade is not sharp, or the motor is underpowered, not only will the cut be inaccurate, but also you'll be putting your safety at risk. Let the saw do the work, guiding it slowly, but surely, along the line. Use an adjustable fence if possible when making straight parallel cuts.

circular saw

## CIRCULAR SAWS

A hand-held circular saw can be used for both cross-cutting and ripping, and many are supplied with a dual-purpose, tungsten-carbide-tipped blade for a long life. It is almost a necessity for the home woodworker and is an excellent investment; there are many quite inexpensive and reliable brands.

## CIRCULAR SAW BLADES

Check that the bore of the blade (the diameter of the central hole that fits over the spindle) is compatible with the machine, as different makes vary. As with hand saws, the type of blade should suit the material and the cutting action, whether ripping along the grain, cross-cutting, or making fine cuts in veneered or laminated panels. Carbide teeth are cheaper for most general-purpose work; tungsten-carbide-tipped blades are sharper and much harder wearing. The latter should be used when cutting composite materials and manufactured boards such as plywood and MDF (medium-density fiberboard).

ABOVE: A circular saw will make light work of cutting wood, but be sure not to overload it, and always have the guards in place. Use a good-quality hand saw for smaller jobs.

## JIGSAWS

Another very handy tool is the jigsaw (saber saw). It is suitable for both straight and curved cuts, saving a lot of hard work.

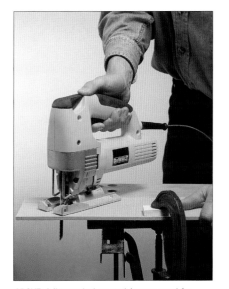

jigsaw (saber saw)

Most jigsaws come into their own when cutting out curved shapes from manufactured boards, such as MDF (medium-density fiberboard) and plywood.

If large amounts of curved or shaped work are envisaged, a small bandsaw is a useful addition to the workshop. These can be inexpensive. Fret/scroll saws are very similar to jigsaws, being fitted with a reciprocating movement. They are used for fine pierced and detail work, and are capable of turning out very delicate results.

ABOVE: A jigsaw (saber saw) is very good for making curved cuts. Most have adjustable cutting angles. Be sure your work is securely clamped to keep it firmly in place.

### JIGSAW BLADES

Jigsaw (saber saw) blades are made for many purposes, but check that the model of jigsaw you buy will accept standard-fitting blades. Many specialized blades are available for cutting all kinds of material, such as wood, manufactured boards, metal, ceramics, plastics and laminates. A knife blade has no teeth, and is designed for cutting leather and rubber sheeting. Bi-metal blades, although more expensive, will last longer and are less inclined to bend. Most blades are 100mm (4in) long, allowing a depth of cut of 50–65mm (2–2½in), but heavy-duty blades are available up to 150mm (6in) long. These should only be fitted to a machine with a powerful motor designed to accept the extra load.

# KNIVES

The do-it-yourself enthusiast will need a variety of knives, some of which have very specific functions. Some do not actually conform to the conventional idea of a knife at all, but all have metal blades and are essentially cutting tools.

### MARKING KNIVES

The purpose of a marking knife is to mark a sawing line, by lightly cutting the surface wood fibres, and assist in the beginning of a saw cut. Not only does this provide a permanent guide line, but it also prevents the fibres from splintering as the saw cuts through. These tools are usually about 200mm (8in) long and make a much finer line than a pencil.

They are normally used in conjunction with a steel rule, straightedge or try square and are bevelled on one side only so that they can be used tightly against the steel edge for accuracy. They are available in both left- and right-handed versions.

Marking knives without pointed ends are also frequently used, and these are bevelled on either the left- or right-hand side, depending on the needs of the user.

Twin-bladed knives are available and are adjusted by a set screw and locking knob. Typically, the blades can be set to a spacing of 3–19mm ( $\frac{1}{8}$–$\frac{3}{4}$in). This type of knife is used for marking parallel lines, gauging mortises and cutting thin strips from veneers for decorative inlay work.

### GENERAL-PURPOSE KNIVES

By far the most common and useful general-purpose knife is the craft knife, which has a store of replacement blades in the handle. This is an indispensable tool which can be used for many purposes.

Another very handy tool is the scalpel. More delicate and invasive than the craft knife, a scalpel is ideal for cutting out templates and particularly useful for cleaning up deeply indented

marking knife with bevel on one side

scalpel

twin-bladed adjustable marking knife

putty knife

craft knife

filling knife

## MARKING OUT

ABOVE: Mark a line across the grain with the knife held firmly against the steel edge of a try square. This gives a very fine line of severed wood fibres, which is ideal to work to with either a saw or a chisel.

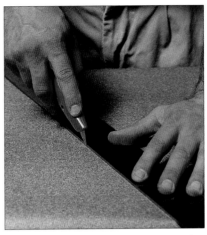

ABOVE: A typical example of a knife being used with a steel rule. Note how the fingers are spread to keep a firm and even downward pressure on the rule, allowing the knife to be used hard against the rule's edge.

cuts in carvings and routed work. Scalpels are made with a variety of handles and have replaceable blades.

### MISCELLANEOUS KNIVES

Putty knives often find their way into the do-it-yourselfer's toolkit. They have specially shaped ends to their blades to make "cutting off" easier. This means withdrawing the knife from the work without damaging the soft putty that is being applied to a window pane or moulding, for example.

The filling knife is a familiar decorator's tool with a flexible spring-tempered blade that is ideal for forcing soft material, such as wood filler, into knot holes, cracks and blemishes in wood, and plaster filler into cracks in walls. These come in a variety of shapes and sizes and are often confused with stripping knives, which have thicker and less flexible blades.

### TIPS

• Never use a scalpel or craft knife with excessive pressure. The blade may shatter and sharp pieces fly up into your unprotected eyes.
• Always place the hand not holding the knife behind the blade. This prevents injury if the blade slips.

# DRILLS AND BITS

Accurate drilling is an important do-it-yourself technique. It is much easier with a hand-held power drill, and even more so with a bench-mounted pillar drill.

### CARPENTER'S BRACE

Drilling by hand with a carpenter's brace still has a place, and a hand drill is useful for smaller jobs, especially in sites far removed from electric power. However, even in these circumstances, the cordless power drill has largely overcome the difficulty of finding a source of electric power.

### CORDLESS DRILL/DRIVER

This tool is worth its weight in gold in situations without power, and it is particularly safe near water. It is rechargeable and usually comes with a spare battery. The variable torque and speed settings make it ideal for doubling as a screwdriver. Although generally not as powerful as a mains-powered drill, it is more than

adequate for most jobs. Use it for drilling clearance holes for screws, fitting and removing screws, and drilling holes for dowels.

Heavier work, especially that which involves using flat bits or Forstner bits to remove very large areas of wood, is best undertaken with a mains-powered electric drill to save time and avoid the need for constant recharging of the battery.

### VARIETIES OF BIT

Great advances have also been made in the pattern of drill bits. For example, there are bits designed for setting dowels. Dowel jointing is often used in projects built with manufactured boards, such as chipboard (particle board) and plywood, and the bits produce flat-bottomed holes.

cordless drill

ABOVE: A carpenter's brace is ideal for boring large holes. Its design provides plenty of leverage to turn flat and auger bits.

Forstner bit

dowel bit          flat bit

plug cutter          countersink bit

from a piece of scrap wood. Then the plugs are glued into holes in the workpiece to conceal fixing screws. Most cutters come with a special matching bit that bores a screw clearance hole and plug countersink in one operation.

Another common drilling accessory is the countersink bit. This allows the head of a screw to be set flush with the surface of the wood. Again, this is best used in a pillar drill with a depth stop to ensure accuracy.

Forstner bits are designed to drill large, flat-bottomed holes that do not pass through the wood, such as holes that might be needed to accommodate kitchen cabinet hinges. The bits will drill deep holes accurately, even in the end grain of the wood, which is usually very difficult.

There are also flat bits that work with a scraping action, cutting large holes very rapidly, although these are not as accurate as conventional twist bits. The latter are used for making small holes in wood, metal and other rigid materials, but specially hardened types are needed for steel. For the do-it-yourselfer on a limited budget, an adjustable bit is a good investment, but these can only be used in a hand brace.

## DRILLING ACCESSORIES
Plug cutters are useful additions to any workshop, especially when quality work is undertaken. The cutter is fitted in a pillar drill and used to remove plugs

ABOVE: Many drill bits can be sharpened with a specialized grinding attachment designed to be run off a hand-held power drill.

# ASSEMBLING TOOLS

Sooner or later, the do-it-yourselfer is likely to be faced with the need to join two or more pieces of a workpiece together. In some cases, this can be done by forming joints and using glue, although some means of clamping the pieces together while the glue dries must be found. Often, however, some form of mechanical fixing is called for. The most commonly used fixings are nails and screws, although occasionally nuts and bolts may be required. There are many types of nail, some of which require special hammers to drive them, while screws have different head designs and need the correct type of screwdriver. Nuts and bolts can be assembled and dismantled with spanners and/or sockets.

# CLAMPS

**M**any do-it-yourself tasks require two or more sections of a workpiece to be held together temporarily while a more permanent fixing is made, often with glue. A variety of clamps is available for this purpose, many of them with specific uses. Keen woodworkers may make their own clamps (or cramps as they are often called) from scrap wood or other materials.

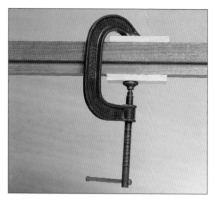

ABOVE: The G-clamp in a typical application. Note the packing pieces beneath the jaws to prevent bruising of the wood.

### COMMONLY USED CLAMPS

The most common clamp in the workshop is the G-clamp. This is a general-purpose tool that is available with a variety of throat sizes. It may be used on its own or in conjunction with others when, for example, working on the surface of a wide board or holding boards together for gluing.

The sash clamp was designed specifically for assembling window frames, or sashes, but it is also often used when edge-jointing boards to form large panels for table tops and similar items.

Sometimes, it is useful to be able to apply a clamp with one hand while holding the workpiece in the other, which is when the single-handed clamp comes into its own. It works on a simple ratchet system, rather like a mastic (caulking) gun.

For picture frames and heavier items with 45-degree mitred joints at the corners, there is the mitre clamp. This can be quite a complex affair with screw handles for tightening or a very

simple "clothes-peg" (pin) type arrangement, that can be applied to the work very quickly.

### SPECIAL-PURPOSE CLAMPS

There are many of these, but one that the do-it-yourself enthusiast may find useful is the cam clamp, which is wooden with cork faces. This is a quickly operated clamp often used by musical instrument makers. Its advantages are its speed in use, its lightness and its simplicity. The cam clamp is ideal for small holding jobs, although it cannot exert a great deal of pressure.

cam clamp

ABOVE: Small wooden picture and mirror frames can be easily assembled with the aid of inexpensive mitre clamps.

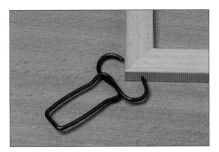

ABOVE: This clever little clamp works by means of spring pressure. It can be applied quickly and easily to small assemblies.

ABOVE: Use sash clamps to edge-joint boards to form a panel such as a table top. Reverse the central clamp to even out the pressure.

ABOVE: Home-made clamps used for the same purpose, but this time the pressure is exerted by means of wedges.

## CLAMPS IN USE

Apply pressure to a joint or the assembly you are working on as soon as possible after gluing – make a habit of preparing everything you need in advance. Keep a box of small scraps of wood handy and use them to protect the surface of the work. It is often said that you can never have too many clamps, and you will soon start collecting a selection of different types and sizes to suit all kinds of assembly technique. Many can be home-made.

### TIPS

• Do not be tempted to release clamps too quickly. Be patient, allowing plenty of drying time for the glue – overnight at least, or as specified by the maker.
• Think through the sequence for the clamping process and make sure you have enough clamps to hand before you apply any glue. With a complex or large structure, you may decide you need another person to help.

# NAILS AND HAMMERS

There is no such thing as an "ordinary" nail. All nails have been derived for specific purposes, although some can be put to several uses. Similarly, various types of hammer are available – always use the correct tool for the job. Wooden-handled hammers have a natural spring in the handles, which makes them easier to control than steel-handled types.

## NAILS

The wire nail can be used for many simple tasks, such as box-making, fencing and general carpentry. Lost-head and oval nails are useful where there is no need for a flat head, or when it is desirable for the nails to be concealed, such as when fixing cladding or boards.

Oval nails can be driven below the surface of the work with less likelihood of them splitting the wood. They should be inserted with their heads in line with the grain.

The cut nail is stamped from metal sheet and has a tapering, rectangular section, which gives it excellent holding properties. It is largely used for fixing flooring.

Panel pins (brads), as their name suggests, are used for fixing thin panels and cladding. They are nearly always punched out of sight below the surface, as are veneer pins.

When there is a need to secure thin or fragile sheet material, such as roofing felt or plasterboard (gypsum board), large-headed nails are used. These are commonly called clout nails, but may also be found under specific names, such as roofing nails and plasterboard nails. Their large heads spread the pressure and prevent the materials from tearing or crumbling. They are usually galvanized to protect them against rust when used outdoors. Zinc nails are used for roofing because they are rustproof and easy to cut through when renewing slates.

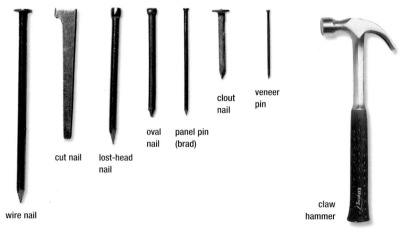

clout nail

veneer pin

oval nail

panel pin (brad)

cut nail

lost-head nail

wire nail

claw hammer

## HAMMERS

The essential hammer for the do-it-yourselfer is the claw hammer, the claw being used to extract nails. About 365–450g (13–16oz) is a good weight to aim for, since the hammer should be heavy enough to drive large nails. It is a mistake to use a hammer that is too light, as this tends to bend the nails rather than drive them.

For lighter nails, a cross-pein or Warrington hammer is useful, since the flat head can be used to start the nail or pin without risk of hitting your fingers. For even smaller panel pins, the pin hammer is used.

## CARPENTER'S MALLET

It should be remembered that the carpenter's mallet, often made from solid beech, is a form of hammer, but it should never be used for striking anything other than wood or similar soft materials, otherwise serious damage will result.

### DOVETAIL NAILING

Cross, or dovetail, nailing is a simple and useful method of holding a butt joint strongly in end grain. When several nails are being driven into one piece of wood, avoid putting them in straight; slanting them will help prevent splitting.

ABOVE: The claw hammer's ability to extract as well as drive nails makes it a useful tool for do-it-yourself projects.

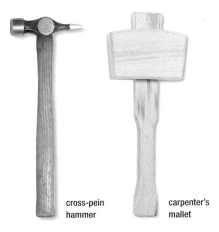

cross-pein hammer

carpenter's mallet

# SCREWS AND SCREWDRIVERS

The holding power of screws is much greater than that of nails, and screwed work can easily be taken apart again without damage to any of the components, unless of course it is also glued. Driving screws does take longer than nailing and they are more expensive, but they will give the appearance of quality and craftsmanship to most work.

### TYPES OF SCREW

The most common woodscrews may be made of mild steel or brass, often with countersunk heads that may be flat or raised. There are many different plated finishes available, ranging from chrome, used for internal fixings such as mirrors, to zinc, which will resist rust.

Brass screws will not rust at all and are often used in woods such as oak, where steel would cause blue staining due to the tannic acid in the sap.

### HEAD PATTERNS AND SCREW SIZES

There are various types of screw head used for both hand and power driving. The most common is the slot-head screw, followed by the Phillips head and the Pozidriv, both of which have a cruciform pattern in the head to take the screwdriver blade.

Screw sizes are complex, combining the length and the diameter (gauge): for example, "inch-and-a-half eight" describes a screw that is $1\frac{1}{2}$in (40mm) long and gauge 8.

### TYPES OF SCREWDRIVER

For woodworking, the traditional hand screwdriver has an oval wooden handle and is used to drive slot-head screws only. It is available in a variety of sizes. A range of plastic-handled tools of

flat and
raised
countersunk
screws

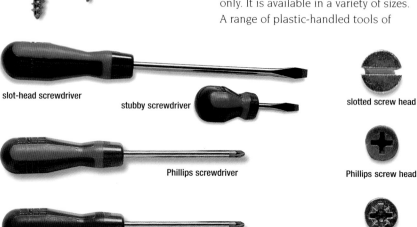

slot-head screwdriver

stubby screwdriver

slotted screw head

Phillips screwdriver

Phillips screw head

Pozidriv screwdriver

Pozidriv screw head

various sizes is also available, designed
to drive Phillips and Pozidriv screws, as
well as slot-heads.

A recent innovation is the screwdriver
bit set, containing a handle and a
number of interchangeable tips to fit
various screw types and sizes.

cordless
electric
drill/driver

Power screwdrivers and drill/drivers
vastly increase the rate of work. They
can offer various torque settings that
allow the screw heads to be set just
flush with the work surface. Power drivers
are also very useful for dismantling
screwed joints and furniture because
they will run in reverse.

Keeping the head of a slot-head
screwdriver correctly ground to prevent
it from slipping is very important.
Remember also that the blade width
must equal the length of the screw
slot for the greatest efficiency and to
prevent both slipping and damage to
the screw head. Always use the correct
size of screwdriver with Phillips and
Pozidriv screws, otherwise both the
screw head and the screwdriver are
likely to be damaged.

## USING SCREWS

Driving a screw is a more skilled task
than nailing. It is usually advisable to
drill pilot holes first to ease the screws'
passage through the wood and to
ensure that they go in straight. In
hardwoods, pre-drilling is vital,
otherwise the screws will shear off
when pressure is exerted by the
screwdriver. Brass screws are
particularly soft, so steel screws of
the same size should be inserted to
pre-cut the threads.

ABOVE: Screw holes should be marked very
carefully when fitting hinges.

ABOVE: Where possible, use the screwdriver with
both hands to prevent slipping.

# PINCERS AND PLIERS

Every do-it-yourself enthusiast's toolkit should include a range of hand tools for gripping small items. Chief among these are pincers, used for removing nails and similar fixings, and general-purpose combination pliers, which offer a variety of gripping and cutting features.

## PINCERS

A good pair of pincers will remove nails and tacks with little trouble. The rolling action required to remove a nail with pincers is very similar to that used with a claw hammer. An ideal length is about 175mm (7in) to ensure good leverage, which is essential. The jaws should touch along their entire width and be properly aligned to provide maximum grip.

It is important that pincers do not damage the work, and for this reason, broad jaws – about 25mm (1in) wide – that will spread the load are best.

Some pincers come with a handy tack lifter at the end of one of the handles. Purpose-made tack lifters are very useful for upholstery work, and if you intend doing any furniture making or restoration, it is well worth investing in such a tool.

Another special tack and nail remover is the nail puller, or "cat's-paw", as it is sometimes known. This tool has a standard tack remover at one end and a large, right-angled claw at the other for getting under the heads of stubborn nails. The claw can be tapped under the head of an embedded nail with a small hammer.

pincers

combination pliers

pincers with a tack lifter

heavy-duty pliers

tack lifter

long-nosed
(needlenose) pliers

nail puller

## PLIERS

These come in a bewildering range of types and sizes, many of which have very specific uses.

Combination pliers and heavy-duty pliers are used for gripping, twisting and cutting. They come in various sizes, but a good pair would be about 200mm (8in) long and probably have plastic or rubber handle grips for comfort and to provide insulation against electric shock.

Long-nosed (needlenose) pliers are rather more specialized and are used for gripping small objects in confined spaces. Some have cranked jaws at various angles for access to awkward places. They come in many sizes.

ABOVE: When using pincers to remove a nail, protect the wood by slipping a piece of hardboard or plywood below the pincer head.

ABOVE: Remove tacks from wood with a tack lifter. Protect the surface with hardboard or a piece of plywood.

ABOVE: The flat behind the claw of this Japanese nail puller can be tapped with a hammer to drive the claw under the nail head.

ABOVE: When using pliers, hold them firmly, keeping your palm away from the pivot, which can pinch your skin as the jaws close.

# SPANNERS AND WRENCHES

Although spanners and wrenches may be thought of as tools for the garage, there are many do-it-yourself tasks that require these gripping and twisting tools, particularly in the kitchen and bathroom, where you are likely to come into contact with pipes and their fittings. All home workshops need at least one comprehensive set of sockets or spanners.

LEFT: Socket sets are extremely useful and offer a choice of types of drive (such as bars and ratchets) as well as sockets in a variety of sizes.

graduated in specific sizes – metric, Whitworth and A/F are the most common. Open-ended spanners are the most usual. Some have jaws that are offset by about 15 degrees to allow them to contact different flats of nuts when working in tight spots.

### SPANNERS

These are necessary in the home workshop where power tools and machinery are involved. They are needed for changing the blades on circular saws, for adjusting and setting bandsaw guides, and for assembling all manner of machinery stands, tool racks and benches.

A good selection of spanners would include open-ended, ring and combination spanners. These are usually purchased in sets; other tools are bought singly.

It is essential to use a spanner that fits a nut or bolt perfectly, otherwise the fixing will be damaged and you run the risk of skinned knuckles. Spanners are

Ring spanners have enclosed heads that give a more secure grip. They may have six or 12 points, and can be used on square and hexagonal nuts and bolts. The 12-point version needs only a very small movement for it to contact new

open-ended
spanner

ring
spanner

combination
spanner

adjustable
spanner

flats on the nut or bolt head, so it is very useful where there is limited room for movement.

Sockets grip in the same manner as a ring spanner, but are designed to fit a variety of drive handles, of which the ratchet handle is the most useful. This enables the user to continue to turn a nut or bolt without having to remove the socket after each turn. Some large sets offer metric, Whitworth, BSF and A/F sizes. Small sets of additional sockets are available to complement your existing set, allowing you to build up a kit that meets your needs exactly.

### WRENCHES

Adjustable spanners and wrenches enable the user to grip various sizes and types of fitting. Some are designed for specific purposes, while others are suitable for more general use.

Basic plumbing tools include adjustable pipe wrenches (known as Stilsons), an adjustable basin wrench and a double-ended basin wrench, both of which will reach up behind a basin to allow removal of the nuts holding taps in place, and water-pump pliers with soft jaws.

Normally, the adjustable spanner is made from forged alloy steel. Self-grip wrenches, or vice grips, can be adjusted to fit pipework or a nut or bolt head, and then can be locked to grip tightly. They are very versatile and useful tools. Water-pump pliers offer five or six settings by virtue of having an adjustable bottom jaw. They are capable of exerting a heavy pressure because of their long handles.

Another variation is the strap wrench, made of a soft pliable material. It is used for gripping container lids.

ABOVE: A strap wrench offers a soft pliable grip that can be used for opening containers.

Stilson wrench

self-grip wrench

---

**TIP**

Never use a wrench on a nut or bolt if a spanner of the correct size is available. Wrenches are essentially for pipe work and will damage the corners of nuts and bolt heads very quickly. Use the correct tool wherever possible.

# FINISHING TOOLS

No matter what type of finish you apply to a surface, in practically all cases, the smoother the surface, the better the finish. A primary method of achieving smoothness is by sanding with abrasive paper, which can be done by hand or by machine. Paint is the most common finish for a variety of surfaces in the home, and you will need a selection of brushes and rollers to apply it. An alternative to paint is wallpaper – there is no limit to the versatility of modern wallpapers, which can be used for decorating both walls and ceilings. A few specialized tools are needed to do the job. Tiles are a good means of providing a durable, waterproof surface to walls and floors. They require skill to lay, but this is not beyond the average do-it-yourselfer.

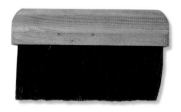

# SANDERS

Although the term "sanding" is generally used for do-it-yourself projects, it is something of a misnomer. A truer description would be "abrading", because what we call "sandpaper" is, in fact, "glasspaper". In addition, we also use garnet paper, and silicon-carbide and aluminium-oxide abrasive papers, all of which shape wood very efficiently.

## GRIT SIZE

One thing abrasive papers all have in common is classification by grit size, and the golden rule is to work progressively down through the grit sizes, from coarse to fine, when smoothing a piece of work. For example, 400 grit is finer than 200 grit and should be employed later in the finishing process. Abrasives can be used by hand or with a variety of machines, both hand-held and stationary. Sanders are also suitable for shaping work, using coarse abrasives for rapid material removal.

## TYPES OF SANDER

A tool commonly used for heavy-duty shaping and sanding is the belt sander. This normally has a 75mm (3in) wide belt, running continuously over two rollers, and a dust collection facility.

A belt and disc sander is an inexpensive alternative. It is used for shaping and trimming rather than smoothing, as the piece of work is taken to them.

Many do-it-yourselfers are likely to own an orbital sander, which is useful for general light sanding work such as finishing boards. These sanders are designed to accept either half or a third of a standard-size abrasive sheet and quite often have dedicated sheets made for them. Random orbital sanders are similar, but may employ self-adhesive abrasive sheets that are easy to fit. They can be small enough to be used with one hand in tight spots, but still give a good finish.

## HAND SANDING

Always wrap abrasive paper around a cork or rubber block when sanding flat surfaces. Clear the dust away as you work to avoid clogging the paper, particularly on resinous and oily wood. To finish off a rounded edge, wrap a square of paper around a section of moulded wood with the correct profile for the job.

belt sander          orbital sander          random orbital sander

ABOVE: You should hold a belt sander with both hands to prevent it from running away.

ABOVE: The belt sander can be inverted and secured in a woodworking vice.

ABOVE: Belt and disc sanders are used for shaping and trimming, and can be aggressive.

ABOVE: The orbital sander is less ferocious than the belt sander and is easy to control.

## MAKING A SANDING BLOCK

**1** Fold your sheet of abrasive paper to size and tear it along a sharp edge.

**2** Wrap the paper around a cork or rubber block before starting to sand.

# PAINTING TOOLS

This is one aspect of do-it-yourself work where you cannot afford to skimp on materials. You will not achieve professional results by using cheap brushes that shed their bristles as you work, or cut-price rollers that disintegrate before the job is finished. Invest in the best quality equipment your budget allows.

## CHOOSING BRUSHES

Paintbrushes come in pure bristle, synthetic fibre and even foam versions. The last guarantees that you will not be left with brush strokes, and they are inexpensive enough to discard when you have finished. All natural brushes shed a few bristles in use, but cheap brushes are the worst offenders. Usually, these have fewer bristles to start with and they are often poorly secured. Regard pure bristle brushes as an investment; you can use them repeatedly, and many painters claim that they improve with age.

Synthetic brushes, usually with nylon bristles, have the advantage of being moult-free, and they perform well with water-based paints. A more expensive version, made of polyester and nylon, is particularly easy to handle and said to give a superior finish.

paintbrushes ranging from 100–25mm (4–1in)

cutting-in
(sash) brush

special-effects brushes

foam brush

roller sleeves

roller handle

paint
pads

radiator brush

## TOOLBOX ESSENTIALS

Serious painters will need a range of brushes: slimline, 12 and 25mm ($\frac{1}{2}$ and 1in), for fiddly areas such as window frames; medium-sized versions, 50 and 75mm (2 and 3in), for doors, floors and skirtings (baseboards); and large types, 100mm (4in), for quick coverage of walls and ceilings. You might like to add a few extras to this basic kit:

• A cutting-in (sash) brush, specially angled to cope with hard-to-reach areas, is particularly useful if you are painting around window frames.

• Special-effects brushes allow you to create distinctive looks such as woodgrain and marbling.

• A radiator brush is designed to reach the wall behind a radiator.

## PAINT PADS

If you are new to decorating, you may find that a paint pad is easier to handle than a brush. Paint pads can be useful for clean, flat painting and precise edges. They give a speedy and even finish, are light to handle and work well with acrylic paints.

Each pad consists of a layer of fibre on top of a layer of foam, attached to a plastic handle. Use paint pads with a paint tray. If you purchase a kit, a tray will usually be provided.

## THE RIGHT ROLLER

If speed is of the essence, a paint roller will be an indispensable part of your decorating toolkit. Once you have a roller, you can simply buy replacement sleeves that fit its existing handle. Many types of specialist roller are used in decorating. Specific covers are suitable for different surfaces and you can buy rollers designed for creating particular patterns.

ABOVE: Load paint on to a paint pad using the tray supplied with it.

ABOVE: A power roller will make painting large areas easier, but watch for drips.

A radiator roller has a long handle for reaching into tight spots. Use small craft and mini-rollers for applying paint in techniques such as stamping.

Power rollers are mains- or battery-operated and, in theory, they can simplify the whole process, with the paint contained in a portable reservoir. Their disadvantage, however, is that they can result in drips and streaks.

Mini-rollers have a cover made from dense foam or pile. Available in several widths, they are used for painting narrow stripes or coating stamps.

Masonry rollers are generally 23cm (9in) wide and have a long pile. Use them for covering rough-textured surfaces and for roller fidgeting.

Sheepskin rollers are used for basic quick coverage of flat paint. They are usually available in 18cm (7in) and 23cm (9in) widths.

Use a sponge roller as a cheaper alternative to a sheepskin one. Sponge rollers are also available in 18cm (7in) and 23cm (9in) widths.

## SPONGES AND CLOTHS

A selection of natural and synthetic sponges is essential for numerous overall decorating techniques, as are lint-free cloths and rags. Each makes its own individual marks.

Natural sponges are mostly used for sponging. Synthetic sponges make a more obvious mark than natural sponges, so use natural examples for producing tight, fine marks and to create special marbled effects.

A chamois, made from real leather, can be scrunched into a ball for ragging. Or use a special ragging chamois, made from strips bound together.

LEFT (clockwise from top left): natural sponge, cloth, pinched-out synthetic sponge, two paint pads, mini-roller, small cellulose sponges, gloss roller, masonry roller, ragging chamois.

# SPECIALIST PAINTING TOOLS

There are many items that will make it easier to plan your decoration. For careful measuring and marking before you start, you may need a spirit (carpenter's) level, long rule, tape measure and pencil. A plumbline, which consists of a small weight suspended on a fine string, is helpful for marking vertical drops. Masking tape is useful for keeping edges straight and covering light switches and sockets.

For certain techniques, special tools are needed. Different shapes of rubber combs will give a variety of woodgrain effects. A heart grainer (graining roller) with its moulded surface will enable you to reproduce the characteristics of a particular wood more accurately. For gilding, a gilder's pad is a useful investment and consists of a soft pad surrounded by a screen of parchment

to shield gold leaf from draughts. Craft knives can be bought with double-ended blades that are screwed into the handle and turned or replaced when blunt. Others have a long retractable strip blade that allows you to break off and dispose of the blunt portion. For safety, keep your fingers behind the cutting edge. Never leave the knife within reach of children or where it will be a danger to animals; a piece of cork makes a good protective cap to put on the end of the blade. Craft knives are ideal for cutting out stencils and stamps.

Keep a supply of different grades of abrasive paper, and a sanding block to use with them. A power sander can also save time when tackling larger jobs. If you need to sand an area of floorboards, the best solution is to hire a purpose-built industrial-quality sander.

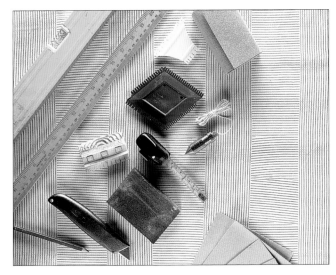

RIGHT (clockwise from top left): spirit (carpenter's) level, long rule, sanding block, two combs, plumbline, tape measure, heart grainer (graining roller), sanding sponge, craft knife, pencil, selection of abrasive papers (far right).

# WALLPAPERING TOOLS

Using the correct tools will make the job of hanging wallpaper much easier, allowing you to achieve a more professional finish. Some are needed specifically for wallpapering; others are likely to be part of your standard do-it-yourself toolkit. When buying decorating tools, opt for quality rather than quantity.

## MEASURING AND MARKING

A retractable steel tape is essential for taking measurements, while a long metal straightedge, a spirit (carpenter's) level or plumbline and a pencil will be needed for marking levels, vertical guidelines on walls and the positions of fixtures.

## CUTTING AND TRIMMING

For cutting wallpaper to length and trimming edges, you will need a pair of paperhanger's scissors, which have long blades and curved tips used for creasing paper into angles. Choose scissors that are at least 250mm (10in) long and made from stainless steel, or which have been specially coated so that they will not rust.

A sharp craft knife can also be used for trimming and will be easier to use with vinyl wallcoverings. Various trimming tools are also available, including the roller cutter, which enables you to crease and cut into edges with a single movement, and is accurate and simple to use.

## PASTING

For mixing and applying paste, you will need a plastic bucket and a paste brush. Proper paste brushes have synthetic bristles and will be easier to clean than ordinary paintbrushes. A pasting table is not essential, but

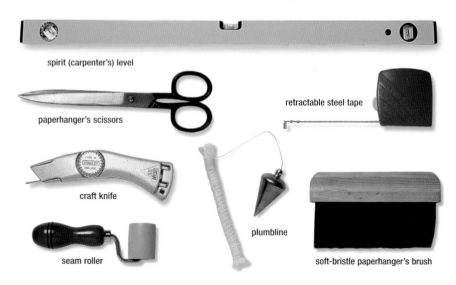

spirit (carpenter's) level

paperhanger's scissors

retractable steel tape

craft knife

plumbline

seam roller

soft-bristle paperhanger's brush

is extremely useful. They are also inexpensive and fold for easy storage. For ready-pasted wallcoverings, a polystyrene soaking trough is required.

## SAFE ACCESS

Hanging wallpaper may also involve working at heights, so safe access equipment will be required. A set of sturdy steps will be suitable for papering walls, but a safe platform will be needed for access to ceilings and stairwells.

## FINISHING

A paperhanger's brush is the best tool for smoothing down wallpaper, although a sponge can be used for vinyl wallcoverings. For the best results, choose a brush with soft, flexible bristles and buy the largest size that you can manage comfortably. Do not use wallpaper brushes with a metal ferrule or collar on them for this job, as you might inadvertently tear or mark delicate wallcoverings.

Use a cellulose decorator's sponge rather than an ordinary household sponge. This type of sponge is made of a higher-density material, which is firmer and will hold water better.

A seam roller will give a neat finish to joints and the edges of borders, but should not be used on wallpaper with an embossed pattern. Types made from wood and plastic are available. A soft plastic seam roller is the best option as it is less likely to leave marks on thin or overpasted wallpapers.

ABOVE: For smooth wall coverings, a seam roller can be used to make sure that the seams are well bonded to the wall. Do not use a seam roller on textured or embossed wall coverings, though, as it will flatten the embossing.

## AVOIDING PASTE DRIPS

A length of string tied tightly across the top of a wallpaper paste bucket makes a handy brush rest. Use the string rather than the side of the bucket for removing excess adhesive from the pasting brush.

# TILING TOOLS

Even the simplest of ceramic tiling jobs will require a small selection of specialized tools, while a major project requires quite a few. In addition, you will have to call on tools from your normal do-it-yourself toolkit, such as a retractable steel tape, a straightedge, spirit (carpenter's) level, a saw and a hammer. You will also need to make a tiling gauge, for setting out the rows of tiles. This should be a wooden batten, 1.2m (4ft) long, marked off in tile widths (with an allowance for the joints between).

**ADHESIVE AND GROUTING TOOLS**

Apply adhesive to the wall with a small pointing trowel, then create a series of ridges in it with a notched spreader. This allows the adhesive to spread when the tile is pressed home, ensuring an even thickness.

Tile spacers are required when using standard field tiles to provide a uniform grouting gap between them. Other types of tile have bevelled edges that create a grouting gap automatically when butted together.

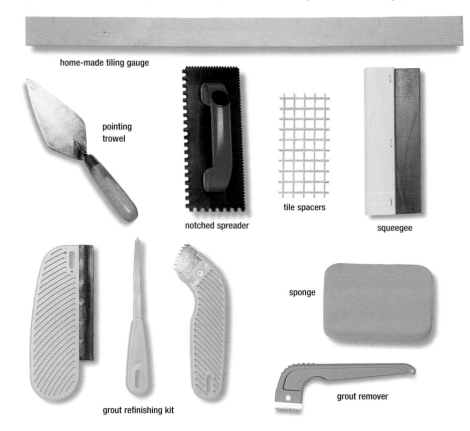

home-made tiling gauge

pointing trowel

notched spreader

tile spacers

squeegee

sponge

grout refinishing kit

grout remover

A squeegee will be needed at the grouting stage to force grout into the gaps between tiles, while a grout finisher will provide the joints with a neat profile. If you don't have a grout finisher, you can substitute it with a short length of wooden dowel. Wipe off excess adhesive from the tiles with a sponge.

Various tools are available for removing old grout when carrying out repairs or renovation work. Take care when using them not to chip the edges of the tiles.

## CUTTING AND SHAPING TOOLS

Straight cuts can be made with a simple tile scorer, straightedge and tile snapper, but an all-in-one tile cutter or tile jig will make life easier for the beginner. Most incorporate a measuring device, trimmer and snapping mechanism in one unit.

Tile nippers can be used for cutting off small pieces of tile, while a tile saw is good for cutting out complex shapes. Once a tile has been cut, you can smooth its edges with a tile file.

tile scorer

tile snapper

tile nippers

tile saw

heavy-duty tile cutter

tile file

tile jig with adjustable width and angle facility

# WOOD AND VINYL FLOOR TOOLS

For laying woodblock and woodstrip floor coverings, you will need general woodworking tools, adhesive and a spreader for woodblock floors, and pins (tacks) or fixing clips for woodstrip floors, plus varnish or sealer if laying an unsealed type. For marking out, you will require a retractable steel tape measure, a pencil and a straightedge. Wooden blocks and strips can be cut to length with a tenon saw, while cut-outs can be made in them to fit around obstacles with a coping saw, pad saw or electric jigsaw (saber saw).

For laying sheet vinyl, a tape measure and sharp utility knife are needed. A long steel straightedge will also be invaluable. For bonding the lengths to the floor along edges and seams, use either double-sided adhesive tape or bands of liquid adhesive, spread with a toothed spreader to ensure that a uniform amount of adhesive is applied.

Lastly, for both wooden and vinyl floor coverings you will need a pair of compasses or a scribing block and pencil, plus a shape tracer with adjustable steel or plastic fingers, to transfer the outlines of the various floor-level obstacles along the edges of the room so that they can be trimmed to fit around them.

Unless they are to be continued into an adjoining room, both types of flooring will need finishing off at doorways, This is achieved by fitting ready-made threshold (saddle) strips.

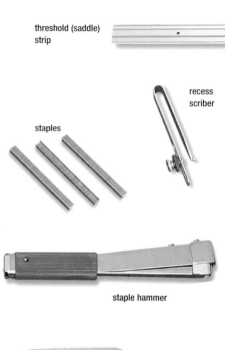

threshold (saddle) strip

recess scriber

staples

staple hammer

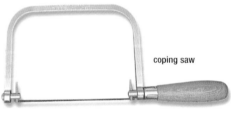

coping saw

tenon saw

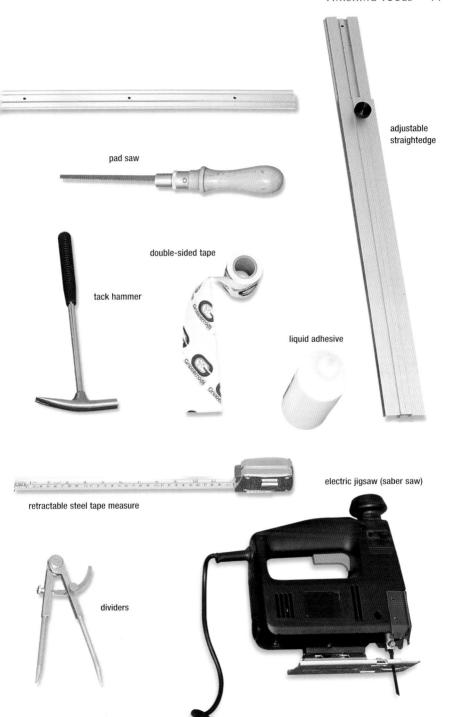

adjustable
straightedge

pad saw

double-sided tape

tack hammer

liquid adhesive

retractable steel tape measure

electric jigsaw (saber saw)

dividers

# CARPET TOOLS

For laying carpet, the basic essentials are a tape measure and a sharp utility knife. As an alternative, special carpet shears can be used.

For a woven carpet, a carpet stretcher is invaluable. This is a device with a horizontal pad of metal spikes at one end, which is locked into the carpet, and a cushioned pad at the other end, which is nudged with the knee to stretch the carpet into place. It is probably best to hire this tool.

Also needed are some carpet gripper strips to hold the carpet in position around the perimeter of the room. These are thin strips of plywood fitted with angled nails that grip the underside of the carpet, and are nailed to the floor about 10mm (³⁄₈in) from the skirting (baseboard). The edge of the carpet is tucked down into the gap, usually with a carpet fitter's bolster. A wide brick bolster (stonecutter's chisel) may be used, as long as it is clean.

Foam-backed carpet may be stapled to the floor or stuck down with double-sided adhesive tape. Adhesive seaming tape may also be needed to join sections of carpet together, and threshold (saddle) strips are used to trim the carpeted edge off at door openings.

Lining paper or cloth underlay is recommended for foam-backed carpets, as it prevents the foam from sticking to the floor surface. For woven carpets, use either a foam or felt underlay: they are available in various grades and should be matched to the carpet.

gripper strips

carpet knife with spare blades

left-handed carpet shears

staples

staple hammer

hessian (burlap) carpet tape

single-sided brass threshold (saddle) strip

aluminium carpet-to-vinyl strip

carpet-to-carpet strip

carpet fitter's bolster

right-handed carpet shears

double-sided tape

recess scriber

tack hammer

dividers

adjustable straightedge

retractable steel tape measure

carpet stretcher

# PAINTING SKILLS

- Painting materials
- Painting preparation
- Painting techniques

# INTRODUCTION

**P**ainting walls, woodwork and other surfaces is, so all the surveys reveal, by far the most popular do-it-yourself job of them all. It can be an extremely satisfying activity, not only because you can completely transform the atmosphere of a room in a relatively short space of time, but also because painting itself is a relaxing and fun activity.

Modern paints and improvements in the design and manufacture of decorating tools have certainly made the task less arduous than it was in the days of traditional oil-bound paints and distemper (tempera), and have also made it easier for the amateur decorator to obtain professional-looking results.

One major shift in paint technology is the trend away from using solvent-based (oil) varnishes and paints for wood, toward water-based (latex) products that do not give off harmful vapours as they dry. Water-based finishes are not as durable as solvent-based ones, but are no longer as far behind them in performance terms as they once were, and they have other advantages, such as faster drying times, virtually no smell and easier cleaning of brushes, rollers and pads. Therefore, it is likely that their use in the home will become much more widespread than previously.

ABOVE: Traditional household paints are either water-based (latex) or solvent-based (oil) and are generally available in three finishes: matt (flat), satin (mid sheen) and gloss.

ABOVE: Careful preparation is one of the keys to successful painting. Buy a dust sheet (drop cloth) and use a sturdy set of steps to reach the tops of walls and ceilings.

No amount of clever technology can eliminate the need for proper preparation of the surfaces to be decorated, even though this part of the job is far less enjoyable and often more time-consuming than the actual painting. In many cases, it involves little more than washing down the surface, but sometimes more thorough preparation will be called for.

The following pages describe the various types of paint, binders, diluents, varnishes and wood stains on the market; which to use where; how to prepare surfaces for redecoration; and how to apply the new finish – especially to the more awkward interior surfaces, such as casement and sash windows and flush and panelled doors.

OPPOSITE: Emulsion (latex) paint is available in a huge range of ready-mixed colours. Most basic wall painting is done with water-based emulsion paint since it is easy to apply with a variety of brushes, rollers, sponges and rags. Several layers can be painted over each other.

RIGHT: Different paints are suitable for different surfaces and effects, so it is very important that you choose the right paint for the right surface.

# PAINTING MATERIALS

There are some basic essentials that you will need for decorating. You can add to this equipment gradually as you work on different effects. For general painting, edging and painting woodwork, use household paintbrushes. The most useful sizes are 50mm (2in) and 25mm (1in). Finer artist's brushes are invaluable for dealing with difficult small spaces and touching up odd areas. Soft sable-haired artist's brushes with rounded edges are best for this purpose. When painting walls and ceilings, you can use larger brushes, but a roller will be quicker and less tiring to use. Good preparation is the secret of all successful painting jobs, so filling and sanding materials are also essential.

# PAINTS

Paint works by forming a film on the surface to which it is applied. This film has to do three things: it must hide the surface underneath; it must protect it; and it must stay put. All paint has three main ingredients: pigment, binder and carrier. The pigment gives the film its colour and hiding power. The binder binds the pigment particles together into a continuous film as the paint dries, and also bonds the film to the surface beneath. In traditional paint, this was a natural material, such as linseed oil in oil paints and glue size in distemper (tempera); but modern paints use synthetic resins such as alkyd, acrylic, vinyl and polyurethane. The third ingredient, the carrier, makes the paint flow smoothly as it is applied and evaporates as the paint dries.

The ratio of pigment to binder in a paint affects the finish it has when it dries: the higher the pigment content, the duller the finish. By adjusting this ratio, paint manufacturers can produce paints that dry to a matt (flat) finish; to a silky sheen, eggshell; or to a high gloss. The choice depends on personal preference, tempered by the condition of the surface:

high-gloss finishes highlight any imperfections, while matt finishes tend to disguise them.

## PAINT TYPES

The paint types used in the home have different carriers. Water-based paint has the pigment and binder suspended in water as tiny droplets. It is an emulsion, like milk, and is usually called emulsion (latex) paint. As the water evaporates, the droplets coalesce to form the paint film. Solvent-based (oil) alkyd paints have pigment and binder dissolved in a petroleum-based solvent, and take longer to dry than water-based paints. These are known as oil or oil-base paints, although the term "alkyd" is used for some primers of this kind. They give off a characteristic "painty" smell as they dry, which many people find unpleasant and to which some are actually allergic. Because of growing awareness of the health risks of inhaling some solvents, the use of these paints is declining in popularity and is already under legal restriction in some countries.

Paint also contains a range of other additives to improve its performance. The most notable is one that makes the paint thixotropic, or non-drip, allowing more paint to be loaded on to the brush and a thicker paint film to be applied; one coat is often sufficient.

LEFT: Emulsion (latex) paints are available in a tempting array of colours.

## PAINT QUALITIES

| | BASE | DILUENT | USES | NOTES |
|---|---|---|---|---|
| Matt emulsion (latex) | water | water, wallpaper paste, acrylic glaze, acrylic varnish; clean with water | basic walls; large choice of colours, flat finish | fast drying, needs varnishing on furniture, marks easily |
| Silk emulsion (latex) | water | as above | as above; faint sheen | fast drying, more hard-wearing than matt, needs varnishing on furniture |
| Soft sheen | water | as above | kitchens and bathrooms; mid sheen | fast drying, moisture-resistant, needs varnishing on furniture |
| Dead flat oil | oil | linseed oil, white spirit (paint thinner), oil glaze, oil varnishes | woodwork; flat/velvet finish | marks easily, not durable |
| Eggshell | oil | as above | woodwork, furniture; faint sheen | more resistant than above, but still marks |
| Satin (mid sheen) | oil | as above | woodwork, furniture; mid sheen | durable, washable finish |
| Gloss | oil | as above | woodwork, exterior furniture; high sheen | tough, hard-wearing finish, washable |
| Primer | oil | not to be diluted; clean with spirits (alcohol) | bare wood | necessary for porous or wood surfaces |
| Undercoat | oil | not to be diluted; clean with spirits (alcohol) | between the primer and top coat | saves on top coats, choose the right colour |
| Masonry | water | not to be diluted; clean with water | exterior masonry | limited colours, apply with a suitable roller |
| Floor | oil | not to be diluted; clean with spirits (alcohol) | floors, light or industrial use | tough, durable, apply with a roller |

### HOUSEHOLD PAINTS

These are available in a wide range of finishes, from completely matt (flat) through varying sheens to high glosses. There is a wealth of colour choice, and in many do-it-yourself stores you can have an exact colour matched and specially mixed for you. Read the instructions on the can to check that it is suitable for your surface. When thinning paint, make sure that you are using the correct diluent.

# PAINT SYSTEMS

A single coat of paint is too thin to form a durable paint film. To provide adequate cover and performance, there must be a paint system consisting of several coats. These will depend on the type of paint system that has been chosen, and on the surface being painted.

The first coat is a sealer, which is used where necessary to seal in things such as the natural resin in wood, or to prevent the paint from soaking into a porous surface.

The second is a primer, which provides a good key for the paint film to stick to. On metal surfaces, this also stops the metal corroding or oxidizing. A primer can also act as a sealer.

The third is the undercoat, which builds up the film to form a flexible, non-absorbent base of uniform colour close to that of the fourth and final layer, the top coat. The latter gives the actual finish and colour.

On walls, for which water-based (latex) paint is generally used, the system consists simply of two or three coats of the same paint, unless there is a need for a sealer or primer to cure a fault in the surface, such as dustiness, high alkalinity or excessive porosity. The first coat is a "mist" coat of thinned paint. A primer is also used if walls are being painted with solvent-based (oil) paints.

On woodwork, the first step is to apply a liquid called knotting (shellac) to any knots to prevent resin from bleeding through the paint film. Then comes a wood primer, which may be water-based or solvent-based, followed by an undercoat, then the top coat. To speed up the painting process, paint manufacturers have perfected combined primer/undercoats, and have also introduced so-called self-undercoating gloss paint, which only needs a primer.

On metal, a primer is generally needed. A zinc phosphate primer is used for iron and steel indoors, but outdoors, it is common to apply a rust-inhibiting primer to these materials as soon as they have been stripped back to bare metal and any existing traces of rust removed completely. There are special primers for aluminium. This is then followed by an undercoat and top coat, as for wood. Copper, brass and lead can be painted directly without the need for a primer, as long as they are brought to a bright finish first and are thoroughly degreased with white spirit (paint thinner).

**BELOW AND RIGHT:** Acrylic primer and knotting (shellac).

# BINDERS AND DILUENTS

Pigment needs a binder so that it will adhere to the surface on to which it is painted. As well as the binder in the paint itself, there are other binders that you can add to modify its consistency and texture. Diluents and solvents are added to thin the paint and to delay the drying time. Glazes also delay drying, and modern products such as acrylic glazes can be used instead of traditional scumble glazes for a more workable consistency.

There are many mediums for glazes such as wallpaper paste, linseed oil, PVA (white glue) and dryers that will change the nature of the paint. Solvents such as white spirit (paint thinner) can also be used to clean paintbrushes. Always use a diluent or solvent that is suitable for the type of paint you are using.

Regardless of how you employ them, remember that solvents other than water give off toxic fumes and are highly flammable. Treat them with respect and make sure your work area is well ventilated. Never smoke nearby.

Take care when disposing of empty containers and any rags soaked in paint. The latter can ignite spontaneously if exposed to even gentle heat. Do not pour solvent used for cleaning brushes into a drain; take it to a proper disposal site.

## BINDERS AND DILUENTS

| | BASE | DILUENT | USES | NOTES |
|---|---|---|---|---|
| PVA (white glue) | water | water | binder for emulsion (latex) washes | makes the mixture more durable |
| Linseed oil | oil | | medium for powder | lengthy drying |
| Dryers | | | add to oil paint to speed drying | |
| Wallpaper paste | water | | dilutes emulsions (latex) | retards the drying a little |
| Acrylic glaze | water | water | as above | retards drying |
| Scumble glaze | oil | water | medium to suspend colour pigments | difficult to tint to the right quantity |
| Methylated spirits (methyl alcohol) | oil | white spirit (paint thinner) | softens dried emulsion (latex) | |
| White spirit (paint thinner) | oil | | paint thinner, brush cleaner | buy in bulk |

# VARNISHES AND WOOD STAINS

**V**arnish is basically paint without the pigment. Most contain polyurethane resins and are solvent-based (like oil paint), although water-based acrylic varnishes are becoming more popular for health and environmental reasons, just as solvent-based paints are losing ground to water-based types.

Varnishes are available with a matt (flat), satin (mid sheen)/silk or a high-gloss finish, either clear or with the addition of small amounts of colour. These coloured varnishes are intended to enhance the appearance of the wood, or to give it some extra colour without obliterating the wood grain, as paint would do.

Varnish is its own primer and undercoat, although it is best to thin the first coat with about ten per cent

ABOVE: Varnishes seal and protect the surface, and add colour to wood.

## VARNISHES

|  | BASE | DILUENT | USES | NOTES |
|---|---|---|---|---|
| Polyurethane/oil-based | oil | white spirit (paint thinner) | strong varnishes in a range of finishes | tough, durable, slow drying |
| Polyurethane (aerosol) | oil | | matt (flat) finish | |
| Acrylic | water | water | range of finishes | not as durable |
| Acrylic (aerosol) | water | | matt (flat) finish | |
| Tinted varnish | oil acrylic | white spirit (paint thinner) water | for bare wood, or antiquing paint; range of colours | slow drying fast drying |
| Button polish | water | methylated spirit (methyl alcohol) | sealing bare wood | quick drying |

white spirit (paint thinner) for solvent-based types, or water for acrylic types, and to apply it with a lint-free cloth rather than a brush so that it can be rubbed well into the wood grain. When this first coat has dried, it is keyed, or roughened, by rubbing very lightly with fine abrasive paper, dusted off, and a second, full-strength coat brushed on. For surfaces likely to receive a lot of wear, it is advisable to key the second coat as before, then apply an additional coat.

## WOOD STAINS

Wood stains, unlike paint and varnish, are designed to soak into the wood. Subsequently, they may be sealed with clear varnish to improve the finish and make the surface more durable. They are available in water-based and solvent-based types, in a wide range of colours and wood shades; different colours of the same type can be blended to obtain intermediate shades, and the stain can be thinned with water or white spirit (paint thinner) as appropriate to give a paler effect.

Stains are often applied with a brush or a paint pad, but often it is quicker and easier to obtain even coverage by putting them on with a clean lint-free cloth. Quick work is needed to blend wet edges together and avoid overlaps, which will leave darker patches as the stain dries.

ABOVE: Pigments and stains can be stirred into water-based (latex) paint mediums to create unique colours and textures.

A water-based stain will raise fibres on the surface of the wood, which will spoil the evenness of the colour. The solution is to sand the surface smooth first, then moisten it with a wet cloth. This will raise the surface fibres. When the wood is dry, these fibres are sanded off with extra-fine abrasive paper, ready to receive the application of stain.

# PAINTING PREPARATION

Perhaps the most important factor in achieving a successful result when decorating is to make sure that the surfaces are clean and smooth. Careful preparation can seem rather tedious, but it is worth the time spent. Wash walls with a solution of sugar soap (all-purpose cleaner), then rinse them well with clean water. Scrape off any flaking paint and fix any dents and cracks in the plaster with filler (spackle). When the filler has hardened, sand it smooth with fine-grade abrasive paper. Similarly, fix any defects in the woodwork. If knots are showing through the existing paintwork, sand them back to bare wood and apply knotting (shellac). When dry, paint on primer and undercoat to bring the area up to the level of the surrounding paintwork.

# PREPARING THE ROOM

Paint is a popular decorative finish for walls and ceilings because it is quick and easy to apply, offers a huge range of colours and is relatively inexpensive compared with rival products, such as wallcoverings. It can be used over plain plaster, or applied over embossed relief wallcoverings and textured finishes.

Before starting to paint, clear the room and prepare the surfaces. Start by taking down curtains and blinds (drapes and shades). Remove furniture to another room if possible, or group it in the middle of the room and cover it with plastic sheeting. Take down lampshades and pendant light fittings (after turning off the power supply). Unscrew wall-mounted fittings and remove the hardware from doors and windows if they are being repainted at the same time.

Protect surfaces not being repainted, such as wall switches and socket outlets (receptacles), with masking tape. Finally, cover the floor with dust sheets (drop cloths), which will absorb paint splashes; vacuum-clean surfaces such as window sills, picture rails and skirtings (baseboards) where dust can settle, and turn off forced-air heating to ensure that dust is not re-circulated into the room.

## ACCESS EQUIPMENT

Normally, most of the surfaces to be painted can be reached from a standing or a kneeling position, but for ceilings, the tops of walls and the upper reaches of stairwells, some access equipment is needed. A stepladder, ideally with a top platform big enough to support a paint kettle (paint pot) or roller tray, will be adequate for walls and ceilings.

For stairwells, use steps or ladder sections plus secured scaffold

### PAINTING WALLS AND CEILINGS

Paint walls and ceilings in a series of overlapping bands. Start painting the ceiling next to the window wall so that reflected light on the wet paint shows whether coverage is even. On walls, right-handed people should work from right to left, and left-handed people from left to right.

boards, or access towers, to set up a platform. Always make sure that you can get to all the surfaces without overreaching.

## PAINT COVERAGE

Paint coverage depends on several factors, including the roughness and porosity of the surface to which it is being applied and the thickness of the coating. For example, the first coat of paint will soak into new plaster, so the coverage will be less than is achieved with subsequent coats. Similarly, a textured surface will hold more paint than a smooth one, again reducing the paint coverage.

Manufacturers usually give an indication of coverage on the container; remember that it is an average figure.

## LIGHT SWITCHES

When painting a wall that contains a light switch, protect the faceplate from splashes with masking tape. Paint around the fitting with a small brush before completing the wall with a larger brush or roller. Remove the tape before the paint has dried completely, otherwise the edges may lift as you pull the tape away.

## ESTIMATING QUANTITIES

| PAINT TYPE | SQ M PER LITRE | SQ FT PER GALLON |
|---|---|---|
| Liquid gloss (oil) paint | 16 | 650 |
| Non-drip gloss (oil) paint | 13 | 530 |
| Eggshell | 12 | 490 |
| Matt (flat) water-based (latex) paint | 15 | 610 |
| Satin (mid sheen)/silk water-based (latex) paint | 14 | 570 |
| Non-drip water-based (latex) paint | 12 | 490 |
| Undercoat | 11 | 450 |
| Wood primer | 12 | 490 |
| Metal primer | 10 | 410 |
| Varnish | 15–20 | 610–820 |

The figures given here are intended as a rough guide only. Always check the manufacturer's coverage figure printed on the container, and use that together with the area to be painted to work out how much paint is required.

# PREPARING PAINTED WOODWORK

Modern paints have excellent adhesion and covering power, but to deliver the best performance they must be given a good start by preparing the surface thoroughly.

Wash surfaces that have previously been painted with a solution of strong household detergent or sugar soap (all-purpose cleaner). Rinse them very thoroughly with clean water, and allow them to dry completely before repainting them.

Remove areas of flaking paint with a scraper or filling knife (putty knife), then either touch in the bare area with more paint or fill it flush with the surrounding paint film by using fine filler (spackle). Sand this smooth when it has hardened.

1 Use fine-grade abrasive paper wrapped around a sanding block to remove "nibs" from the paint surface and to key the paint film ready for repainting.

2 Wash the surface down with detergent or sugar soap (all-purpose cleaner) to remove dirt, grease, finger marks and the dust from sanding it. Rinse with clean water, ensuring that no detergent residue is left, as this will inhibit the new paint film.

3 Use a proprietary tack rag or a clean cloth moistened with white spirit (paint thinner) to remove dust from recessed mouldings and other awkward corners.

# STRIPPING WITH HEAT

Every time a surface is repainted, this adds a little more thickness to the paint layer. It does not matter much on wall or ceiling surfaces, but on woodwork (and, to a lesser extent, on metalwork) this build-up of successive layers of paint can eventually lead to the clogging of detail on mouldings. More importantly, moving parts, such as doors and windows, start to bind and catch against their frames. If this happens, it is time to strip off the paint back to bare wood and build up a new paint system from scratch.

It may also be necessary to strip an old paint finish if it is in such poor condition – from physical damage for example – that repainting will no longer cover up the faults adequately.

1 Play the airstream from the heat gun over the surface to soften the paint film. Scrape it off as it bubbles up, and deposit the hot scrapings in an old metal container.

2 Use a shavehook (triangular scraper) instead of a flat scraper to remove the paint from mouldings. Take care not to scorch the wood if it is to be varnished afterwards.

3 Remove any remnants of paint from the wood surface with wire wool (steel wool) soaked in white spirit (paint thinner), remove any loose particles, then sand the surface lightly. Wipe with a clean cloth moistened with white spirit.

# STRIPPING WITH CHEMICALS

As an alternative to stripping paint using a heat gun, you can use a chemical paint remover, which contains either dimethylene chloride or caustic soda. Heat works well on wood, but may scorch the surface and can crack the glass in windows; it is less successful on metal because the material conducts heat away as it is applied. Chemical strippers work well on all surfaces, but need handling with care; for safety, always follow the manufacturer's instructions.

You can choose between liquid and paste-type chemical strippers. The former are better on horizontal surfaces, while the latter are good for intricate mouldings since they take longer to dry. Whichever type you select, neutralize the chemical by washing it off in accordance with the manufacturer's instructions.

Both types of chemical stripper will cause injury if splashed on to bare skin or into the eyes, so be sure to cover up well when using them. Wear old clothes or overalls and vinyl gloves, together with safety spectacles or a similar form of eye shield. Make sure you work in a well-ventilated area and never smoke near the workplace until the stripper has been removed, as the

## USING LIQUID REMOVER

1 Wear rubber gloves and old clothing. Decant the liquid into a plastic container or an old can, then brush it on to the surface. Leave it until the paint film bubbles up.

### HOMEMADE PASTE REMOVER

Add caustic soda to water until no more will dissolve. Thicken to a paste with oatmeal and use as for proprietary paste remover. Be particularly careful when using this corrosive solution. If it splashes on the skin, rinse at once with plenty of cold water.

fumes given off can be toxic when inhaled through a cigarette. If you should accidentally splash your skin, wash off the stripper immediately with plenty of cold water.

2 Use a flat scraper or shavehook (triangular scraper) as appropriate to remove the softened paint. Deposit the scrapings safely in a container.

3 Neutralize the stripper by washing the surface down with water or white spirit (paint thinner), as recommended by the manufacturer. Leave to dry.

## USING PASTE REMOVER

1 Paste removers are especially good for removing paint from intricate mouldings because they dry very slowly. Apply the paste liberally to the surface.

2 Give the paste plenty of time to work, especially on thick paint layers. Then scrape it off and wash down the surface with plenty of water to neutralize the chemical.

# REMOVING TEXTURED FINISHES

Textured finishes are tackled in different ways, depending on their type. Texture paints are basically thick water-based (latex) paints, normally used to create relatively low-relief effects, and can be removed with specially formulated paint removers. Some textured effects formed with a powder or ready-mixed compound are best removed with a steam wallpaper stripper, which softens the compound so that it can be scraped from the wall.

Never attempt to sand off a textured finish. There are two reasons. One is that it will create huge quantities of very fine dust; the other is that older versions of this product contained asbestos fibres as a filler, and any action that might release these into the atmosphere as inhalable dust must be avoided at all costs.

**1** Strip texture paint by brushing on a generous coat of a proprietary texture paint remover. Stipple it well into the paint and leave it to penetrate.

**2** When the paint has softened, scrape it off with a broad-bladed scraper. Wear gloves, and also safety goggles if working on a ceiling.

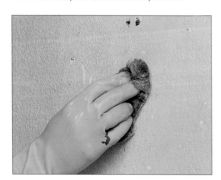

**3** Once the bulk of the coating has been removed, use wire wool (steel wool) dipped in the paint remover to strip off any remaining flecks of paint.

**4** Remove powder-based and ready-mixed types using a steam stripper, which will soften the finish. Never try to sand off this type of finish.

# REMOVING TILES

When faced with a tiled surface, complete removal or a cover-up with plasterboard (gypsum board) are the two options. The former will leave a surface in need of considerable renovation, while the latter will cause a slight loss of space within the room, as well as some complications at door and window openings, where new frames, architraves (trims) and sills may be necessary. In addition, the skirtings (baseboards) will need removing from the walls and refitting to the plasterboard surface.

## CERAMIC TILES

ABOVE: On a completely tiled wall, use a hammer to crack a tile and create a starting point for the stripping. On partly tiled walls, start at the tile edge. Use a broad bolster (stonecutter's chisel) and a club (spalling) hammer to chip the old tiles off the wall. Replaster afterwards.

## POLYSTYRENE (STYROFOAM) TILES

1 Lever the tiles away from the ceiling with a scraper. If they were fixed with a continuous coat of adhesive, consider covering the tiles with heavy lining paper as a temporary measure. For the best finish, fit a new plasterboard (gypsum board) ceiling, nailing through the tile layer into the ceiling joists.

2 If the tiles were fixed in place with blobs of adhesive, use a heat gun to soften the old adhesive so it can be removed with a broad-bladed scraper.

# STRIPPING WALLPAPER

Once the room is cleared, and dust sheets (drop cloths) are spread over the floor and any remaining furniture, the next step is to identify what type of wallcovering is to be removed. An ordinary printed paper will absorb water splashed on it immediately; other types will not. To tell washables from vinyls, pick and lift a corner, and try to strip the wallcovering dry. The printed plastic layer of a vinyl wallcovering will peel off dry, but the surface of a washable paper will not come off in the same way unless it is a duplex paper made in two layers. With paper-backed fabric wallcoverings, it is often possible to peel the fabric away from its paper backing; try it before turning to other, more complicated methods of removal.

Printed papers can usually be stripped relatively easily by soaking them with warm water containing a little washing-up liquid or a stripping compound. This will soften the adhesive, allowing the paper to be scraped off. Resoak stubborn areas and take care not to gouge the wall with the scraper.

Washable papers will not allow water to penetrate to the paste behind, so must be scored to break the surface film. Then they can be soaked, but removal will still be difficult; using a steam stripper will speed the process.

Wash all traces of adhesive from the wall and allow to dry before painting.

**1** To strip printed wallpaper, wet the surface with a sponge or a garden spray gun. Wait for the water to penetrate, and repeat if necessary.

**4** After removing the bulk of the old wallpaper, go back over the wall surface and remove any remaining "nibs" of paper with sponge/spray gun and scraper.

2 Using a stiff wallpaper scraper – not a filling knife (putty knife) – start scraping the old paper from the wall at a seam. Wet it again while working if necessary. Hold the scraper blade flat against the wall to stop it digging in.

3 Turn off the power before stripping around switches and other fittings, then loosen the faceplate screws to strip the wallpaper from behind them.

5 To strip a washable wallpaper, start by scoring the plastic coating with a serrated scraper or toothed roller, then soak and scrape as before.

6 For quicker results, use a steam stripper to remove washable papers. Press the steaming plate to the next area while stripping the area just steamed. Once the wallcovering has been removed, wash the wall to remove all traces of adhesive.

# FILLING DEFECTS AND CRACKS

**A** perfectly smooth, flat surface is essential for a good paint finish, and regardless of whether you intend painting a wood or plaster surface, there are likely to be cracks and other minor blemishes that need filling before you can begin painting.

If you have chosen an opaque finish, cracks and small holes in wood can be filled with cellulose filler (spackle). However, if you intend applying a varnish or similar translucent finish, a tinted wood stopper (patcher) would be more appropriate, since it will disguise the damage. Cracks in plaster should be treated with cellulose filler.

Always apply filler so that it is a little proud of the surrounding surface. Then, when it has dried, sand it back to leave a perfectly smooth surface.

## FILLING DEFECTS IN WOOD

1 Fill splits and dents in wood using filler (spackle) on painted surfaces, and tinted wood stopper (patcher) on new or stripped wood that will be varnished.

2 Use the corner of a filling knife (putty knife), or even a finger, to work the filler into recesses and other awkward-to-reach places. Smooth off excess filler before it dries.

3 When the filler or wood stopper has hardened completely, use abrasive paper (sandpaper) wrapped around a sanding block to sand the repair down flush with the surroundings.

## FILLING CRACKS IN PLASTER

1 Use a filling knife (putty knife) to rake out loose material along the crack, and to undercut the edges so that the filler (spackle) grips well.

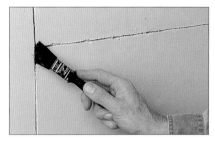

2 Brush out dust and debris from the crack, using an old paintbrush. Alternatively, use the crevice nozzle attachment of a vacuum cleaner.

3 Dampen the surrounding plaster with water from a garden spray gun to prevent it from drying out the filler too quickly and causing it to crack.

4 Mix up some filler on a plasterer's hawk (mortarboard) or a board offcut to a firm consistency. Alternatively, use ready-mixed filler or wallboard compound.

5 Use a filling knife to press the filler well into the crack, drawing the blade across it and then along it. Aim to leave the repair slightly proud.

6 When the filler has hardened, use fine-grade abrasive paper (sandpaper) wrapped around a sanding block to smooth the repair flush with the surrounding wall.

# PAINTING
# TECHNIQUES

The most important requirement for successful results when painting is the proper use of the correct materials and tools. Make sure that you have the right type of brush, sponge, cloth, pad or roller for the specific technique you are planning. Read carefully through the steps to check that you have everything you need before you start.

In particular, make sure that you have enough paint to complete the job; running out could be disastrous. Remember that the quality of the finish will be determined by the effort you put into it. Don't rush or overload brushes in an attempt to speed the work, but bear in mind that you need to keep working from a "wet edge" to prevent seam lines from showing in the finish.

# USING A PAINTBRUSH

The paintbrush is the most versatile and, therefore, the most widely used tool for applying paint. Choose the brush size to match the surface being painted. For example, for painting glazing bars (muntins) on windows or narrow mouldings on a door, use a slim brush – or perhaps a cutting-in (sash) brush if painting up to an adjacent unpainted surface, such as glass where a neat edge to the paint film is needed. For expansive, flat areas, select a larger brush for quick coverage. Remember that the largest wall brushes can be tiring to use, especially with solvent-based (oil) paints.

Get rid of any loose bristles in a new brush by flicking it vigorously across the palm of the hand before using it for the first time. Wash previously used brushes that have been stored unwrapped to remove any dust or other debris from the bristles, and leave them to dry out again before applying a solvent-based paint.

Always check that the metal ferrule is securely attached to the brush handle, and hammer in any projecting nails or staples. Check, too, that the ferrule is free from rust, which could discolour the paint. To remove rust, use either wire wool (steel wool) or abrasive paper (sandpaper).

## PREPARING THE PAINT

1 Wipe the lid first to remove any dust. Then prise it off with a wide lever, such as the thicker edge of a table knife to avoid damage to the lip.

2 Decant some paint into a clean metal or plastic paint kettle (paint pot), or small bucket. This will be easier to handle than a full container, especially one without a handle.

3 Remove any paint skin from partly used containers. Then strain the paint into the paint kettle through a piece of old stocking or tights (pantyhose), or cheesecloth.

## USING A BRUSH

1 To load the brush with paint, dip it into the paint to about a third of the bristle depth. An overloaded brush will cause drips, and paint will run down the brush handle.

2 Tie a length of string or wire across the mouth of the paint kettle (paint pot) between the handle supports, and use it to scrape excess paint from the bristles.

3 Apply the paint to the wood in long, sweeping strokes, brushing the paint out along the grain direction until the brush begins to run dry.

4 Load the brush with more paint and apply it to the next area. Blend the two together with short, light strokes, again along the grain direction.

5 Repeat this process while working across the area, blending the edges of adjacent areas together with light brush strokes to avoid leaving visible joins.

6 At edges and external corners, let the brush run off the edge to prevent a build-up of paint on the corner. Repeat the process for the opposite edge.

# USING A PAINT ROLLER

**G**enerally, paint rollers are used to apply water-based (latex) paints to large, flat areas, such as walls and ceilings. Choose a sleeve with a short pile for painting plaster, a medium pile for painting embossed or textured wall coverings and a long pile for deeply sculpted surfaces, such as those created with textured finishes (texture paints). Rollers can also apply solvent-based (oil) paint to flat surfaces, such as flush doors, but tend to leave a distinctive "orange peel" texture rather than the smooth finish left by a paintbrush.

There are some drawbacks with paint rollers: they cannot paint right up to internal corners or wall/ceiling angles, so these need to be painted first with a brush or pad. They can also splash if "driven" too fast, and the sleeves take a lot of time and effort to clean thoroughly, especially if they have been used for a long period and there is dried paint in the pile. Repeated cleaning eventually causes the sleeve to peel from its core.

It is possible to buy a roller washer for removing emulsion (latex) paint. It is designed to stand in a sink and be connected to a tap (faucet). When the tap is turned on, the running water causes the roller to spin and flush the paint from its pile. Oil-based paints should be removed by rolling the sleeve back and forth in white spirit (paint thinner).

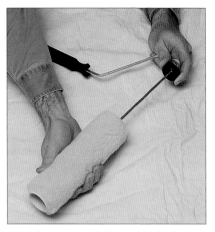

**1** Select a sleeve with the required fibre type and pile length, and slide it on to the sprung metal cage until it meets the stop next to the handle. If painting a ceiling, fit an extension to the handle if possible.

**4** Load the roller sleeve with paint by running it down the sloping section into the paint. Then roll it up and down the slope to remove the excess. Make sure the tray is placed out of harm's way so that it cannot be upset accidentally.

2 Decant some paint (previously strained if from an old can) into the roller tray until the paint level just laps up the sloping section.

3 Brush a band of paint about 50mm (2in) wide into internal corners and wall/ceiling angles, around doors and windows, and above skirtings (baseboards). Brush out the edge of the paint to feather it so that it does not form a seam.

5 Start applying the paint in a series of overlapping diagonal strokes to ensure complete coverage of the surface. Continue until the sleeve runs dry. Do not "drive" the roller too quickly, as it may cause the paint to splash.

6 Reload the sleeve and tackle the next section in the same way. Finish off by blending the areas together, working parallel to corners and edges.

# USING A PAINT PAD

**P**eople either love or loathe paint pads. They tend to apply less paint per coat than either a brush or a roller, so an additional coat may be needed in some circumstances, but they make it easy to apply paint smoothly and evenly with no risk of brush marks.

For best results, pads should be used with the correct type of paint tray. This incorporates a loading roller that picks up the paint from the reservoir in the tray and applies it evenly to the pad as the latter is drawn across the roller.

If you do not have the correct tray, a roller tray will suffice. Dip the pad carefully into the paint, then run it over the ridged section of the tray to ensure that the paint is evenly distributed on the pad sole and that the pad is not overloaded.

New pads should be brushed with a clothes brush to remove loose fibres. As with brushes, always select the correct size for the job, using the largest for painting walls and ceilings.

After use, dab the pad on newspaper to remove as much paint as possible. Then wash thoroughly in water, white spirit (paint thinner) or brush cleaner as appropriate. Work the fibres between your fingertips to clean them, finishing off by washing in hot, soapy water.

**1** Pour some paint into the special applicator tray. Then load the pad by running it backward and forward over the ridged loading roller.

**4** Special edging pads are designed for painting right up to internal angles. They have small wheels that guide the pad along the adjacent surface as you work. Make sure the wheels remain in contact with that surface.

2 On walls, apply the paint in a series of overlapping parallel bands. Make sure the sole of the pad remains flat on the wall. Use a small pad or a special edging pad (see step 4) to paint right up to corners and angles.

3 Use smaller pads for painting narrow areas such as mouldings on doors or glazing bars (muntins) on windows, brushing out the paint along the direction of the grain. The pad will produce neat, straight lines.

## USING AEROSOL PAINT

5 Some larger pads can be fitted to an extension pole to make it easier to paint ceilings and high walls. Make sure the pad is attached securely.

Aerosol paints and varnishes are ideal for hard-to-decorate surfaces such as wickerwork. Always follow the maker's instructions when using them.

# USING TEXTURE PAINTS

Texture paints are water-based (latex) paints thickened with added fillers. Once the paint has been applied to the decorating surface, a range of three-dimensional effects can be created using various patterning and texturing techniques. These paints are ideal for covering surfaces in poor condition. Most have a natural white finish, but they can be overpainted with ordinary water-based paint for a coloured effect. Avoid using texture paints in kitchens – the textured surface will trap dirt and grease, which is difficult to clean.

**1** Start applying the paint to the wall or ceiling surface in a series of overlapping random strokes, recharging the roller or brush at intervals. Do not push the roller too quickly, as it may flick the paint about.

**4** Use a texturing comb to create overlapping swirls, working across the area. Practise the effect on paint applied to a piece of heavy cardboard first. When you are happy with your technique, begin on the wall.

**5** Twist a sponge before pulling it away from the wall surface to create a series of small, overlapping swirls in the paint finish. Rinse the sponge regularly.

2 When an area of about 1 sq m (11 sq ft) is covered, go over the whole area with a series of parallel roller/brush strokes to create an even surface texture. This can be left for a subtle effect or given a more obvious pattern, as shown here.

3 Give the textured finish the appearance of tree bark by drawing a flat-bladed scraper or similar edged tool over the surface to flatten off the high spots.

6 You can buy patterning roller sleeves in a range of different designs for use with texture paints. This one creates a regular diamond pattern.

7 This patterning sleeve gives a random streaked effect when rolled down the wall. Apply the texture paint with a brush first if using a patterning sleeve, but do not spread it too thinly, otherwise there will be insufficient to create a pattern.

# PAINTING DOORS

The main problem with painting doors – or indeed any woodwork with a large surface area – involves keeping what professional decorators call a "wet edge". Obviously the door has to be painted bit by bit, and if the edge of one area begins to dry before it is joined to the next area, the join (seam) will show when the paint dries completely.

The secret of success is to work in a sequence, as shown in the accompanying drawings of flush and panelled doors, and to complete the job in one continuous operation, working as fast as reasonably possible.

Before starting to paint a door, wedge it open so there is room to walk through the doorway without touching wet paint, and also so that the hinged edge of the door can be reached easily. Remove handles, locks and other fittings; wedge a length of dowel in the latch hole to make a temporary handle for use until the paint has dried. Slide a dust sheet (dust cover) underneath the door to catch any drips. Finally, warn everyone else in the house that

## PAINTING FLUSH DOORS

 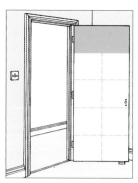 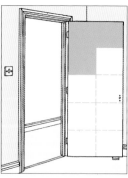

**1** Remove the door furniture and wedge open the door. Then divide it into eight or ten imaginary squares, and start painting at the top of the door by filling in the first square. Brush the paint out toward the door edges so it does not build up on the external angles.

**2** Move on to the next block at the top of the door, brushing paint out toward the top and side edges as before. Carefully blend the two areas together with horizontal brush strokes, then with light vertical laying-off strokes.

**3** Continue to work down the door block by block, blending the wet edges of adjacent blocks as they are painted. Complete a flush door in one session to prevent the joins (seams) between blocks from showing up as hard lines. Replace the door furniture when the paint is dry.

the door is covered with wet paint, and keep children and pets out of the way in another room or out of doors.

If you intend painting the door frame and surrounding architrave (trim) as well as the door, do so after you have painted the door itself and the paint has dried. That way, you will only have one area of wet paint to avoid at a time when passing through the door opening.

## PAINTING DOOR EDGES

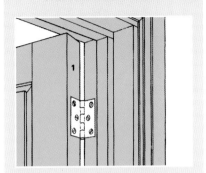

If each side of the door is to be a different colour, match the colour of the hinged edge (1) to that of the closing face of the door – the one facing the room – and the leading edge to the outer face.

## PAINTING PANELLED DOORS

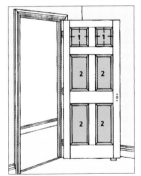

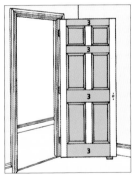

**1** Tackle panelled doors by painting the mouldings (1) around the recessed panels first. Take care not to let paint build up in the corners or to stray on to the faces of the cross-rails at this stage. Then paint the recessed panels (2).

**2** Next, paint the horizontal cross-rails (3), brushing lightly in toward the painted panel mouldings to leave a sharp paint edge. Feather the paint out thinly where it runs on to the vertical stiles at the ends of the rails.

**3** Finish the door by painting the vertical centre rail (4) and the outer stiles (5), again brushing toward the panel mouldings. Where the centre rail abuts the cross-rails, finish with light brush strokes parallel to the cross-rails. Work as quickly as possible.

# PAINTING WINDOWS

**W**indows are more difficult to paint than doors because they contain so many different surfaces, especially small-paned types criss-crossed with slim glazing bars (muntins). There is also the additional problem of paint straying on to the glass. The ideal is a neat paint line that covers the bedding putty and extends on to the glass surface by about 3mm (⅛in) to seal the joint and prevent condensation from running down between putty and glass.

With hinged windows, the edges of the casement or top opening light (transom) should be painted to match the colour used on the inside of the

window. With double-hung sliding sash windows, the top and bottom edges of each sash and the top, bottom and sides of the frame are all painted to match the inner face of the sashes.

Remove the window hardware before you start painting. On casement windows, tap a nail into the bottom edge of the casement and into the lower frame rebate (rabbet), and link them with stiff wire to stop the casement from swinging open or shut while you are working.

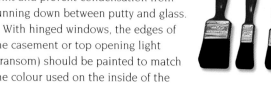

## PAINTING A CASEMENT WINDOW

**1** Remove the window furniture from the opening casement and wedge the window open while you work. Tackle the glazing bars (muntins) and edge mouldings first (1), then the face of the surrounding casement frame (2), and finally the hinged edge of the casement. Paint the remaining top, bottom and opening edges from outside.

**2** Move on to paint the glazing bars and edge mouldings (3) of the fixed casement. Use masking tape or a paint shield to ensure neat, straight edges here and on the opening casement; the paint should overlap the glass by about 3mm (⅛in) to ensure a good seal. Paint the face of the surrounding casement frame (4).

**3** Paint the outer frame (5), then the centre frame member between the opening and fixed casements (6). Complete the job by painting the window sill (7) and the rebate (rabbet) into which the opening casement closes.

## PAINTING A SASH WINDOW

For best results, sash windows should be removed from their frames before painting. Modern spring-mounted windows are easy to release from their frames. With older cord-operated types, remove the staff beads (window stops) first to free the sashes. Although quite a major task, take the opportunity to renew the sash cords (pulley ropes). This makes it possible to cut the cords to free the window. Some making good and finishing off will have to be done after the window is reassembled.

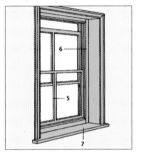

**1** To paint sash windows without removing the sashes, start by raising the bottom sash and lowering the top one. Paint the lower half of the top sash (1), including its bottom edge, and the exposed parting beads (2) and the exposed sides of the frame.

**2** When the paint is touch-dry, reverse the sash positions and paint the upper half of the top sash (3), including its top edge, and the exposed and unpainted parting beads and frame sides (4).

**3** Finish off by painting the face and edges of the inner sash (5), the staff beads (window stops) and any other trim mouldings around the window (6). Finally, paint the window sill (7). Leave the sashes ajar until the paint has dried to prevent components from sticking.

## PAINTING AROUND GLASS

◀ Stick masking tape to the glass with its edge 3mm (⅛in) from the wood. Paint the wood, then remove the tape.

▶ Alternatively, hold a paint shield against the edge of the glazing bar (muntin) or surrounding moulding. Wipe the shield to prevent smears.

# VARNISHING WOOD

Varnish is a useful means of providing a protective finish for wood while allowing the pattern of the grain to show through. The more coats of clear varnish applied, the darker the wood will appear, but coloured varnishes are also available that can give the wood the appearance of another species or simply make an attractive finish in their own right. Again, the more that is applied, the darker will be the appearance of the wood, so if possible test coloured varnish on scrap wood first to determine the number of coats you need to obtain the desired finish.

1 On bare wood, use a clean lint-free cloth to wipe the first coat of varnish on to the wood, working along the grain direction. This coat acts as a primer/sealer. Allow the varnish to dry completely.

2 Sand the first coat lightly when dry to remove any "nibs" caused by dust particles settling on the wet varnish, then wipe off the sanding dust.

3 Apply the second and subsequent coats of varnish with a brush, working along the grain and blending together adjacent areas with light brush strokes. Sand each coat, except the last, with very fine abrasive paper (sandpaper).

# STAINING WOOD

Wood washing actually stains wood with a colour, so that the beauty of the grain shows through and is enhanced by the colour. The technique can only be used on totally bare, stripped wood once all traces of varnish, wax or previous paint finishes have been removed completely. If they are not, the result will be patchy. Depending on the product used, the surface may or may not need varnishing to seal it, so make sure you read the manufacturer's information on the container. Usually a matt (flat) finish looks appropriate for this technique.

Colours that often work well include yellow ochre, blue, Indian red, violet, cream and pale green.

## WOOD WASHES

yellow ochre

blue

Indian red

violet

cream

pale green

1 Pour the pre-mixed wash into a paint kettle (paint pot). Then brush the stain evenly on the wood in the direction of the grain.

2 While the stain is still wet, wipe off the excess with a cloth. This will even the effect and expose slightly more of the grain. Then leave the stain to dry completely before varnishing the wood if required.

# PAINT FINISHES

- Basic paint finishes

- Patterned paint effects

- Faux paint finishes

# INTRODUCTION

**F**or many people, decorating with paint means nothing more than applying solid colours to their walls, ceilings and woodwork, but there is so much more to be achieved with this material if a few techniques are learned and a little imagination applied. There are many types of paint to choose from, never mind a vast kaleidoscope of colours, and you may be surprised at the variety of effects that are possible. What's more, decorating with paint allows you to create unique, one-off decorative effects that you could never achieve with other materials, such as wallpaper. And, when the time comes for a new look, paint is the quickest to prepare and the easiest of materials to cover with something fresh.

There are many types of decorative paint effect to choose from, some being more difficult to create than others, but all are well within the scope of the determined and competent do-it-yourselfer. They can be applied to a variety of surfaces, but some lend themselves particularly to large areas,

ABOVE: Colourwashing is a simple technique for applying an overall pattern to a large surface area; it can be done with a brush or sponge.

LEFT: In roller fidgeting, two different colours are applied by the same roller in one operation to give an interesting two-tone effect.

LEFT: Some items of furniture can look particularly attractive if given a distressed appearance. This is easy to achieve with paint.

RIGHT: With care, it is even possible to use paint to re-create the appearance of wood grain. In this case, an oak finish has been applied.

such as walls, while others are more effective on smaller items, such as pieces of furniture.

Among the simplest of paint effects is the application of one colour over another in such a manner that the first can show through in some areas, usually in a random pattern. That pattern is created by using a variety of applicators – thick-bristled brushes, sponges or balls of cloth – and mixing additives into the paint that make it hold the marks that these leave.

More uniform patterns can be produced by using stencils or stamps to print motifs on the wall, or by masking certain areas before painting them. There are techniques, too, for painting surfaces to look like natural materials, such as wood or marble. These require a degree of skill, but can be achieved with practice and confidence.

Naturally, as with any painted finish, thorough preparation is crucial for any decorative paint effect; surfaces must always be sound and clean, while choosing the right tools is a must

(some effects require special tools). The type of paint you use is important too, since all have specific properties that make them suitable for particular situations. Knowing what you can and cannot do with a paint is vital.

In the following pages, not only will you learn about using specialist paint equipment, but also a variety of decorative techniques, ranging from simple sponging to complex wood-graining and marbling. Study them carefully and use your imagination to choose the right ones for your situation. If you follow the step-by-step techniques, you will be able to give your home a new look that reflects your personality in a unique manner.

RIGHT: Trompe l'oeil effects are intended to deceive the eye into thinking that a flat surface has depth. Clouds provide a tranquil backdrop.

# BASIC PAINT FINISHES

The techniques demonstrated in this section show you how to achieve a variety of traditional paint effects, most of which can be used to obtain an all-over impact. In the main, they are suitable for decorating large surface areas, such as walls, quickly and with ease. Several, such as distressing and wood washing, are ideal for putting your own personal stamp on furniture, while others – for example, applying crackle glaze – will enable you to transform small items and home accessories into something decorative and special. Spend some time practising the various techniques on pieces of scrap board until you are happy that you can achieve exactly the effect you want.

# COLOURWASHING

You can dilute emulsion (latex) paint with water, wallpaper paste and emulsion glaze to make a mixture known as a wash. The effect varies depending on the consistency of the paint mixture and the method of applying the colour, but it is usually done with a broad brush.

In this instance, a large paintbrush has been used, but you could also employ a synthetic sponge to achieve a different effect.

## Materials

| | |
|---|---|
| emulsion (latex) paint | paint pot |
| wallpaper paste | large paintbrush |

**COLOUR EFFECTS**

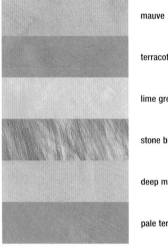

mauve

terracotta

lime green

stone blue

deep mustard

pale terracotta

**1** Using a paint pot, mix 50 per cent emulsion (latex) paint with 50 per cent wallpaper paste (premixed to a thin solution). Using at least a 10cm (4in) brush (up to 15cm/6in), dip the tip into the mixture and wipe off the excess on the side of the pot. Add the first dashes on to the wall, well spaced.

**2** Without adding more paint, brush out these dashes in random directions, using broad sweeping strokes. Continue working along the wall, adding a little more paint as you go and using quite a dry brush to blend the seams between areas of paint.

# COLOURWASHING LAYERS

This is done in the same way as colourwashing one layer, but once the first layer is dry a second colour is applied on top. This layering will soften the overall effect of the brush or sponge marks. Experiment with different colour variations (contrasting and complementary) and layering combinations until you have achieved the effect you want, using a large piece of board as your "canvas".

## Materials

| | |
|---|---|
| emulsion (latex) paint in two colours | paint pot |
| | large paintbrush |
| wallpaper paste | |

## COLOUR EFFECTS

camel under cream

purple under mauve

jade green under pale green

blue under cream

terracotta under yellow

red under pale yellow

1 Mix the paint in a paint pot, using 50 per cent emulsion (latex) paint and 50 per cent wallpaper paste (premixed to a thin solution). Apply the paint to the wall with random strokes, varying the direction as you go. Continue until you have covered the whole surface.

2 When the first layer has been allowed to dry completely, repeat step 1, using a second colour of paint. Add more paint and soften the joins between areas. The overall colourwash effect will be much softer than when applying only one colour.

# SPONGING

Large areas can be covered quickly and easily using the simple technique of sponging, perfect for beginners. Varied effects can be made by using either a synthetic sponge or a natural sponge. A natural sponge will produce smaller, finer marks, while heavier marks can be created with a synthetic sponge. Pinching out small chunks will avoid straight edges. You may find edges and corners are a bit tricky with a large sponge, so use a smaller piece of sponge for these.

## Materials

emulsion (latex) paint     natural sponge

## COLOUR EFFECTS

cream over terracotta

blue over lilac

mustard over white

grey over white

lime green over white

lilac over mauve

1 Pour the paint into a shallow container and dip the sponge into it; scrape off the excess paint on the edge of the container, ensuring that there are no blobs left on the sponge. Lightly dab the paint on to the surface, varying the angle of application to prevent a uniform appearance.

2 Add more paint to the wall, continuing to work over the surface until you have covered it completely. If necessary, fill in any gaps and make sure that the overall pattern is of similar "weight" – not too heavy in some areas or too light in others.

# SPONGING LAYERS

The technique is the same as for sponging one layer, but the overall effect is deepened by the addition of one or more other colours. After the first has been applied and allowed to dry, you can proceed with the second, taking care not to put on too much paint, otherwise you will obliterate the colour below. Experiment with colour combinations, and perhaps try using a natural sponge for one layer and a synthetic sponge for another.

## Materials

emulsion (latex) paint    natural sponge
  in two colours

## COLOUR EFFECTS

turquoise
and lime green

pale terracotta
and yellow

purple
and grey

cornflower blue
and grey

orange, red
and yellow

pale green, jade
and grey

1 Apply a single layer by dipping the sponge into the paint, then scrape off the excess and dab on to the wall for an even pattern. Making the pattern even is not quite so important when applying two colours because the second layer will soften the effect. Allow the surface to dry completely.

2 Make sure the sponge is completely clean and dry. Dip it into the second colour paint, scraping off the excess as before and dabbing on to the surface. Do not apply too much paint, however, as you must make sure the first colour isn't totally covered.

# DRAGGING

A special dragging brush is often used to achieve this effect, but it can also be done with a household paintbrush or even the end of a sponge. The technique is very simple – the brush is pulled down over wet paint in a clean line to produce a striped effect. These lines must be unbroken, so painting a full-height room may prove extremely difficult. To overcome this, a horizontal band can be added to break up the height of the room.

### Materials

| | |
|---|---|
| pencil | paint pot |
| rule | large paintbrush |
| emulsion (latex) paint | dragging brush |
| wallpaper paste | damp cloth |

### COLOUR EFFECTS

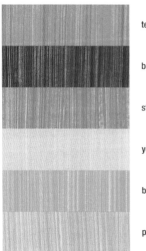

terracotta

brown

stone blue

yellow

biscuit

powder blue

**1** Draw a horizontal baseline across the wall at dado (chair rail) level. Mix emulsion (latex) paint with 50 per cent wallpaper paste (premixed to a thin solution) in a paint pot and brush on in a lengthways band, slightly overlapping the baseline. Work on one small section at a time, about 15–25cm (6–10in) wide.

**4** Drag straight over the join between the two areas of paint and carry on dragging. Continue in this way from one end of the wall to the other.

2 Dampen the dragging brush with the wash before use, as initially it will take off too much paint if used dry. Then take the brush in one hand and flatten the bristles out with your other hand. Pull the brush down in as straight a motion as possible. This will create deep groove lines in the paint mixture.

3 Brush on another band of paint mixture, adjacent to the last one and overlapping it slightly. Do not cover too large an area at a time, otherwise the paint may become unworkable as it begins to dry.

5 Once this top section has been done, take a damp cloth and, pulling along the pencil line, remove the excess paint.

6 Drag in a horizontal motion across the bottom of the baseline, creating subtle stripes in a different direction.

# STIPPLING

A delicate and subtle finish can be achieved by stippling. The technique consists of making fine, pinpoint marks over a wash of emulsion (latex) paint, and it creates a soft, mottled effect. However, it can be quite tiring to do, as the brush has to be dabbed over the surface many times, using firm, even pressure. Two people can speed up the process, one person applying the paint and the other stippling the surface.

## Materials

emulsion (latex) paint    household paintbrush

paint pot    stippling brush

wallpaper paste

## COLOUR EFFECTS

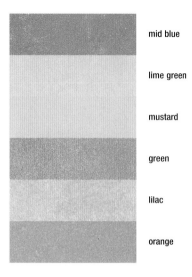

mid blue

lime green

mustard

green

lilac

orange

1 Mix a wash of 50 per cent emulsion (latex) paint and 50 per cent wallpaper paste, premixed to a thin solution, in a paint pot. Brush on a thin, even coat of the mixture, covering an area of about 0.2 sq m (2 sq ft).

2 Take the stippling brush and dab over the surface with the tips of the bristles until the effect is even all over. Continue stippling the surface until there are no obvious joins (seams) and the whole effect looks soft and even.

# ROLLER FIDGETING

This is a quick and simple technique and consists of pouring two undiluted emulsion (latex) paint colours into a roller tray, one at each side. You will find that the two paints will sit quite happily together and do not instantly mix. Then, a long-pile masonry roller is skimmed over the surface of these colours until a good thick coat is applied. This is rollered on to the wall at varying angles.

## Materials

| | |
|---|---|
| paint tray | long-pile masonry roller |
| emulsion (latex) paint | 2.5cm (1in) household |
| in two colours | paintbrush |

## COLOUR EFFECTS

red and camel

mid blue and grey

grey and cream

yellow and cream

pale mauve and dark mauve

mid blue and green

**1** Pour two colours, one on each side of the pool of the roller tray. Apply a thick coat from here on to the roller so that it will create a two-tone effect. Apply the roller to the wall at varying angles, using short strokes.

**2** Continue without applying more paint to the roller until the colours are slightly softened together. Keep the angles as random as possible. Go over the whole effect with the roller to soften it. Add more paint when starting another area.

# RAGGING

There are two methods of ragging – ragging on and ragging off – and both techniques are as simple as they sound. With ragging on, you dab the rag into the paint, then dab on to the surface. The technique is similar to sponging, but leaves a sharper effect. The effect will vary depending whether you use a similar colour to the base or a strongly contrasting one. Make sure that the ragging is applied evenly.

## Materials

| | |
|---|---|
| emulsion (latex) paint | roller tray |
| wallpaper paste | large paintbrush |
| paint pot | chamois |

Ragging off produces a stronger effect, like crumpled fabric. You brush paint on to the surface, then use a rag to remove some of the paint, leaving a ragged print. The recommended "rag" to use is a chamois, as it creates a definite print, although you can use most types of cloth for a particular effect.

When using either of the techniques, it is important to apply the rag to the wall with firm, but gentle, pressure. When you remove it, lift it cleanly from the surface without any vertical or sideways movement that might smear the paint and spoil the finished effect. The chamois leather should be squeezed out periodically.

### RAGGING ON

1 Mix 50 per cent emulsion (latex) paint with 50 per cent wallpaper paste in a paint pot. Pour into a roller tray. Scrunch up a chamois, dip it into the paint and dab off the excess, then dab the "rag" on to the wall.

2 Continue re-scrunching the chamois and dipping it into the paint as before, then dabbing it on to the wall in a random manner. Carry on in this way until the surface has been covered evenly and completely.

## RAGGING OFF

1 Mix 50 per cent emulsion (latex) and 50 per cent wallpaper paste as before. Brush the wash over a large area.

2 Take a chamois, scrunch it up and dab on to the wall to remove small areas of paint. Vary the angle with each dab.

## COLOUR EFFECTS

mid blue

deep mauve

biscuit

grey

pale mauve

terracotta

3 Continue working over the surface until the entire effect is even. If you find you are taking off too much paint, apply more immediately with a brush, then dab the chamois over the surface in the same manner as before.

# DISTRESSING

This is a way of ageing paint to create chips and scratches that would occur naturally on a painted piece of furniture over a matter of time. The method shown here employs petroleum jelly and candle wax, but you can use just one or the other. This creates a barrier between the surface and the paint, so once the paint is dry it can be lifted away in certain areas where the medium has been applied.

## Materials

| | |
|---|---|
| petroleum jelly | paint scraper |
| artist's paintbrush | soapy water |
| emulsion (latex) paint | wax candle |
| household paintbrush | varnish |

1 Using an artist's paintbrush, load it with petroleum jelly and apply long blobs in the direction of the grain of wood over a suitably coloured base coat. Even if the surface is not wooden, rub in a lengthways direction.

## COLOUR EFFECTS

blue over
yellow
over wood

mauve over
blue over wood

green over
blue over wood

orange over
yellow
over wood

purple over
red over wood

blue over
burnt orange
over wood

4 Wash down thoroughly with soapy water, as the paint that is sitting on top of the petroleum jelly will not actually dry and you will not be able to totally remove the petroleum jelly surface by using the scraper alone.

2 Carefully paint the surface, making sure it is covered completely, but ensuring that the petroleum jelly is not dragged about too much, since it will spread readily under the action of the paintbrush. Allow the paint to dry thoroughly.

3 Once the paint has dried completely, carefully go over the surface with a paint scraper. This will lift off the areas of paint where the petroleum jelly has prevented contact between the top coat and base coat.

5 Once dry, rub over with a wax candle and then paint again, using a contrasting colour. (You could use another layer of petroleum jelly, following the same procedure as before, but the finished effect would not look as subtle.)

6 When the paint is dry, go over the surface once more with a paint scraper to lift off the areas over the candle wax. Wipe down to remove all the flakes of paint, then apply a coat of varnish to protect the surface.

# WOOD WASHING

You can stain wood with a colour while allowing the beauty of the grain to show through, using wood washing (wood staining). The wood must be bare, either new or stripped of all traces of varnish, wax or previous paint. Depending on the product used, the surface may or may not need varnishing – read the manufacturer's instructions. Usually a matt (flat) finish looks appropriate for this technique.

## Materials

| | |
|---|---|
| specialist wood wash (wood stain) | household paintbrush |
| paint pot | cloth |

## COLOUR EFFECTS

yellow ochre

blue

Indian red

violet

cream

pale green

1 Pour the premixed wash (stain) into a paint pot. Then brush the wash evenly on to the wood, working in the direction of the grain. Keep a "wet" edge and do not overlap areas.

2 While wet, wipe off the excess with a cloth. This will even the effect and expose slightly more of the grain. Then leave to dry before varnishing if required.

# CRACKLE GLAZE

This technique reproduces the effect of old, crackled paint, but it can only work if you use a special crackle-glaze medium. A base coat is applied first, and when dry, a layer of crackle glaze is added. This is followed by a top coat of paint, which will not be able to grip the base coat while drying and subsequently will shrink and crack to produce a crackled effect. You can achieve some striking colour combinations with this technique.

## Materials

| | |
|---|---|
| emulsion (latex) paint in two colours | household paintbrush crackle-glaze medium |

## COLOUR EFFECTS

mustard over red

navy over pale blue

mid blue over yellow

turquoise over lime green

lilac over purple

yellow over red

**1** Apply a coat of base colour and leave to dry thoroughly. Then apply a second coat of base colour and allow to dry again. Apply a good solid coat of crackle-glaze medium. The timing for applying the various coats will vary according to the manufacturer, so follow the instructions given on the container.

**2** Apply the top coat. Generally, the thicker the top coat of paint, the larger the cracks in the final effect. Make sure the top coat contrasts greatly with the one underneath so that the cracks are obvious. Do not overbrush when applying the top coat, as the effect occurs quite quickly and you could spoil it.

# PATTERNED PAINT EFFECTS

There is a long tradition of using both simple and complex patterns as forms of decoration, but in the main these have been provided by wallpaper, which is a quick and convenient way of doing the job. However, using paint to make patterns allows you to create something quite unique. There are many ways of applying pattern as a decoration, whether freehand or using a template. With stencilling and stamping, you can add an individual touch to your schemes by choosing designs from a wealth that are available commercially or by drawing, cutting, and using your own stencils and stamps. Classic lines and stripes never seem to go out of fashion, and grid patterns are a fun way of combining colours.

# STENCILLING

The decorative possibilities of stencilling are endless, so it is not surprising that it is one of the most popular of paint effects. It is an ideal way to create an interesting border or all-over pattern using motifs that relate to the theme of your room. Stencilling also enables you to co-ordinate furnishings and accessories by picking out details in similar or contrasting colours. Or you can use the patterns and colours of your stencilling as a starting point for the style and colours of your home. The fleur-de-lis and rose design shown here is typical of what can be achieved.

## Materials

| | |
|---|---|
| household sponge | masking tape |
| emulsion (latex) paint | spray adhesive |
| in three colours | tracing paper |
| rule | stencil card or acetate |
| spirit (carpenter's) | two motif stencils |
| level | stencil brush and fine |
| pencil | lining brush |

1 Using a large sponge, rub the first emulsion (latex) colour on the wall. Leave to dry. Repeat using a second colour to cover the base. Using a rule and spirit (carpenter's) level, draw a line at dado (chair rail) height and place masking tape above it. Sponge your third colour below this.

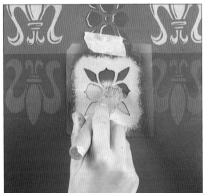

4 When you have completed a line of motifs above the dividing line, make sure that the paint on the faces of the stencils is completely dry (or cut new ones), then flip the stencils over and position them as mirror images below the original motifs. Stencil the roses in the base colour and the fleur-de-lis in the second colour.

2 If necessary, cut stencils from stencil card or acetate. Secure the rose stencil above the dividing line and stencil in your third colour with a stencil brush. When dry, position the fleur-de-lis stencil next to the first and paint in the colour of the base coat. Alternate stencils around the room.

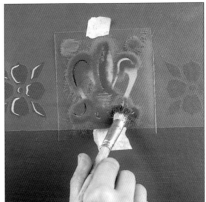

3 Make some highlighting stencils, using the originals as templates. Place them over the painted motifs and, with a stencil brush, add highlights in the base colour to the first stencilled design, and highlights in the third colour to the second design.

5 Allow the paint to dry, then go back and add highlights to the motifs as before, using base colour on the fleur-de-lis and the third colour on the roses. Again, make sure that there is no wet paint on the faces of the flipped stencils, since this could be transferred to the wall and spoil the overall effect.

6 Using a fine lining brush and the base colour paint, paint a narrow line where the two different colours on the wall meet. If you do not have the confidence to do this freehand, position two lines of masking tape on the wall, leaving a small gap between them. When the line of paint is dry, carefully remove the masking tape.

# STAMPING

Like stencilling, stamping allows you to create your own decorative motifs. It is easy and inexpensive to cut out shapes in relief from high-density sponge and to use them to apply paint. However, you can also achieve quite sophisticated effects with this simple technique, and the steps here show how to add a special touch to a room by stamping panels with gold leaf. This is achieved by stamping the wall with gold size first, then rubbing on gold leaf, which will adhere to the tacky surface.

## Materials

| | |
|---|---|
| card (card stock) | household sponge |
| rule | plumbline |
| pencil | tape measure |
| scissors | small paint roller |
| high-density sponge | gold size |
| craft knife | Dutch Metal |
| emulsion (latex) paint | (simulated gold leaf) |
| in jade green and | soft brush |
| purple | |

1 Fold a 30cm (12in) square piece of card in half, cut an arc from corner to corner and unfold to create a symmetrical arch template.

4 Using a plumbline as a guide, and beginning 23cm (9in) from a corner, mark a vertical line up the wall to a height of 1.8m (6ft). Use the plumbline to draw vertical lines every 60cm (2ft).

7 When the size is tacky, apply Dutch Metal (simulated gold leaf) by rubbing over the backing paper with a soft brush. Peel the backing away.

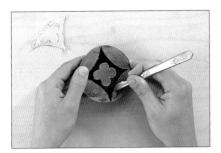

2 Transfer a design on to a piece of high-density sponge. Using a craft knife, cut away excess sponge from around the shape.

3 Apply jade green emulsion (latex) paint to the wall using a sponge and working in a circular motion. Allow the paint to dry.

5 Measure 15cm (6in) to each side of each line and draw two more vertical lines to mark the edges of the panels. Place the template at the top of each panel and draw in the curves.

6 Load the stamp with gold size and apply it to the areas within the outlined panels, beginning at the centre top and working down in horizontal lines. Reload the stamp as necessary.

8 Once the panel has been gilded completely, go over it with a soft brush to remove any excess gold leaf.

9 Using the centre of the stamp, fill in the spaces between the gold motifs with purple emulsion paint.

# STRIPES

A classic design for decorating schemes, stripes are extremely versatile, as you can vary their width for any number of effects. If you are aiming for a symmetrical, formal look, it is important to measure out the available space accurately first so that you can be sure the stripes will fit. It is helpful to draw out the design in a small scale on a piece of paper to work out the correct balance.

## Materials

| | |
|---|---|
| emulsion (latex) paint in two colours | pencil |
| | masking tape |
| paint roller | acrylic scumble |
| paint tray | nylon stocking |
| paintbrushes | cardboard |

1 Paint the walls. Mark the centre of the most important wall with a pencil. Make marks 7.5cm (3in) on each side of this, then every 15cm (6in). Continue around the room until the marks meet at the least noticeable corner.

4 Dilute some of the second colour with about 25 per cent water and 25 per cent acrylic scumble. Complete each stripe in two or three stages, blending the joins to achieve an even result.

7 Working on one stripe at a time, place masking tape between the top corners and the mark. Brush on the second colour, then dab the stocking over the wet paint. Leave to dry.

2 Hang a short length of plumbline from one of the marks, and mark with a dot where it rests. Then, hang the plumbline from this dot and mark where it rests. Continue down the wall. Repeat for each mark below the picture rail.

3 Starting in the centre of the wall, place strips of masking tape on alternate sides of the marked rows of dots to give 15cm (6in) wide stripes. Repeat until you have taped all the walls.

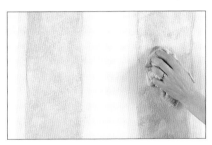

5 Dab the wet paint lightly with the stocking to smooth out the brush marks. Complete all the stripes, peel off the masking tape and leave the paint to dry.

6 From a piece of cardboard, cut a triangle with a 15cm (6in) base and measuring 10cm (4in) from base to tip. Use this to mark the centre of each stripe.

8 Dilute some of the second colour paint with 20 parts water to one part paint. Brush this over the wall, working in all directions to give a hint of colour to the first colour stripes.

9 Add a little paint to the remaining diluted mixture to strengthen the colour. Using a paint guard or strip of card to protect the painted wall, brush the paint on to the picture rail.

# PRINTED TILES

This is an inexpensive and clever way to create a tiled effect with simple painted squares. Fine tape separates the tiles and is removed when the effect is finished to give the illusion of grouting. Leave some of the squares plain, but add extra effects to others by sponging them or dabbing them with a nylon stocking. Experiment with different colours to create your own design, or leave some of the squares white as a contrast. You could also experiment with mosaic patterns by measuring and masking much smaller squares with fine lining tape before applying the second colour. You need not restrict yourself to creating squares either; you could try oblongs, triangles or diamonds, or perhaps even combinations of these shapes.

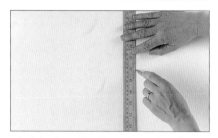

**1** Paint the wall in white, using a paint roller to achieve an even texture. Decide on the width of your "tiled" panel. Mark the wall 45cm (18in) above your work surface and in the centre of the width measurement.

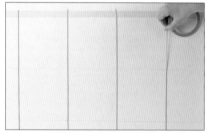

**4** Place fine masking tape over the lines in both directions. Smooth the tape into place with your fingers, pressing it down well to ensure that paint does not seep underneath it.

## Materials

| | |
|---|---|
| emulsion (latex) paint in white and a second colour | standard, fine and low-tack masking tape |
| paint roller | sponge |
| paint tray | kitchen paper (paper towels) |
| paintbrush | |
| rule | nylon stocking |
| pencil | eraser |
| spirit (carpenter's) level | |

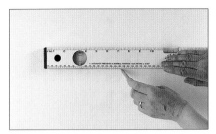

2 Draw a horizontal line across the wall at this height, using a spirit (carpenter's) level to make sure that it is straight and level. Apply a strip of standard masking tape to the wall above the line, making sure that it butts up to it accurately.

3 Mark dots along the tape at 15cm (6in) intervals on each side of the centre mark. Use the spirit level to draw vertical lines down the wall. Mark along the vertical lines at 15cm (6in) intervals and connect them with horizontal lines.

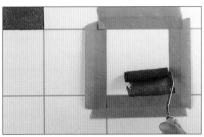

5 Place low-tack masking tape around one square. Pour the second colour into the paint tray and add 25 per cent water. Roll an even coat over the square. Repeat for all plain squares.

6 Mask off a square to be sponged. Dampen the sponge, dip it into the second colour and dab the excess on to kitchen paper (paper towels). Sponge the square. Repeat for other squares.

7 Mask off a square to be dabbed with the nylon stocking. Apply the paint with a brush, then use the stocking to blend it. Repeat for all the squares needing this effect.

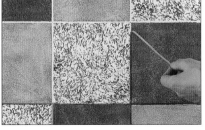

8 Allow the paint to dry partially, then remove the tape while it is still soft. When the paint is completely dry, clean off all the pencil marks with an eraser.

# FAUX PAINT FINISHES

Techniques that reproduce the look of a particular surface or material are often very challenging, but they can be great fun too, and when done correctly they can produce very realistic and satisfying results. The following pages will show you how to achieve a number of wood and stone finishes that will allow you to create imaginative decorative effects throughout your home. Effects include pine, oak, mahogany, beech and marbling. Artist's oil colours are used, since their lengthy drying periods allow more time to work on the effect, and their colours are intense and translucent.

# PINE

Woodgraining and wood effects can seem difficult and daunting to the beginner, but the right choice of colours and suitable base coats can be half the battle. The only specialist tools used are a heart grainer (graining roller) and comb, which are necessary as the patterns they create cannot be imitated in any other way. Both are relatively simple to use with a little practice and create convincing effects.

Look at pieces of real wood so that you can learn to replicate the grain accurately. Pine is readily available and you can use a pine effect surface in many locations throughout your home.

## Materials

| | |
|---|---|
| satinwood paint in pale yellow | white spirit (paint thinner) |
| household paintbrush | heart grainer (graining roller) |
| paint pot | comb |
| artist's oil colour paint in yellow ochre and burnt umber | large paintbrush varnish |

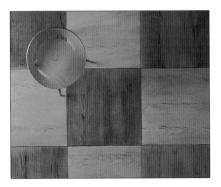

**1** Prepare the surface to be woodgrained in the normal manner. Brush on two coats of pale yellow satinwood paint, allowing each coat to dry thoroughly before proceeding.

**4** Following the direction of the dragging, pull the heart grainer (graining roller) down gently, rocking it as you work, to create the effect. Butt one line straight over the other.

2 Mix yellow ochre artist's oil colour paint with a tiny amount of burnt umber to dirty the colour slightly. Then mix with white spirit (paint thinner) to create a thick cream, and brush over the surface.

3 Drag the brush in a lengthways direction over the wet paint. This will allow streaks of the base colour to show through, which is the basis for the woodgrain effect.

5 Use the comb to make graduated cone shapes in random positions across the surface between the heart graining, slightly overlapping it in some areas.

6 Soften the surface while wet with a large dry brush, applying only light pressure and brushing in the direction of the effect. Varnish the finish when dry.

# OAK

Perhaps nothing speaks more of a traditional style than solid oak wood furniture or panelling. Here is a way of disguising inexpensive white wood or modern pine and giving it the look of dark oak. If you are painting bare wood, remember to give it a coat of primer before starting the paint effect. This technique requires a heart grainer (graining roller) and a comb to re-create the details of the woodgrain, both of which can be bought from most good craft shops and specialist decorating shops.

## Materials

| | |
|---|---|
| gloss or satin paint in beige | paint pot |
| | graduated comb |
| paintbrush | fine graduated comb |
| artist's oil colour paint in burnt umber | heart grainer (graining roller) |
| | cloth |
| white spirit (paint thinner) | large paintbrush |
| | varnish |

1 Prepare the surface to be woodgrained in the normal manner. Apply two coats of beige for the base coat in either gloss or satin finish, allowing each to dry thoroughly.

4 Use a heart grainer (graining roller) to start creating the detailed figuring of the grain. Do this by pulling the tool down gently over the surface with a slight rocking motion, to create the hearts with random spacings. Butt one line straight over the other as you go.

2 Mix burnt umber artists' oil colour paint with white spirit (paint thinner) in a small paint pot until it is the consistency of thick cream. Brush on and drag in a lengthways direction.

3 Using a graduated comb, pull down on the surface. Do not work in totally straight lines, but make them curve slightly, butting one up against the other.

5 When you are satisfied with the effect that the heart graining produces, take the fine graduated comb and go over all the previous combing. As the work progresses, you will begin to see the finish take on the appearance of genuine oak.

6 Wrap a piece of clean, lint-free cloth around the comb and dab it on to the surface in a random manner to create the angled grain, pressing it into the wet paint. Then soften the overall effect by going over the entire surface with a large dry brush. Varnish when dry.

# MAHOGANY

This beautiful hardwood has a rich, warm colour that seems to suit most styles of home, whether traditional or modern. It was extremely popular during the Victorian era when it was complemented by deep-toned furnishings and fabrics. These days it is not ecologically desirable to use mahogany, and it is also hard to come by and expensive, so all the more reason to paint some for yourself. Practise on sample pieces first, then progress to larger furniture when you have more confidence in the technique.

## Materials

| | |
|---|---|
| satin or gloss paint in dusky pink | white spirit (paint thinner) |
| artist's oil colour paint in burnt sienna, crimson and burnt umber | paint pots |
| | paintbrushes in different sizes |
| | varnish |

1 Apply two coats of dusky pink and leave to dry. Tint burnt sienna oil paint with crimson, adding white spirit (paint thinner) to make a thick creamy consistency. Brush on in long strips. Thin burnt umber to a thick cream. Fill gaps with long strips.

2 Stipple the surface gently with a dry paintbrush to soften the overall effect.

3 Starting at the bottom, with a 10cm (4in) paintbrush held almost parallel to the surface, drag through the wet paint in elongated arcs. Use the burnt umber area as the middle section. Before completely dry, soften in one direction using a large dry brush. Varnish when dry.

# BEECH

In recent years, beech has become popular for both furniture and home accessories such as trays, and mirror and picture frames. It is a light-coloured, straight-grained wood, and its close patterning gives it a look of solidity. Its soft, warm colour and generally matt (flat) finish adds a quiet, but modern, tone to a room as well as helping to lighten it up. Like oak, beech is sometimes given a limed effect, so if this is what you require allow more of the base coat to show through when painting.

## Materials

| | |
|---|---|
| satinwood paint in white | white spirit (paint thinner) |
| household paintbrush | heart grainer (graining roller) |
| paint pot | fine graduated comb |
| artist's oil colour paint in Naples yellow and white | narrow comb |
| | varnish |

**1** Apply two coats of white satinwood and leave to dry. Mix the yellow and white oils with white spirit (paint thinner) until a thick cream; brush on the surface. Drag in a lengthways direction.

**2** Use a heart grainer (graining roller) to start graining, pulling it down gently and rocking it slightly, working in spaced lines. Do not butt them together. Use a graduated comb in the same direction to fill in between the heart graining.

**3** Again, working in the same direction, soften the effect with a large dry brush. Now take a narrow comb and go over the entire surface in the same direction to add detail. Varnish when dry.

# MARBLING

There are many specialist techniques for achieving a marble effect, but here is a very simple method. Types of marble vary greatly in colour and pattern, and it may be a good idea to use a piece of real marble as a reference source. Aim for a general effect of marbled patterning that is subtle in colour, with most of the veining softened to create depth.

Try colour variations of crimson and ultramarine; raw sienna and black; Indian red, yellow ochre and black; raw sienna, yellow ochre and Prussian blue; or Prussian blue and ultramarine.

## Materials

| | |
|---|---|
| satinwood paint in white | small paint pots |
| household paintbrush | white spirit (paint thinner) |
| artist's oil colour paint in ultramarine and yellow ochre | stippling brush |
| | swordliner brush |
| | gloss varnish |

1 Paint a base coat of white satinwood paint on to the surface and leave to dry. Squeeze a long blob of ultramarine artist's oil colour paint into a paint pot and add some white spirit (paint thinner) to form a thick cream. Brush on patches of this.

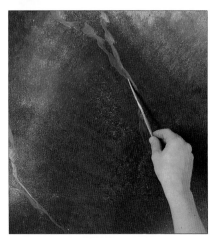

4 Dip a swordliner brush into white spirit and drag it through the wet surface, applying no pressure, but just letting the brush stroke the surface of the paint. Slightly angle the bristles while you pull the brush down.

2 Squeeze some yellow ochre artist's oil colour paint into a second paint kettle and dilute it with white spirit until it is the consistency of thick cream. Fill in the patches where the blue has not been painted with this mixture.

3 While the oil colours are still wet, take a stippling brush and work over the entire surface, blending them gently together. The idea is to make one colour fade gradually into the next without any hard lines.

5 Dip the brush back into the white spirit for each line. The white spirit will finally separate the oil glaze surface. Make sure there are not too many lines and only add the odd fork – the less complicated the pattern, the better the effect will be.

6 Dip the swordliner into the dark blue glaze remaining from step 1 and draw down the side of each painted line with a very fine line. When you are happy with the effect, allow the paint to dry completely, then coat with gloss varnish.

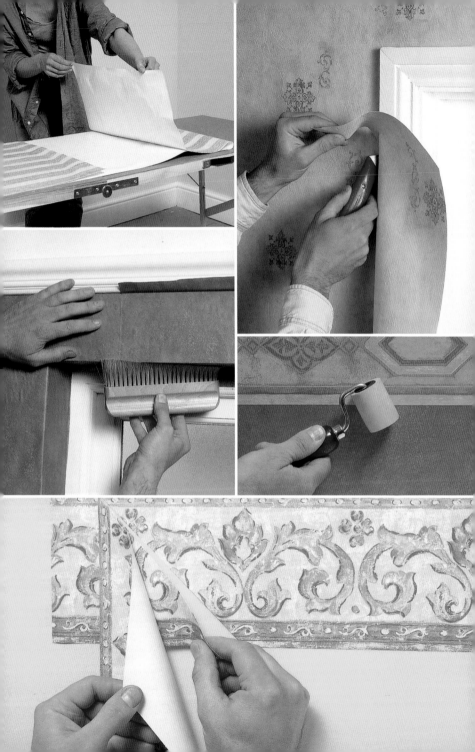

# PAPERING WALLS & CEILINGS

- Wallcovering materials
- Wallcovering preparation
- Wallcovering techniques

# INTRODUCTION

**F**ifty years ago, practically all of the rooms of almost every home would have had papered walls, and many would have had papered ceilings too. When decorating, few people would have even considered not hanging wallpaper; it was how things were done. In more recent times, however, the popularity of wallcoverings has diminished, and today many look upon them as a more luxurious finish to be reserved for the more important rooms in the home. That said, modern wallcoverings – not all of which are paper based – are far more versatile than their forerunners, offering not only a wide range of colours and patterns, but also in some cases high wear and moisture resistance, making them particularly suitable for kitchens, bathrooms and children's rooms, where traditional wallpapers would not be an ideal choice.

Many of today's do-it-yourselfers may be put off by the thought of hanging a wallcovering. But hanging wallcoverings is actually quite a straightforward task that, in the main, requires only care to achieve very professional-looking results.

While it is true that wallcoverings are not as popular as they once were, there is no doubt that a well-chosen example

LEFT: Hanging wallcoverings requires the use of a few specialized tools, which are readily available. You will also need an inexpensive folding pasting table and at least one set of sturdy stepladders.

ABOVE: When joining border papers that have intricate patterns, professional results can be achieved by cutting around a prominent shape in the pattern and butting the ends together.

While practically all wallcoverings are printed by machine, hand-printed examples are still available, often offering traditional patterns. Not surprisingly, they are expensive, but for the restoration of a period property they offer the perfect decorative solution.

You don't need many special tools for hanging wallcoverings, unlike many other do-it-yourself jobs: pasting and hanging brushes, some paperhanger's scissors and a pasting table, all of which are inexpensive. With this equipment, a roll of wallpaper and this chapter, you'll soon be giving your rooms a new look.

can give a far more impressive finish to a room than paint alone. Whether you want a subdued delicate pattern, a wildly flamboyant design, muted colours or bold tones, there will be a wallcovering to meet your needs. Moreover, you need not restrict yourself to flat coverings either, since there is a good choice of textured materials to be had. As with colours and patterns, textures may be light or heavy, and several can be over-painted, offering even greater decorative possibilities.

There are special finishes, too, that may be based on foils, fabrics and natural materials such as grasses. While these are more difficult to hang than conventional wallcoverings, they may be just what is required to add a final feature to a decorative scheme.

## AVOIDING PASTE DRIPS

A length of string tied tightly across the top of a wallpaper paste bucket makes a handy brush rest. Use the string rather than the side of the bucket for removing excess adhesive from the pasting brush.

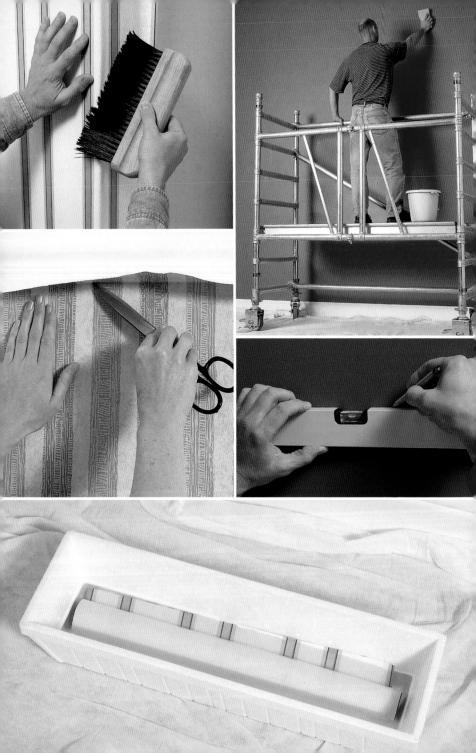

# WALLCOVERING MATERIALS

These days, there are wallcoverings for every room in your home, offering a wide choice of colourways, patterns and textures. Some offer good wear resistance, and many are washable. So when considering this type of decorative finish, the first decision to make is what type of wallcovering suits your needs; then you can select from the colours and patterns on offer. Estimating quantities is important, as you don't want to end up with too many rolls; equally, too few could cause problems, as subsequent rolls you buy may come from later batches and display colour differences. Fortunately, estimating is a simple task. You will need some special tools and equipment, but these are widely available.

# CHOOSING WALLCOVERINGS

Wallcoverings offer a wide range of patterns and colourways, from very traditional to the most modern designs. Choose with care, particularly if you are new to hanging wallpaper, as some will be much easier to hang than others. Check the manufacturer's guidelines before buying to determine the suitability of the paper.

## BUYING WALLCOVERINGS

When shopping for wallcoverings, ask for a large sample of any design that catches your eye so you can examine it in the room that is to be decorated. Look at the samples in both natural and artificial light, near a window and in a dark corner, as some colours and patterns alter dramatically when viewed in different lights.

Test a sample for durability by moistening it under a tap. If it tears easily or the colours run when rubbed lightly, the paper could be difficult to hang and maintain. Avoid thin papers, particularly if you are an inexperienced decorator, as they are likely to tear when moistened by the paste and may be difficult to hang.

Never skimp on the number of rolls you buy, and check that the batch number on all rolls is the same, as there may be a slight colour variation between batches that may not be noticeable on the roll, but could become obvious after hanging. However, the batch system is not infallible, so check rolls again for a good colour match before cutting and hanging. It is also worth buying at least one extra roll. Many retailers offer a sale-or-return service.

## CHOOSING A PATTERN

Take a critical look at the room you plan to decorate and make a note of any aspects that could make hanging a wallcovering difficult. Uneven walls and

ABOVE: A freematch wallpaper or one with a continuous pattern, such as stripes, will not need an allowance for pattern matching.

ABOVE: A straight-match pattern has the same part of the pattern running down each side of the paper, making the cutting of drops simple.

ABOVE: An offset pattern has motifs staggered between drops, which must be taken into account when cutting and measuring the paper.

awkward corners, for example, can make pattern matching particularly problematic, while some types of wallcovering will conceal a poor surface better than others.

Regular patterns, such as vertical stripes, checks and repetitive geometric designs, will emphasize walls that are out of true, whereas random florals and paint-effect papers will not encourage the eye to rest on any one point and, therefore, will help to disguise awkward angles. Trimming can also ruin the appearance of a large pattern, so in a room that has a sloping or uneven ceiling, or several windows, cabinets and doors, a design with a small pattern may be a better choice. If a poor surface is the problem, avoid thin or shiny wallcoverings, which will highlight every blemish.

If you are not an experienced decorator, avoid complicated patterns, as any mismatching will be obvious; instead consider using one of the many easy-to-hang, freematch designs that are readily available.

BELOW: Wallcoverings are available in many different designs and finishes, so choose with care.

# ESTIMATING QUANTITIES

Standard wallcoverings are sold in rolls that measure approximately 10m long by 530mm wide (33ft x 21in). Use the tables to calculate the number of rolls that you require for walls and ceilings, remembering to add 10 per cent for waste, especially if the design has a large pattern repeat. Lining paper is usually 560mm (22in) wide and is available in standard 10m (33ft) and larger roll sizes. You can calculate the number of rolls required from the tables, but there is no need to add any extra for a pattern repeat. For walls, measure around the room and include all the windows and doors in your calculation, except for very large picture windows and patio doors. It is easier to measure the perimeter of the floor to calculate the size of a ceiling.

Depending on where they were manufactured, you may find papers in non-standard sizes, so do check. This could well be the case with handmade wallcoverings. These often have the added complication of an unprinted border down each edge, which must be removed before hanging, although some suppliers may be able to do this for you. In the USA, wallcoverings vary in width and length, but are usually available in rolls sized to cover specific areas.

In fact, it is not that difficult to calculate your requirements for a non-standard wallcovering. When papering walls, measure the height of the wall first and divide the length of a single roll by that figure. This will give you the number of drops you can cut from a single roll. Multiply that number by the width of the roll to determine the width of wall that will be covered by a roll. Then divide the total width of all the walls to be covered by that figure. This will give you the total number of rolls needed. As before, include windows and doors and add 10 per cent for waste.

If in any doubt, approach your supplier; many will be happy to make the calculation for you.

## CALCULATING THE NUMBER OF ROLLS NEEDED FOR A CEILING

| MEASUREMENT AROUND ROOM | | NUMBER OF ROLLS |
|---|---|---|
| 10m | (33ft) | 2 |
| 11m | (36ft) | 2 |
| 12m | (39ft) | 2 |
| 13m | (43ft) | 3 |
| 14m | (46ft) | 3 |
| 15m | (49ft) | 4 |
| 16m | (52ft) | 4 |
| 17m | (56ft) | 4 |
| 18m | (59ft) | 5 |
| 19m | (62ft) | 5 |
| 20m | (66ft) | 5 |
| 21m | (69ft) | 6 |
| 22m | (72ft) | 7 |
| 23m | (75ft) | 7 |
| 24m | (79ft) | 8 |
| 25m | (82ft) | 8 |

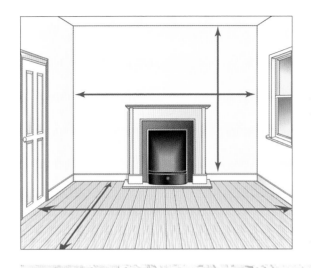

LEFT: Measuring up for wallcovering. Measure the height of the walls and their total width. Then refer to the tables to determine the number of standard-size rolls required. There is no need to deduct the area of doors and windows, unless they are very large. If you want to paper the ceiling, it will be easier to measure the floor to calculate the area.

## CALCULATING THE NUMBER OF ROLLS NEEDED FOR WALLS

| WIDTH OF WALLS | HEIGHT OF ROOM FROM SKIRTING (BASEBOARD) | | | | | | | |
|---|---|---|---|---|---|---|---|---|
| | 2–2.25m (6ft 7in– 7ft 5in) | 2.25–2.5m (7ft 5in– 8ft 2in) | 2.5–2.75m (8ft 2in– 9ft) | 2.75–3m (9ft– 9ft 10in) | 3–3.25m (9ft 10in– 10ft 8in) | 3.25–3.5m (10ft 8in– 11ft 6in) | 3.5–3.75m (11ft 6in– 12ft 4in) | 3.75–4m (12ft 4in– 13ft 1in) |
| | NUMBER OF ROLLS | | | | | | | |
| 10m (33ft) | 5 | 5 | 6 | 6 | 7 | 7 | 8 | 8 |
| 11m (36ft) | 5 | 6 | 7 | 7 | 8 | 8 | 9 | 9 |
| 12m (39ft) | 6 | 6 | 7 | 8 | 8 | 9 | 9 | 10 |
| 13m (43ft) | 6 | 7 | 8 | 8 | 9 | 10 | 10 | 10 |
| 14m (46ft) | 7 | 7 | 8 | 9 | 10 | 10 | 11 | 11 |
| 15m (49ft) | 7 | 8 | 9 | 9 | 10 | 11 | 12 | 12 |
| 16m (52ft) | 8 | 8 | 9 | 10 | 11 | 11 | 12 | 13 |
| 17m (56ft) | 8 | 9 | 10 | 10 | 11 | 12 | 13 | 14 |
| 18m (59ft) | 9 | 9 | 10 | 11 | 12 | 13 | 14 | 15 |
| 19m (62ft) | 9 | 10 | 11 | 12 | 13 | 14 | 15 | 16 |
| 20m (66ft) | 9 | 10 | 11 | 12 | 13 | 14 | 15 | 16 |
| 21m (69ft) | 10 | 11 | 12 | 13 | 14 | 15 | 16 | 17 |
| 22m (72ft) | 10 | 11 | 13 | 14 | 15 | 16 | 17 | 18 |
| 23m (75ft) | 11 | 12 | 13 | 14 | 15 | 17 | 18 | 19 |
| 24m (79ft) | 11 | 12 | 14 | 15 | 16 | 17 | 18 | 20 |
| 25m (82ft) | 12 | 13 | 14 | 15 | 17 | 18 | 19 | 20 |

# BASIC WALLCOVERINGS

When choosing a wallcovering, it is important to take into consideration how practical it will be in the room you wish to decorate. Each room in your home has very different requirements and by choosing the right type of wallcovering, you will be sure of a decorative surface that will wear well and look good for years to come.

## LINING PAPER

This provides a smooth base for wallpaper or paint on walls and ceilings. It is made in several grades from light 480 grade, suitable for new or near-perfect walls, to extra-thick 1200 grade for use on rough and pitted plaster. A good-quality lining paper will be easier to handle than a cheap, thin paper and less likely to tear when it has been moistened by paste.

## WALLPAPERS FOR PAINTING

Woodchip paper is made by sandwiching particles of wood between two layers of paper. The thicker grades are easy to hang and cover uneven surfaces quite well, but woodchip paper is not easy to cut and can be difficult to remove, while the thinner grades tear easily. Woodchip paper is a budget buy, but it is not particularly attractive or durable.

Relief wallpaper is imprinted with a raised, decorative surface pattern and is available in a wide choice of designs, as well as pre-cut dado (chair) rail panels and borders. It is quite easy to hang, although the thinner grades can tear when wet. It hides blemishes well and is durable once painted.

Textured vinyl has a deeply embossed surface pattern that masks flaws and is uncrushable, so it is suitable for hardwearing areas such as the hall (lobby) and children's rooms. It is more expensive than relief wallpaper, but is very easy to hang and usually dry strippable.

Embossed wallcovering comes in rolls and pre-cut panels made from a solid film of linseed oil and fillers fused on to a backing paper. It requires a special adhesive and will crack if folded. It is very expensive, but is extremely hardwearing and durable, and the deeply profiled, traditional designs are particularly suited to use in older and period properties. It can also be painted over.

## IMPORTANT CONSIDERATIONS

While woodchip and relief papers are ideal for disguising minor blemishes and irregularities in the wall surface, they cannot be used to hide a poor-quality surface. This should be borne in mind when choosing the wallcovering, and steps should be taken to make good any substantial damage, or an unstable surface, before hanging.

In addition, the heavier types of embossed wallcovering require special hanging techniques that may, in the long run, make it preferable to repair the wall and use a more conventional wallcovering. For example, some types may require the wall to be covered with

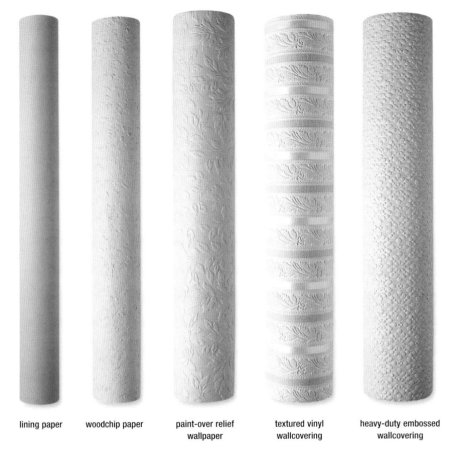

| lining paper | woodchip paper | paint-over relief wallpaper | textured vinyl wallcovering | heavy-duty embossed wallcovering |

lining paper first, and soaking times can be quite long. The back of some papers must be thoroughly soaked with hot water before applying paste. These papers are very stiff and must be handled with care; they cannot be folded, as this would break the relief pattern, leaving a permanent mark.

A seam roller cannot be used, as this would flatten the edges between drops, damaging the relief pattern and making the joins between drops really obvious. Instead, careful work with a paperhanger's brush is required to ensure that edges are pressed down. Because the papers cannot be folded, they cannot be brushed around internal and external corners. Therefore, drops must be cut to fit exactly up to the angles; at an external corner, the join must be disguised by applying a small amount of conventional cellulose filler (spackle) once the paper has dried.

# PRINTED WALLCOVERINGS

Printed wallcoverings offer a wide variety of designs and finishes to suit every situation in your home. Choose them with care.

## PATTERNED WALLCOVERINGS

Printed wallpaper is available in an extensive choice of patterns and colours. The cheapest are machine-printed, but top-price designs are hand-printed and often untrimmed, so hanging is best left to the professionals. Printed wallpaper can be sponged, but is not particularly durable and is best used in rooms where it will not be subjected to much wear. The thinner grades tear easily when pasted.

Washable wallpaper also comes in a good choice of designs, but is more durable and has a thin plastic coating that allows the surface to be washed clean when necessary. It is priced competitively, is fairly easy to hang and in some cases is dry strippable.

Vinyl wallcovering has a very durable surface layer of PVC that creates a hardwearing, often scrubbable, finish that resists steam, moisture and mould. There is a good choice of colours and patterns, as well as pearlized and embossed textured designs. Vinyl wallcovering is usually ready-pasted and dry strippable; paste-the-wall ranges are also available.

Sculptured vinyl is a thick, very hardwearing vinyl imprinted with a decorative design or tile effect. The waterproof finish resists steam, condensation, grease and cooking splashes, so it is a good choice for kitchens and bathrooms. It requires a heavy-duty adhesive, but is easy to hang and is dry strippable.

When buying wallcoverings, check the labels carefully to determine whether the covering you like will be suitable for the situation in which you want to hang it. If in doubt, seek the advice of your supplier. He or she will also be able to tell you if any special adhesives or hanging techniques will be required for what you have in mind. Be wary of opting for "fashionable" patterns, particularly if they are flamboyant, as they may soon lose their appeal.

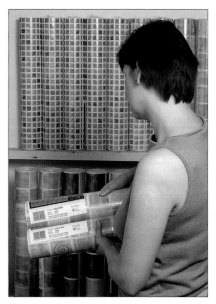

ABOVE: Some wallcoverings are more hardwearing than others. Bear this in mind when choosing a pattern and material.

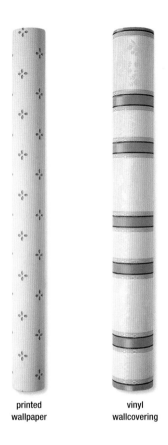

| printed wallpaper | vinyl wallcovering | paste-the-wall wallcovering | sculptured vinyl wallcovering |

## SPECIAL WALLCOVERINGS

Metallic foils and wallcoverings made from natural materials such as cork, silk and grasscloth can often be ordered from dedicated decorating outlets. They are expensive and difficult to hang, so employing a professional is advisable. In general, they are hard to clean, so they are best for low-wear areas of the home.

Some special wallcoverings will actually hide minor imperfections in the wall surface; others will highlight them, so choose with care.

special metallic wallcoverings

# WALLCOVERING PREPARATION

As with any decorative scheme, wallcoverings rely on the quality of the surface to which they are applied for their final appearance. While some papers and vinyls are thick and will disguise minor irregularities in a wall or ceiling, most will not, so it is essential to repair all surface defects if you want the finish to look its best. Although an existing sound papered finish can be papered over, it is far better to remove the old covering and apply the new one to a clean surface. And if that surface is dusty, it should be washed off and sealed so that the wallpaper paste can adhere well. For some wallcoverings a lining paper should be hung on the wall first to provide the best finish.

# REMOVING TEXTURED FINISHES

If the wall or ceiling to be given a new covering is painted or wallpapered, preparing the surface for its new finish is quite straightforward.

However, if it was previously covered with materials such as texture paint, ceramic or polystyrene (Styrofoam) tiles or wall panelling, more work will be needed to remove the old finishes and return the surface to its original condition.

Textured finishes are tackled in different ways, depending on their type. Texture paints are basically thick water-based paints, normally used to create relatively low-relief effects, and can be removed with specially formulated paint removers. Some textured effects formed with a powder or ready-mixed compound are best removed with a steam wallpaper stripper, which softens the compound so that it can be scraped from the wall.

Never attempt to sand off a textured finish. There are two reasons. The first is that it will create huge quantities of very fine dust; the second is that older versions of this product contained asbestos fibres as a filler, and any action that might release these into the atmosphere as inhalable dust must be avoided at all costs.

### PRACTICAL CONSIDERATIONS

Whichever method you use for stripping old texture paint, it will be messy, so you must take steps to protect yourself and areas of the room

that you are not working on. Preferably wear overalls; at the very least old clothes. Rubber gloves are a must, as is some form of eye protection if you are working on a ceiling, while the latter is also essential when using a chemical stripper. A hat will keep your hair clean.

Ideally, remove all furniture from the room, but if you can't or don't want to do this, place it all together in the centre of the room and cover it with dust sheets (drop cloths). When working on a ceiling, you will have to move the furniture to another part of the room at some stage. Cover the floor with dust sheets, too, and provide yourself with a supply of plastic bags for collecting the paint scrapings. Bear in mind that chemical strippers can give off toxic fumes, so open windows to ensure good ventilation, but close doors to other rooms to prevent the fumes from spreading through your home. Make sure you clean up before leaving the room to prevent tracking paint scrapings through the house.

Always follow the instructions given with a chemical stripper, allowing the required soaking time before scraping off the softened paint. In some areas, you may need a second application of stripper to remove all the paint. Don't cover too large an area at one time, as this will cause an unnecessary build-up of fumes. You should be able to get into a rhythm of scraping one area while the stripper soaks into the next. Make sure you wash off all traces of stripper before hanging your paper.

## REMOVING TEXTURED FINISHES

1 Strip off old texture paint by brushing on a generous coat of a proprietary texture paint remover using an old paintbrush. Stipple it well into the paint and leave it to penetrate for the specified amount of time.

2 When the paint has softened, scrape it off with a broad-bladed scraper. At all times, wear gloves and also safety goggles as protection against splashes.

3 Once the bulk of the coating is removed, use wire (steel) wool dipped in the paint stripper to remove any remaining flecks of paint.

4 Remove powder-based or ready-mixed types using a steam stripper, which will soften the finish. Never try to sand off this type of finish.

# REMOVING TILES AND PANELLING

For tiles and wall panelling, complete removal or a cover-up with plasterboard (gypsum board) are the two options available. The former will leave a surface in need of considerable renovation, while the latter will cause a slight loss of space within the room, as well as some complications at door and window openings. If you are faced with removing a layer of ceramic tiles from a wall, it is unlikely that you will be able to do so without causing a fair amount of damage to the surface below. In this situation, it will be better to add a skim coat of fresh plaster to the entire surface, rather than try to make good individual areas of damage. Unless you are confident that you can achieve a perfectly flat finish, entrust this work to a professional plasterer.

## REMOVING WALL PANELLING

1 The last board to be attached will have been nailed to the fixing grounds through its face. Use a hammer and nail punch to drive the nails right through the board and free it. Lift it off the wall.

## REMOVING CERAMIC TILES

1 On a completely tiled wall, use a hammer to crack a tile and create a starting point for the stripping. On partly tiled walls, start at the tile edge.

2 Use a broad bolster (stonecutter's chisel) and a club (spalling) hammer to chip the old tiles off the wall.

2 The other boards will have been secret-nailed through their tongues. Use a crowbar (wrecking bar) to prise them away from their grounds, taking care not to cause too much damage to the wall.

3 Finally, prise the grounds off the wall. Use a claw hammer with some protective packing to lever them out of the wall. Some nails may come away with the grounds; others may be left in the wall.

## REMOVING POLYSTYRENE (STYROFOAM) TILES

1 Lever the tiles away from the ceiling with a scraper. If the tiles were fixed with a continuous coat of adhesive, consider fitting a new ceiling.

2 If the tiles were stuck in place with blobs of adhesive, use a heat gun to soften the old adhesive so it can be removed with a scraper.

# REMOVING OLD WALLPAPER

**A**lthough a sound wallcovering can be papered over, it is far better to remove all traces of it.

### REMOVING WALLPAPER

Ordinary wallpaper is not difficult to remove and requires only wetting and soaking for 10–15 minutes before stripping with a broad-bladed scraper. Adding wallpaper stripper or a few drops of washing-up liquid (dishwashing detergent) to the water will help it to penetrate the paper. Wallpaper that has been over-painted or has a washable finish needs scoring with the edge of a scraper before soaking, but hiring a steam stripper is the easiest method, and you are less likely to damage the plaster surface.

If walls are faced with plasterboard (gypsum board), take care not to saturate the surface or hold a steam stripper in place for too long. Dry-strippable papers can simply be peeled from the wall, leaving the backing paper in place. If this is still adhering well and remains intact, a new wallcovering can be hung over the top, but if it tears, the backing should also be removed.

### PREPARING SURFACES

Once all the old paper has been removed, walls should be washed thoroughly with a solution of sugar soap (all-purpose cleaner) to remove dust, grime and traces of old adhesive.

Rinse and allow the surface to dry. Cracks and gaps should also be repaired, and any stains that remain after cleaning should be sealed. For settlement cracks between walls and the ceiling or woodwork, use a flexible decorators' filler, and seal stains with an aluminium primer or proprietary aerosol stain block.

New porous plaster and old walls that are dusty will require sealing. A PVA adhesive (white glue) solution of one part PVA to five parts water is ideal for sealing these surfaces and will stabilize them before papering. A coat of size or heavy-duty wallpaper paste ensures good adhesion of the wallcovering and allows paper to be manoeuvred freely on the wall.

### PREPARING WALLS

**1** Use abrasive paper wrapped around a sanding block to remove any remaining "nibs" of wallpaper.

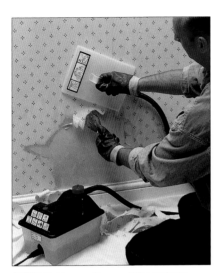

ABOVE: Stubborn wallpaper will be easier to remove with a steam stripper. You can hire one if you don't expect to be doing much stripping.

ABOVE: Vinyl wallcoverings can usually be stripped dry and will peel off the wall, leaving the backing behind; strip this off if it tears.

2 Repair any cracks with cellulose filler (spackle) and seal persistent stains with a stain block or aluminium paint.

3 A coat of size will make the wallpaper easier to hang on new plaster; it prevents moisture being absorbed too quickly from the paste.

# HANGING LINING PAPER

Lining paper helps to disguise surface blemishes and provides a good surface for decorating. It is usually hung horizontally so that the joints do not coincide with those of the decorative paper, but hanging vertical lengths will be easier in narrow alcoves and where there are wall fixtures such as pipes. On poor walls, two layers of lining paper may be necessary; the first layer should be hung vertically, and the second horizontally.

The basic paperhanging techniques shown on the following pages can also be used for lining paper, but it should be left to soak for only five minutes to become pliable. Treat each surface separately and trim the paper to fit into internal and external corners. Do not use a ceiling as a guideline, expecting it to be level; mark a horizontal guideline for the lower edge of the first length (immediately below the ceiling) with a spirit (carpenter's) level and long straightedge. If you are lining both walls and ceiling, start with the ceiling, working from one end of the room to the other.

Work from right to left if right-handed and left to right if left-handed, folding each length of lining paper concertina-fashion to make it manageable. Allow a slight overlap on to the adjacent wall at each end and on to the ceiling if this is uneven. When the paper has been

**1** Normally, lining paper is hung in horizontal lengths across each wall, preventing the joints from coinciding with those of the decorative paper, as this could cause them to open up as the paste dries.

brushed out, crease these overlaps with the back of the scissors, peel back and trim to the crease before brushing back. Work down the wall, trimming the last length so that it butts against the top edge of the skirting (baseboard).

## TIPS

• Allow at least 24 hours for lining paper to dry out completely before hanging the final wallcovering.
• Lining paper may shrink as it dries. Fill small gaps between lengths with fine surface filler and sand smooth. In corners, use a bead of flexible filler (spackle) and smooth with a wet finger.

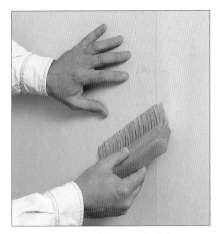

2 Lining paper can be hung vertically in narrow alcoves or behind pipework, however, if this makes the job easier. It should also be hung vertically if you intend over-painting it, as the joins will be less obvious.

3 To line a ceiling, work across the longest dimension of the room, marking an initial guideline. You may find it easier if someone else holds the concertina of pasted paper while you brush it into place.

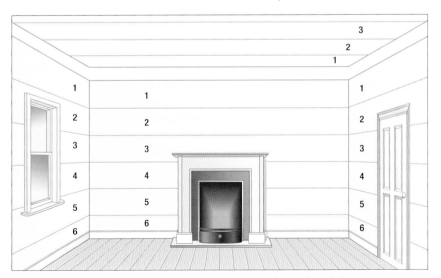

ABOVE: The correct sequence of work when hanging lining paper: for a wall, begin just below the ceiling and move downward; for a ceiling, work across the longest dimension from one end of the room to the other. In each case, trim the last length to width.

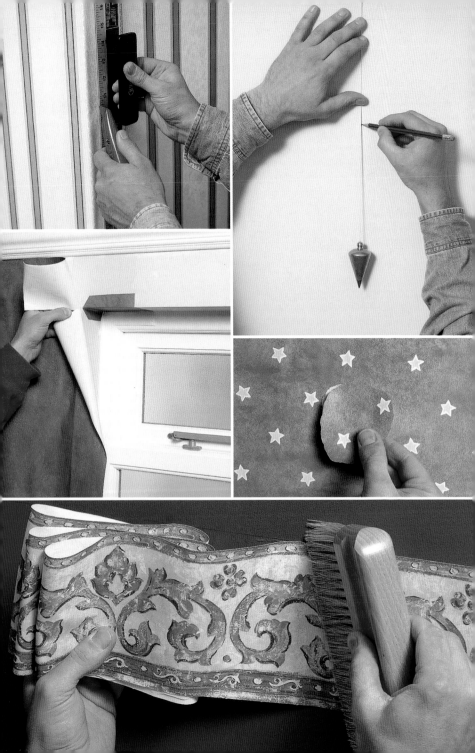

# WALLCOVERING TECHNIQUES

Contrary to what many people think, hanging wallpaper is actually quite a simple process. You do need to take care, though, since you will be dealing with long strips of wallcovering, which in practically all cases will be covered in sticky paste on one side. The potential for mishaps is quite high, so work in an unhurried, logical manner, keeping the work area tidy. The following pages show you all the techniques you need to know to paper walls and ceilings successfully, and how to cope with difficult areas, such as corners, doors, windows and alcoves. Common problems are described, together with the methods for overcoming them.

# PREPARING WALLPAPER

Wallpaper can be hung using one of three methods, depending on whether you are using a ready-pasted, paste-the-wall or traditional unpasted paper. However, the most important step with any paperhanging task is to prepare fully before cutting the paper by carefully measuring the lengths and making an allowance for pattern matching to avoid mistakes.

## PREPARING UNPASTED PAPER

Measure the height of the wall from the ceiling to the top of the skirting (baseboard) and add 100mm (4in) for trimming the top and bottom. Measure and cut the first drop to length. To ensure a square cut, lay the paper flush with the long edge of the pasting table and use a straightedge to mark the cutting line.

If the ceiling is quite level, you can cut a number of lengths. Match the pattern of each length dry off the roll against the first cut length to avoid problems with pattern matching as the job progresses.

Use the paperhanger's brush to weigh one end down, and line up the edge of the paper with the edge of the pasting table, then apply a thin, even coat of paste brushing outward toward the edges.

Fold the ends of the pasted length in to the centre and leave it to soak, checking the manufacturer's guidelines for the exact length of time. Long lengths of paper should be lightly folded concertina-style.

## READY-PASTED PAPER

To activate ready-pasted papers, fill a trough two-thirds with water and put it on the floor at the end of the pasting table. Roll a length of paper with the decorative face inside and immerse for the recommended soaking time. Draw it on to the pasting table, patterned side down so that excess water can drain into the trough.

For paste-the-wall papers, apply a coat of paste to an area wider than the paper – it can be hung directly from the roll or using cut lengths.

### PREPARING PRE-COATED WALLCOVERINGS

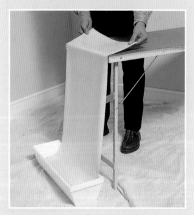

You can buy many wallcoverings pre-coated with adhesive. The adhesive is activated by soaking a length of paper in a trough of cold water. Once immersed and soaked for the recommended length of time, drain the paper into the trough. Mix ordinary paste to recoat any dry edges.

## CUTTING, PASTING AND FOLDING WALLPAPER

1 Measure carefully, allowing for pattern matching, and cut the paper to length. Cut several more drops from the same roll and to the same length, marking their tops.

2 Brush on an even coat of paste, working out from the centre to the edges. Align each edge with the table edge in turn to prevent paste from getting on to the table.

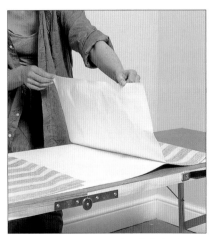

3 When you have pasted about half of a short drop, fold the pasted end into the middle. Then slide the paper along the table and paste the rest. Fold the end in to meet the first.

4 Fold longer lengths of wallpaper concertina-fashion to make them more manageable. Leave the folded drops of paper for the required time so that the paste soaks in.

# HANGING THE FIRST LENGTH

In a room with no focal point, work clockwise around the room. Start and finish near the least obtrusive corner so that any pattern mismatch will not be obvious.

To ensure the end result is well balanced, centre a pattern over a chimney breast (fireplace projection) or other prominent feature and work outward in both directions.

## WHERE TO START

Use a plumbline and spirit (carpenter's) level to mark a guideline on the wall. The distance from a corner to the guideline should be one roll width less 25mm (1in), and the first length should be hung so that you are working away from (and not into) the corner.

## HANGING THE PAPER

Place the first length next to the guideline, then adjust the top so that there is 50mm (2in) of paper lapping on to the ceiling and slide the vertical edge into its final position.

Lightly brush out the top half of the paper, working downward to expel air bubbles and firmly push the top trimming allowance into the angle with the ceiling. Make sure that the vertical edge is aligned with the guideline then continue to work down the wall, brushing outward from the centre of the length.

Crease the paper into the junction between wall and ceiling by running the blunt edge of the scissors along the

paper, then gently peel back the paper and trim neatly to fit along the creaseline. Brush the trimmed edge firmly back into position.

Ease the bottom half of the paper away from the wall and smooth it into place. Make sure that it is aligned with the guideline, then crease the bottom edge of the paper into the skirting (baseboard) and trim to fit, as before, using scissors.

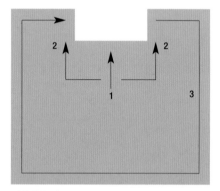

ABOVE: Begin by centring a pattern over a prominent feature, then work outward in both directions.

## TIPS

• Hang papers with a large design so that any loss of pattern occurs at floor level, not at the ceiling.

• Agitate pre-pasted papers during soaking to expel any air bubbles and ensure that all the paper comes into contact with water. Make sure the paper is loosely rolled.

• Edges can dry out during trimming – keep a little extra paste handy.

1 Place the edge of the first drop against the vertical guideline, making sure that it is aligned accurately. When you are happy, begin brushing the paper on to the wall.

2 Brush out the top half of the length and push it into the angle with the ceiling, using a dabbing action with the paperhanger's brush. Make sure you brush out all air bubbles.

3 Using the back edge of the scissors blade, run along the wall/ceiling angle to crease the paper into it. This will provide an accurate trimming line.

4 Gently peel back the paper and cut along the crease line to remove excess paper. Then brush the end of the drop back into place. Repeat at the skirting (baseboard).

# EXTERNAL CORNERS

Corners are unlikely to be completely square, so never try to hang a full width of wallpaper around them as it will not hang straight. Hanging two separate lengths of paper and overlapping them slightly at the corners will produce a far better result, although some small loss of pattern will be inevitable on walls that are not perfectly true.

## PAPERING AN EXTERNAL CORNER

Hang the cut length as usual, matching the pattern down the full length, then lightly brush the paper around the corner. Do not apply too much pressure, as the paper could tear, but make sure that there are no bubbles and the paper has adhered well along the edge of the corner.

Use scissors to make a release cut top and bottom where the wall meets the skirting (baseboard) and ceiling. This will allow the paper to be smoothed on to the wall on both sides of the corner and trimmed along the skirting and ceiling. Using a craft knife, trim the length vertically to leave an overlap of about 25mm (1in) brushed around the corner. Discard the waste.

Cut another length and hang this to a vertical guideline on the second wall so that it overlaps the strip of paper brushed around the corner, with its edge about 12mm ($\frac{1}{2}$in) from the corner and the pattern matching as closely as possible.

To do this, you may need to hang the new length so that it overlaps the previous length substantially. The width of the pattern will determine how much the two lengths may have to be overlapped. Make a vertical cut with a craft knife through both layers, from ceiling to skirting. Pull away the waste strip of the overlapping drop, then carefully peel back the edge of that drop until you can remove the waste strip of the overlapped drop. If necessary, add a little more paste, then brush back the paper to leave a neat butt join between the two drops. Finally, trim to fit the top and bottom as normal.

When working with a very thin paper, especially if it has a white ground, you can simply leave one drop overlapping the other at an external corner. This will not be very noticeable. However, if you are hanging a vinyl wallcovering, you must make the vertical cut through both drops to produce a butt join, as the pasted overlapping drop will not adhere to the vinyl surface of the drop below, unless you use special overlap adhesive.

If the wall is not completely square, the pattern may not match exactly along the full drop where the two lengths cross over. This cannot be avoided and should be taken into account when planning the order of the work. Always aim for the overlap to be where it is least noticeable. On a chimney breast (fireplace projection), for example, the overlaps should be on the side walls, not the face.

1 Hang the last drop on the first wall and brush the wallpaper smoothly around the external corner.

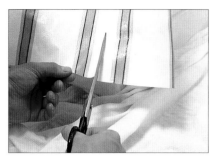

2 Make vertical release cuts at the top and bottom, into the skirting (baseboard) and ceiling junctions.

3 Trim off the excess paper to leave an overlap of about 25mm (1in). Make sure the edge is brushed down firmly.

4 Hang the first drop on the second wall so that it overlaps the turned paper and the pattern matches as closely as possible.

5 When working with a thick paper or a vinyl wallcovering, make a single cut down through both layers using a sharp knife. Keep the cut as straight as possible.

6 Peel back the edges, remove the waste and brush the edges back into place. You should be left with a neat butt join and minimal disruption to the pattern.

# INTERNAL CORNERS

As with external corners, internal corners should be papered with two separate pieces of wallpaper, overlapping them slightly.

Hang the last full-width length, then measure the distance from the edge of the paper into the corner, taking measurements from the top, centre and bottom of the wall. Add a 12mm ($\frac{1}{2}$in) overlap allowance to the widest measurement and cut a strip of this width from the next full length. Do not discard the offcut (scrap) – put it to one side for use later.

Hang the cut length, brushing the overlap allowance on to the adjacent wall. Make sure the paper is brushed firmly into the corner by dabbing the wallpaper into the angle with the tips of the brush bristles.

Measure the width of the offcut and use a plumbline to mark a vertical guideline on the adjacent wall that distance from the corner.

If the internal corner is badly out of true, take measurements from the top, centre and bottom of the wall, and adjust the guideline for the offcut so that it will not overlap on to the previous wall.

Hang the offcut against the guideline, overlapping the strip of paper turned on to the wall. Although there will be a slight mismatch of the pattern, it should not be too noticeable. Trim the top and bottom of the length neatly with scissors. Treat a vinyl in the same manner as for an external corner, or use overlap adhesive.

**1** When you come to an internal corner, hang the last full-width drop, then measure from the edge of the wallcovering into the corner at the top, middle and bottom.

## TIPS

• If an overlap allowance puckers in an internal corner, make small horizontal cuts in the paper so that it lays flat.
• Keep a tube of overlap adhesive handy to ensure that overlapping edges of vinyl wallcoverings adhere properly.
• Paper with a straight-match pattern can be difficult to align in an internal corner. Hold a spirit (carpenter's) level horizontally across the corner to check that the design is level.

2 Using the widest of the three measurements, and adding an allowance to turn around the corner, cut a strip from the next pasted length of paper. Do not discard the waste length.

3 Hang the strip of paper, butting its edge up to the last drop hung and brushing the overlap allowance on to the facing wall. Make sure to brush it well into the corner.

4 Measure the width of the waste length cut from the drop and make a mark at this distance out from the corner. Use a plumbline to position a vertical guideline at this point.

5 Hang the offcut against the line, overlapping the strip turned around the corner and making sure that the edge is brushed down well. Trim at top and bottom.

# AROUND DOORS

If you follow the correct sequence for hanging and trimming the lengths of wallpaper, you should be able to paper around a door frame with little trouble.

Mark out the walls in roll widths first so that you know exactly where each length falls. Thin strips beside a door or window will be difficult to hang and are likely to peel, so adjust the starting point if necessary, perhaps moving it half a roll's width in one direction or the other. When you are happy that you will not be left with awkward strips on either side of the door, begin hanging full drops in the normal manner. Continue until you have hung the last full drop before the door.

Hang a full length so that it overlaps the architrave (trim), matching the pattern to the last length hung. Lightly brush the paper on to the wall where possible, and then use the bristle tips of the brush to press the paper into the top of the architrave. Take great care not to tear the wallcovering at this point, particularly if you are using a thin paper.

Locate the external corner of the door frame and make a diagonal release cut into this point with scissors. As you cut toward the corner, press the paper against the wall to prevent it from tearing. Smooth the paper down the wall and brush the vertical overlap of paper into the edge of the architrave. Brush out the section of paper above the door frame, pressing it into the wall/ceiling angle and the angle between architrave and wall.

Make sure the paper does not separate from the previous length as you do this. Crease the paper against the architrave with the back of the scissors, then ease the paper away from the wall and cut along the creases, or trim with a craft knife held at a 45-degree angle to the wall. Trim the top of the door frame first, cutting inward from the outer edge of the architrave. Brush the paper back into place against the side and top of the architrave. Then crease the paper against the ceiling and trim it to fit. Wipe the paste from the woodwork and the paper. Hang the next drop in a similar manner, butting it against the last drop above the door and making a release cut so that it will fit around the frame. Trim and brush into place.

1 Hang the drop on the wall, butting it up to the last full drop hung. Then drape the paper over the frame and brush it gently into the top of the architrave (trim).

2 Take the paperhanger's scissors and make a diagonal release cut through the paper into the external corner of the frame. Be careful not to tear the damp paper.

3 Brush the resulting flaps of paper into the side and top of the architrave, using a dabbing action with the bristles of the paperhanger's brush. Crease them with the scissors.

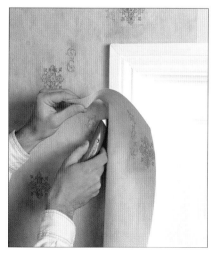

4 Trim the paper flush with the architrave using a sharp craft knife, or pull it back gently and cut it with the scissors. Hang the next drop around the other side of the frame.

# AROUND WINDOWS

**H**anging wallpaper around a window that is set flush in the wall with a decorative frame around it requires a similar technique to that used for papering around a door. However, many windows are set into the wall to leave a shallow recess that must be tackled in a slightly different manner. Fortunately, any small mishaps or irregularities in the papering around a window can often be concealed by curtains or blinds (drapes or shades).

Hang the first length overlapping the window, matching the pattern to the last length hung. Smooth the paper on to the wall, then make horizontal cuts into the corners of the reveal – the first level with the top of the window sill, and the second level with the top of the reveal.

Locate the corners of the window sill and make diagonal release cuts toward these points so that the paper can be eased around the shape of the sill. Brush the paper below the sill on to the wall, and trim to fit. Brush the remaining flap of paper around the corner into the reveal and trim to fit against the window frame. Make sure air bubbles are expelled, but do not apply too much pressure. If the overlap is not deep enough for the reveal, hang a narrow strip to fit between its edge and the window frame.

Cut an oversized patch to fit the head of the reveal, matching the pattern to the paper above the reveal. Make a release cut in the outer corner, then slip the pasted patch into place. Tuck

**1** Drape the paper over the window reveal, and make horizontal cuts at top and bottom so that the paper can be brushed into the reveal. Cut only as far as the corners of the reveal.

the edges of the patch under the paper above and inside the reveal, and trim through both layers with a wavy stroke. Peel back the paper to remove the waste and brush down firmly – the joint should be almost invisible. Complete the rest of the window in the same way, hanging short lengths above and below the reveal. Lengths above the window can be brushed into the reveal complete, provided that it is not deep and the edge is square. With a deep reveal, or one where the edge is not square, cut strips to fit the reveal, turning them slightly on to the face of the wall, then overlap their edges with drops hung on the face. Make a wavy cut through both layers, as before, remove the waste and brush flat.

2 Cut along the top of the window sill and make diagonal release cuts around the sill.

3 Brush the remaining flap of wallpaper into the reveal and trim to fit.

4 Ease back the paper, and cut and fit a patch in the corner of the reveal.

5 Cut through both layers and remove the waste to create an unobtrusive butt join.

6 Hang short lengths above and below the window, matching the pattern.

7 Cut lengths long enough to be brushed into the reveal at the top.

# AROUND SWITCHPLATES

Before wallpapering around sockets and switches, turn off the electricity supply and hang the paper over the fitting. Press it firmly against the faceplate so that you can see a clear impression and make a pencil mark 6mm (¼in) in from each corner. Make diagonal cuts to each pencil mark with scissors, trimming the flaps of paper 6mm (¼in) in from the outer edge of the faceplate.

Loosen the screws of the faceplate and ease it from the wall, then use a paperhanger's brush to gently push the flaps of paper behind the faceplate. Push the faceplate back into position and tighten its screws. Wipe off any adhesive from the fitting and allow the paste to dry before restoring the power.

1 Turn off the electricity supply. Use a pencil to mark the corners on the paper where it overhangs the fitting.

2 Make a diagonal cut from the centre to each corner of the faceplate. Loosen the screws and pull the faceplate back.

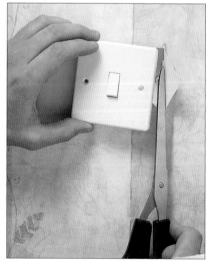

3 Trim the flaps of paper and push them under the edges of the loosened faceplate. Retighten the screws.

# AROUND LIGHT FITTINGS

If there is a ceiling rose, turn off the electricity supply before brushing the paper over the casing and then locate its exact centre with your finger. Make a small cut in the paper at this point and gently pull the pendant through the cut, taking care not to tear the paper.

Ease the paper around the shape of the rose by making a series of small radial cuts from the centre of the rose to the edge of the casing. Smooth the paper into place on the ceiling around the rose and finish hanging the rest of the paper. Crease the paper into the edge of the rose before restoring the electricity supply. The paper can be trimmed neatly with a knife once the paste has dried but turn the electricity supply off again before doing this. Where there is a large ceiling centrepiece, it is easier to hang and trim the paper if you plan your starting point so that a join runs through the middle of the fitting. Make radial cuts as for a normal rose to fit the paper up to the edges of the centrepiece.

## WALL LIGHT FITTINGS

Turn off the electricity supply and remove the fitting. Bind the wires with electrical insulating or masking tape. Hang the paper to the cable, mark its position on the paper and make a small incision. Feed the cable through the hole, taking care not to tear the paper. Finish hanging the drop and allow the paste to dry before replacing the fitting.

1 Turn off the electricity supply. Make a series of cuts in the paper toward the edge of the ceiling rose. Brush down.

2 Crease the paper around the edge of the rose, then trim neatly with a knife. Finally, brush the paper smooth.

# AROUND FIREPLACES

**F**ireplaces come in a variety of forms; some are very simple and rectangular in outline; others are very ornate. When faced with papering around a simple fireplace, you can use the same techniques as you would for papering around a door frame – make diagonal cuts to the corners and brush the paper into the angles between the fireplace and the wall. However, an ornate frame will require a little more effort.

Hang a full length so that it drapes over the fireplace and match the pattern above the mantel shelf to the last length hung. Lightly brush the paper into the junction of the wall and shelf and trim. Cut inward from the outer corner of the mantel shelf, and support the rest of the length to prevent it from tearing.

Press the paper against the wall at the point where the corner of the shelf meets the wall, gently easing the paper around the contours with your fingers. Make a series of small cuts to allow the paper to lie flat, then use the tips of a paperhanger's brush to mould the paper into the precise shape. Trim each small flap of paper, then crease and trim the paper down the side of the fireplace and wipe any adhesive from the surface.

In some cases, the mantel shelf may span the entire chimney breast (fireplace projection), in which case you need only paper down to the shelf, then cut strips to fit at the sides, making release cuts as necessary to match the shape of the fireplace. You could also use this technique for a fireplace that has a very complex shape to the sides.

**1** Hang the drop above the fireplace, draping the paper over the mantel shelf. Brush it into the angle and trim along the back edge.

**2** Ease the paper around the contours of the mantel shelf by making small release cuts. Brush it into place and trim off the excess.

# BEHIND RADIATORS

If a radiator is too heavy to remove, turn it off and allow it to cool completely. Measure and make a note of the position of each wall bracket from the outer edges and top of the radiator, then hang the paper on the wall so that it drapes over the radiator. Match the pattern with the last length hung.

Measure out the position of the wall bracket and make a pencil mark on the wallpaper at this point. Make a vertical slit with scissors from the bottom edge of the paper up to the mark, and use a radiator roller to feed and smooth the paper down on each side of the bracket. Trim the paper neatly along the skirting (baseboard) and wipe off any adhesive left on the face of the wallpaper, skirting and radiator. Repeat for the other bracket.

## WALL FITTINGS

When removing wall fittings, mark the position of each screw hole with a wooden match and carefully press the tip through the pasted paper before it is smoothed into place.

1 Use paperhanger's scissors to make a vertical cut from the bottom of the paper in line with the radiator bracket.

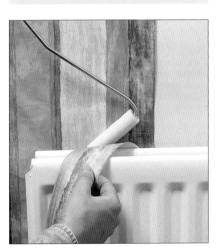

2 Carefully feed the paper down behind the radiator with a radiator roller, smoothing it on to the wall at the same time.

# HANGING BORDERS

A decorative border can add the finishing touch to a wallpaper or paint scheme. You can choose from a wide variety of patterns, colourways and sizes, all of which are quick and easy to hang. The key to a professional-looking result is to make sure that the border is absolutely straight and hung against accurate guidelines, and that all the joins are neat.

## BASIC TECHNIQUES

Use a spirit (carpenter's) level to mark the position of the border on the walls at 300mm (12in) intervals, joining the pencil marks with a long straightedge. Measure from one corner of the wall to the other and add 50mm (2in) for trimming. Paste by brushing out from the centre, and fold concertina-style, leaving the paper to soak for ten minutes. Brush the back of a ready-pasted border with tepid water, rather than immersing it in a trough. A self-adhesive border needs to be re-rolled so that the decorative face is facing outward.

To hang, place 300mm (12in) of the border against the guideline at a time, allowing the folds to drop out as you work. If using a self-adhesive border, peel away the backing paper and smooth it into place. Before cutting and hanging the next length, match the pattern on the roll. Do not attempt to hang a continuous length of border around an external or internal corner; instead use the same technique as for hanging conventional paper.

## DEALING WITH CORNERS

**1** Draw a guideline for the border on the wall using a spirit (carpenter's) level.

### TIPS

• Hang a border by working from right to left if you are right-handed, and left to right if left-handed.
• Positioning a border is easier if the guideline is above a horizontal border, and on the inner edge around windows and doors.
• Hang a border below an uneven ceiling and paint the gap to match.

If you have to use more than one length on a wall, a butt join can be used for borders with a simple repeat pattern. For more complex designs, overlap the two lengths so that the pattern matches exactly and carefully cut around a motif through both layers. When the waste paper has been removed and the cut edges smoothed into place, the join should be almost invisible. Use a seam roller to press down the edges.

2 Fold a pasted border concertina-style so that it is ready to hang and easy to handle.

3 Match the pattern in a corner using a dry length, before cutting and pasting.

## CREATING A BUTT JOIN

1 Form a butt join between two lengths of a border that has a simple pattern.

2 Use a seam roller to press edges and joins down firmly.

## CREATING AN INVISIBLE JOIN

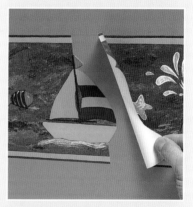

An intricate pattern gives you the option of disguising a join between lengths of border. Simply overlap the end of one length over the other, matching the patterns accurately, then cut through both layers, following the outline of part of the pattern. Remove the waste and brush down; the join will disappear.

# DIVIDING A WALL WITH A BORDER

**A** border will allow two different wallpaper patterns to be applied to a wall, one above and one below, by concealing the joint between them. Mark a guideline on the wall, approximately 900mm (3ft) from the floor, and hang a length of each design at the same time so that it overlaps the pencil line by 50mm (2in). Before hanging the next lengths, hold a long straightedge on the guideline and cut through both layers of paper with a knife. Remove the waste strips and smooth down the cut edges to form a neat butt join.

When the room has been papered, the border can then be hung. Centre it over the butt join using an overlap adhesive for vinyl wallcoverings.

### AROUND A WINDOW OR DOOR
Draw a horizontal guideline to the full width of the border above the frame, and then mark a vertical guideline down each side. Cut the horizontal length 50mm (2in) longer than required and hang it, making sure that it overlaps the side guidelines evenly.

Add the vertical lengths, overlapping the horizontal strip squarely at the corners. Use the trimming allowance on the vertical lengths to adjust the border so that you will be cutting through the busiest part of the design. Holding a steel rule at a 45-degree angle, cut through both layers of paper from the external to internal corner of the border, using a craft knife. Peel back the cut edges and remove the

waste paper from the wall. Brush the border back into place to create a neat mitred join at each corner.

You can use this technique of making mitred right-angled joins between lengths to allow for changes in floor or ceiling level, or to use the border to

### DIVIDING A WALL

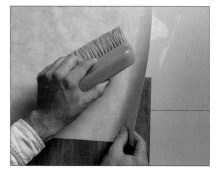

**1** Hang a drop of each patterned paper so that they overlap the pencil guideline. Work on one pair of drops at a time.

### MITRING A CORNER BORDER

**1** Mark out horizontal and vertical guidelines for the lengths of border, using a spirit (carpenter's) level.

outline other features such as fireplaces or perhaps even pictures.

In some cases, you might want the border to run along the wall above the stairs. In this situation, the technique of making an angled cut through both layers of the border where they overlap is the same, but the actual angle will be shallower. You need to mark the wall with a pencil guideline that runs parallel to the flight of stairs, then hang the border. Where it overlaps at the top and bottom of the stairs, cut from corner to corner as before and brush flat.

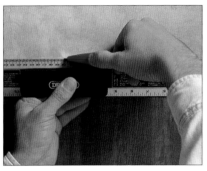

2 Brush the ends of the paper flat, trim through both layers along the guideline and remove the waste. Brush the ends back.

3 When you have completed the wall, centre the border over the butt join between the two papers and wipe away any traces of adhesive.

2 Overlap the ends of the lengths of border and cut through both layers from corner to corner, using a straightedge and sharp knife.

3 Remove the waste pieces of paper and smooth down the cut edges to form a neat mitred join.

# PAPERING CEILINGS

**W**allpapering a ceiling is not as difficult as it may appear. The techniques used are the same as for walls and there are few obstacles or awkward angles to deal with. Although the job will be easier with two people, it is possible to achieve good results on your own. Adequate access equipment, however, is essential and will make the job very much easier.

## ACCESS EQUIPMENT

Before tackling this job, it is important to consider how you plan to reach the ceiling safely. Access equipment will be needed that allows you to hang a full length across the room. Scaffold boards supported at either end by sturdy stepladders or trestles will create a flat, level walkway spanning the full width of the room, and can be adjusted to a working height to suit you. Use two boards tied together for a distance of more than 1.5m (5ft) and provide support in the centre.

## PAPERING SEQUENCES

Plan the papering sequence so that a paper that has a definite pattern is centralized across the room. A sloping ceiling can be papered either to match the ceiling or the walls, but do not attempt to hang a single length down the sloping surface on to the wall below. Treat the wide angle between the two surfaces as an internal corner.

## HANGING THE FIRST LENGTH

Assemble your work platform across the main window of the room. Ceilings should be papered by hanging lengths across the room parallel to the window, working away from the light so that you are not in your own shadow and daylight will not emphasize the joins between lengths.

To mark a guideline for the first length, measure one roll width less 25mm (1in) out from each corner and drive in a nail at each point. Tie a taut, chalked length of string between the nails, then snap the string against the ceiling to create a guide for the first length. If hanging paper on a white ceiling, make sure you use coloured chalk to coat the string. ▶

### HANDLING PAPER

As long lengths of paper are often needed for a ceiling, fold these concertina-style after pasting. When papering, they are easier to handle if you support them with a spare roll of wallpaper.

1 Measure out from each corner to a distance equal to the width of a roll and mark the positions with nails.

2 Tie a chalked length of string between the nails, making sure it is taut. Snap it against the ceiling to leave a chalk guideline.

3 Hang the first length against the chalk line, brushing it into place as you go. If possible, have someone else support the folded paper.

4 Use the bristles of a paperhanger's brush to ease the paper into the angle between the wall and ceiling.

5 Use the back of the scissors blade to crease the paper. Then pull it back from the ceiling and trim along the long edge. Brush the cut edge back into place firmly. Treat each end of the length in the same manner.

Cut the first strip of paper to length, allowing an extra 100mm (4in) for trimming, then paste and fold it concertina-style. Place one end so that about half of the trimming allowance laps on to the wall and the edge of the paper is aligned with the chalk line, then brush it firmly into place.

If you are papering around a bay window or alcove, make diagonal release cuts at the external corners to allow the paper to lay flat. Brush the paper into the side wall of the recess and trim the edges to fit along the edge of the ceiling.

Once the first length of wallpaper is in position, crease and trim the long edge into the angle between the wall and ceiling first, followed by each end, using normal wallpapering techniques. Continue hanging lengths of paper across the ceiling, trimming their ends where they meet the walls. Finally, cut the last length roughly to the width required, making sure you allow 25mm (1in) for trimming along the edge of the paper. Hang and trim it in the same manner as the first length.

### DEALING WITH PROBLEM AREAS

If you are faced with papering around a bay window or an alcove, make diagonal release cuts in the paper at the external corners of the recess to allow the paper to lay flat against the ceiling. Brush the paper into the side walls of the recess, crease it and trim it to fit along the edges of the ceiling.

### PAPERING AN ALCOVE

ABOVE: Paper into a bay window or an external corner by making a diagonal cut to ease the paper around the external angle.

### A SLOPING CEILING

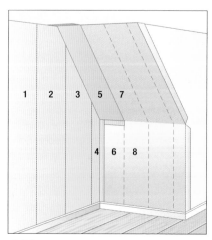

ABOVE: The sequence for papering a wall and a sloping ceiling. Do not try to hang a complete length on the sloping surface and down the wall.

# PAPERING ARCHES

If possible, arrange your starting position on the wall containing the arch so that you will be left with an even width to fill between the arch and each full-width drop on each side of it.

1 Trim away excess paper from the arch to leave a trimming allowance of 25mm (1in).

This will ensure a balanced appearance. Hang the paper so that it overlaps the arch, matching the pattern to the last length hung, then trim off the waste to within 25mm (1in) from the edge of the arch. Brush the trimming allowance on to the inner face of the arch, making right-angled cuts into the paper every 12mm (½in) around the curve of the arch so that it lays flat. Paper across the rest of the arch, length by length, using the same method of cutting to cope with the curved edge.

For the inner face, cut a strip of paper 35mm (1¼in) wider than the arch. If the paper has a definite pattern, use two strips with a butt joint at the highest point. Align the manufactured edge of the cut strip with one edge of the arch and trim the other edge with a knife once the paper has been smoothed into place.

2 Make right-angled cuts to ease the paper around the curve of the arch.

3 Paper the inner face of the arch last, joining strips at the highest point.

# PAPERING STAIRWELLS

When working in stairwells, safety is the main priority. Access equipment suitable for use on stairs may be hired, but you can also construct your own safe work platform.

### ORDER OF WORK

Hang the longest length first, and work upward from the foot of the stairs.

Hang the top half of each length, but leave the rest of the folded length hanging while you move the work platform out of the way. Then smooth the lower half of each length into place.

When measuring lengths for a well wall, make sure that you allow for the gradient of the stairs.

Tackle the head wall next, hanging the top portions of the two or three drops needed, leaving the remainder of the folded lengths hanging. Adjust the work platform so that the planks rest on a stair or ladder and are supported by a ladder at the bottom. Smooth the lower portions of the lengths on to the head wall, and trim neatly in line with the hallway ceiling. Hang lengths along the lower head wall from the foot of the stairs.

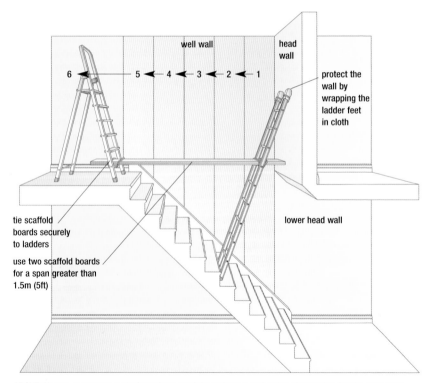

ABOVE: How to construct a platform for a straight staircase and order of papering for the well wall.

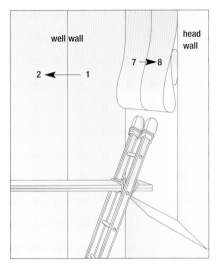

ABOVE: The order of papering for the head wall of a stairwell. Note that the ends of the straight ladder have been padded to prevent damage to the wall. Adjust the access equipment before brushing the lower half of the wall.

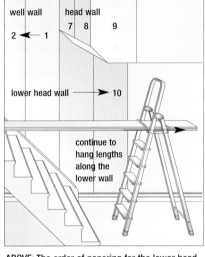

ABOVE: The order of papering for the lower head wall of a staircase. Work off the foot of the stairs, using a scaffold board and stepladders as necessary. Trim the paper neatly at the angles between ceiling, stairs and wall.

ABOVE: Be especially careful to take accurate measurements. Mistakes can be costly when working with very long lengths.

ABOVE: Hang the longest length first and work upward from the foot of the stairs. Hang the top half of each length first.

# COMMON PROBLEMS

Inadequate preparation and poor papering techniques, rather than faults with the paper itself, are the cause of most wallpapering problems. Some minor mistakes such as air bubbles are quite easy to remedy, but if the problem is extensive, it is better to strip off the affected area and start again.

## DEALING WITH BUBBLES

Bubbles that remain after the paste has dried are caused by not allowing the paper to soak for long enough, not having brushed out the

paper properly, or by poor preparation, which prevents the paper from sticking to the wall.

With a small bubble, you may be able to cut a slit in the paper and inject a little paste behind it with a syringe. Then press the paper down and carefully wipe off any excess paste.

For a larger bubble, make two diagonal cuts with a sharp knife. Carefully peel back the flaps and use a small paintbrush to apply paste to the back of each. Press the flaps back against the wall and brush flat, again wiping off any excess paste.

## REPAIRING A BUBBLE

**1** When faced with the occasional large bubble in a papered surface, make diagonal cuts across its face with a sharp knife. Then peel back the resulting flaps.

**2** Apply more paste to the wall or the backs of the cut flaps of paper. Press back into place and brush down firmly. If there are lots of bubbles, it may be better to replace the drop.

### REPAIRING TEARS

Often, tears are not as bad as they look. If the tear is small, carefully apply some overlap adhesive to the torn piece and ease it back into place with the tips of a brush.

When faced with a large tear in wallpaper, remove loose and damaged paper by tearing it gently from the wall. Tear, rather than cut, a patch from a new piece of paper so that the pattern matches the surrounding area, then feather the edge by tearing away a 6mm (¼in) strip from the back. Paste the patch and lightly brush it into place.

With a vinyl wallcovering, cut a patch so that the pattern matches the surrounding area and tape it to the wall over the damage. Cut through both layers to form a square, remove the damaged vinyl from the wall, then paste and fit the patch.

### REPAIRING DAMAGED WALLCOVERINGS

1 Carefully tear away any loose or damaged wallpaper, feathering the edges.

2 Make a matching patch by carefully tearing the paper. Feather the edges and stick it down.

### REPAIRING VINYL

1 Cut out damaged vinyl and a new patch taped on to the wall to match in one go.

2 Remove the old vinyl from within the cut square and apply the patch.

# OTHER WALLPAPERING TIPS

By and large, hanging a wallcovering is a straightforward process which, in most cases, will go without a hitch. However, now and again you may come across a difficult situation that needs overcoming. Some of the most common problems are covered here, and if you follow the techniques you will be able to give your decorative scheme a professional-looking finish.

### LONG LENGTHS

In the stairwell the drop from ceiling to floor will be considerable in places. Get someone to support the weight of the wallcovering while you hang the top portion.

### BULKY OVERLAPS

Overlapped edges can create bulky seams in relief and embossed wallpapers. Feather the trimming allowance by carefully tearing down the edge, then flatten the torn paper with a seam roller before hanging the overlapping length.

### GAPS IN SEAMS

Paper shrinking as it dries, due to poor pasting technique or poor butt joins, can cause gaps at the seams. To avoid this, disguise the gaps with a fine felt-tipped pen, paint or crayon in a similar shade to the base colour.

### CURLING EDGES

These are caused by inadequate pasting, paste drying out during hanging or, on overlapped vinyl, the wrong paste having been used. Lift the edge of the paper with the back of a knife blade and apply a small amount of paste with a fine brush. Smooth the paper firmly into place with a damp sponge. For overlapping edges on vinyl wallpaper, use vinyl overlap adhesive.

### POOR PATTERN MATCH

Usually the result of inaccurate cutting and hanging, patterns not matching may also be caused by variations in the paper along the seams. Check the whole batch and return faulty rolls to the retailer. Straight-match patterns can be difficult to match, especially in internal corners where the edge has been trimmed. Use a level to check that prominent motifs are level across the corner.

### SHINY PATCHES

Brushing matt (flat) finish wallpapers too vigorously can cause shiny patches. Normally, they cannot be removed, but rubbing gently with a piece of fresh white bread may disguise them. Bread is also useful for removing greasy fingermarks from non-washable papers.

### STAINS ALONG SEAMS

Paste that has been allowed to dry on the face of the paper can result in stains. These are difficult to remove, but if the paper is washable, try wiping with a sponge and a solution of mild detergent. Bear this in mind while working and sponge off splashes before they have a chance to dry.

ABOVE: Supporting the weight of long lengths will help prevent the wallpaper tearing.

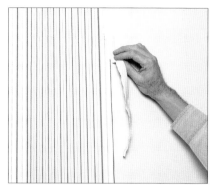

ABOVE: Feather the edge of relief wallpaper at external and internal corners.

ABOVE: Disguise gaps with a felt-tipped pen, a crayon or watercolour paint.

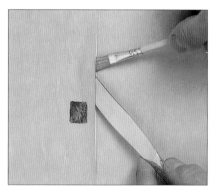

ABOVE: Apply wallpaper adhesive to curling edges with a fine brush.

ABOVE: Use a spirit (carpenter's) level to check that motifs are level across a corner.

ABOVE: Rubbing with a ball of white bread may make shiny patches less obvious.

# HOME TILING

- Tiling materials

- Tiling preparation

- Tiling techniques

- Decorative tiling layouts

# INTRODUCTION

Tiles have a long pedigree in the interior decoration business. Faience (glazed earthenware) plaques have been found in Cretan buildings dating from around 1800 BC, and a tradition of ceramic wall and floor decoration was established soon after this farther east in Syria and Persia (now Iran). Mosaic wall and floor decorations, incorporating stone (usually marble), glass and ceramic tesserae, were a major feature of Roman interiors. The technique spread to North Africa and thence to Spain, and the Renaissance soon led to widespread use of decorative tiling all over Europe.

Probably the most important centre of ceramic tile making in Europe was Holland, where the creation of individually hand-painted tiles in a unique blue-grey colour soon made Delft famous in the early 17th century. From there, the use of tiles spread rapidly, and it was not long before mass production was introduced.

The end product is the familiar ceramic tile we use today. The manufacturing and printing technology may have changed, and the adhesives and grouts used may have improved, but the result would be familiar to a 17th-century Dutchman.

The 20th century brought new kinds of tile, notably vinyl, linoleum and cork tiles, which owe their existence to advances in plastics and resins technology. They offer a combination of properties that make them useful alternatives to ceramics in a wide range of situations, and they are generally much less expensive.

Here in the 21st century there is a huge range to choose from – in every style imaginable – but the techniques for working with them remain the same.

The following pages concentrate on working with ceramic wall tiles, since these are the most popular of the types available. A wide range of situations is dealt with, from splashbacks to whole walls, including information on working around obstacles such as door and window openings and on creating special effects with tiled borders and feature panels. There are also sections on using other types of wall tiles, and on tiling floors.

ABOVE: Tile friezes and panels have been used to clad walls since the Renaissance, and can make a stunning focal point in a garden or courtyard.

LEFT, BELOW AND OPPOSITE: Tiles have never before been available in such a profusion of styles and designs. These range from highly glazed plain types to more rustic versions with matt (flat) or textured surfaces, and patterns that look as though they have been hand-painted.

# TILING
# MATERIALS

Ceramic tiles provide the most durable of all finishes in the home, whether for walls, floors or worktops, and there has never been a bigger choice of colours, designs, shapes and sizes. Vinyl, lino and cork floor tiles offer an alternative floor finish to ceramics, and offer the advantages of ease of laying combined with a surface finish that is warmer to the touch and also less noisy underfoot than ceramic tiles. For a hard-wearing and attractive floor, there are also quarry tiles, ideal for areas that receive a lot of foot traffic. For most tiling jobs, you will need tools for measuring, spacing and cutting the tiles, and adhesive and grout for attaching the tiles. Notched spreaders and grout finishers are usually sold with adhesives and grouts.

# WALL TILES

In today's homes, the surfaces that are tiled more often than any other are walls, especially in rooms such as kitchens and bathrooms, where a hard-wearing, water-resistant and easy-to-clean decorative finish is required. Often the tiling protects only the most vulnerable areas such as splashbacks above wash basins and shower cubicles; but sometimes the whole room is tiled from floor to ceiling.

Tiles used for wall decoration are generally fairly thin, measuring from 4 to 6mm (³⁄₁₆ to ¼in) thick, although some imported tiles (especially the larger sizes) may be rather thicker than this. The commonest kinds are square, measuring 108mm (4¼in) or 150mm (6in) across, but rectangular tiles measuring 200 x 100mm (8 x 4in) and 200 x 150mm (8 x 6in) are becoming more popular.

Tile designs change with fashions in interior design, and current demand seems to be mainly for large areas of neutral or small-patterned tiles interspersed with individual motif tiles on a matching background. Plain tiles, often with a simple border frame, are also popular, as are tiles that create a frieze effect when laid alongside one another. Some sets of tiles build up into larger designs (known as feature panels), which can look quite striking when surrounded by an area of plain tiling.

The surface of ceramic wall tiles is no longer always highly glazed, as it was traditionally. Now there are semi-matt finishes, often with a slight surface texture that softens the harsh glare produced by a high-gloss surface.

Tile edges have changed over the years too. Once, special round-edged tiles were used for the exposed edges of tiled areas, and plain ones with unglazed square edges elsewhere. Nowadays, tiles are either the universal type or the standard square-edged variety. Both types usually have two adjacent edges glazed so they can be used as perimeter tiles, and sometimes all four edges are glazed.

LEFT: Wall tiles can be used to make eye-catching schemes, mixed geometrically or at random.

# MOSAICS

**M**osaics are just tiny tiles – usually plain in colour, sometimes with a pattern – that are sold made up in sheets on an open-weave cloth backing. These sheets are laid like larger tiles in a bed of adhesive, and all the gaps, including those on the surface of the sheet, are grouted afterwards. Square mosaics are the most common, but roundels, hexagons and other interlocking shapes are also available. Sheets are usually square and 300mm (12in) across, and are often sold in packs of five or ten. The best way of estimating quantities is to work out the area to be covered and to divide that by the coverage figure given on the pack to work out how many packs to buy. Note that wall and floor types are of different thicknesses, as with ordinary ceramic tiles.

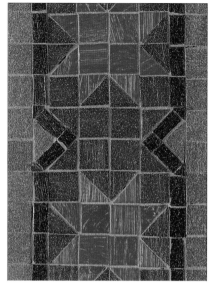

**ABOVE AND BELOW:** Mosaic tiles are regaining the popularity they enjoyed in times past, but laying them is definitely a labour of love.

# FLOOR TILES

Although less widely used than wall tiles, ceramic floor tiles are a popular choice for heavy traffic areas such as porches and hallways. They are generally thicker and harder-fired than wall tiles, to enable them to stand up to heavy wear without cracking. Again, a wide range of plain colours, simple textures and more elaborate designs is available. Common sizes are 150mm (6in) and 200mm (8in) squares and 200 x 100mm (8 x 4in) rectangles; hexagons are also available in plain colours, and a popular variation is a plain octagonal tile that is laid with small square coloured or decorated inserts at the intersections.

Quarry tiles are unglazed ceramic floor tiles with a brown, buff or reddish colour, and are a popular choice for hallways, conservatories and country-style kitchens. They are usually laid in a mortar bed, and after the joints have been grouted the tiles must be sealed with boiled linseed oil or a recommended proprietary sealer. Common sizes are 100mm (4in) and 150mm (6in) square. Special shaped tiles are also available for forming upstands at floor edges.

Terracotta tiles look similar to quarry tiles, but are larger and are fired at lower temperatures, so they are more porous. They are sealed in the same way as quarry tiles. Squares, ranging in size between 200 and 400mm (8 and 16in), and rectangles are the commonest shapes, but octagonal versions with small square in-fill tiles are also popular.

Cork tiles come in a small range of colours and textures. Their surface feels warm and relatively soft underfoot, and they also give some worthwhile heat and sound insulation – particularly

FAR LEFT: Ceramic floor tile with a painted medieval design.

MIDDLE: Ceramic tiles provide a durable and waterproof surface for bathroom floors.

LEFT: Quarry tiles provide a durable and attractive floor covering, and are especially suited to kitchens and conservatories.

useful in bathrooms, kitchens, halls and even children's bedrooms. The cheapest types have to be sealed to protect the surface after they have been laid, but the more expensive vinyl-coated floor types can be walked on as soon as they have been stuck down. They need little more than an occasional wash and polish to keep them in good condition. However, even the best cork floor tiles are prone to damage from sharp heels and heavy furniture, for example.

Vinyl tiles come in a very wide range of plain and patterned types, and generally resist wear better than cork, so they can be used on floors subject to fairly heavy wear. However, they are a little less gentle on the feet. Some of the more expensive types give very passable imitations of luxury floor coverings such as marble and terrazzo. Most are made in self-adhesive form and very little maintenance is needed once they have been laid.

Modern lino tiles, made from natural materials rather than the plastic resins used in vinyl tiles, offer far better performance than traditional linoleum. They come in a range of bright and subtle colours and interesting patterns, often with pre-cut borders.

All these types generally come in 300mm (12in) squares, although larger squares and rectangles are available in

**ABOVE LEFT:** Cork is the warmest of tiled floor coverings underfoot, and when sealed is good-looking and durable too.
**MIDDLE:** The more expensive types of vinyl floor tile offer superb imitations of other materials, such as wood, marble and terrazzo.
**ABOVE RIGHT:** Lino tiles offer a warm, attractive and durable alternative to cork and vinyl floor coverings in rooms such as kitchens and hallways.

some of the more expensive ranges. They are generally sold in packs of nine, covering roughly 0.84 sq m (1 sq yd), although many kinds are often available singly.

# ADHESIVE AND GROUTING

Both adhesive and grout for wall tiling are now usually sold ready-mixed in plastic tubs complete with a notched plastic spreader. For areas that will get the occasional splash or may suffer from condensation, a water-resistant adhesive and grout is perfectly adequate, but for surfaces such as shower cubicles, which will have to withstand prolonged wetting, it is essential to use both waterproof adhesive and waterproof grout. Always use waterproof grout on tiled worktops; ordinary grout will harbour germs. Some silicone sealant or mastic (caulking) may also be needed for waterproofing joints where tiling abuts baths, basins and shower trays.

## ADHESIVE

Ceramic floor-tile adhesive is widely available in powder form as well as ready-mixed. It is best always to use a waterproof type (plus waterproof grout), even in theoretically dry areas.

Special water-based adhesive is the type to choose for both cork and lino tiles; solvent-based contact adhesives were formerly the first choice, but their fumes are extremely unpleasant and also dangerously inflammable, and they are no longer recommended. For vinyl-coated cork tiles, a special vinyl acrylic adhesive is needed. For vinyl tiles, an emulsion-type latex flooring adhesive is the best choice.

It is important that you allow adhesive to dry for at least 24 hours before applying grout.

## GROUTING

Grout is generally white, but coloured grout is on sale and will make a feature of the grout lines (an effect that looks best with plain or fairly neutral patterned tiles).

Adhesive and grout are both sold in a range of quantities, sometimes labelled by weight, sometimes by volume; always check the coverage specified by the manufacturer on the packaging when buying, so as not to buy too much or run out halfway through the job.

## TOOLS FOR ADHESIVE AND GROUTING

Notched spreaders are used for creating a series of ridges in the adhesive, allowing it to spread when the tile is pressed home, and ensuring that an even thickness of adhesive is applied. They are available in various sizes. Grouting tools include a grout spreader, grout finisher and grout remover.

## OTHER MATERIALS

A damp sponge or cloth is needed to remove excess grout from the faces of the tiles, and a clean, dry cloth is needed to polish the tiles afterwards.

For protection, a face mask, safety goggles and leather gloves should be worn, especially when cutting and smoothing tiles, and when handling cut tiles. Rubber gloves should be worn when using tile adhesive, grout and grout colourant. If your skin is very sensitive, use a barrier cream also.

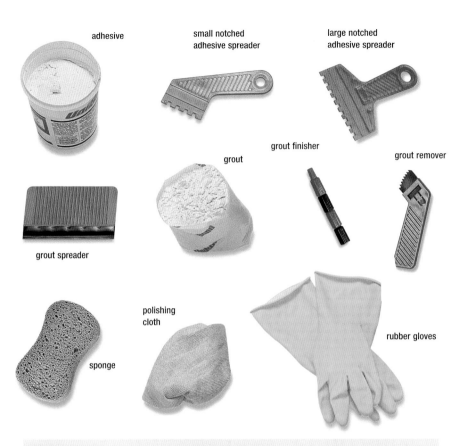

adhesive

small notched adhesive spreader

large notched adhesive spreader

grout spreader

grout

grout finisher

grout remover

sponge

polishing cloth

rubber gloves

## RENEWING GROUT

Over the years, the grout in an existing tiled surface may become discoloured or cracked, which could cause serious problems in a shower. Fortunately, it can be renewed without having to strip off all the tiles. However, being very hard, it is difficult to remove and you will need a proper grout remover. This has a hardened, sharp serated blade.

If the grout is only discoloured, it can be removed to a depth of about 3mm (¹⁄₈in), then new grout applied on top; if it is cracked, however, go to the thickness of the tile before regrouting.

Take care when using a grout remover, as it may chip the glaze along the edges of the tiles, which will be difficult to disguise and may lead to water penetrating the tiled surface.

A grout remover is also useful for removing a damaged tile prior to replacing it. After raking out all the grout around the damaged tile, chip out the tile carefully with a hammer and cold chisel. Wear safety goggles and thick leather gloves to protect your eyes and hands from flying shards of tile, which will be sharp.

# TILING
# PREPARATION

The best way to practise tiling skills is to begin by covering just a small area such as a washbasin splashback, where setting out the tiles so that they are centred on the area concerned is a simple job, and there is very little tile cutting to do. For a larger area – a whole wall, or perhaps even a complete room – exactly the same techniques are used. The big difference is the sheer scale of the job, which makes the preliminary setting-out by far the most important part. The problem is that walls are seldom blank surfaces, and there may be a number of obstacles to tile around. Care must be taken to get the best fit with these inflexible tile squares, without needing to cut impossibly thin slivers to fill in gaps.

# PLANNING

The most important thing to do is to plan precisely where the whole tiles will fall. On a flat, uninterrupted wall this is quite easy; simply find the centreline of the wall and plan the tiling to start from there. However, there will probably be obstacles such as window reveals, door openings and built-in furniture in the room, all competing to be the centre of attention, and it will be necessary to work out the best "centre-point" while all the time trying to avoid having very thin-cut tile borders and edges.

It is best to use a device called a tiling gauge – a batten (furring strip) marked out in tile widths – to work this out. The gauge is easy to make from a straight piece of timber about 1.2m (4ft) long, marked off with pencil lines to match the size of the tile. Use this to ensure that the tiles will be centred accurately on major features such as window reveals, with a border of cut tiles of equal width at the end of each row or column of tiles.

The next stage is the actual setting-out. With large areas of tiling, two things are vitally important. First, the tile rows must be exactly horizontal; if they are not, errors will accumulate as the tiles extend across the wall, throwing the verticals out of alignment

with disastrous results. When tiling right around a room, inaccurate levels mean that rows will not match up at the start and finish points. Second, the tiles need some support while the adhesive sets; without it, they may slump down the wall.

The solution is to fix a line of battens across the wall – or right around the room – just above the level of the skirting (baseboard), securing them with partly-driven masonry nails (tacks) so that they can be removed later when the adhesive has set. The precise level will be dictated by setting-out with the tiling gauge, but usually will be between half and three-quarters of a tile width above the skirting. Do not rely on this being level; it may not be. Draw the line out in pencil first, using the spirit (carpenter's) level, then pin the battens up and check the level again. If everything is straight, it is time to start tiling.

## ESTIMATING QUANTITIES

When working out how many tiles you will need, first select the tile size. Then set out the area to be tiled on the wall and use the setting-out marks to count how many tiles are needed in each horizontal row and each vertical column. Count cut tiles as whole tiles, then multiply the two figures together to obtain the total required. Always add a further 5 per cent to the total to allow for breakages and miscalculations.

## NUMBER OF TILES NEEDED

| TILE SIZE | NO/SQ M | NO/SQ YD |
|---|---|---|
| 108 x 108mm<br>(4¼ x 4¼in) | 86 | 71 |
| 200 x 100mm<br>(8 x 4in) | 48 | 41 |
| 150 x 150mm<br>(6 x 6in) | 43 | 36 |

## MAKING AND USING A TILING GAUGE

1 Use a pencil and one of the chosen tiles to mark up a length of wood for use as a tiling gauge. Allow for the width of tile spacers if they are to be used.

2 Hold the tiling gauge horizontally against the wall to see how many tiles each row will take, and also to centre the tiling on a wall feature or window opening.

3 Similarly, hold the gauge vertically to assess how many tiles will fill each column, and where best to position any cut tiles that may be needed at top or bottom.

# SETTING OUT TILED WALLS

Careful setting-out is essential to the success of any tiling job. The object is to obtain a balanced look to each tiled surface, with the rows of tiles being centred on the wall itself or on some prominent feature, much like you would centre a wallpaper pattern. This will ensure that any cut tiles at the margins or around a feature are of equal size.

Doors and window openings particularly can cause problems and often require quite a bit of thought.

## TILING AROUND A DOOR

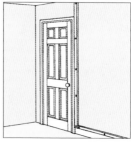

**1** If the door is close to the room corner, start with whole tiles next to the frame. Use a vertical tile guide if the architrave (trim) is not truly vertical (it may not be).

**2** Tile the whole of the main wall area, adding cut tiles next to the room corner and at ceiling level. Remove the tile supports when the adhesive has had time to set.

**3** Fit a tile support above the door, in line with the tile rows, and another between it and the other room corner, just above skirting (baseboard) level.

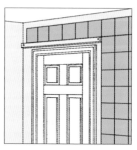

**4** Carry on placing whole tiles above the door opening, filling in with cut tiles at the room corner and at ceiling level, as in step 2.

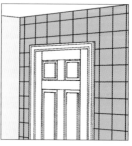

**5** Remove the tile support above the door opening and fill in all around it with cut and whole tiles as required. Grout the tiles when the adhesive has set.

**6** If the door opening is near or at the centre of the wall, centre the tiling on it and fix tile support battens (furring strips) as required.

## TILING AROUND A WINDOW

1 For tiling a wall with a window opening, first decide on where to centre the tiling. On a wall with one window, centre the tiling on a line drawn through its centre.

2 If there are two window openings in a wall, centre the tiles on a line drawn through the centre of each window, provided an exact number of whole tiles will fit between them.

3 Otherwise, centre the tiling on a line drawn midway between the windows. Always work across and up the wall, placing whole tiles up to window-sill level, then up the wall at each side of the window. Fit a tile support above the opening to support whole tiles there.

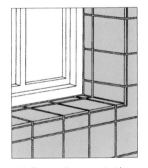

4 Remove the support strips and cut tiles to fit on the face wall at each side and across the top of the window. To tile a window reveal, place whole tiles so they overlap the edges of the tiles on the wall face. Then fill in between these and the frame with cut tiles.

## POSITIONING CUT TILES FOR PANELS

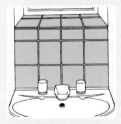

If the height of a tiled splashback is determined by a feature such as a mirror or window, position a row of cut tiles along the top of the panel. Make sure their top edges are overlapped by any tiles in a window recess.

If the width of the tiling is defined, as with a bath panel, always position cut tiles of equal size at each side.

# SETTING OUT TILED FLOORS

Tiled floors need careful setting-out if the end result is to look neat and professional. This is especially important with glazed ceramic and quarry tiles and also patterned vinyl and lino tiles, but matters rather less with plain vinyl or cork tiles where the finished effect is of uniform colour and the joints between the tiles are practically invisible.

Fortunately the necessary setting-out is much easier with floor tiles than wall tiles, since the tiles can be dry-laid on the floor surface and moved around until a starting point is found that gives the best arrangement, with cut border tiles of approximately equal size all around the perimeter of the room.

In a regularly shaped room, start by finding the centre-point of the floor by linking the midpoints of opposite pairs of walls with string lines. In an irregularly shaped room, place string lines as shown in step 2 so that they avoid obstructions, then link the midpoints of opposite pairs of strings to find the room's centre. Now dry-lay rows of tiles out toward the walls in each direction, allowing for any joint thickness, to see how many whole tiles will fit in and to check whether this results in over-narrow border tiles or awkward cuts against obstacles. Move the rows slightly to improve the fit if necessary, then chalk the string lines and snap them against the floor to mark the starting point.

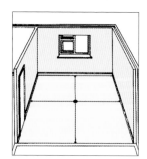

1 In a regularly shaped room, find the centre by linking the midpoints of opposite pairs of walls with string lines.

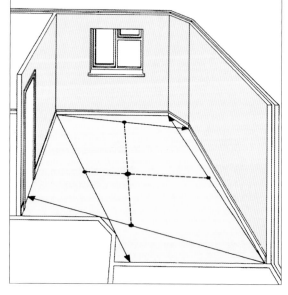

2 In an irregularly shaped room, use string lines that avoid obstacles, and link their midpoints to find the centre.

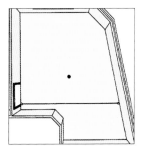

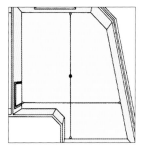

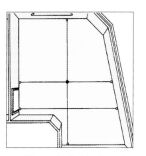

3 To ensure that tiles will be laid square to the door threshold if the walls are out of square, place a string line at right angles to the door opening across the room to the opposite wall.

4 Place a second string line at right angles to the first so that it passes through the room's centre-point.

5 Place a third string line at right angles to the second, again passing through the centre-point, to complete the laying guide.

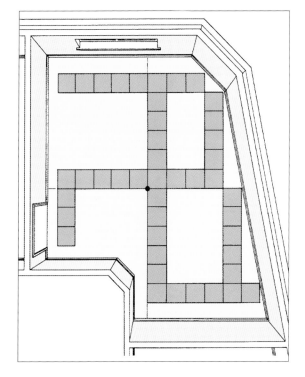

6 Dry-lay rows of tiles out from the centre of the room toward the walls, allowing for the joint width, as appropriate, to determine the width of the border tiles and the fit of the tiles around any obstacles.

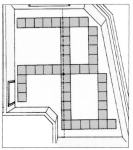

7 Adjust the string lines to obtain the best possible fit, chalk them and snap them against the floor to mark the laying guidelines.

# PREPARING A SURFACE FOR TILING

The surface for tiling should be clean and dry. It is possible to tile over painted plaster or plasterboard (gypsum board), but old wallcoverings should be removed and brick walls must be rendered. Note that modern tile adhesives allow tiling over existing tiles, so there is no need to remove these if they are securely bonded to the wall surface. There is also no need to fill minor cracks or holes; the tile adhesive will bridge these as it is applied to the wall surface. Printed wallpaper can easily be removed because it will absorb water splashed on it immediately; other types will not. With paper-backed fabric wallcoverings, it is often possible to peel the fabric away from its paper backing; try this before turning to other methods.

## WASHING WALLS AND CEILINGS

Wash wall surfaces down with sugar soap (all-purpose cleaner) or detergent, working from the bottom up, then rinse them with clean water, working from the top down. Wash ceilings with a floor mop or squeegee, after disconnecting and removing light fittings. Again, rinse off with clean water.

## REMOVING WALLPAPER

1 To strip printed wallpaper, wet the surface with a sponge or a garden spray gun. Wait for the water to penetrate, and repeat if necessary.

4 After removing the bulk of the old wallpaper, go back over the wall surface and remove any remaining "nibs" of paper with sponge/spray gun and scraper.

2 Using a stiff wallpaper scraper – not a filling knife (putty knife) – start scraping the old paper from the wall at a seam. Wet it again while working if necessary.

3 Turn off the power before stripping around switches and other fittings, then loosen the faceplate screws to strip the wallpaper behind them.

5 To strip a washable wallpaper, start by scoring the plastic coating with a serrated scraper or toothed roller, then soak and scrape as before.

6 For quicker results, use a steam stripper to remove washable papers. Press the steaming plate to the next area while stripping the area just steamed.

# TILING TECHNIQUES

Tiling is relatively straightforward and does not require a lot of expensive equipment. It pays to plan each tiling project carefully and not to rush it. The more you practise, the more skilled you will become – tiling the walls or floor of a whole room is too large an undertaking for a beginner, but tiling a skirting (baseboard), window recess or splashback can be accomplished after only a little experience. Having thoroughly prepared the surface to be tiled, you will need to work quite quickly, as the adhesive and grout will begin to go off quite rapidly. Tackle small sections at a time, cleaning off any excess as you go before it has a chance to harden. This is particularly important with combined adhesives and grouts.

# BEGINNING TO TILE

## FITTING TILE SUPPORTS

Use masonry pins (tacks) to fix the support to the wall, aligned with the guideline. Drive the pins in only part of the way so that they can be pulled out to remove the batten (furring strip) later.

When tiling large areas or whole walls, pin a vertical guide batten to the wall as well to help keep the tile columns truly vertical.

### FIXING TILES

Once all the necessary setting-out work has been done, the actual technique of fixing tiles to walls is quite simple: spread the adhesive and press the tiles into place. However, there must be an adhesive bed of even thickness to ensure that neighbouring tiles sit flush with one another. To obtain this, use a toothed spreader (usually supplied with the tile adhesive; buy one otherwise). Scoop some adhesive from the tub with the spreader, and draw it across the wall with the teeth pressed hard against the plaster to leave ridges of a standard height on the wall. Apply enough adhesive to fix about ten or twelve tiles at a time.

Bed the tiles into the adhesive with a pressing and twisting motion, aligning the first tile with the vertical guideline or batten. If using tile spacers, press one into the adhesive next to the top corner of the first tile, and place the second tile in the row.

## MARKING OUT A SPLASHBACK

1 When tiling a small area with rows of whole tiles, use the tiling gauge to mark the extent of the tiled area on the wall. Here each row will have five tiles.

Carry on placing spacers and tiles until the end of the row is reached. Add subsequent rows in the same way until all the whole tiles are in place.

2 Next, use a spirit (carpenter's) level to mark a horizontal base line, above which the first row of whole tiles will be fixed. Cut tiles will fit below it.

3 Then use the spirit level again to complete a grid of horizontal and vertical guidelines on the wall surface, ready for a wooden tile support to be fixed.

## FIXING TILES

1 Use a notched spreader to spread adhesive on the wall. Press the teeth against the wall to leave ridges of even height. Place the first tile on the tile support, with its side against the pencilled guideline or vertical guide batten (furring strip).

2 Insert a tile spacer at the tile corner and place the second tile. Add more tiles to complete the row, then build up succeeding rows in the same way.

# CUTTING TILES

It is now time to tackle any cut tiles that are needed at the ends of the rows, and along the base of the tiled area beneath the horizontal tile support. Remove this, and the tile spacers, only when the adhesive has set; allow 24 hours.

When cutting border tiles, measure each cut tile individually at top and bottom or each side as necessary. The walls, floors and ceilings of houses are rarely true and you are likely to find that the gaps to be filled will vary from one tile to the next. Straight cuts can be made with a small cutter or cutting jig, while shapes will need to be nibbled out with nippers or cut with a tile saw.

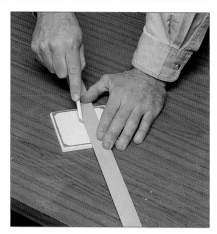

1 Use a pencil-type tile cutter and a straightedge to make straight cuts. Measure and mark the tile width needed, then score a line across the glaze.

4 The traditional way of making a cut-out in a tile is to score its outline on the tile, then gradually nibble away the waste material with pincers or tile nippers.

5 An alternative is to use a special abrasive-coated tile saw. This is indispensable for making cut-outs – to fit around pipes and similar obstructions.

2 Place a nail or matchstick (wooden match) under the scored line at each side of the tile, and break it with downward hand pressure on each half of the tile.

3 Use a cutting guide or tiling jig if preferred, especially for cutting narrow strips. This type holds the tile securely and also guides the tile cutter accurately.

## USING A TILE-CUTTING JIG

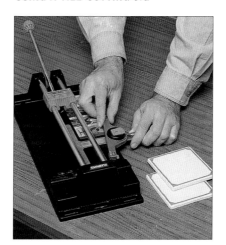

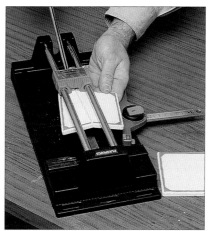

1 For making angled cuts as well as straight ones, a tile-cutting jig is invaluable. To set it up, first fix the side fence to the angle required.

2 Draw the cutting point across the tile, scoring the tile only once. Snap the tile by holding it against the guide bars and lowering the cutter handle with its tip under the tile.

# ADDING CUT TILES

When tiling a whole wall, cut tiles are likely to be needed at the corners at each end of the wall, and at the skirting (baseboard) and ceiling. If the tiling is to extend on to an adjacent wall, the horizontal rows must align, so extra care is needed when setting out.

At an internal corner, tile up to the angle completely on one wall so that its tiles overlap the edges of the tiles on the first wall. You can do the same thing at an external corner, using glazed-edge tiles on one wall to conceal the edges of the tiles on the other, provided the angle is truly vertical. If it is not, bed corner strip in the adhesive, set it vertical, then tile up to it.

1 Measure, mark and cut the sections of tile needed to complete each row of tiling. Spread a little adhesive over their backs and press them into place.

2 When tiling adjacent walls, place all the cut pieces on the first wall. Repeat on the second, overlapping the original cut pieces. If cut tiles are only needed on one wall, make sure they are overlapped by the whole tiles on the adjacent wall.

3 When tiling external corners, set out the tiles so that, if possible, whole tiles meet on the corner. Overlap the tiles as shown, or to fit plastic corner trim.

# GROUTING

When all the tiles are in place, including any cut tiles that are required, it is time to tackle the final stage of the job – filling in the joint lines between the tiles with grout. You should leave adhesive to dry for at least 24 hours before grouting. Ready-mixed grout is a little more expensive than powdered, but more convenient to use. You need a flexible spreader (usually supplied with the grout) to force the grout into the gaps, a damp sponge or cloth to remove excess grout from the faces of the tiles, and a short length of wooden dowel or a proprietary grout shaper to smooth the grout lines. A clean, dry cloth will be needed to polish the tiles afterwards.

1 Apply the grout to the tile joints by drawing the loaded spreader across them at right angles to the joint lines. Scrape off excess grout and reuse it.

2 Use a damp sponge or cloth to wipe the surface of the tiles before the grout dries out. Rinse it in clean water from time to time.

3 Then use a short length of wooden dowel or a similar tool to smooth the grout lines to a gentle concave cross-section. Allow the grout to harden completely, then polish the tiles with a dry cloth to remove any remaining bloom.

# ALTERNATIVE EDGING TECHNIQUES

Most ceramic wall tiles have two glazed edges, making it possible to finish off an area of tiling or an external corner with a glazed edge exposed. However, there are alternative ways of finishing off tiling. It can be edged with wooden mouldings or plastic trim strips.

Wooden mouldings can be bedded into the tile adhesive on walls; to edge worktops they can be pinned (tacked) or screwed to the worktop edge.

Plastic edge and corner mouldings (nosings) have a perforated flange that is bedded in the tile adhesive before the tiles are placed. These mouldings come in a range of pastel and bright primary colours to complement or contrast with the tiling. Take care when fitting them to make sure they are vertical, checking with a spirit (carpenter's) level, otherwise they will cause problems when you come to add the tiles. Remember to allow a grouting gap between the moulding and the tiles.

Another method of finishing off the edge of a tiled area is to use proprietary border tiles. These are special narrow tiles that come in a variety of widths, normally coinciding with standard tile widths, and usually have a glazed edge that can be exposed. Border tiles offer a wide range of patterns to choose from, and some even have moulded relief patterns for added interest. They can be used horizontally or vertically.

ABOVE: Bed plastic edge or corner trim into the adhesive, then position the tiles so that they fit flush against the curved edge of the trim strip.

## EDGING A COUNTER TOP

1 Wood can be used to edge a tiled counter top. Start by attaching the moulding to the edge of the worktop so it will fit flush with the tiled surface. Mitre the ends of the lengths of moulding to produce neat internal and external corners.

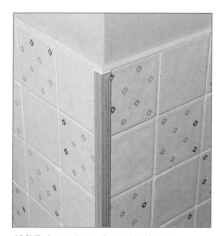

ABOVE: As an alternative to plastic, use wooden mouldings bedded in the tile adhesive. Here, an L-shaped moulding forms a neat external corner trim.

ABOVE: When tiling over existing tiles, some way of disguising the double thickness along exposed edges will be needed. A quadrant (quarter-round) moulding is ideal.

2 Spread the tile adhesive and bed the tiles in place, checking that they lie level with the top edge of the moulding and flush with each other.

3 Plug the counter-bored screw holes by gluing in short lengths of dowel and chiselling them off flush with the moulding. Sand them smooth. Finally, grout the tile joints for a neat finish and paint, stain or varnish the mouldings.

# LAYING CERAMIC FLOOR TILES

**B**oth glazed ceramic and quarry tiles can be laid directly over a concrete floor, as long as it is sound and dry. They can also be laid on a suspended timber floor if it is strong enough to support the not inconsiderable extra weight (check this with a building surveyor). In this case, cover the floorboards with exterior-grade plywood, screwed down or secured with annular nails (spiral flooring nails) to prevent it from lifting; this will provide a stable, level base for the tiles.

Glazed ceramic floor tiles are laid with specially formulated adhesive, which should be a waterproof type in bathrooms and a flexible type if tiling on a suspended floor. Quarry and terracotta tiles are laid on mortar over a solid concrete floor, and in thick-bed tile adhesive over plywood.

Old floor coverings should be lifted before laying ceramic or quarry tiles, but if a solid floor is covered with well-bonded vinyl or cork tiles, these can be left in place and tiled over, using tile adhesive. First remove any wax polish used on them.

Set out the floor as described previously, but transfer the starting point to the corner of the room farthest from the door once the setting-out has been completed.

1 Pin tiling guides to the floor in the corner of the room at right angles to each other, then spread some adhesive on the floor with a notched-edge trowel.

4 To cut border tiles to the correct size and shape, lay a whole tile over the last whole tile laid, butt another against the skirting (baseboard) and mark where its edge overlaps the tile underneath.

2 Place the first tile in the angle between the tiling guides, butting it tightly against them and pressing it down firmly into the adhesive bed.

3 As the tiles are laid, use the spacers to ensure an even gap between them. Use a straightedge and spirit (carpenter's) level to check that all the tiles are horizontal.

5 Cut the marked tile and use the cut-off piece to fill the border gap. Repeat step 4, using the same tile until it becomes too narrow to fill the border gap.

6 Spread grout over the tiles to fill all the joint lines. Wipe excess grout from the surface of the tiles with a damp cloth. Use a piece of dowel or similar rounded tool to smooth the grout. Polish the tile with a clean, dry cloth.

# LAYING QUARRY TILES

Quarry tiles offer a hard-wearing floor surface, which is ideal for areas that will receive a lot of foot traffic such as hallways. However, they are quite thick, which makes them difficult to cut, so consider carefully where you want to use them; an area that requires a lot of cut tiles may be impractical. Some suppliers will offer to cut quarry tiles for you, which can solve the problem. However, make sure you measure them carefully and mark them clearly.

As with tiling a wall, guide battens (furring strips) will be needed and should be nailed to the floor in one corner, making sure they make a right angle. Their thickness should be about double the thickness of the tiles to allow for the mortar on which the tiles are bedded.

When laying the tiles, it is necessary to work in bays so that the mortar thickness can be kept uniform. This is achieved by nailing a third batten to the floor parallel with one of the other two and four tile widths away from it. Then a board is cut as a spreader for the mortar, with notched ends that fit over the parallel battens so that an even thickness of mortar is achieved as the board is drawn along them. This should be the thickness of a tile plus 3mm (⅛in).

Before laying the tiles, soak them in a bucket of water, as this will prevent them from sucking all the moisture out of the mortar and weakening it.

1 Add a third tiling guide to form a bay four tiles wide. Put down a thin mortar bed and place the first row of tiles, using a tiling gauge to space them.

4 Complete the second bay in the same way as the first. Continue in this fashion across the room until all the whole tiles are laid. Allow the mortar to harden so that you can walk on the tiles before finally removing the guide battens (furring strips).

2 Complete four rows of four tiles, then check that they are level. Tamp down any that are proud, and lift and re-bed any that are lying low.

3 Complete the first bay, then remove the third tiling guide and reposition it another four tile widths away. Fill the second bay with mortar and tamp it down.

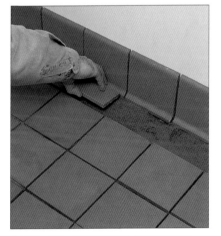

5 If installing a tiled upstand, place this next, aligning individual units with the floor tiling. Then cut and fit the border tiles.

6 Mix up a fairly dry mortar mix and use a stiff-bristled brush to work it well into the joints between the tiles. Brush away excess mortar while working before it has a chance to harden, otherwise it will stain the faces of the tiles.

# VINYL, LINO AND CORK FLOOR TILES

Vinyl, lino and cork floor tiles are available in both plain and self-adhesive types. Cork tiles may be unsealed or vinyl-coated. For plain vinyl tiles, an emulsion-type latex flooring adhesive is used, while plain cork tiles and lino tiles are best stuck with a water-based contact adhesive. For vinyl-coated cork tiles, use a special vinyl acrylic adhesive.

Since these tiles are comparatively thin, any unevenness in the sub-floor will show through the tiles. Cover timber floors with a hardboard underlay first. Concrete floors may need localized repairs or treatment with a self-smoothing compound.

If laying patterned tiles, set the floor out carefully. With plain tiles, setting out may not appear to be so important, but nevertheless the floor should still be set out carefully to ensure that the tile rows run out at right angles from the door.

**1** If using self-adhesive tiles, simply peel the backing paper off and place the tile in position on the sub-floor against the marked guidelines.

**2** Align self-adhesive tiles carefully before sticking them down; the adhesive grabs positively and repositioning may be difficult.

**3** If using non-adhesive tiles, spread the appropriate type of adhesive on the sub-floor, using a notched spreader to ensure that an even thickness is applied.

**4** After laying an area of tiles, use a smooth block of wood to work along the joints, pressing them down. This will ensure that they are all bedded firmly in the adhesive.

**5** At the border, lay a tile over the last tile laid, butt another against the skirting (baseboard) and mark its edge on the tile underneath.

**6** Place the marked tile on a board and cut it with a sharp knife. The exposed part of the sandwiched tile in step 5 will fit the gap perfectly.

**7** Fit the cut piece of border tile in place. Trim its edge slightly if it is a tight fit. Mark, cut and fit the other border tiles in exactly the same way.

**8** At an external corner, lay a whole tile over the last whole tile in one adjacent row, butt another against the wall and draw along its edge.

**9** Move the sandwiched tile to the other side of the corner, again butt the second whole tile against the wall and mark its edge on the sandwiched tile.

**10** Use the utility knife to cut out the square waste section along the marked lines, and offer up the L-shaped border tile to check its fit before fixing it.

# USING CORK WALL TILES

Cork wall tiles are usually sliced into squares – 300mm (12in) is the commonest size – or rectangles. They come in a range of natural shades, and may also be stained or printed with surface designs during manufacture. They are stuck to the wall surface with a special water-based contact adhesive, and since they are virtually impossible to remove once placed, they should be regarded as a long-term decorative option and their use carefully planned.

Cork tiles are not rigid like ceramic wall tiles and will follow the contours of the wall, so it is essential that this is prepared properly before the tiles are applied. The surface must be sound and as flat as possible, with all major cracks and holes filled and sanded down.

As with ceramic tiles, careful setting out will allow you to minimize the amount of cutting required, although this is not as difficult as cutting rigid tiles – a sharp knife is all that is required. To avoid problems of slight colour changes between batches of tiles, mix them all thoroughly before beginning.

---

**TIP**

If using cork tiles on walls, change the faceplate screws on light switches and socket outlets (receptacles) for longer ones; the originals may be too short to reach the lugs in the mounting box.

---

1 To ensure that the tile rows and columns build up correctly, draw horizontal and vertical pencil guidelines on the wall. Place the first tile.

4 Fit the cut piece of border tile in place on the wall. Shave or sand its cut edge down a fraction if it is a tight fit. Cut and fit others in the same way until you have filled all the border areas completely.

**2** If border tiles are to be cut, hold a whole tile over the last whole tile fixed, butt another against the frame and mark where its edge overlaps the tile underneath it.

**3** Place the marked tile on a board and cut it with a sharp utility knife. The exposed part of the sandwiched tile in step 2 should fit the border gap precisely.

**5** To fit a tile around an obstacle such as a light switch, make a paper or card template and test its fit before cutting the actual tile.

**6** Run a kitchen rolling pin or a length of broom handle over the completed cork surface to ensure that all the tiles are well bonded to the wall, paying particular attention to the joints between tiles.

# USING MOSAIC TILES

S mall mosaic tiles are an attractive alternative to square and rectangular tiles, especially for small areas of tiling where their size will look particularly appropriate. Modern mosaic tiles come in a range of shapes and sizes, from simple squares and roundels to interlocking shapes such as hexagons. They are generally sold in sheets backed with an open-mesh cloth that holds the individual mosaic pieces at the correct spacing and greatly speeds up the installation process, since the entire sheet is stuck to the wall in one go. If cut pieces are needed to fill in the perimeter of the tiled area, simply cut individual mosaic tiles from the sheet with scissors, trim them to size with a tile cutter and position them one by one. Mosaic tiles are fixed and grouted with ordinary tiling products.

**1** Start by putting up a horizontal tile support and a vertical tiling guide, as for ordinary tiling. Then apply an area of tile adhesive to the wall.

## CUTTING MOSAIC TILES

As well as using sheets of tiles, you can create mosaics with tesserae. Small pieces of tile can be shaped with mosaic nippers: wearing protective leather gloves and safety goggles, place the jaws of the nippers at right angles to the tile and press them together to make a clean cut. Clear away small, sharp shards of tile immediately and dispose of them safely. Alternatively, wrap each tile separately in heavy sacking and place on a wooden cutting board. Wearing protective leather gloves and safety goggles, tap the tile smartly several times with a hammer. Unwrap carefully and dispose immediately of small, unusable shards.

2 Position the first sheet of mosaic tiles on the wall, in the angle between the tiling support and the tiling guide, and press it firmly into place.

3 After placing several sheets, use a mallet and a piece of plywood to tamp the mosaics down evenly. Use a towel or a thin carpet offcut as a cushion. Ensure the grouting spaces between each sheet are equal.

4 To fill in the perimeter of the area, snip individual mosaic tiles from the sheet, cut them to the size required and bed them firmly in the adhesive.

5 When the adhesive has dried, spread grout over the tiled area, working it well into the gaps between the individual mosaics. Wipe off excess grout with a damp sponge, and polish the surface with a cloth when dry.

# TILING A WINDOW RECESS

Tiling a small area of a room will focus attention and add colour and pattern without being overpowering. Here, two different designs of hand-painted tiles have been used to accentuate a window recess, the colours complementing the bright-coloured wall.

For a completely different effect, plain terracotta tiles with curved edges would give a Mediterranean look to the window. Plain, matt-glazed tiles in rich shades of blue would create a very different note of Moorish magnificence.

Before you begin, measure the window recess carefully to determine how many tiles you will need. Allow a whole tile for each cut one to be on the safe side.

1 Wearing a face mask and gloves, sand the paintwork on the window sill and walls to remove any loose paint. Key (scuff) the surface to provide a base for the adhesive.

4 Place the first two tiles in position on the wall, butting them closely together and lining up the outside edge of the outer tile with the edge of the wall. Hold the tiles in place with masking tape until set. If the recess is less than two whole tiles deep, place the cut tiles next to the window frame.

2 Wearing rubber gloves, spread a thick layer of tile adhesive in one corner of the window. Using a damp sponge, remove any adhesive that gets on to the wall.

3 Using the notched edge of the spreader, key the surface only halfway through, leaving a thick layer of adhesive.

5 Spread adhesive in the opposite corner of the window and key as before. Position two vertical tiles as in step 4. Lay tiles along the window sill, overlapping the edges of the vertical tiles at each end.

6 Spread adhesive up the sides of the window recess and key. Position the contrasting tiles, lining up the edges with the edges of the recess. Tape in place as before until set. Grout all the tiles, removing any excess with a damp sponge. Polish with a dry, lint-free cloth.

# DECORATIVE TILING LAYOUTS

The preceding pages have dealt with tiling walls in the technical sense of planning the layout and fixing the tiles. However, tiles are more than just wallcovering units; they come in a range of sizes and designs that can also be used creatively in a variety of ways. Tile manufacturers offer a range of mass-produced designs you can choose from, which can be used to great effect with the application of a little imagination, or you can select from a variety of unique hand-painted tiles available from better tile suppliers, antique tiles from salvage companies, or even commission a motif panel from a specialist tile supplier. Plan the motif's position on the wall carefully, and build it in the usual way as tiling progresses.

# CHECKED PATTERN

If you have your heart set on a particular tile, but find it is outside your budget, do not despair; you can create quite dramatic results with the cheapest of tiles as long as you use them imaginatively. Here, basic wall tiles in two shades of blue have been used to create a stunning chequerboard effect that is topped with a thin, decorative band of tile strips. The strips make a visual "dado rail" (chair rail) that divides the tiles' surface quite naturally into two distinct areas. The upper portion of the wall is then finished using lighter blue tiles. The strips can be cut from ordinary tiles, or use proper dado tiles.

1 Prepare the wall properly, then attach a pair of batten (furring strip) guides at right angles where the first row of tiles will start.

4 Lay the light coloured tiles in place above the border, using tile spacers as before. Cut any tiles you need to complete the edges and set them in place. Use a damp sponge to remove any excess adhesive and leave to dry.

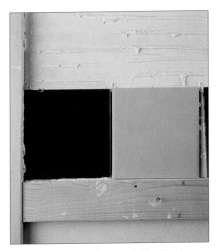

2 Wearing rubber gloves, apply tile adhesive using a notched spreader to key (scuff) the surface. Position the tiles, alternating light and dark.

3 When you have laid as many tiles as you want, cut 5cm (2in) strips of the darker tiles. Apply and key the tile adhesive as before, then set the strips in position using tile spacers.

5 When the adhesive has set, grout the tiles thoroughly, wearing rubber gloves. Press the grout down into the gaps between the tiles.

6 Remove any excess grout using a damp sponge and leave to dry. When the grout has set, polish the surface of the tiles with a dry, lint-free cloth.

# GEOMETRIC CHEQUERBOARD

Shades of blue and ivory Venetian glass tiles make a lovely cool splashback for a bathroom basin. They are arranged here in a simple geometric design, but you can experiment with other patterns – position the tiles diagonally to make a diamond shape, or use alternate coloured squares like a chequerboard.

For a co-ordinated look, use one of the tile colours to make a thin border around the bath or repeat the design on the door of a bathroom cupboard. You could also continue the design around a window.

1 Using a craft knife, score the surface of a piece of waterproof chipboard to provide a key (scuffed surface) for the tiles.

4 Clamp the board firmly and drill the screw holes. Put a drinking straw in each hole to keep them open. Wearing rubber gloves, spread waterproof tile adhesive over about one-third of the board.

**2** Seal both sides with diluted PVA (white glue) to prevent it from warping.

**3** Plan the design on the board. Mark a point in each corner for the screw holes, for hanging the splashback on the wall.

**5** Position the tiles on the board, pressing them firmly into the adhesive. Repeat over the rest of the board, working on one-third of the board at a time. Remove excess adhesive with a damp sponge. Leave to dry.

**6** Spread waterproof grout over the surface of the tiles, taking care not to dislodge them. Remove excess with a damp sponge, then polish with a dry, lint-free cloth. Seal the back with two coats of yacht varnish. Mark the screw positions on the wall, and drill and plug them. Screw the board to the wall with chromed mirror screws.

# PATTERNED WALL PANEL

Flowers have always been a popular theme for tiled wall panels, from the ornate vases of flowers produced at the Iznik potteries in Ottoman Turkey to the blue and white tulip panels made by Delft potters in Holland. Flowers are also a recurring theme in folk art in many countries.

These handmade and hand-painted tiles from the South of France are set directly on to the wall. A border of plain tiles in toning colours makes a perfect frame for the design. You could even edge the tiles with wooden moulding for a picture-frame effect.

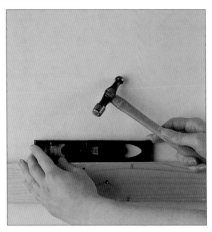

**1** Prepare the surface of the wall thoroughly. Decide on the position of the panel, then fix two guide battens (furring strips) to the wall.

**4** Start to build up the bottom and side of the border with plain tiles. Use tile spacers or space the tiles by eye.

2 Wearing rubber gloves, spread a layer of tile adhesive over the wall between the battens.

3 Using the notched edge of the spreader, key (scuff) the surface of the adhesive.

5 Begin to fill in the space between the bottom and side of the border with the floral tile panel. Continue to build up the panel and border gradually, moving diagonally from the starting point and making sure that the floral panel pieces are properly aligned. Remove excess adhesive with a damp sponge. Leave to dry overnight.

6 Wearing rubber gloves, grout the tiles, pushing the grout down well into the gaps between the tiles. When the grout has set slightly, remove the excess with a damp sponge. When completely dry, polish with a dry, lint-free cloth.

# WALL BORDER

These long, star-studded Spanish tiles are a modern version of the tiles made by medieval Islamic potters. They were widely used in place of the more time-consuming tile mosaics that decorate buildings such as the Alhambra Palace in Granada.

Tiles with interconnecting patterns look wonderful as an all-over wall decoration. Here they are used to add a touch of Spanish style in a simple border along the base of a wall.

When using tiles in this manner, bear in mind that they are not designed to take knocks (unless you use thicker worktop or floor tiles), so consider carefully where you will put them.

1 Measure the length of one tile. Using a pencil, mark the wall into sections of this measurement.

4 Using the notched edge of the spreader, key (scuff) the surface only halfway through, leaving a thick layer of adhesive.

2 Using a set square (T square), draw a vertical line at each mark to help position the tiles accurately.

3 Wearing rubber gloves, spread a thick layer of tile adhesive along the base of the wall. Cover enough wall to apply four or five tiles at a time.

5 Slide each tile into position. You may wish to use tile spacers or you could space them by eye. Wipe the surface of the tiles and the wall with a damp sponge to remove any excess adhesive. Leave to dry.

6 Grout the tiles thoroughly, pushing the grout down well into the gaps between the tiles. Using a damp sponge, remove any excess grout from the surface of the tiles. Use a length of dowel with a rounded end, or a grout shaper, to smooth the grout joint. Leave to dry. Polish the surface of the tiles with a dry, lint-free cloth.

# LAYING FLOORS

- Flooring materials

- Flooring preparation

- Flooring techniques

- Flooring variations

# INTRODUCTION

The wide range of floor coverings available to choose from includes decorative wood panels and strips, sheet vinyl and carpets.

There are two main types of wooden floor covering: woodblock, sometimes called wood mosaic, and woodstrip. The former consists of small slivers of wood (usually a hardwood) laid in groups and stuck to strong cloth to form wooden "tiles", while the latter is just what its name implies: narrow tongued-and-grooved hardwood planks laid over an existing floor.

Sheet vinyl floor coverings come in a huge range of colours and patterns, and may also have a surface embossed along the lines of the design to give plausible imitations of other floor coverings such as tiles, marble, wood and cork. Some more expensive types have a cushioned underside formed by incorporating small air bubbles during manufacture, which makes them warmer and softer underfoot than their solid counterparts.

Carpets laid loose have been used on floors for millennia, but it was only a few decades ago that wall-to-wall fitted carpeting became popular. Traditional woven carpets made from natural fibres have been challenged by carpets made from synthetic fibres and by alternative methods of manufacture. There is now a huge choice of colours and patterns in types to suit all locations and wear conditions, available in a variety of widths.

While some floor coverings require more skill than others to lay,

LEFT: Subtle variations of colour make wooden floorboards particularly attractive. To make the most of the grain pattern of the boards, after sanding you could use a clear or tinted varnish, or a stain followed by a varnish.

ABOVE: Sheet vinyl is durable and easy to clean, and is available in a range of colours and patterns.

BELOW: Carpeting provides luxury underfoot, and it is therefore ideal for bedrooms.

with care and forethought all can be installed by the determined do-it-yourselfer. Moreover, with a little imagination, many floor coverings can be used to produce eye-catching and unusual effects to match or complement the décor of a room.

Remember that practicality is important when choosing a floor covering. Always consider whether the area to be covered will be exposed to water, as in a bathroom, or to heavy wear, as in a kitchen, and whether durability is paramount or a more whimsical surface would suffice. Above all, choose projects that appeal to you and that will produce floors you will enjoy creating and living with.

# FLOORING MATERIALS

When choosing new floor coverings,
remember that there is more to it than
simply ordering wall-to-wall carpet
throughout, and mistakes can be expensive.
Floor coverings have to withstand a great
deal of wear and tear in certain areas of the
average home, especially if there are
children or pets in the family, so choosing
the right material is very important.
Luckily, there is a wide choice of materials,
and laying them is well within the capability
of most people. Shopping for floor coverings
has never been easier either. All the major
do-it-yourself suppliers stock a huge range
of materials – plus all the tools needed to
lay them. If they do not stock what you need,
try specialist flooring and carpet suppliers.

# WOOD FLOOR COVERINGS

These come in two main forms: as square woodblock panels made up of individual fingers of wood stuck to a cloth or felt backing for ease of handling and laying; or as woodstrip flooring – interlocking planks, often of veneer on a plywood backing. They are laid over the existing floor surface. Most are tongued-and-grooved, so only occasional nailing or clipping is required to hold them in place.

Woodblock panels are usually 300 or 450mm (12 or 18in) square, while planks are generally 75 or 100mm (3 or 4in) wide and come in a range of lengths to allow the end joints to be staggered from one row to the next so that they all line up.

LEFT: Wooden flooring materials can be used like tiles, creating a combination of interlocking shapes and natural textures.

BELOW: Parquet is created by laying blocks of wood in a variety of geometric patterns.

ABOVE: Give a contemporary interpretation to traditional parquet flooring by colourwashing the blocks. This provides a subtle means of matching the floor to your decorative scheme.

RIGHT: Hard-wearing and elegant, woodstrip flooring is a practical choice for living rooms and hallways.

FAR RIGHT: Wood squares can be painted in alternate colours, creating a chequerboard design. It is also possible to combine different wood effects, such as walnut and maple.

# VINYL, LINOLEUM AND CORK

Vinyl is available as sheets and tiles. Sheet vinyl is a relatively thin material that provides a smooth, hygienic and easy-to-clean floor covering, which is widely used in rooms such as kitchens, bathrooms and hallways. It is made from layers of plastic resin, with a clear wear layer protecting the printed design and frequently an air-cushion layer between this and the backing for extra comfort and warmth underfoot. Vinyl tiles come in a wide range of plain and patterned types, and are laid with double-sided adhesive.

Linoleum (lino) is becoming popular again for domestic use, and is also available in sheet form and as tiles, in some stylish designs and colourways with optional contrasting border designs. Lino is more difficult for the amateur to lay, however, being heavier, less flexible and harder to cut than vinyl.

ABOVE: Vinyl flooring is available in a wide range of decorative designs, including realistic imitations of ceramic tiles, wood panels, cork tiles and stone. The covering shown here is imitating an intricate wooden pattern.

Cork is frequently used in work areas such as kitchens and bathrooms. It offers a unique combination of warmth and resilience underfoot, coupled with an easy-to-clean surface that looks attractive too.

ABOVE: Sheet vinyl can offer excellent imitations of a wide range of other floor coverings, including marble, terrazzo and, shown here, woodstrip.

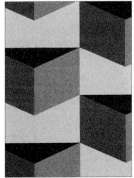

ABOVE: Linoleum shapes can be cut and adhered to the floor to produce patterns. Lino is ideal for kitchens, with its hard-wearing, easy-to-clean surface.

# CARPETS

Carpets consist of fibre tufts or loops woven or stuck to a durable backing. Woven carpets are generally the most expensive. Modern types are made by either the Axminster or the Wilton method, which differ in technical details, but both produce a durable product that can be either patterned or plain. Tufted carpets are made by stitching tufts of fibre into a woven backing, where they are secured by attaching a second backing under the first with adhesive. Some of the less expensive types have a foam underlay bonded directly to the backing; others require a separate underlay to be laid.

A wide range of fibre types is used in carpet construction, including wool, nylon, acrylic, polypropylene and viscose rayon, as well as modern natural materials such as coir, sisal and seagrass. Fibre blends can improve carpet performance; a mixture of 80 per cent wool and 20 per cent nylon is particularly popular for providing a combination of warmth, resilience, low flammability and resistance to soiling.

Pile length and density affect the carpet's performance as well as its looks, and most carpets are classified to indicate the sort of wear they can be expected to withstand. The pile can be cut, often to different lengths, giving a sculptured effect; looped (shag), that is, uncut and left long; corded, which means uncut and pulled tight to the backing; or twisted, which gives a tufty effect. A dense pile wears better than a loosely woven one, which can be parted to reveal the backing.

Carpet widths are described as broadloom, more than 1.8m (6ft) wide; or body (stair carpet), usually up to 900mm (3ft) wide. The former are intended for large areas, the latter for corridors and stairs. Broadloom carpet is available in various metric and imperial widths.

**ABOVE AND LEFT:** The range of colours and patterns of carpet available makes it possible to complement and enhance any style of interior. Carpets are made in qualities to match the requirements of every room in the house.

# CARPET TILES

These are small squares of carpet of various types, designed to be loose-laid. Cheaper tiles resemble cord and felt carpets, while more expensive ones may have a short or long cut pile. Common sizes are 300, 450, 500 and 600mm (12, 18, 20 and 24in) square.

Along with lino tiles, carpet tiles are real winners in the practicality stakes. Almost unbeatable in areas that need to be hard-wearing and where children and their attendant wear and tear are concerned, carpet tiles have the single disadvantage that they never look like fitted carpet, no matter how well they are laid. Rather than fighting the fact that they come in non-fraying squares, make use of this very quality and create a fun floor-scape, such as a giant board game. Carpet tiles are very forgiving, allowing for slight discrepancies in cutting, and are very easy to replace if an area is damaged. A geometrical design is easiest; it is advisable to leave curves to the experts, but anything else – even the elegance of a painting by Mondrian – is possible.

ABOVE: Carpet tiles have a long commercial pedigree, and can be a clever choice in the home too, since they can be lifted for cleaning and rotated to even out the effects of wear.

LEFT: Small carpet tiles can be used to create intricate patterns, such as this large backgammon board game. Such patterns need working out carefully on paper first and can be fiddly to lay, but the finished effect is well worth the effort.

# MATERIALS FOR DIFFERENT ROOMS

In principle, it is possible to lay any floor covering in any room of a home. However, custom and the practicalities of life tend to divide the home into three broad areas.

Access areas, such as halls, landings and stairs, need a floor covering that is able to cope with heavy traffic and muddy shoes. Ideal choices for hallways are materials with a water-repellent and easy-clean surface – for example, sheet vinyl, vinyl tiles, a woodstrip or woodblock floor, sanded and sealed floorboards, or glazed ceramic or quarry tiles. For stairs, where safety is paramount, the best material to choose is a heavy-duty carpet with a short pile, which can also be used on landings.

Work areas, such as kitchens and bathrooms, also need durable floor coverings that are easy to clean and, especially in the case of bathrooms,

ABOVE: Plain carpets are the key to simple, yet sophisticated, colour schemes. Neutral tones can be offset with the subtlest of colour contrasts.

LEFT: Cork is the warmest of tiled floor coverings underfoot, and when sealed is good-looking and durable too.

water-resistant as well. Sheet vinyl is a popular choice for both rooms, but tiles of various types can also provide an excellent surface – sealed cork, with its warm feel underfoot, is particularly suitable in bathrooms. However, if carpet is preferred for these rooms, there are extremely hard-wearing kitchen carpets available, with a specially treated short nylon pile that is easy to keep clean, and also

RIGHT: Solid
woodstrip
flooring, shown
here in beech,
provides a luxury
floor covering
that looks
stunning and
will also last
for a lifetime.

water-resistant bathroom carpets that give a touch of luxury underfoot without turning into a swamp at bath time.

Leisure areas – living rooms, dining rooms and bedrooms – are commonly carpeted wall to wall. Do not be tempted to skimp on quality in living rooms, which receive the most wear and tend to develop distinct traffic routes. However, it is reasonable to choose light-duty types for bedrooms.

Alternatives to carpets depend simply on taste in home décor. Options include sanded and sealed floorboards teamed with scatter rugs, or a parquet perimeter to a fine specimen carpet. Woodstrip, sheet vinyl or cork tiles may also be worth considering for children's rooms.

ABOVE: Wood is an excellent choice for entrance halls too, where a durable, yet good-looking, floor surface is essential.

# FLOORING PREPARATION

All floor coverings must be laid on a sound, flat surface. With a wooden structure, the older the floor, the more likely it is that there will be loose or damaged boards, or protruding nail heads. With a concrete floor there may be cracks, an uneven surface or, worse, damp patches. All of these conditions must be rectified before laying your new floor covering. If wooden boards are in reasonable condition, they may need only sanding to remove high spots; otherwise, they can be covered with sheets of hardboard, plywood or chipboard (particle board). Concrete can also be covered in this manner or finished with a self-levelling floor screed. If you are in any doubt about your ability in this respect, seek professional help.

# REMOVING OLD FLOOR COVERINGS

Generally speaking, old floor coverings should always be lifted before laying new ones. This also provides an opportunity to inspect the floor itself and to carry out any repairs that may be necessary. However, there are some situations where it may not be practical or necessary to lift an existing floor covering – for example, where vinyl tiles have been laid over a concrete floor and they are firmly stuck to it. Stripping such a large area will be an extremely time-consuming job unless a professional floor tile stripping machine is hired.

Woodblock or woodstrip floors should be lifted if damaged or loose, otherwise cover them by pinning on hardboard sheets.

**1** The backing of old foam-backed carpets may remain stuck to the floor surface after the carpet has lifted. Scrape and brush it up, and also remove any remaining staples and remnants of seaming tape.

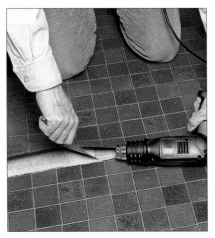

**2** To lift vinyl tiles or sheet vinyl that has been stuck along edges and seams, use a heat gun to soften the adhesive and quickly pull up the flooring. Work the blade of a scraper beneath the edges so that you can lift them.

**3** If vinyl or cork tiles have been stuck on to a hardboard underlay, lift a few tiles to expose the board edges, then lever up the boards in one piece.

# RENOVATING FLOORBOARDS

For suspended wood floors – boards laid over floor joists – start by lifting the old floor covering and checking that all the boards are securely fixed to their joists, and that they are reasonably flat and level. Loose boards will creak annoyingly when walked on, and raised edges or pronounced warping may show as distinct lines through the new floor covering.

Use either cut nails or large oval-headed nails to secure loose boards. When driving them near known pipe or cable runs, take care not to pierce them; it is best to drive the new nails as close to existing nail positions as possible for safety. If there are only one or two loose boards, secure them with screws rather than nails.

Another problem with floorboards, particularly if they are very old, is that gaps can open up between them. When laying a flexible floor covering over them, such as carpet or vinyl, the gaps may cause irregularities in the surface, leading to noticeable wear patterns. One solution is to glue strips of wood into the gaps, planing them flush with the boards when the glue has dried. If they are really bad, however, it may be worth lifting all the boards and relaying them, clamping them tightly together as you do so with hired flooring cramps. Any remaining gaps will need filling with a narrow board. Obviously, this is quite a drastic solution, and it may be simpler to clad the floor with hardboard sheets.

**1** Drive in any nails that have lifted due to warping or twisting of the floorboards, then recess their heads slightly using a nail punch. If existing nails have pulled through a board, drive in new ones, slightly to one side.

**2** If nails will not hold the floorboard flat against the joist, drill pilot and clearance holes, and use wood screws to secure the board firmly in place. Countersink the holes so that the screw heads sit below the surface of the board.

# LAYING HARDBOARD

Covering existing floorboards with a hardboard underlay is an alternative to floor sanding as a way of ensuring a smooth, flat surface ideal for thin sheet floor coverings. Lay the boards in rows with the joints staggered from row to row, and pin them down with hardboard pins (brads) driven in at 150mm (6in) spacings. Lay separate strips above known pipe runs so that you can get to them easily should the need arise.

Before you begin, condition the boards to the temperature and humidity conditions in the room so that they will not become warped after laying. Soak the textured sides of the boards with warm water, then stack them back to back in the room for

at least 24 hours. It is best to lay the hardboard textured side uppermost to provide an additional key (scuffed surface) for the flooring adhesive. In addition, the indentations in the board will accommodate the nail heads, preventing them from damaging the floor covering.

Dry-lay the boards first, working out from the centre of the room and making sure that their edges do not coincide with the gaps between floorboards. Check also that you will not be left with impossibly narrow gaps to fill at the walls. If necessary, shift the position of the first board to one side or the other.

If preparing to lay glazed ceramic or quarry tiles on a suspended wood floor, put down exterior-grade plywood.

1 If hardboard sheets are used as an underlay for a new floor covering, start by punching in any raised nail heads all over the floor.

2 Nail the hardboard sheets to the floorboards at 150mm (6in) intervals along the edges and also 300mm (12in) apart across the face of each sheet. Lay the boards in rows, staggering the joints from one row to the next.

# LAYING A CHIPBOARD FLOOR

To level and insulate a concrete floor, you can cover the concrete with a floating floor of chipboard (particle board), if raising the floor level will not cause problems at door thresholds. The chipboard can be laid directly on the concrete over heavy-duty plastic sheeting, which acts as a vapour barrier. If additional insulation is required, put down polystyrene (plastic foam) boards first, then lay the new flooring on top of them.

Treat damp floors with one or two coats of a proprietary damp-proofing liquid and allow to dry before laying the vapour barrier. Widespread rising damp may require more radical treatment, in which case, it is best to seek professional help.

**1** Before you begin laying the chipboard (particle board) panels, prepare the floor surface. First, remove the skirtings (baseboards). Next, put down heavy-duty plastic sheets to prevent moisture rising through the floor.

**2** Tape the sheets to the walls; they will be hidden behind the skirting later. Then butt-joint 25mm (1in) polystyrene (plastic foam) insulation boards over the floor, staggering the joints in adjacent rows.

**3** Cover the insulation with tongued-and-grooved flooring-grade boards. Use cut pieces as necessary, and add a tapered threshold (saddle) strip at the door. When finished, replace the skirtings.

# LAYING SELF-SMOOTHING COMPOUND

Ground floors of solid concrete are prone to two main problems: cracking or potholing of the surface, and rising damp caused by a failure in the damp-proof membrane within the floor structure. Cracks and depressions may show through new floor coverings, especially thinner types such as sheet vinyl, while dampness will encourage mould growth beneath the covering, so both these problems must be eradicated before laying a new floor.

Relatively narrow cracks can be patched with either a repair mortar of one part cement to three parts sand or with an exterior-quality masonry filler.

If the floor surface is uneven or pitted, it can be covered with a thin layer of self-smoothing compound. There are two types available; both are powders and are mixed with either water or with a special latex emulsion. The compound is mixed in a bucket and poured on to the floor surface, trowelling it out to a thickness of about 3mm (⅛in). The liquid finds its own level and dries to give a hard, smooth surface that can be walked on in about 1 hour. Leave it to dry for 24 hours before laying a floor covering over it.

At a door opening, it is necessary to nail a thin strip of wood across the threshold to contain the levelling compound and prevent it from spreading beyond the room. Use masonry nails to hold the wood in place, leaving their heads proud so that they can be prised out and the wood removed once the compound has dried.

1 Start by sweeping the floor clear of dust and debris. Then scrub away any patches of grease from the surface with strong detergent solution. Fill any cracks or holes deeper than 3mm (⅛in) with mortar or filler.

4 Mix up the self-smoothing compound in a bucket, following the manufacturer's instructions carefully to ensure that the mix is of the right consistency and free from lumps.

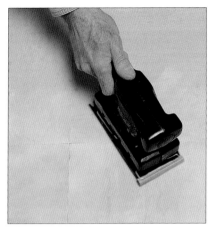

2 Key the surface of vinyl floor tiles by sanding them before laying the compound. Wipe away the dust with a damp cloth.

3 If the concrete surface is very dusty or appears unduly porous, seal it by brushing on a generous coat of PVA building adhesive (white general-purpose adhesive) diluted with about five parts water.

5 Starting in the corner of the room that is farthest from the door, pour the self-smoothing compound on to the floor surface to cover an area of about 1 sq m (11 sq ft).

6 Use a plasterer's trowel to spread the compound out to a thickness of about 3mm (⅛in). Mix, pour and level further batches as required until the entire floor has been covered. Leave to dry for 24 hours.

# FLOORING TECHNIQUES

A variety of techniques can be used to give a floor a new lease of life, whether it is simply brightening up an existing boarded floor with a coat of varnish or paint, laying a practical, hard-wearing covering or putting down a thick carpet to provide some underfoot luxury. Always consider the type of wear and tear the flooring will be subjected to and choose appropriately. Take the time to work out the quantities of materials needed – your supplier will often be able to help you in this respect – and make sure that you have everything to hand before you begin work. Clear the room of all furnishings and keep children and pets out of the way until you have finished.

# SANDING WOOD FLOORS

Where old floorboards are very uneven, or it is planned to leave them exposed but they are badly stained and marked, you will need to sand them. Hire a floor sanding machine to do this. It resembles a cylinder (reel) lawnmower, with a drum to which sheets of abrasive paper are fitted. A bag at the rear collects the sawdust; however, always wear a face mask and goggles when sanding floors. Also hire a smaller disc or belt sander for finishing off the room edges.

If necessary, drive any visible nail heads below the surface. Start sanding with coarse abrasive paper, running the machine at 45 degrees to the board direction, then use medium and fine paper in turn with the machine running parallel to the boards. Use the disc or belt sander to tackle the perimeter of the room where the large sander cannot reach. Even so, this will not sand right up to the skirtings (baseboards) or into the corners, and the only solution in these areas is to use a hand scraper.

### FINISHING

Once the floor has been sanded, sweep up the remaining dust and vacuum the floor. If you intend laying a floor covering, you need do no more. If you want to leave the boards exposed, wipe them with a cloth moistened with white spirit (paint thinner). This will remove any remaining dust.

If you want to make the most of the grain pattern of the boards, use a clear or tinted varnish, or a stain followed by

**1** Use a floor sander to smooth and strip old floorboards. Drape the power cord over one shoulder and raise the drum before starting the machine up.

a varnish. Brush stain on to two or three boards at a time, keeping a wet edge so that any differences in shade will be less noticeable. Brush on three coats of varnish, thinning the first with 10 per cent white spirit and allowing six hours between coats. Keep the room well ventilated.

### TIPS

Sanding creates lots of dust, so wear a facemask and goggles. When sanding, raise the drum at the end of each pass to prevent damage to the boards while the machine is stationary. For safety, drape the power cord of the sander over one shoulder.

2 Run the machine at 45 degrees to the board direction to start with, first in one direction, then in the other, at right angles to the original passes made.

3 Then switch to a medium-grade abrasive and run the sander back and forth, parallel to the board direction. Finish off with fine-grade abrasive.

4 Use a smaller disc or belt sander to strip areas close to the skirtings (baseboards) and door thresholds.

5 Use a scraper to remove paint or varnish from inaccessible areas such as around pipework, then sand the stripped wood smooth by hand.

# LAYING WOODSTRIP FLOORING

**W**oodstrip flooring is available in two main types: as solid planks, and as laminated strips (rather like plywood) with a decorative surface veneer. Lengths range from as little as 400mm (16in) up to 1.8m (6ft), and widths from 70mm (2¾in) up to around 200mm (8in). Solid planks are usually about 15mm (⅝in) thick; laminated types are a little thinner.

Both types are generally tongued-and-grooved on their long edges for easy fitting. Some are designed to be fixed to a wooden sub-floor by secret nailing; others are loose-laid, using clips to hold the strips together. Laminated strips are generally pre-finished; solid types may also be, but some need sealing once they have been laid.

All the hard work involved in putting down woodstrip flooring lies in the preparation; the actual laying, like so many decorating jobs, is simple.

Always unpack the strips and leave them in the room where they will be laid for at least seven days to acclimatize to the temperature and humidity levels in the home. This will help to avoid buckling due to expansion, or shrinkage due to contraction, when laid.

Should the manufacturer recommend the use of a special underlay – which may be plastic sheeting, glass fibre matting or foam – put this down first, taping or stapling the seams together for a smooth finish.

**1** Remove the skirtings (baseboards) and make sure that the sub-floor is clean, dry and level. Unroll the special cushioned underlay across the floor, taping one end to keep it in place. Tape or staple the seams together to prevent them from rucking up.

**4** The last board is fitted without clips. Cut it to width, allowing for the spacers as in step 2, and apply adhesive along its grooved edge.

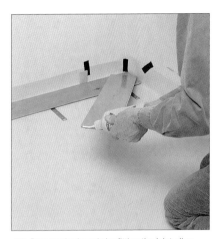

2 Prepare the boards by fitting the joint clips into their grooves. Lay the first length, clips outward, using spacers to create an expansion gap at the wall. Glue the ends of the boards together.

3 Position the second row of boards, tapping them together with a hammer and an offcut so that the clips on the first row engage in the groove of the second. Stagger the boards so that the joints don't coincide with those of adjacent rows.

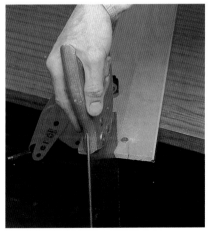

5 Insert some protective packing against the wall before levering the strip into place. Tap it down level with a hammer and protect the floor with a board offcut. Replace the skirtings to hide the expansion gaps.

6 To fit a board around a pipe, mark its position and drill a suitably sized hole. Then cut out a tapered wedge, which can be glued back after fitting the board.

# LAYING WOOD MOSAIC FLOORING

The least expensive way of creating a decorative timber floor finish is by laying mosaic floor tiles, which are square tiles made from a number of small fingers of decorative hardwood mounted on a cloth or felt backing sheet. This acts as an underlay as well as a means of bonding the fingers together; the result is a sheet that will bend along the joint lines, so it is easily cut to size if required. Alternatively, the fingers may be wired or stuck together to produce a rigid tile. In either case, tiles are generally 300mm (12in) or 450mm (18in) square.

The fingers themselves may be solid wood or veneer on a cheaper softwood backing, and are usually arranged in a basketweave pattern; however, other patterns are also available. A wide range of wood types is available. Some tiles are supplied sealed; others have to be sealed after being laid.

Laying woodblock floor tiles is a comparatively straightforward job, similar to any other floor tiling project in terms of preparation and setting-out. Store the panels unpacked in the room where they will be laid for at least seven days, to allow them to acclimatize to indoor temperature and humidity levels. This will help to reduce shrinkage or expansion after the tiles are laid. However, an expansion gap should always be left around the perimeter of the room.

1 Work from the centre of the floor outward, stretching strings between the centres of opposite walls to find the starting point. Mark out guidelines and spread some adhesive over a small area of the floor.

4 To cut edge pieces, lay a whole tile over the last whole tile laid and place another on top, butted against the skirting (baseboard). Draw along its edge on the middle tile. Over-cut to allow for the expansion gap.

2 Align the first tile carefully with the tiling guidelines and press it firmly down into the adhesive. Bed it down with a hammer, using a scrap of wood to protect the surface of the panel from the hammer head.

3 Lay the next panel in the same way, butting it up against its neighbour. Wipe off any adhesive from the tile faces immediately, otherwise it will spoil the finish.

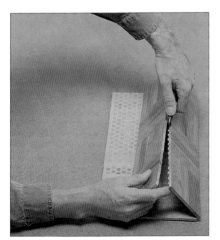

5 The tile can be bent along the main joint lines between the fingers, then sections can be separated by cutting through the backing fabric with a sharp utility knife.

6 More complicated cuts running across the fingers of wood can be made with a tenon saw, using very light pressure to avoid splitting or tearing the thin strips. Sand the edges lightly to remove wood fibres. ▶

7 At door architraves (trims) and other similar obstacles, make a paper template or use a proprietary shape tracer to copy the required shape and mark the tile. Cut along the outline with a coping saw.

8 Cover the cut edges of the tiles by pinning (tacking) lengths of quadrant beading (base shoe) to the skirtings. Alternatively, fit expansion strips cut from cork tiles along the edges to finish.

9 On new work, do not fix the skirtings until the flooring has been laid. They will then hide the expansion gap.

10 Sweep and dust unsealed panels, then apply two or three coats of clear varnish or floor sealer, sanding the surface lightly between coats. Work from the corner farthest away from the door so that you do not become trapped.

# PARQUET

**G**ood parquet is a very manageable kind of flooring. There are numerous patterns to be made by combining these wooden blocks. A good trick is to work out the pattern starting from the centre and making it as big a perfect square as you can; then lay a simple border to accommodate all the tricky outside edges. Parquet is often made in oak, but you could dye it with stain or varnish for a richer effect.

TOP RIGHT: You can make up lots of different patterns. The example here would be easy to do.

RIGHT: Classic herringbone presents problems at the edges if the room is not perfectly square, but it can be combined with a simpler pattern around the outside.

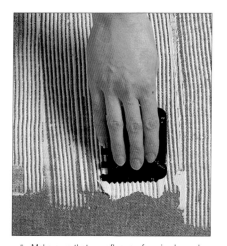

**1** Make sure that your floor surface is clean, dry and level. Find your starting point as for laying wood mosaic flooring and draw guidelines on the floor. Using a ridged spreader, coat a manageable area of floor in the specified floor adhesive.

**2** Apply wood blocks to the adhesive. Use a length of timber laid across the blocks to check that they all lie flush. Repeat until the floor is covered. Seal the floor with two or three coats of varnish, sanding between coats.

# LAYING SHEET VINYL

Sheet vinyl flooring can be difficult to lay because it is wide and comparatively stiff, and edge cutting must be done accurately if gaps are not to be noticeable against skirtings (baseboards). Lengths of quadrant beading (base shoe) can be pinned (tacked) around the perimeter of the room to disguise any serious mistakes.

Most rooms contain at least one long straight wall, and it is often easiest to press the vinyl into the angle between wall and floor and cut along it with the knife held at a 45-degree angle. Then press the ends of the length neatly against the walls at right angles to the first wall, make small diagonal cuts at internal and external angles, and trim the edges to fit there.

1 Unless the wall is perfectly straight, make a cut at the corner and trim the adjacent edges of the sheet with a sharp knife along the angle of wall and floor.

4 To join sheet vinyl edge to edge, overlap the two sheets so that the pattern matches and cut through both layers against a steel straightedge. Discard the waste strips.

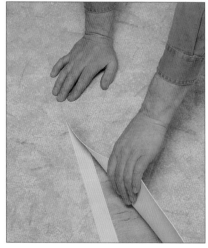

5 Place a strip of double-sided adhesive tape underneath the joint line, peel off the backing paper and press the two cut edges firmly down on to the tape.

2 At door architraves (trims), make cuts into the edge of the sheet down to floor level so the sheet will lie flat, and trim off the tongues of excess material.

3 Use a similar technique for trimming the sheet around larger obstacles, such as washbasin pedestals.

6 To fit the vinyl sheet around pipework, make a cut into it at the pipe position and then trim out a circle of the material to fit around the pipe.

7 At door openings, fit threshold (saddle) strips to anchor the edges of the sheet. Here, an existing strip has been prised up and is being hammered down again to grip the vinyl.

# TEMPLATES FOR SHEET VINYL

Where sheet vinyl flooring is being laid around unusually shaped obstacles, such as washbasin pedestals and piping, the best way of obtaining an accurate fit is to make a template of the obstacle so that its shape can be transferred on to the vinyl. Tape together sheets of paper and cut them roughly to the outline of the room and the obstacle. Tape the template to the floor, and use a block of wood and a pencil (or a pair of compasses) to draw a line on the template parallel with the outline of the obstacle. Next, transfer the template to the vinyl, and use the same block of wood or compass setting to scribe lines back on to the vinyl itself. These lines will accurately represent the shape of the room and the obstacle. Cut along them and remove the waste, then stick down edges and seams as before.

A shape tracer, which incorporates a series of adjustable plastic or metal fingers, can also be used to transfer the shapes of obstacles to the vinyl.

**1** Use a small block of wood and a pencil to scribe the wall outline on to the paper template laid on the floor.

**4** Repeat step 2 to scribe the outline of the obstacle on to the vinyl. Fix the pencil to the block with tape or a rubber band if that makes it easier to use.

## PREPARING THE TEMPLATE

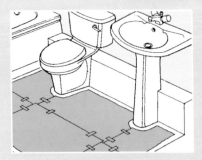

To make a cutting template for a room full of obstacles, such as a bathroom, tape sheets of paper together with their edges about 50mm (2in) from the room walls all around. Tear in from the edges to fit the template around the obstacles as shown, ready for the outline of the room and the obstacles to be scribed on to the template with a block of wood and a pencil.

2 Tape the template over the sheet vinyl and use the same block with a pencil to scribe a copy of the room outline back on to the vinyl.

3 Use the same scribing technique to transfer the outline of obstacles such as washbasin pedestals on to the paper template.

5 Using a sharp utility knife, cut carefully around the outline of the obstacle. Make a cut into the waste area, test the cut-out for fit, and trim it slightly if necessary.

6 To make cut-outs around pipes, use a slim block and a pencil to scribe the pipe position on to the template as four lines at right angles to each other.

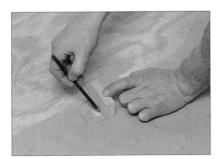

7 Place the template over the vinyl at the pipe position, and use the same block and pencil to mark the cut-out on the vinyl as a small square.

8 Use compasses or a pipe offcut to draw a circle inside the square, then cut around the circle and into the waste area from the edge.

# LAYING FLEXIBLE FLOOR TILES

Flexible vinyl and lino floor tiles are available in plain and self-adhesive types. For plain vinyl tiles, an emulsion-type latex flooring adhesive is used, while lino tiles are best stuck with a water-based contact adhesive.

Because these tiles are thin, any unevenness in the sub-floor will show through the tiles. Cover wooden floors with a hardboard underlay first. Concrete floors may need repairs or treatment with a self-smoothing compound.

Set the floor out carefully. Find the centre-point of the floor by linking the midpoints of opposite pairs of walls with string lines. Dry-lay rows of tiles to see how many whole tiles will fit, move the rows if necessary, then chalk the string lines to mark the starting point.

1 At the border, lay a tile over the last tile laid, butt another against the skirting (baseboard) and mark its edge on the tile underneath.

4 At an external corner, lay a whole tile over the last whole tile in one adjacent row, butt another against the wall and draw along its edge.

5 Move the sandwiched tile to the other side of the corner, butt the second whole tile against the wall and mark its edge on the sandwiched tile.

2 Place the marked tile on a board and cut it with a sharp knife. The exposed part of the sandwiched tile in step 1 will fit the gap perfectly.

3 Fit the cut piece of border tile in place. Trim its edge slightly if it is a tight fit. Mark, cut and fit the other border tiles in exactly the same way.

6 Use the utility knife to cut out the square waste section along the marked lines, and offer up the L-shaped border tile to check its fit before fixing it.

7 After laying an area of tiles, use a smooth block of wood to work along the joins, pressing them down. This will ensure that they are all bedded firmly in the adhesive.

# LAYING FOAM-BACKED CARPET

Laying traditional woven carpet can be difficult for the amateur, because if it is to wear well it has to be correctly tensioned across the room by using gripper strips and a carpet stretcher. However, there is no reason why the do-it-yourselfer should not lay less expensive foam-backed carpet in, for example, a spare bedroom. It is possible to disguise any slight inaccuracies that creep into the cutting and fitting process more easily here than with a sheet vinyl floor covering.

Start by putting a paper or cloth underlay on the floor, taping the seams and stapling the underlay in place so that it cannot creep as work continues. Unroll the carpet across the room, with the excess lapping up the walls. Roughly trim the excess all around the room, leaving 50mm (2in) for final trimming. Make small cuts at external corners, such as around chimney breasts (fireplace projections), and let the tongues fall back into the alcoves, then trim off the waste across the face of the chimney breast. Next, press the carpet into internal corners and mark the corner point with a finger. Make cuts to remove the triangle of carpet from the internal angle. Finally, trim the perimeter with a knife drawn along the angle between skirting (baseboard) and wall, and secure the edges with double-sided adhesive tape. Fit threshold (saddle) strips across door openings.

1 Before laying a foam-backed carpet, put down a paper or cloth underlay to keep the foam from sticking to the floor. Tape the seams and staple it in place to prevent it from creeping and rucking up as you work.

4 Work the carpet across the floor to the opposite wall to ensure that it is laying flat. Then trim that edge against the skirting (baseboard) and tape it down too.

2 Put double-sided adhesive tape all around the perimeter of the room, then unroll the carpet and position it so that it laps up the room walls.

3 Butt the edge of the carpet against the longest straight wall in the room. Peel the backing paper off the adhesive tape and press the edge of the carpet into place, working along the wall from one end to the other.

5 Make cuts at internal and external corners to bed the carpet on to the tape. Trim excess carpet by drawing a knife along the angle. Take care not to over-trim.

6 Use adhesive seaming tape to join sections of carpet together where necessary in particularly large rooms. Pressure from a wallpaper seam roller ensures a good bond with the tape, preventing the edges from lifting.

# LAYING WOVEN CARPET

The laying and trimming technique used for fitting woven carpets is broadly similar to that described for foam-backed carpets, with two main exceptions: the edges are secured on toothed gripper strips instead of by double-sided adhesive tape, and the carpet must be tensioned across the room to ensure that it wears evenly and cannot ruck up in use.

Start by nailing the gripper strips to the floor all around the room, using a hardboard or cardboard spacer to set them about 10mm (³⁄₈in) away from the skirtings (baseboards). Then put down a good-quality foam underlay, paper side up, cutting it to fit just inside the gripper strips. Tape any seams and staple the underlay to the floor at regular intervals.

Now unroll the carpet, trim it roughly and make small diagonal cuts at internal and external corners. Use a carpet fitter's bolster or a clean brick bolster (stonecutter's chisel) to press one edge of the carpet down on to the gripper strips, then trim off excess carpet and use the bolster to tuck the carpet edge into the gap between the strips and the wall.

Use the carpet stretcher to tension the carpet along the adjacent walls and across the room, hooking it on to the gripper strips as each section is stretched. Trim along the other walls too, and fit the carpet neatly into the doorway, securing it with a threshold (saddle) strip.

**1** Nail gripper strips around the perimeter of the room, using a spacer to set them slightly away from the skirting (baseboard). The edge of the carpet will be tucked into the gap.

**4** Press one edge of the carpet on to the gripper strips with a carpet fitter's bolster (stonecutter's chisel) to ensure that the angled teeth are able to grip the carpet backing securely.

2 Lay underlay, trimmed to butt up to the gripper strips. Tape pieces together as necessary, then staple the underlay to the floor at regular intervals.

3 Unroll the carpet and trim it roughly all around. Then make cuts at external corners so that tongues of carpet will fit around them.

5 Cut off the excess carpet along this edge by running a sharp utility knife along the angle between the gripper strip and the skirting, as shown. Take care not to damage the skirting with the knife by holding the blade at an angle away from it.

6 Use the blade of the bolster to tuck the trimmed edge of the carpet into the angle between the gripper strip and the skirting. Then tension the carpet along adjacent walls with the carpet stretcher. Attach the carpet to the gripper strips in the same manner. ▶

**7** Make release cuts at all the internal corners, then trim the waste carpet along the other walls of the room as before and tuck the cut edges into the perimeter gaps. This will provide a neat finish to the edges of the carpet.

**8** At door frames and similar obstacles, trim the carpet to follow the contours of the obstacle as closely as possible, and press it on to the gripper strips.

**9** Complete the installation by fitting a door threshold (saddle) strip. Different types are available for linking carpet to carpet, and carpet to smooth floor coverings.

### STRETCHING CARPET

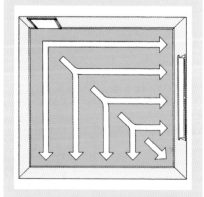

Stretch a carpet along two adjacent walls of the room, hooking it on to the gripper strips. Then stretch it across the room, first in one direction, then in the other.

# LAYING STAIR CARPET

The technique of carpeting a flight of stairs is similar in principle to that used for carpeting a room, with gripper strips being used to hold the carpet securely to the treads. The job is easiest on a straight flight, but it is not too difficult to cope with winding flights or projecting bullnose steps because cuts can be made across the carpet at any point on the flight and the seams hidden neatly at the back of the tread.

Start by nailing on the gripper strips, just above the bottom edge of each riser and just in front of the rear edge of each tread. The space between them should be about the same as the thickness of a single fold of the carpet. Instead of two lengths of the normal plywood-based strip, special one-piece L-section metal grippers can be used here. Add short lengths of ordinary gripper strip to the sides of the treads,

the thickness of the carpet away from the sides of the flight. Next, cut pieces of underlay to cover each tread and the face of the riser below, and fix them in position with the aid of a staple gun or carpet tacks.

Start laying the carpet at the top of the flight of stairs. If the same carpet is being used on the landing, this should be brought over the edge of the top step and down the face of the first riser. If you do this, the top edge of the stair carpet should be tucked into the gripper strips at the bottom of the first riser. Trim the edges of the carpet on the first tread, then on the next riser, and tuck them in before locking the fold of carpet into the gripper strips at the back of the next tread with a carpet fitter's bolster (stonecutter's chisel). Continue in this way to the bottom of the flight, where the stair carpet always finishes at the base of the last riser, whether or not the floor below is covered with the same carpet.

1 Cut lengths of carpet gripper strip to fit across the width of the flight, and nail them in position at the foot of each riser and also at the back of each tread.

2 Next, cut and fit a short length of gripper strip to the sides of each tread. Position them just less than the carpet thickness away from the sides of the flight. ▶

**3** Cut underlay to fit adjacent treads and risers, and tack them in place so that they fit smoothly over the nosing at the front of the tread.

**4** As an alternative to using two lengths of plywood gripper strip in the tread/riser angle, fit a one-piece L-section metal strip.

**5** Begin fitting the carpet at the top of the flight, trimming each tread and riser in turn, then forcing a fold of carpet into the angled gripper strips.

**6** On an open-string staircase, either trim the carpet to fit around each baluster or fold over the edge and tack it to fit against the baluster, as shown here.

**7** On winder (curved) stairs, cut carpet to cover each tread and the riser below. Align the weave at right angles to the riser.

**8** Secure each piece of carpet to the gripper strip at the rear of the tread first, then stretch it over the tread and down to the next gripper strip.

**9** Trim off the waste from the bottom edge of the riser and tuck in the carpet at the sides. Repeat the cutting and fitting sequence for any other winder steps on the flight.

**10** If the flight finishes with a projecting bullnose step, trim and tack the carpet to the riser, as shown, and cover the riser with a separate strip.

## ALTERNATIVE FIXINGS

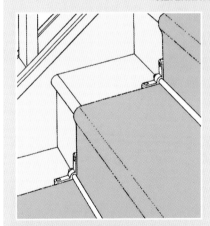

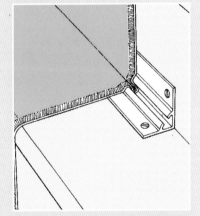

ABOVE: When laying a stair runner rather than a full-width carpet, paint or stain the stair treads and anchor the runner in place with stair rods.

ABOVE: If you are using foam-backed carpet on your stairs, fit special gripper strips for foam-backed carpet into the angles between treads and risers.

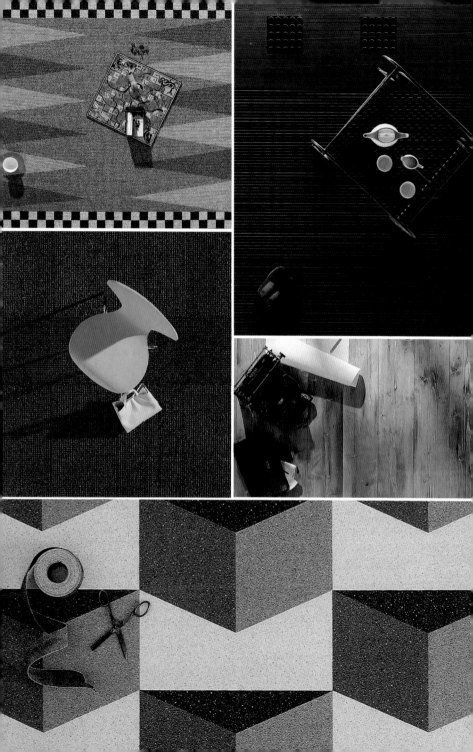

# FLOORING
# VARIATIONS

In years gone by, people wanted floors to
last a lifetime. Today we change our
furnishings – and our homes – more often,
so the need is for chic, inexpensive flooring
with instant design impact. If in doubt about
a room's final use or colour scheme, a
beautiful neutral floor will allow you to alter
either. The scale of a room is also important:
large patterns are seen to best advantage
only in large rooms with the minimum of
furniture. However, floors are often the main
feature of halls and passages, even more so
when seen from an upper landing. In this
situation, go for a really eye-catching
treatment. The following pages will give
you a taste of what is possible with the
application of a little imagination.

# DISTRESSED FLOORBOARDS

Wooden floors are often appealing because of their subtle variations of colour, which improve with age. Your wooden floors may not be in a great state to begin with, though, or may look uninteresting, and you don't really want to wait for the years to work their magic naturally. Wood stains can help to imitate that look in only a few hours. You can create the look of driftwood, weathered teak or other hardwood decking, as found in beach houses. All you need is three different dyes and a thin wash of white emulsion (latex) paint. This technique would give a bleached effect to any wood stain; for example, over a warm mahogany, a wash of cream or white instantly gives the faded look of maturity.

**1** First prepare the surface by knocking in any protruding floorboard nails with a nail punch, and removing any old paint spills with a sander.

**4** With either a lint-free cloth or a brush, apply the stain. This will colour anything porous, so protect your hands with rubber gloves and wear old clothes.

**7** While the stain is still wet, brush on a wash of the diluted white or cream emulsion (latex) paint, about one part emulsion to four parts water.

2 Brush the boards with a wire brush, along the direction of the grain, with the occasional cross stroke to give a distressed effect.

3 Experiment with the stains, mixing colours together – a little should go a long way. Use scrap wood to test the effect.

5 Apply a generous quantity of stain, but rub off the surplus. For an even finish, complete in one session, keeping the joins between areas random and avoiding overlapping bands of stain.

6 It's better to apply one thin coat all over, then go back and add further coats, perhaps working the stain into knots or grooves with a brush, to give an uneven, weathered look.

8 Using a dry cloth, rub off surplus paint or apply more until you have achieved the effect you want.

9 Seal the finish by applying two coats of clear varnish, brushing along the grain and sanding very lightly between coats.

# WOOD-GRAIN CHEQUERBOARD

Painted chequerboards are a recurrent theme for flooring, yet they are rarely seen in natural wood. If you are starting from a concrete or wooden floor, have the new floor covering cut into squares of the size you want, and either screw them in place or stick them down. If your floor is already covered in sheets of plywood or hardboard, mark out a chequerboard pattern, ignoring the natural joins. Wood-graining doesn't have to be done painstakingly carefully; you can alter the effect produced in oil paint until it starts to dry.

Obtain some reference for the wood effect; oak was the inspiration here. The grain effects resemble the wood treated in different ways, half "polished" and half "rough-sawn and sand-blasted". You could also use two different wood effects, such as walnut and maple.

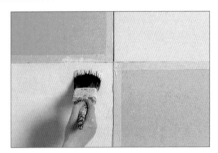

1 Mark out the floor, edging alternate squares with masking tape. Paint them with two shades of cream.

4 After a few minutes, drag a dry graining brush over the finish, to give the grain effect.

7 Then repeat step 4, using a graining comb rather than a dry graining brush, so the grain looks wider.

2 Mix oil colours into an oil-based glaze, to match the wood reference. Thin the result with white spirit (paint thinner), if necessary.

3 For the "lighter" squares, brush the glaze in the direction of the "grain", leaving brush marks. Add cross-hatched strokes.

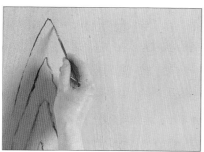

5 Using a darker oil paint and a fine artist's brush, gently draw in the chevrons of the wood grain.

6 Soften with a brush, adding white spirit if the paint has dried. Allow to dry. For the "darker" squares, repeat step 1.

8 Paint on more noticeable chevrons in the same way, following the grain.

9 Soften the effect, using the graining comb before the brush. Allow to dry. Apply two coats of satin varnish and allow to dry. If you like, burnish with a little non-slip polish.

# LINOLEUM IN 3-D PATTERNS

inoleum now comes in many thicknesses, colours and patterns, and by cutting it into *trompe l'oeil* patterns and playing with slight colour variations, you can create quite grand effects. Lino is hard-wearing, water-resistant and relatively inexpensive and, given this dramatic treatment, reminiscent of the optical effects in the drawings of Escher, it can become the centrepiece of any hall, kitchen or bathroom. Rolls of lino and floor adhesive were used in this project but you could also use self-glued tiles to make a floor reminiscent of a Venetian palazzo.

Before you begin, draw a plan of the design on squared paper and transfer this to the floor by laying out grid lines. To provide a means of cutting the linoleum to shape, make hardboard templates and cut around them with a sharp knife. Take great care to make your cuts accurate, otherwise you will be left with unsightly gaps between the pieces, which will collect dirt.

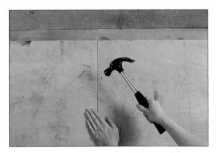

1 You need a smooth, flat surface on which to apply the lino. If necessary, lay a plywood or hardboard floor.

4 Draw grid lines on the floor to act as a guide when laying the lino shapes.

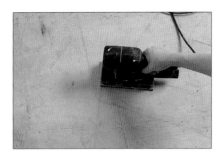

2 Having made sure no nail heads are exposed, lightly sand the floor, to make sure that it is perfectly flat.

3 Measure the floor. To ensure a good fit, it is very important to work out your pattern on paper first.

5 Draw each of the pattern shapes on to a sheet of hardboard and cut them out carefully with a saw.

6 Use the templates to cut out the lino shapes. Remember that lino isn't very forgiving and accuracy is all-important.

7 Try out your pattern in pieces of lino to see if any need trimming. If necessary, number them on the back to help you fit them together.

8 Apply contact adhesive to the floor and the backs of the tiles, then carefully fit them in place; you cannot adjust them once they are laid.

# PATTERNS WITH CARPET TILES

Carpet tiles are among the simplest of floor coverings to lay, because they are highly tolerant of any slight inaccuracy in cutting to fit. The cheapest types are usually plain in colour and have a very short pile or a corded appearance, while more expensive tiles may have a longer pile and are available in patterns as well as plain colours. Most are designed to be loose-laid, with just the edges secured with bands of adhesive or double-sided tape. This makes it easy to lift individual tiles for cleaning or to even out wear.

Most carpet tiles are marked on the back with an arrow to indicate the pile direction. Align these for a plain effect, or lay them at right angles to create a chequerboard effect. When satisfied with the layout, lift perimeter tiles and put down double-sided tape all around the room. Peel the backing paper off the top of the tape and press the tiles into place. Finish doorways with threshold (saddle) strips.

Another possibility with carpet tiles is to make eye-catching patterns by choosing a selection of different coloured tiles and cutting them into a variety of shapes. Plan the design on paper first and do not start cutting the tiles until you are completely happy with it. If you need to cut very small pieces, make sure all of them are secured with double-sided tape.

**1** Measure your room and make sure that the floor is level and all protruding floorboard nails have been driven in.

**4** With a steel straightedge and a rigid-bladed knife, score along the marked lines. Don't attempt to cut the tile through in one action.

**7** Stick the cut tiles in place, making sure not to pack them too tightly. In this case, the chequered border was laid first, followed by the central pattern. Tread the tiles down.

Plan your design on paper. Most rooms are not perfectly square or rectangular, so leave room for an area of plain tiles to edge the pattern.

Measure the tiles to work out how many will be needed. Draw the pattern on the backs of the tiles.

Starting at the top of the tile, cut down the scored lines. Do this on a solid surface and take great care in doing it.

Lay carpet tape and remove the backing. Cut all the tiles for one complete run and fit them, rather than laying little bits at a time.

# HIGH-TECH RUBBER FLOORING

Available from specialist rubber manufacturers, rubber mats are valued for their non-slip and protective qualities, and, since they are waterproof, they are particularly useful in, say, a shower room. Rubber is sold from the roll in a broad spectrum of colours, widths and textures. In addition, it doesn't fray and will happily absorb any lumps or strange joins in a floor. To keep it looking good, clean and seal with a silicone spray polish.

1 Rubber matting in two different designs and rubber tiles have been used here. Measure the floor and the rubber matting, then carefully trim the long runners for the border to size.

2 For each corner, cut a square from the same matting. Divide diagonally and fit them so that the grooves run at right angles to the grooves in the runners. Place the long runners between them.

3 Lay the second matting for the central area. Cut this second type into squares, then cut holes in the runners at regular intervals for them.

4 Secure all the pieces with rubber adhesive, applied to both surfaces. Spray with silicone polish and buff lightly.

# CHEQUERBOARD CARPET TILES

Floor mats are easy and cheap to come by, and you can often cut them without the edges fraying. They come in many finishes, some even incorporating words or pictures, and all in manageable rectangles. When these very textured grey polypropylene mats are arranged with the pile running in different directions, a chequerboard effect is achieved. Alternatively, a variety of colours could be used to make an eye-catching pattern.

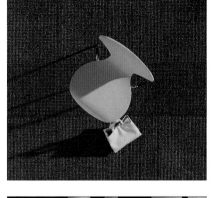

**1** Use strings to find the room's centre and mark with a cross. Measure the floor and work out how many mats you will need. Mark the cuts with a white crayon or chalk on the reverse of the mats.

**2** If the mats are of carpet quality, score along the lines with the craft knife, working from the back of the mat. Then cut the mats to size.

**3** Using a notched spreader, apply floor adhesive to the floor, working on a small area at a time.

**4** Starting at the centre, carefully lay the mats in position, remembering that, for the effect shown here, you need to alternate the weaves.

# WOODWORK IN THE HOME

- Woodwork materials
- Wall woodwork
- Doors, locks & windows
- Wood finishing

# INTRODUCTION

**A**s a constructional material, wood is invaluable. It is very strong for its weight, and it can be used to create quite complex structures at relatively low cost. Properly looked after, wood will last for years, as an examination of your surroundings will confirm. All homes, no matter how they have been built, will contain a large amount of wood. The basic framework of the house may be made of wood, as well as at least some internal walls and the structure supporting the roof. Floors often have wooden surfaces – the material is warmer underfoot than concrete and stone; walls will be trimmed at floor level and around door openings with wooden mouldings, while the doors themselves will almost certainly be wood; window frames, too, are commonly of wooden construction. Then there is the furniture – shelves, cabinets, chairs, tables and so on. So sooner or later the do-it-yourselfer will be faced with tackling some form of woodworking task.

Fortunately, wood is an easy and forgiving material to work with, requiring few specialized tools unless undertaking cabinet-making or similar complex jobs. Taking the time to develop a few basic, practical

LEFT: Wood possesses a wide range of characteristics in varying degrees – strength, durability, flexibility, brittleness and, of course, beauty. Woodwork is involved in all sorts of jobs around the home, such as putting up shelves, fitting architraves (trims), replacing doors and drawers, and fitting locks.

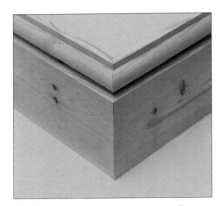

ABOVE: Skirtings (baseboards) protect wall surfaces at floor level from accidental damage. They receive a lot of wear and tear from feet, vacuum cleaners and furniture legs, and may need replacing.

ABOVE: Renewing old drawer fronts is neither a complex nor a very expensive job. Remove the old drawer front from the carcass with a screwdriver, drill pilot holes in the new front, and screw it into position.

woodworking skills will allow you to tackle a wide variety of do-it-yourself tasks – from simply giving a wooden surface (such as a floor) a new finish, through putting up the simplest of fixtures, to carrying out all manner of repairs around the home.

The following pages contain a selection of simple indoor projects that involve working with wood. By using the information provided, you will gain the confidence you need to

complete many do-it-yourself tasks. Just remember that, as with so many things, care and patience are the most important keys to success.

RIGHT: Shelving systems such as these adjustable brackets are capable of holding heavy weights, and have the advantage of being portable when you need to move them. The bracket positions can be adjusted to vary the spacing between the shelves, but remember that a shelf's capacity depends on the strength of the wall fixings employed.

# WOODWORK MATERIALS

Wood can be purchased in two basic forms: as sections of natural timber (lumber) sawn and/or planed to shape, or as manufactured boards made from thin veneers, wood particles or blocks. All have their specific uses, and it is important to choose the right type, size and thickness for the job in hand. When joining and hinging pieces of wood, you will also need to choose the correct fittings. Commonly used joint plates include the L-shaped corner plate and the T-shaped fixing plate. There is a wide variety to choose from, as browsing through any catalogue will reveal, and the following pages include most of the types in common use.

# WOOD AND MANUFACTURED BOARDS

A s they are expensive, hardwoods are often used as veneers over cheaper materials, as lippings around flat surfaces such as shelving and table tops, and for picture framing.

Softwoods, such as pine and, to a lesser extent, Douglas fir, are the most commonly used types of wood for do-it-yourself jobs, such as wall frames, flooring, skirtings (baseboards), picture and dado (chair) rails, and a great variety of cladding, framing and fencing applications. In addition to softwoods, there is a range of inexpensive manufactured boards.

### PRACTICAL USES

The two boards most often used are plywood and chipboard (particle board). The former, which has good mechanical strength and can be sawn easily, is suitable for structural work.

Chipboard is more friable and less easy to work accurately, but is cheap. It is adequate for some flooring applications and a host of carcassing jobs, such as kitchen cabinets and bookcases. It is unwise to drive screws or nails into the edge of a chipboard panel, as the material will crumble.

Both plywood and chipboard are available faced with hardwood and coloured melamine veneer for improved appearance.

Blockboard, which consists of solid wooden blocks sandwiched between plywood skins, is a stable and strong

ABOVE: Beech hardwood.

structural material often used where some form of weight-bearing capacity is required. As with all manufactured boards, the extremely hard resins used to bond blockboard together rapidly blunt tools unless they are tungsten (carbide) tipped.

Pineboard is like the core of blockboard, but without the outer layers. Small strips of pine are glued together on edge and sanded smooth. It is ideal for shelving and carcassing.

MDF (medium-density fiberboard) is another useful material. Unlike most other boards, it can be worked to fine detail with saws and chisels, and it is often used for delicate mouldings.

Hardboard is ideal for covering floors prior to tiling or carpeting and, as it is light, for making back panels for cabinets and pictures. It can be used for making templates to establish correct shapes, helping to avoid mistakes when using expensive material for a finished piece.

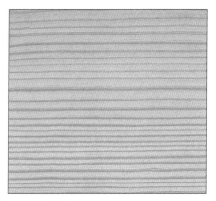

ABOVE: Pine softwood.

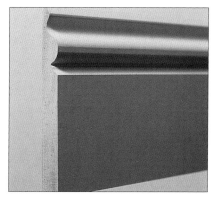

ABOVE: Paper-coated MDF skirting (baseboard).

## STANDARD SIZES

Nearly all manufactured boards have a standard size of 1220 x 2440mm (4 x 8ft). Some suppliers offer a metric size, which is smaller (1200 x 2400mm), so always check, as this can make a critical difference to your cutting list. Special sizes of plywood and MDF, up to 3m (10ft) in length, are available from some suppliers. Many stores will offer part sheets or cut large sheets into smaller sizes if requested at the time of purchase.

## GRAIN DIRECTION

The direction in which the grain runs on the outer layers is always given first when describing plywood. This can be important when planning your cutting list. With birch plywood, for example, 1220 x 2440mm (4 x 8ft) in a supplier's catalogue will indicate that the grain runs across the width of the board, not down its length. Most veneered decorative boards have the grain running across the length, so their catalogue entry would read 2440 x 1220mm (8 x 4ft).

## COMMON THICKNESSES OF MANUFACTURED BOARDS

| TYPE | 3mm 1/8in | 6mm 1/4in | 9mm 3/8in | 12mm 1/2in | 16mm 5/8in | 19mm 3/4in | 22mm 7/8in | 25mm 1in | 32mm 1 1/4in |
|---|---|---|---|---|---|---|---|---|---|
| Plywood | ✓ | ✓ | ✓ | ✓ | ✓ | ✓ | ✓ | ✓ | |
| Plywood (D. fir) | | | ✓ | | ✓ | | | | |
| Blockboard | | | | | | ✓ | | ✓ | |
| Chipboard | | | | ✓ | ✓ | ✓ | ✓ | ✓ | |
| Hardboard | ✓ | ✓ | | | | | | | |
| MDF | | | ✓ | ✓ | ✓ | | ✓ | | ✓ |

# JOINT PLATES AND HINGES

There is a huge range of fittings available for making joints and connecting different materials. These will often prevent the need for making complex joints in wood, allowing the less skilled to produce strong structures or repairs with relative ease.

Hinges will be found all around the home on doors and cabinets, and replacing or refitting them is a common do-it-yourself task.

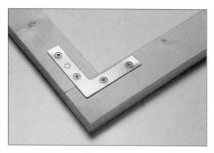

ABOVE: An L-shaped corner plate.

### JOINT PLATES AND BRACKETS

Flat mild-steel plates, drilled and countersunk to take woodscrews, are a common means of making and strengthening butt joints in wooden framing. Some commonly used joint plates are L-shaped corner plates and T-shaped fixing plates.

Brackets such as corner plate fixings, 90-degree angle brackets and joist hangers are also available. They can be used to make right-angled joints, overlapping joints and for hanging joists.

ABOVE: A simple 90-degree angle bracket.

### HINGES

Any device that includes a pivot action can be called a hinge, and there are many different variations. Some are designed to be concealed within the framework of a cabinet, or the carcass, while others are intended to act as decorative features in their own right.

It is important to fit the correct number of hinges of a suitable size and robustness when hanging a door so that it is well supported when it swings open. If a hinge or hinge pin is strained

in any way, the door will not fit in the frame properly and may even become detached, possibly causing injury.

ABOVE: Hinges are available in a wide range of types, finishes, sizes and materials for a variety of tasks. Some are functional, while others make decorative features in their own right.

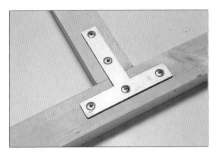

ABOVE: A T-shaped fixing plate.

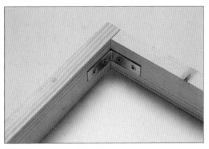

ABOVE: A corner plate fixing.

ABOVE: An overlapping fixing plate.

ABOVE: A joist hanger.

## KNOCK-DOWN JOINTS

These fittings are often used with manufactured boards, such as chipboard (particle board) and plywood. They ensure good, square connections, usually by means of pegs, and allow the assembly to be dismantled and reassembled as required. For the best results, at least two joints should be fitted between each pair of panels.

ABOVE: The knock-down joint in its separate parts ready for assembly.

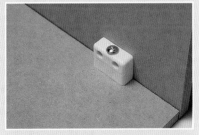

ABOVE: When the parts are connected, they form a strong and accurate joint.

# WALL WOODWORK

All walls incorporate wooden fixtures of one form or another. At the very least, there will be skirtings (baseboards) at floor level and wooden trims around door openings. In some cases, there may be dado (chair) rails and, in older properties, picture rails near the ceiling. At some stage, you may find that you need to replace these items, either to effect repairs or give the room a new look. Cladding the walls with wooden boards or panels is another means of giving a room a fresh look, and can provide thermal and acoustic insulation too. Other wall woodwork jobs featured in the following pages include fitting tongued-and-grooved boarding and boxing-in pipes.

# USING MOULDINGS

**M**oulding is the term used to describe any section of wood that has been shaped, either by hand or by machinery, to alter the square profile of the original piece. This may range from simply rounding over the sharp edges of the finished work to adding more decorative detail.

### TYPICAL APPLICATIONS

Mouldings have many uses, not only providing protection to vulnerable surfaces, but also adding decoration. The larger mouldings include architraves (trims), dado (chair) rails, picture rails and skirtings (baseboards). Architraves are fitted around flush door and window openings to create decorative and protective borders. Dado and picture rails are horizontal mouldings fixed to wall surfaces, the former to protect the plaster from damage by the backs of chairs, and the latter to allow pictures to be hung. Skirtings are boards fixed at ground level to protect the plaster from damage by feet or furniture.

### FIXING MOULDINGS

Generally speaking, it is wise to drill pilot holes in hardwood mouldings before nailing, especially when fixing close to the ends, since small-section hardwoods, especially ramin, which is often used, will split readily.

Softwoods are far more forgiving, and it is unnecessary to drill a softwood architrave before nailing it in place. Simply drive the nails in, punch the heads below the surface, and fill before finishing. Panel pins (brads) or lost-head oval wire nails are the preferred fixings for architraves.

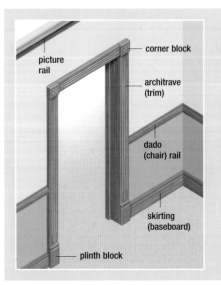

picture rail

corner block

architrave (trim)

dado (chair) rail

skirting (baseboard)

plinth block

### PRACTICALITIES

This is a typical layout showing how architectural mouldings are put to use. They are so called because they would be used to produce a certain effect in the interior of a room rather than for individual items of furniture.

Notice how they combine a decorative effect with good practical points: the plinth blocks and corner blocks around a door frame convey a classic formality, but they also avoid the need to form complex joints where two wooden components meet.

The plinth blocks provide useful protection to more intricate mouldings at floor level where they may be damaged easily.

## FITTING A SHELF MOULDING

**1** Using a try or combination square, check that the corners of the board are square. If necessary, plane or re-cut the edges to ensure that they are square.

**2** Mark the mouldings to length and, using a tenon saw and mitre box, cut their ends at 45 degrees to fit neatly together at the corners of the board.

**3** Check the fit of the mouldings, then apply glue to them and the edges of the board. Hold them in place with plenty of masking tape and leave for the glue to dry.

**4** When the glue has dried, clamp the board securely to your bench top and carefully clean up any rough edges or slight overlaps with a plane. Finish by sanding lightly.

# FITTING AN ARCHITRAVE

**T**rimming a door is fairly straightforward. Measure the internal width of the door frame and mark out the top piece of architrave (trim) so that its bottom edge is 12mm (½in) longer. Mitre the ends at 45 degrees, using a mitre box, so that the top edge is longer than the bottom.

Pin (tack) the top piece of architrave to the top of the frame so that it projects by an equal amount at each side and is 6mm (¼in) up from the bottom edge of the top frame member. All architrave should be set about 6mm (¼in) back from the inside edge of the door frame.

Measure for each side piece separately, as they can vary quite considerably over the width of a door, especially in older houses. Cut each to length, mitring the top ends to match the horizontal section already fitted. Sand the ends to remove any splinters, then offer them up, checking the fit of

the mitred ends. If all is well, pin the mouldings to the frame.

Drive all the pin (tack) heads below the surface of the wood with a nail punch. Then fill the holes and any gaps between the mitred ends of the architrave, using a coloured wood filler if you intend applying a translucent finish. Finally, when the filler is dry, sand it flush with the surrounding surface.

**1** Remove the old architrave (trim) with a crowbar (wrecking bar). Place a block of wood beneath the tool's blade to protect the adjacent wall from damage.

**4** Pin the new piece of architrave in place, making sure that it is horizontal and about 6mm (¼in) above the bottom face of the top internal frame member.

2 Pull out any remaining nails and scrape away any old wood filler or paint from the face of the opening's frame. Take care, however, not to gouge the wood.

3 Measure the internal width of the door frame and cut the top section of architrave to length, allowing for the 6mm (¼in) projection at each end. Mitre the ends at 45 degrees.

5 Measure, cut and fit the side pieces of architrave in the same manner. Pin (tack) them in position, butting their mitred ends against the ends of the top piece.

6 Punch all the pin (tack) heads below the surface of the wood, apply filler and sand it down. Any gaps between the mitred ends should also be filled and sanded smooth.

# REPLACING SKIRTINGS

Skirtings (baseboards) receive a lot of wear and tear from scuffing by feet and furniture, which is why they are there in the first place, of course. From time to time, after replacing floorboards or laying new woodstrip or laminate flooring, for example, the damage may be so great that sections of skirting or even complete lengths of it need to be replaced.

Skirtings may vary from simple rectangular sections of wood to quite ornate moulded profiles.

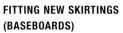

### FITTING NEW SKIRTINGS (BASEBOARDS)

In a rectangular room, it is always best to fit the two long sections of skirting board first, then fit the shorter ones to them. It makes handling, lifting and fixing much easier. ·

### REPLACING STRAIGHT SECTIONS

To replace sections of skirting, first prise the old board partially away from the wall, using a crowbar (wrecking bar), then insert wedges to hold it far enough away to allow you to get at it with a saw. Place a mitre box tight against the board and, with a tenon saw, nibble away at it at 45 degrees until the board is cut in half. Repeat the 45-degree cut at the other end of the section to be replaced and remove the length of old skirting. Then offer up the replacement section, mark each end with a pencil and mitre accordingly. Mitring the ends will make the joints between the new and old boards less obvious and easier to fill if there is any subsequent shrinkage.

A good way to hold the new section in position is to lay a plank so that it butts up against the skirting and kneel on it while driving the nails home. Set all nail heads below the surface before filling and sanding.

### DEALING WITH CORNERS

When fitting a moulded shape into a corner, the best way to achieve the joint is to scribe it. This is done by marking the profile of one board on to the back of the other with the aid of a small offcut of the moulding. Then a coping saw is used to cut along the marked line, allowing the board to fit neatly over its neighbour. This technique avoids the mismatch of ends that can occur when some mouldings are mitred at 45 degrees, using a mitre box or mitre saw. However, to form an external corner for a wall return, use a mitre saw or mitre box in the normal way.

---

**TIP**

Many skirtings (baseboards) are fixed with flooring, or cut, nails, which are square-edged and grip extremely well. However, they may split a small section of replacement skirting, so use masonry nails instead and drill pilot holes through the skirting.

## REPLACING A SECTION OF SKIRTING

1 Prise away the old skirting (baseboard) with a crowbar (wrecking bar) and wedges.

2 Cut away the damaged section with a mitre box and a saw.

3 Hold a new length of board in place and mark it for cutting.

4 Hammer nails into the new section of board while holding a plank against the wood.

## INTERNAL AND EXTERNAL MITRES OF A SKIRTING

ABOVE: An internal corner with mitred joint.

ABOVE: A mitred external corner.

# REPLACING RAILS

Picture rails and dado rails, sometimes called chair rails because they protect the walls from damage by chair backs, may need to be renewed or repaired. This task is essentially the same as replacing skirtings (baseboards).

### REMOVING AND REPLACING RAILS

Use a crowbar (wrecking bar) to prise the old picture or dado (chair) rail away from the wall, inserting a block of wood under its head to protect the plaster and to give extra leverage.

Remove any nails that remain in the wall with a pair of pincers, again using a block of wood to protect the wall. Make good the nail holes with filler, leaving it slightly proud at this stage. When the filler is completely dry, sand it down with abrasive paper wrapped around a cork block, or block of wood, to give a perfectly flat, smooth surface. Fit the new length of rail, scribing or mitring the ends as necessary to ensure a neat finish at the corners.

### FIXING METHODS

Cut-nails, such as those used to fix skirtings, have long been used to fix picture rails, dado (chair) rails and the like, but you may find that they are not available in your local store. Any ordinary wire lost-head nail is a good alternative when fixing through plasterwork into stud (dry) walling, as long as you know where the studs are. With a brick or blockwork wall, use masonry nails, drilling clearance holes in the wood to prevent splits.

## REPLACING A DADO RAIL

**1** Prise the old rail from the wall using a crowbar (wrecking bar) and levering against a block of wood. This will provide additional leverage and prevent damage to the wall.

### CUTTING A SCRIBED JOINT

Use a scrap of the moulding as a guide. Hold a pencil against the scrap of wood and run it over the back of the board to transfer the outline. Cut out the waste with a coping saw.

2 Remove any nails that remain in the wall with pincers. Again, lever against a block of wood to prevent the plasterwork from becoming damaged, reducing the amount of making good required.

3 Brush off all dust and loose paint and plaster. Fill any cracks or holes in the plasterwork with filler, working it in well with a filling or putty knife and leaving it slightly proud.

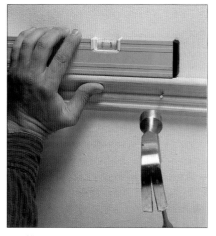

4 Leave the filler to dry. Then sand it with abrasive paper wrapped around a cork or wooden sanding block to obtain a smooth, flat finish. You may need to fill any low spots again.

5 Nail the new rail to the wall, making sure that it is horizontal with a spirit (carpenter's) level. Punch the nail heads below the surface of the wood, fill and sand smooth.

# FIXING CLADDING

**W**ooden cladding may be fixed to walls and ceilings for a variety of reasons. These include: cosmetic, to hide the existing finish; acoustic, to deaden sound; and thermal, to insulate against heat loss. Sometimes cladding has a structural purpose, for example, when it forms part of a stud (dry) wall.

The framework of battens needs to be designed around obstacles (windows and doorways), electrical switches and sockets, and positioned so that whole sheets of cladding join on a stud.

### BATTENING A WALL

Drill pilot holes in the battens for the masonry nails, as this will prevent the wood from splitting. Hammer a masonry nail home at one end, level the batten with a spirit (carpenter's) level and drive home a nail at the other end. Finish by driving in more nails along the batten. If the wall is crumbly, you can attach the battens with screws and wall plugs. Secure battening is essential.

### FITTING SHEET PANELLING

Cladding can be fixed to the framework of battens using either nails or screws. If screws are used, especially brass ones, a feature can be made of them, so they should be equally spaced to form a pattern. Alternatively, a panel adhesive can be used. If it fails to adhere immediately, tap nails part way through into the battens. The nails can be removed when the panels are secure.

To cut cladding, use either a hand saw or power saw. If using a hand saw,

**ABOVE:** Cladding comes in a range of profiles and can be fixed to a framework of battens using nails, screws or adhesive.

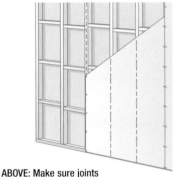

**ABOVE:** Make sure joints coincide with the centres of studs.

have the decorative face uppermost and cut on the downstroke to limit the chances of damaging it. With a power saw, turn the decorative face of the wood downward. Before using the saw, score the cutting line carefully using a straightedge as a guide. If you need a perfectly straight edge on a cut sheet, where it is to be butted against another board, clamp a straightedge to the board as a guide for the saw.

After cutting, use a fine abrasive paper wrapped around a wood or cork block to smooth down the rough edges.

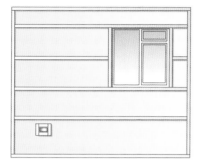
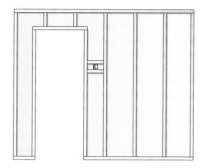

ABOVE: The framework of battens has to be tailored to suit the size and position of obstacles such as doors, windows and electrical fittings. Shown are layouts for vertical cladding (left) with a likely cable point and horizontal cladding (right).

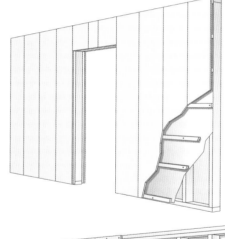

LEFT: Work from each end of the surface to be covered, using cut panels in the middle to retain symmetry.

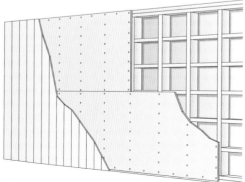

LEFT: Vertical boards fitted to stud (dry) walling with optional intermediate backing sheets. Note how the sheets meet in the centres of the studs.

# TONGUED-AND-GROOVED BOARDING

Fitting tongued-and-grooved boarding is more time-consuming than using sheet materials, but the supporting framework can be made simpler because the boards are relatively narrow and rigid. As with all cladding, it is essential to ensure that the battens are fixed securely, and are reasonably spaced for adequate support.

### FITTING THE BOARDING

First, square off the ends of the board to ensure that it is at 90 degrees, or 45 degrees if you want to set the boards at an angle. Mark off the length of board required with a craft knife or pencil and cut it to size with a tenon saw.

Place the board in position on the battens, making sure that the tongue is left exposed for the next board to slot over, and in the case of TGV (tongued, grooved and V-jointed) that the correct face side with the chamfer is showing.

Secret nail the board by driving panel pins (brads) through the tongue. Repeat this procedure with the remaining boards, tapping each firmly home with a mallet and an offcut of wood to prevent damage to the tongue before nailing.

Leave the second to last board slipped over the previous tongue, but before nailing, use an offcut and pencil to scribe the cutting line on the final board if it needs trimming to fit. Cut and plane the board to width. You might need to fit the last two boards by springing them into place, in which case, both will have to be nailed through the face, since the tongues will not be accessible. Punch the nail heads down and fill.

At internal and external corners, the joints between boards can be concealed by pinning (tacking) on a decorative moulding, which can also be used along the ceiling. Fit normal skirtings (baseboards) at floor level.

## DEALING WITH CORNERS

ABOVE: Neaten internal corners by pinning or gluing a length of scotia (cove) moulding into the angle. Use this at ceiling level too.

ABOVE: Butt-join the two boards that form an external corner, and conceal the joint with a length of birdsmouth (corner bead) moulding.

1 Tap fixing nails into each support batten at 300mm (12in) intervals. Check the batten is level and drive in the nails.

2 If the walls are out of true, insert slim packing pieces between the battens and the wall to ensure that the faces of the strips are vertical.

3 Scribe the wall outline on to the face of the first board by holding its grooved edge to the wall and running a block and pencil down it.

4 Fix the boards by interlocking their tongued-and-grooved edges and driving nails through the exposed tongue of each board into the battens.

5 When fixing subsequent boards, close up the joints by tapping the board edges with a hammer and a scrap of wood.

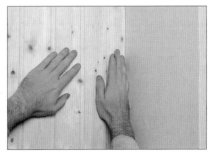

6 Saw or plane the final board down to the required width and spring the last two boards into place. Secure the last board.

# BOXING-IN PIPES

Some people regard visible pipes in the home as an eyesore, but with a little time and minimal woodworking skills they can be hidden from view.

## ACCESSIBILITY

Bear in mind that stopcocks, drain taps, pumps, hand-operated valves and the like will need to be readily accessible and require some form of removable box system. For this reason, the boxing around them should be assembled with screws rather than nails. If a panel needs to be regularly or quickly removed, turn buttons or magnetic catches are a good idea.

## BOXING BASICS

Steel anchor plates and screws can be used to secure the sides of boxing to walls. Battens, either 50 x 25mm (2 x 1in) or 25 x 25mm (1 x 1in), can be used to fix boards at skirting (baseboard) level.

Measure the distance the pipes project from the wall. Cut the side panels from 25mm (1in) plywood or MDF (medium-density fiberboard) slightly over this measurement and to their correct length. Fix small anchor plates flush with the back edge of each panel and spaced at about 600mm (2ft) intervals.

Hold the panels against the wall and mark the screw holes. Drill them and fix the panels with plugs and screws.

Cut the front panel to size from 6mm (¼in) plywood. Drill screw holes in the panel and fix it in place.

1 Measure the distance that the pipes protrude from the wall, making an allowance for any clips, brackets or fittings such as valves. Make the side panels slightly wider than this measurement.

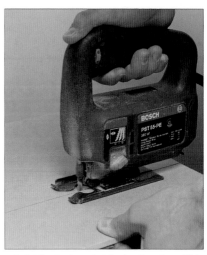

4 Cut the front panel of the box from 6mm (¼in) plywood, using a jigsaw or circular saw. Offer it up and check the fit. If the panel does not need to be removed again, it can be nailed in place.

2 If the panels are narrow, you may be able to drive the screws through their edges – mark the positions with a pencil. If not, fix anchor plates flush with the back edges of the panels.

3 Attach the side panels, screwing them firmly into position. If screwing to a plywood panel, you may need to make pilot holes; in masonry, you need to drill and plug the holes.

5 If the panel needs to be removable, drill screw holes and secure it with 19mm (¾in) screws. Cup washers under the screw heads will protect the panel if it is likely to be removed often.

6 Trim the edges of the front panel flush with the side panels with a block plane. Then drive any nail heads below the surface and fill. Sand the entire box prior to applying a finish.

# DOORS, LOCKS & WINDOWS

Among the wooden items in the home that receive a considerable amount of wear and tear are the doors. In time, you may need to replace them, either because they are damaged or to spruce up a room. Their hinges, too, can become worn and loose, or even broken. Even the doors of cabinets can suffer the same ailments, while their drawer fronts may have to be changed to match any new doors fitted. An important consideration for every householder is security – making sure that the doors and windows of your home are fitted with sturdy locks and catches that will deter a thief from breaking in. Fortunately, a wide range is available and they are not difficult to fit. A weekend's work is all that is necessary to ensure that your home is well protected.

# HANGING DOORS

Installing a new door is not a difficult task, but the job does need patience, precision and organization if it is to go smoothly. A methodical step-by-step approach will pay off. The following sequence relates to hanging a new door, which may or may not need trimming on one or more sides.

### TYPES OF DOOR

Many modern internal doors are hollow structures with "egg-box" centres and solid edges. They offer little flexibility for trimming to fit frames that are out of square, which is often a problem in old buildings. For this reason, as well as for aesthetic appeal, use only solid doors in older houses.

### PUTTING IN A NEW DOOR

Measure the frame top to bottom and side to side, then choose a door that will fit as closely as possible. Even so, it will probably need to be cut to fit.

Joggles, or horns, may project from the ends of the door to protect it in transit. Mark these off level with the ends of the door, using a try square. Place the door on a flat surface and cut the joggles flush with the ends of the door, using a hand saw. Offer up the door to the frame, placing wedges underneath (chisels are handy) to raise it off the floor by about 12mm (½in) to allow for a carpet or other floor covering.

Mark the door in pencil while it is wedged in place to allow for a 3mm (⅛in) clearance at the top and sides.

Place the door back on the flat surface and saw off the bulk of the waste, leaving the marked lines still visible. Plane down the edges of the door to the marked lines, working with the grain, then plane the top, working in from each side to avoid splintering the wood. Replace the door in the frame, wedging it once more to hold it. If you are satisfied with the fit, you can hang it.

Hold each hinge in position, about 150mm (6in) from the top and 225mm (9in) from the bottom of the door, with the knuckle projecting just beyond the face of the door; mark it with a knife. For a heavy door, a third hinge will be needed, positioned centrally between the other two.

Working around the outline, cut down vertically into the wood to the depth of the hinge flap with a chisel. Make a series of cuts across the width of the recess, to the same depth, and remove the waste. Place the hinge in the recess, drill small pilot holes for the screws, then screw the hinge to the door. Repeat with the other hinge.

Offer the hinge side of the door to the frame, placing wedges under it to raise it to the correct height. Press the free flap of each hinge against the frame and mark around it in pencil. Cut the recesses. Drill pilot holes and hang the door, fitting only one screw in each hinge flap. When you are satisfied with the operation of the door, insert all the screws, making sure that the heads lie flat in the countersinks of the hinges, otherwise the door will not close properly.

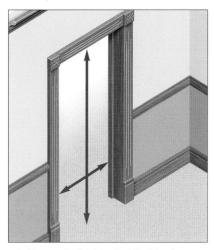

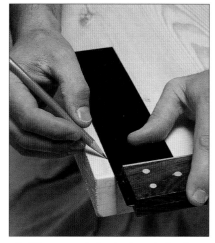

1 Measure the height and width of the door frame to assess the size of the door you require. If you cannot find the exact size needed, choose one that is slightly larger.

2 If there are protective joggles projecting from the top and bottom of the door, square them off accurately with the ends of the door, using a pencil and try or combination square.

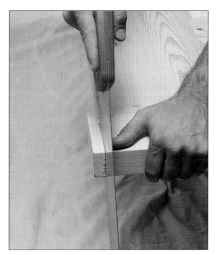

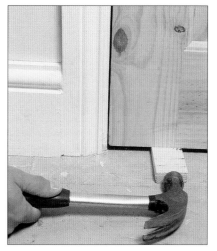

3 Remove the joggles with a hand saw, making a clean, square cut. Saw on the waste side of the line and finish off with a plane or sanding block, working in toward the centre of the door.

4 Offer the door into the frame. Use wedges to square it up if necessary. Make sure you allow a gap of about 12mm (½in) at the bottom to accommodate the thickness of any floor covering. ▷

5 Mark the clearance between the door and frame across the top and along the sides, using a pencil and a 3mm (⅛in) washer as a guide. Join the pencil marks with a straightedge.

6 Support the door on sturdy trestles or a similar firm surface. Then saw off the bulk of the waste, using a hand saw and keeping to the waste side of the marked lines.

9 Set a marking gauge to the thickness of the hinge flap and use the gauge to mark this dimension on the face of the door, allowing the flap recess to be cut to the correct depth.

10 Chop out the waste with a sharp chisel, cutting vertically along the scribed lines first, then across the waste before scooping it out. Work carefully down to the depth of the flap.

7 Plane the edges of the door down to the marked lines. When planing the top edge, work in from both sides to prevent splintering at the ends. Offer the door into the frame to check its fit.

8 Hold each hinge on the edge of the door so that its knuckle projects just beyond the face of the door. Mark around the flap with a sharp knife or pencil.

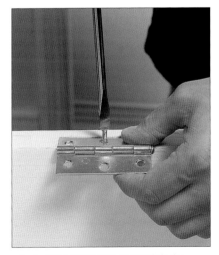

11 Check that the flap fits snugly in the recess, flush with the door edge, making any necessary adjustments. Then make pilot holes for the screws and fix the hinge securely.

12 Mark the positions of the hinges on the door frame with a pencil. Cut the recesses and offer up the door. Fix each hinge with one screw only until you are happy with the fit.

# REPLACING CABINET FRONTS

Even if they are not damaged or worn, changing the doors and drawer fronts of storage cabinets is an easy way of giving a room a new look.

### NEW DRAWER FRONTS

The drawers of modern furniture are often made with false fronts that allow a basic carcass to be used in a number of different styles. To replace a front, open the drawer or, better still, remove it completely. From inside the drawer, slacken the screws holding the false front to the carcass and remove it. Place the old front over the new one, aligning it exactly, drill down through the screw holes and into the new front to make pilot holes for the fixing screws. Take care not to drill right through the new face and spoil the finish. Use a depth stop to prevent this. Finally, screw the new front to the carcass from the inside.

### NEW DOORS

Replacing a chipboard (particle board) door may be necessary if the hinges have failed, which can occur with kitchen furniture after a number of years because of its heavy workload. If you replace old chipboard doors with new ones, they must be exactly the same size and be hung in the same way as the originals, since they cannot be trimmed to fit. Doors such as these are readily available, along with the chipboard hinges necessary to fit them. It is important to ensure that the hinge positions are perfectly accurate and

### REPLACING A DRAWER FRONT

**1** Remove the old drawer front by unscrewing it from behind.

### REPLACING A DOOR

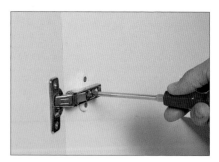

**1** Remove the old hinge simply by unscrewing it from the side.

that their recesses are of the correct depth, so careful measuring and a reliable drill stand or pillar drill is essential. You will also need a special bit to cut the blind hole for the hinge in the door. Transfer the hinge positions from the old door.

2 Drill pilot holes in the new front, using the existing holes in the old one as a guide.

3 Screw the new drawer front into position from behind. Offer up the drawer and check the fit.

2 Measure accurately from the edge of the old door to the centre of the hinge hole.

3 Transfer the position to the new door to ensure that the new hinge is placed accurately.

4 Drill a new hole, preferably using a drill stand for accuracy.

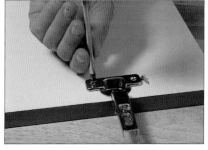

5 Attach the new hinge to the new door. Then fit the door.

# FITTING MORTISE DOOR LOCKS

**D**oors, especially those at the rear of the house, often provide an easy entrance and exit point for intruders. Good locks, properly fitted to a strong door and door frame, are the basic requirements for ensuring that house doors are secure, while additional security devices may help you feel safer at home. A mortise lock is fitted into a slot cut in the edge of a door, where it cannot easily be tampered with.

### INSTALLING MORTISE LOCKS

Align the mortise lock with the centre rail of the door and use the lock body as a template for marking the top and bottom of the mortise.

Draw a line down the middle of the door edge and, using a drill bit the width of the lock body, drill a series of overlapping holes along the centre-line to the depth of the lock. Chisel out the mortise so that the lock body fits snugly. Insert the lock, mark the outline of the faceplate with a pencil and chisel out a recess so that it fits flush with the door edge.

Mark and drill the holes for the key and spindle; enlarge the keyhole with a padsaw. Assemble and check the lock works.

With the latch and bolt open, mark their positions on the frame. Measure from the outside of the door to the centre of the bolt, mark that distance on the jamb and cut mortises in this

**1** Mark out the dimensions of a mortise lock on the door edge.

**4** Insert the lock, then mark and chisel out the recess for the faceplate.

position. Chisel a recess for the striking plate (keeper) and check that the door closes properly before fixing.

---

### TIP

"Measure twice and cut once." Accuracy is vital when marking out for door locks, so take your time with this part of the job and you will experience fewer problems later.

2 Using a mortise gauge, mark a vertical line in the centre of the door between the pencil lines.

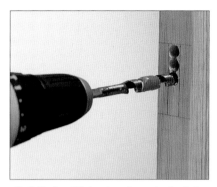

3 Drill a line of holes along the centre-line to the depth of the lock body.

5 Using the lock as a guide, mark the positions of the spindle and keyholes.

6 Drill the holes, then use a padsaw to form the keyhole. Fit the covers.

7 Cut mortises for the latch and the deadbolt on the door jamb.

8 Cut out a recess for the striking plate (keeper) so that it fits flush in the door jamb.

# FITTING RIM DOOR LOCKS

A rim door lock is an alternative to a mortise lock. It locks automatically as the door is closed, and the bolt cannot be forced back without a key.

### INSTALLING RIM LOCKS

Mark the position of the lock on the door, using any template provided, and bore a hole with a flat bit for the key cylinder. Push the cylinder into the hole, connect the lock backplate and secure it with screws. The cylinder connecting bar will protrude through the backplate. If necessary, cut it to length using a hacksaw.

If necessary, mark and chisel out the lock recess in the door edge, then fit the lock and screw it to the door, making sure that the cylinder connecting bar has engaged in the lock.

With the door closed, mark the position of the striking plate (keeper), then chisel out the recess so that the plate fits flush with the frame. Fix the striking plate with the screws provided and check that the door closes properly.

**1** Mark the position of the cylinder on the door and drill its hole.

**4** If necessary, mark the length of the connecting bar to be cut off.

## FITTING A RACK BOLT

A rack bolt allows you to lock a door from the inside, and is unobtrusive and secure.

Mark the position of the rack bolt in the centre of the door edge and on the inner face of the door, using a try or combination square to ensure that the two marks are level. Drill a hole of suitable size horizontally into the door edge to the depth of the body of the bolt. Push the bolt into the hole, mark the outline of the faceplate, then withdraw the bolt and chisel out a recess for the plate. Hold the bolt level with the guideline on the inside of the door, and mark and drill a hole for the key.

Fit the bolt, check that it works properly and screw the keyhole plate to the door. Close the door and wind out the bolt so that it leaves a mark. Drill a hole at this point and fit a recessed cover plate.

2 Insert the barrel of the lock cylinder into the drilled hole.

3 Fit the backplate to the door and secure it tightly with screws.

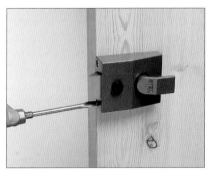

5 Fit the lock case to the connecting plate and screw together.

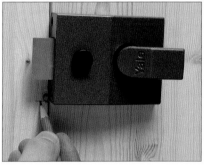

6 Mark the position of the striking plate (keeper). Chisel out its recess in the frame.

1 Use tape to mark the drilling depth and keep the bit horizontal. Push in the bolt.

2 Mark the outline of the faceplate, then withdraw the bolt to chisel out the recess.

# WINDOW SECURITY

Over half of all home burglaries occur through a window, and even the smallest is vulnerable, so good locks are very important. The first line of defence is to fit good-quality handles and stays, followed by key-operated locks to all ground-floor windows, and those first-floor windows that are easily accessible. It is also essential to provide a secure means of ventilation around your home.

## BASIC HARDWARE

The most common items of hardware fitted on hinged windows are a rotating cockspur handle, which is used simply to fasten the window, and a casement stay, which props it open in several different positions. On sliding sash windows, the basic hardware is a catch that locks the two sashes together when they are closed.

## CHOOSING AND FITTING WINDOW LOCKS

Many window locks are surface-mounted, using screws, and are quick and easy to fit, although for some types a drilled hole for a bolt or recess chiselled for a striking plate (keeper) may be required. Mortised locks and dual screws that fit into holes drilled in the window frame take longer to install, but they are very secure.

When buying locks for windows, bear in mind the thickness of the frames. In some cases, these may be too thin to accommodate a recessed lock without seriously weakening the frame. If in any doubt, buy surface-mounted fittings.

All window locks are supplied with fixing screws, but these should often be discarded in favour of longer, more secure fixings. Some locks come with special security screws that can only be tightened, but not unscrewed. In this case, the lock should be fitted with ordinary screws first and the proper screws only added when you are happy that the lock functions correctly. In other cases, the screws are concealed by plastic plugs. For extra security, it is also a good idea to fit two locks on casement windows more than 1m (3ft) high, while all locking devices for sash windows are best used in pairs.

For secure ventilation, if the window has a stay pierced with holes, you can replace the plain peg with a casement stay lock. Attach the screw-on lock to the threaded peg with the key supplied. This will allow you to secure the window in any position.

If fitting lockable window catches and stays, do not leave keys in the locks where they might be seen by an intruder; they may also fall out as the window is opened and closed. Instead, hang them on a hook close to the window where they are readily accessible, but can't be seen from outside.

### TIP

Ensure you have the right screws: a lock intended for wooden window frames requires woodscrews; metal window frames will require self-tapping screws.

## FITTING A WINDOW HANDLE AND STAY

1 Choose the position of the cockspur handle on the casement and make pilot holes through it with a bradawl (awl). Then screw the handle firmly to the casement.

2 Fit the striking plate (keeper) to the frame so that it will engage with the cockspur. Drill out the frame to a depth of 20mm (¾in) through the slot in the plate.

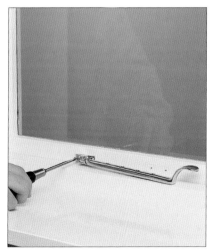

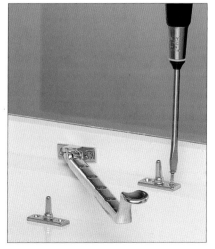

3 Fit the casement stay by screwing its baseplate to the bottom rail of the casement, about one-third along from the hinged edge.

4 Open the window to find the correct position for the pegs on the frame. Attach the pegs, then fit the stay rest to the casement rail.

# CASEMENT WINDOW LOCKS

Locks for wooden casement windows may be surface-mounted or set in the frame. If surface-mounted, the lockplate is attached to the fixed frame, and the body of the lock to the opening frame. With the window closed, mark the positions of the lock and plate on both frames, then screw them in place. For those with a locking bolt, you will have to cut a rebate (rabbet) or drill a hole to receive the bolt. Some surface-mounted locks are also suitable for fitting to metal casement windows. Check the instructions.

Locks that are designed to be set in the frame normally require holes to be drilled in both fixed and opening frames. Also, a hole must be drilled through the face of the frame to allow insertion of the key.

1 With the lock assembled, mark its position on the fixed and opening frames. Separate the two parts of the lock and screw the body to the opening frame.

2 Fit the cover plate and insert the screws. You may want to use longer screws than those provided to ensure a strong fixing.

3 Some makes come with small covers or plugs to hide the screws. Tap these into place when you are happy with the fit of the lock.

# SASH WINDOW LOCKS

Some types of casement window lock will also work with sash windows. An effective security device for sash windows is the sash stop, which actually allows the window to be opened slightly for ventilation. To fit the device, it is necessary to drill a hole in the upper sash to accommodate its bolt. Then a protective plate is added to the top of the lower sash. In operation, turning the key releases the spring-loaded bolt, which prevents the sashes from sliding past each other.

Another option is key-operated dual screws (shown below), which bolt both sashes together. Use a flat bit the width of the lock barrel to drill through the inner meeting rail (mullion) into the outer rail to the required depth, then tap the barrels into place with a hammer and piece of wood. Fit the longer barrel into the inner rail, the shorter into the outer rail, and screw the bolt into the barrel with the key.

## FIRE SAFETY

Wherever possible, fit window locks that all use the same standard key so that any key can be used to open a window in the event of an emergency. Keep keys in accessible positions.

1 Mark the drill bit with tape to the required depth and drill through the inner meeting rail (mullion) of a sash window, into the outer rail.

2 Separate the two sections of the lock and tap the barrels of the dual screw into place in the meeting rails.

# WOOD FINISHING

Practically all wooden structures need finishing with some form of protective film that prevents them from becoming dirty, discoloured, or damaged by moisture or slight knocks. Some finishes, such as wax, allow the decorative pattern of the grain to show through, while others, such as paint, conceal it. Although there are many techniques for finishing wood, a number of basic steps are common to all of them. Carry out preparation work well away from the finishing area, and be prepared to move the work back and forth several times as you apply and rub down successive coats. Remember that any finish on wood will enhance defects as well as good points, so preparation is important.

# PREPARING WOOD FOR FINISHING

Many different types of wood will need filling. This can be as simple as rubbing in a grain filler, which will give a more even and less absorbent surface. It may involve using a wood filler, which can be bought to match the colour of the wood being used, to fill cracks, blemishes and knot holes. Soft interior stopping is fine for tiny cracks, and a two-part exterior-grade wood filler for making good large holes.

The tools required for finishing are simple, and most of the work can be done entirely by hand. A few scrapers, some abrasive paper in various grades, wire (steel) wool, soft cloth, a cork sanding block and some filler or stopping are the basic requirements.

Apply any filler that is necessary to knot holes and blemishes in the wood, allow to dry and remove the excess gently with a chisel. With this done, the wood can be rubbed down with abrasive paper wrapped around a cork block, working along the grain.

Wipe over the surface with a clean, damp rag to raise the grain very slightly, allow it to dry, then cut it back lightly with 400-grit abrasive paper, again working along the grain.

### ESSENTIAL REQUIREMENTS

Not often mentioned is the fact that wood must be dry, regardless of the treatment applied. Another requirement is that when several applications of a finish are called for, they must be rubbed down, or "flatted", between coats.

1 Apply filler to match the colour of the wood. Scrape away any excess with a sharp chisel.

2 Sand down with abrasive paper wrapped around a cork block, working along the grain, not across it.

3 To remove dust, wipe down with a soft, damp cloth, using long strokes parallel to the grain.

# STAINING AND VARNISHING WOOD

If you want to stain your wood, test the stain on a spare piece of the same wood to check the final colour and depth.

Remember that end grain will absorb a lot more of the stain and will be much darker. Stain can be applied with a soft cloth or brush. Keep a wet edge all the time to avoid a patchy finish. Apply the stain in short circular motions.

Varnishes, such as polyurethane or acrylic, which are quick drying, should be applied along the grain with a soft brush. Be sure to get into all recesses, but do not leave pools or runs. Allow to dry and flat down with 320-grit abrasive paper or a fine grade of wire (steel) wool.

Varnish is best applied in a cool environment; otherwise problems with a "ripple" finish can occur.

## APPLYING STAIN

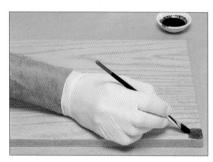

1 Use a small brush to test the colour on a spare piece of wood. Dilute the stain when treating end grain, otherwise it will be too dark.

2 If satisfied with the colour, apply the stain with a soft cloth in quick, circular motions. Don't allow the stain to "puddle".

## APPLYING VARNISH

1 For large panels, use a wide brush to apply varnish with long strokes.

2 Rub down the surface using 320-grit silicon-carbide paper, varnish and repeat.

# WAXING WOOD

**W**ith the wood sanded down, apply a coat of sanding sealer, lightly sanding it when dry. This provides a good base for the wax, preventing it from soaking too deeply into the wood and improving the durability of the final finish.

Apply a coat of wax to the wood with a soft cloth or a ball of very fine wire (steel) wool, using a circular motion, followed by strokes along the grain, to work it well into the wood.

Allow the wax to dry for an hour or so, then polish off with a soft cloth. Add a second, thinner, coat of wax, working in the direction of the grain only. Polish this off lightly and leave for a few hours before giving it a final vigorous polishing.

1 Apply a thin coat of clear shellac or a proprietary sanding sealer to the wood to provide a stable base for the wax. Leave this to dry, then sand lightly.

2 Apply the wax with a ball of fine wire (steel) wool, using a strong circular motion to work it into the wood. Then finish off with strokes in the direction of the grain. Allow the wax to dry.

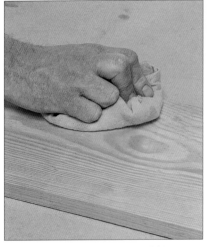

3 Buff the wax vigorously with a polishing pad made from a soft duster. Add a second, thinner coat of wax and polish it off lightly before leaving it for a few hours. Finally, buff well.

# PAINTING WOOD

Start by priming any bare areas, then apply an undercoat and finally one or two coats of gloss (oil) paint. With a standard gloss paint, begin by applying the paint vertically, and then use sideways strokes to blend it well. Work in the direction of the grain, blending in the wet edges for a uniform finish. If you are using a one-coat paint, apply the finish quite thickly in close, parallel strips and do not over-brush.

| new or stripped wood | primer to seal | undercoat (1 or 2 coats) | gloss topcoat |
| --- | --- | --- | --- |

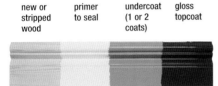

**ABOVE: The sequence for painting wood.**

1 Apply a suitable primer to all areas of bare wood and allow to dry completely before overpainting. The primer will prevent the paint from soaking into the wood and leaving a patchy finish.

2 Apply one or two undercoats and lightly rub down with fine-grade abrasive paper between coats. To avoid problems, always use the same make of undercoat as topcoat.

3 Finally, apply the topcoat. When painting a panelled door, do the mouldings and panelled areas first, then move on to the cross rails, and finish with the vertical stiles.

# SHELVES & STORAGE

- Shelves
- Cabinets & wardrobes
- Storage projects

# INTRODUCTION

**F**inding suitable storage space around the home for all the personal and household belongings every family accumulates can be quite a challenge. One difficulty is making a sensible compromise between tidiness and accessibility; it is no good having a place for everything if that means spending hours each day laboriously taking things out and putting them back again.

The solution is to tailor-make storage to suit its purpose. Some things need a temporary resting place where they remain readily accessible. Others need long-term storage, perhaps being retrieved and used only occasionally. And there is a third storage category, that of display – simply to show things off.

In a typical home, possessions are stored in one of three main ways: on shelves, in cupboards (closets) or in drawers. These may be combined in a variety of storage or display units, and the amount of each type of space that is required will vary from one house to another. For example, the avid bookworm will have miles of bookshelves, while the clothes horse will need more wardrobe space.

The storage that is needed can be provided in one of two ways. One is to buy or make pieces of freestanding furniture that match the required storage function. The other is to use raw materials such as wood and manufactured boards plus the

BELOW: Planned storage is essential in a kitchen to make the most of available space.

ABOVE: A system of shelves provides a useful means of storage in a living room.

ABOVE: For an office/study area, consider using wire baskets for storage.

appropriate hardware to create built-in storage space – arrays of shelving, cupboards in alcoves and so on. The former is the best solution for those who value furniture more than function, since the pieces can be moved from one home to another. However, built-in storage is generally more effective in providing the most space for the least money, since the walls of a room can often be used as part of the structure. In this chapter, you will find a wide variety of storage options that you can use to good effect.

Apart from obvious places such as kitchen cabinets and bedroom wardrobes, there are many places in the main rooms of the home where items can be stored. This can be done without spoiling the look of the room. Properly planned storage space can be not only practical and capacious, but positively elegant.

## LIVING ROOM

Here, storage needs are likely to be firmly leisure-oriented. There has to be room for books, tapes, CDs, videotapes and DVDs, not to mention display space for ornaments and other treasures. The choice is between freestanding and built-in furniture, and it is worth spending time looking at different possibilities because here looks are as important as performance.

Built-in furniture can make optimum use of alcoves and other recesses. A more radical option is a complete wall of storage units, which could incorporate space for home entertainment equipment, as well as features such as a drinks cabinet. This also offers the opportunity to include a home office section – some desk space, room for a computer, plus somewhere to file away all the essential paperwork that every household generates.

## KITCHEN

Storage is a serious business here, and what is needed and how it is provided depends on what kind of kitchen it is and how it is used. The fully fitted kitchen is still popular because it packs the most storage into the least space, although there is now a discernible movement back to farmhouse-style kitchens fitted with freestanding rather than built-in furniture. This is suitable only for people who are either very tidy and well organized or, on the other hand, happy to live in chaos. The style of such kitchens restricts the amount of storage space they can offer at the expense of the look of the room, so for those who have a lot of kitchen utensils and like to keep large stocks

ABOVE: A fitted kitchen unit provides made-to-measure storage space under a work counter.

ABOVE: The traditional dresser is ideal for creating the country kitchen look.

of food, a fitted kitchen is a better idea. However, there is one big advantage with freestanding furniture: it can be taken along when moving house.

In deciding what is wanted, analyze storage needs thoroughly. Think about food, utensils and small appliances for a start; all need a place close to cooking and food preparation areas. Move on to items like china, cutlery and glassware; do they need to be in the kitchen at all, or would the dining room be a better place to keep them? Then consider non-culinary items – things like cleaning materials, table linen and so on – and make sure there is enough space for them.

Remember that ceiling-height cupboards (closets) are always a better bet than ones that finish just above head height, even if some small steps or a box are needed to reach them. It is best to use the top shelves for storing seldom-used items.

Always aim to make the best possible use of cupboard space. Fit extra shelves where necessary, use wire baskets for ventilated storage, hang small racks on the backs of cupboard doors and use swing-out carousels to gain access to corner cupboards.

If there is a separate laundry room, it is often easier to split cooking and non-cooking storage needs by moving all home laundry and cleaning equipment out of the kitchen altogether. Such a room can also act as a useful back porch if it has access to a garden.

## DINING ROOM

Here, storage needs relate mainly to providing places for china, glassware and cutlery – especially any that is kept for special occasions. Think too about storage for tablemats, cloths and other table accessories. There may also be a need for somewhere to store small appliances such as toasters, coffee makers and hotplates. Once again, the choice is between built-in storage units and freestanding furniture; this is largely a matter of taste.

## HALLWAY

Simple hooks and an umbrella stand are the bare minimum, but consider providing an enclosed cupboard (closet) that is built-in rather than freestanding. It is simple to borrow

ABOVE: A collection of glasses can be seen to best advantage in a glass-fronted display case.

some porch or hall floor space to create an enclosure. If it is fitted with a door to match others leading to the rest of the house, it will blend in perfectly. Make sure it is ventilated so that damp clothes can dry.

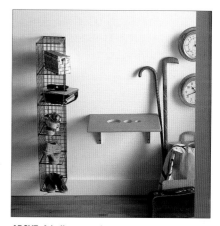

ABOVE: A hallway needs storage for items you will use outdoors, such as umbrellas and shoes.

## BEDROOM

Now take a look at your storage requirements in the bedroom. Here, the main need is for space to store clothes, and this is one area where built-in (and ideally, walk-in) storage is the perfect solution. If there are two bedrooms, space can often be poached by forming a deep partition wall, accessible from one or both rooms. This can actually save money in the long run, as there is no furniture to buy. If you have bedrooms upstairs and

**ABOVE: Wardrobes need an arrangement of hanging rails, shelves and drawers.**

the overall upstairs floor space is large enough, you could also consider creating a separate dressing room.

Bedrooms built under the roof slope offer an opportunity to make use of the space behind the walls by creating fully lined eaves cupboards (closets). These are particularly useful for long-term storage of items such as luggage, which may be needed only occasionally, as well as providing a home for toys and games in children's rooms.

Do not just restrict bedroom storage to clothes and bedlinen, though. There is no reason why it should not also allow for books, ornaments, or even a small television or computer.

**LEFT: In a bedroom, small shelves can provide useful room for a variety of bits and pieces.**

RIGHT: In a home workshop, use perforated wall boards to store hand tools.

## BATHROOM

Next, look at the bathroom. Here requirements are likely to be relatively low-key – somewhere to keep toiletries and cleaning materials, for example. It is not a good idea to store towels and the like in a potentially damp and steamy atmosphere. The choice is likely to be between a floor-standing vanity unit and some wall cabinets, although if space permits some thought might be given to the growing number of fully fitted bathroom furniture ranges.

## ROOF SPACE

It is worth boarding over at least the area around the access hatch so that luggage, boxes and the like can be put there. If the roof construction permits, however, there is a chance to create almost unlimited storage capacity. Fit a proper ladder for safe and easy access.

## WORKSHOP

An area where some storage space is certainly needed is a home workshop, whether this is a spare room, an area at the back of the garage or a separate building. The basic need is for shelf space, to take everything from cans of paint to garden products, and also some form of tool storage to keep everything in order.

LEFT: A corner cabinet makes a versatile bathroom storage unit because it uses literally every corner of space. In this bathroom, bottles and soaps have been neatly stored in an aluminium accessory holder.

RIGHT: Storage can be stylish and attractive as well as functional, as these painted bathroom hooks show.

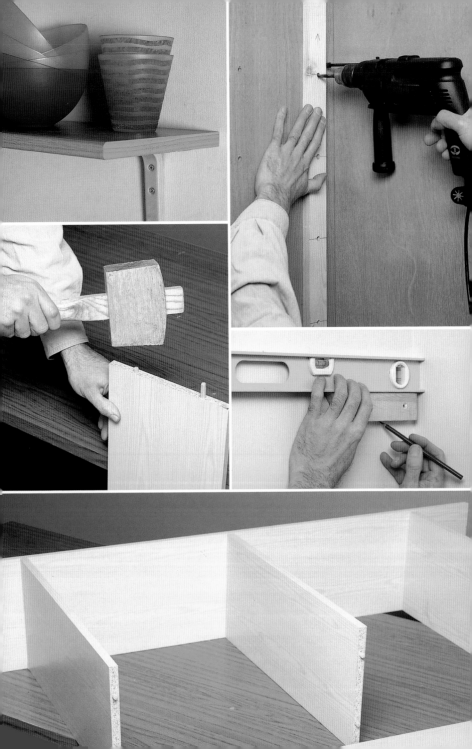

# SHELVES

The most basic form of storage is shelving, but even so, there are options to consider. Adjustable shelving systems are very versatile, making use of slotted wall uprights that accept special shelf brackets. They allow you to add or remove shelves or adjust their spacing at will. Individual brackets are ideal for single shelves, but can be utilitarian in appearance. If you intend fitting shelves into an alcove, they can be fixed to battens screwed to the wall. In a freestanding unit, shelves can be held by special studs, bookcase strips or dowel-reinforced butt joints. In a garage or home workshop, shelves can be supported on sturdy "ladder" frames to create flexible storage systems.

# ADJUSTABLE SHELVING

Shelving systems abound in do-it-yourself stores for those who prefer simply to fit rather than to make the shelving. There is a range of brackets on the market to cater for every need, and these clip into slotted uprights screwed to the wall. The bracket positions can be adjusted to vary the spacing between the shelves to accommodate your needs.

Shelving systems are a versatile way of dealing with changing requirements, and they have the distinct advantage of being portable when you need to move them. They are capable of holding heavy weights, but remember that ultimately a shelf's capacity depends on the strength of the wall fixing employed.

First measure the distance between the shelving uprights, bearing in mind the thickness and material to be used for the shelf. Books can be very heavy, so do not set the uprights too far apart, otherwise the shelf will sag in the middle. About a quarter of the length of the shelf can overhang each end. If necessary, cut the uprights to length. Drill and plug the wall so that you can attach one upright by its topmost hole. Do not tighten the screw fully at this stage. Simply allow the upright to hang freely.

Hold your spirit (carpenter's) level against the side of the upright, and when you are satisfied that it is vertical, mark its position lightly on the wall with a pencil. Mark in the remaining screw positions, then drill and plug the rest of the screw holes.

You may find that when you tighten the screws, the upright needs a little packing here and there to keep it vertical in the other plane. If these discrepancies are not too large, this adjustment can be done by varying the relative tightness of the screws, which will pull the upright into line. You can mark off the position for the second upright and any others, using a spirit level on top of a shelf with a couple of brackets slipped into position. Fitting the second upright entails the same procedure as before.

## PLANNING SHELVES

Aim to keep everyday items within easy reach and position deep shelves near the bottom so that it is easy to see and reach the back. Allow 25–50mm (1–2in) of clearance on top of the height of objects, so that they are easy to take down.

Think about weight too. If the shelves will store heavy objects, the shelving material must be chosen with care. With 12mm (½in) chipboard (particle board) and ready-made veneered or melamine-faced shelves, space brackets at 450mm (18in) for heavy loads or 600mm (2ft) for light loads. With 19mm (¾in) chipboard or 12mm (½in) plywood, increase the spacing to 600mm (2ft) and 750mm (2ft 6in) respectively. For 19mm (¾in) plywood, blockboard, MDF (medium-density fiberboard) or natural wood, the bracket spacing can be 750mm (2ft 6in) for heavy loads, 900mm (3ft) for light ones.

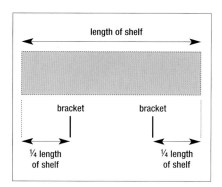

Measure the distance between the uprights. Allow a quarter length of shelf at each end.

Fix the first screw loosely in the top hole and let the upright hang.

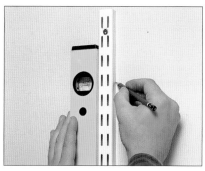

Check the bracket is absolutely vertical with a spirit (carpenter's) level.

A little packing card may be necessary if the wall is uneven.

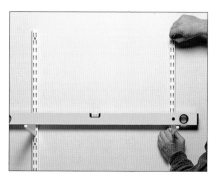

Mark the position for the second upright using the first as a guide.

The shelf brackets can be inserted at different heights and can be easily moved.

# USING SHELF BRACKETS

With a little thought, shelving can be made to be decorative as well as functional, and a variety of materials, including wood, metal and glass, can be used to good effect.

All require firm wall fixings. Always use a spirit (carpenter's) level when fitting shelves.

### SIMPLE SHELVING

Ready-made shelving systems can be employed, both wall-mounted and freestanding. The basic methods of fitting shelving are the same, no matter what material is used. Essential requirements are establishing a truly level surface with a spirit level, obtaining firm fixings in the wall, and being able to fit the shelving accurately into an alcove.

The simplest form of shelf is a wooden board supported by a pair of metal or wooden brackets. The latter are available in a range of sizes and in styles that vary from purely functional to quite decorative. Consider carefully before buying; the brackets will be in plain view, so make sure they fit in with their surroundings. You can make them less obvious, however, by painting them to match the wall colour.

Make sure that you match the size of bracket to the width of board you intend using – if too narrow, the shelf will not be

1 Mark the position of the shelf by drawing a line across the wall, using a long, straight batten as a guide. Make sure it is perfectly horizontal with a spirit (carpenter's) level.

supported fully and may actually collapse when loaded. Choose brackets that will span between two-thirds and three-quarters of the width of the board.

Use your spirit level to ascertain the height and horizontal run of the shelf, then mark the positions for the brackets. Mark the positions of the screws through the holes in the brackets, drill with a masonry bit and insert wall plugs. Hold each bracket in place and start all the screws into the wall plugs before tightening them fully.

If fitting more than one shelf on an uninterrupted run of wall, mark them out at the same time, using a try or combination square. Cut them to size, then screw them to the shelf brackets.

2 Mark the positions of the fixing screws on the wall through the bracket holes. For accuracy, lay a short piece of wood on top of each bracket, aligning it with the pencil line.

3 Drill the holes for the screws, using a masonry bit if necessary, and insert wall plugs. Hold each bracket in place and start all of its screws before tightening them fully.

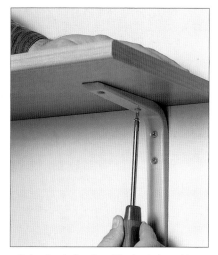

4 Lay the shelf on top of the brackets, making sure the overhang is equal at each end. Use a bradawl (awl) to make pilot holes and screw through the brackets into the shelf.

5 You can also attach the shelf to the brackets before mounting the brackets to the wall. If you do this, make sure that the back edge of the shelf aligns with the bracket mounting faces.

# FITTING SHELVES IN ALCOVES

Alcoves beside chimney breasts (fireplace projections) or other obstructions make perfect sites for shelves, since the back and side walls can be used as supports. Although it is easy to use fixed shelf brackets or an adjustable shelving system to support shelves here, it is cheaper to fix slim wood or metal support strips directly to the alcove walls and rest the shelves on top of these.

If using wooden supports, cut their front ends at an angle so that they are less noticeable when the shelves are fitted. Paint them the same colour as the walls (or to tone with the wall covering) to make them even less obtrusive. If using L-shaped metal strips for the supports, choose a size that matches the shelf thickness so they are almost invisible once the shelves have been fitted.

The actual job is quite simple. Mark the shelf level on the alcove walls, cut the supports to the required lengths and screw them to the walls. Then cut your shelf to size and slip it into place, resting on the supports. It can be nailed, screwed or glued in place for extra stability. The only difficult part is in making the shelf a good fit, since the alcove walls may not be truly square. Accurate measuring of the alcove width at front and back, plus some careful scribing of the rear edge of the shelf, will ensure good results.

When fitting more than one shelf, measure for each separately, since the alcove may not be uniform in size.

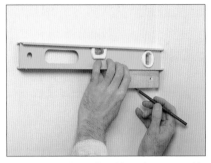

**1** Decide on the shelf positions, then use a spirit (carpenter's) level to mark the position of the first shelf support on one alcove wall.

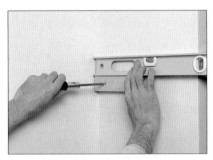

**4** Screw the second support in place as before, marking the positions of the fixing holes on the wall. Check again that it is level.

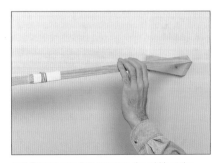

**7** Repeat step 5 to measure the width at the point where the front edge of the shelf will be, then transfer the measurement to the shelf.

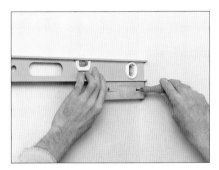

**2** Drill clearance holes in the supports, and use one to mark its fixing hole positions on the wall. Drill the holes and fix this support.

**3** Rest a shelf on the first support, hold it level and mark the shelf position on the opposite wall. Then prepare the second shelf support.

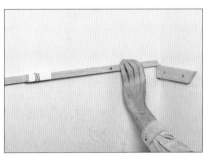

**5** Make a set of gauge rods from scrap wood, held together with a rubber band. Extend the rods to span the rear wall of the alcove.

**6** Lift the rods out carefully without disturbing their positions and lay them on the rear edge of the shelf. Mark the width of the alcove on it.

**8** Cut the shelf to width and lay it in place. If the fit is poor against the back wall, use a block and pencil to scribe the wall outline on it.

**9** Saw carefully along the scribed line with a power jigsaw (saber saw). Sand the cut edge smooth and fit the shelf back in position.

# USING SHELF SUPPORT STRIPS

This is an ingenious method of providing support for single shelves. It consists of a specially shaped channel that is screwed to the wall at the required position; then the shelf is simply knocked into place with a soft-faced mallet.

The channel grips the shelf securely and can support surprisingly heavy loads. For lighter loads such as ornaments you can use small shelf support blocks. The shelf is clamped in place by tightening a locking screw underneath the block.

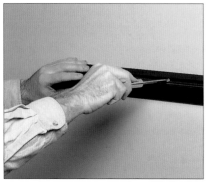

**1** Hold the support strip against the wall at the desired level and mark the position of the central screw hole. Drill and plug the hole, then attach the strip.

**2** Place a spirit (carpenter's) level on top of the strip. Swivel the strip until it is precisely level, then mark the positions of the remaining screw holes on the wall.

**3** Swivel the strip out of the way and drill the other holes. Insert wall plugs. Then secure the strip with the remaining screws and slot the shelf into place.

**4** Shelf support blocks are also available for mounting small display shelves. The shelf is clamped in the block by tightening a locking screw from underneath.

# USING STUDS AND BOOKCASE STRIPS

Adjustable shelves may also be wanted inside a storage unit. There are two options. The first involves drilling a series of carefully aligned holes in each side of the unit, then inserting small plastic or metal shelf support studs. The second uses what is known as bookcase strip – a metal moulding with slots into which small pegs or tongues are fitted to support the shelves. Two strips are needed at each side of the unit. In both cases, accurate marking out is essential to ensure that the supports line up.

## USING SHELF SUPPORT STUDS

1 Use a simple predrilled jig to make the holes for the shelf supports in the sides of the unit. A depth stop will prevent you from drilling too deep and breaking through.

2 Drill two sets of holes in each side of the unit, with the top of the jig held against the top of the unit to guarantee alignment. Insert the supports and fit the shelves.

## USING BOOKCASE STRIPS

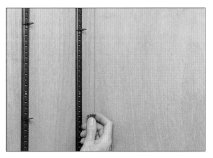

1 Mark the positions of the top ends of the strips to ensure that they are level, then mark the screw positions to a true vertical. Make pilot holes and screw on the strips.

2 Insert pairs of pegs into the bookcase strip at each shelf position, checking that their lugs are properly engaged in the slots. Then lift the shelf into place on the pegs.

# FREESTANDING SHELVING

Freestanding shelf units can easily be moved if the room layout is changed or when painting or papering. However, they have drawbacks too. Some manufactured shelving and display units are rather flimsy, and may twist out of square or sag if they are heavily loaded. In general, better results come from building units from stronger materials such as natural wood and plywood.

The other problem is getting units to stand upright against the wall; skirtings (baseboards) prevent standard units from being pushed back flush with the wall surface, and carpet gripper strips make them lean forwards slightly. The answer is to design the side supports on the cantilever principle with just one point of contact with the floor. This point should be as far as possible from the wall, so that the unit presses more firmly against the wall as the load on the shelves is increased. Fix the unit to the wall with brackets for safety, particularly if there are children around.

Since a shelf unit is basically a box with internal dividers, it can be constructed in several different ways, using simple butt joints or more complicated housings. Perhaps the best compromise between strength and ease of construction is to use glued butt joints reinforced with hardwood dowels, which give the joints the extra rigidity they need in a unit of this sort.

Start by deciding on the dimensions of the unit, then select materials to suit the loading the shelves will support.

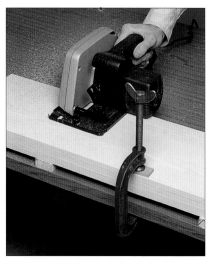

**1** Clamp groups of identical parts together. Mark them to length and cut them in one go to ensure that they are all the same.

**4** Glue the dowels and tap them into the holes in the shelf ends. Check that they all project by the same amount, and cut down any that may be too long.

2 Mark the positions of the shelf dowel holes on the unit sides. Drill them all to the required depth, using a drill stand if possible.

3 Use a dowelling jig to drill the dowel holes in the shelf ends. This ensures that the holes are correctly positioned and are drilled straight.

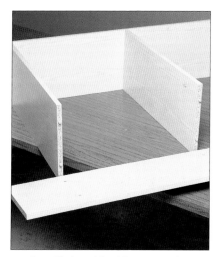

5 Assemble the unit by gluing one end of each of the three shelves and joining them to one of the side panels. Then glue the other ends and add the second side panel.

6 Cut a hardboard or plywood backing panel. Use a try square to check that the angles are correct, then pin the board into position on the back of the unit.

# MAKING UTILITY SHELVING

Storage space in workshops, garages, basements and attics is best provided by building simple but sturdy shelves from inexpensive materials. Use wood that is sawn, not planed (dressed), for the framework, and cut the shelves from scrap plywood. Damaged boards and offcuts (scraps) are often available cheaply from timber merchants (lumberyards).

The shelving units shown here are made from 50mm (2in) square wood, with shelves of 19mm (¾in) plywood.

The only other materials needed are some scraps of 9mm (⅜in) thick plywood for the small triangular braces that help to stiffen the structure.

The uprights should be spaced about 760mm (2ft 6in) apart so that the shelves will not sag; they can reach right to ceiling level if desired. Match the depth of the unit to whatever is to be stored and to the amount of space available. Remember that it can be difficult reaching things at the back of deep shelves.

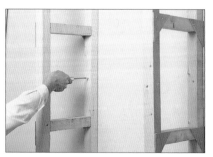

**1** Start by deciding on the height the uprights should be, and on how many "ladders" are needed. Cut them all to length with a power saw.

**2** Make up the ladders by gluing and nailing the rungs between pairs of uprights. Reinforce the joints by gluing and screwing on plywood triangles.

**3** Stand the assembled ladders against the wall, check that they are truly vertical, and screw them to the wall into wooden studs or masonry anchors.

**4** Cut as many plywood shelves as are needed so they span between the centre lines of the rungs; notch the corners so they will fit neatly.

# MAKING A STORAGE RACK

**T**his tool storage rack is basically a wall-mounted backing board of 19mm (¾in) thick plywood. Tools are hung on various supports, as shown in the illustration. These are located in, and slide along, horizontal channels formed by pinning 38 x 12mm (1½ x ½in) plywood to the backing panel and then pinning 75 x 19mm (3 x ¾in)

softwood strips to the plywood. Make the trays for small tools from 12mm (½in) plywood, and use hardwood dowel pegs or old wire coat hangers to form support hooks for larger tools. Slide the backplate of each support into its channel at the sides of the rack, and push them to where they are needed.

BELOW: This versatile storage rack is easy to make and can be tailored exactly to accommodate a variety of hand tools. Its design allows the arrangement of fixtures to be adjusted at any time to meet changing needs.

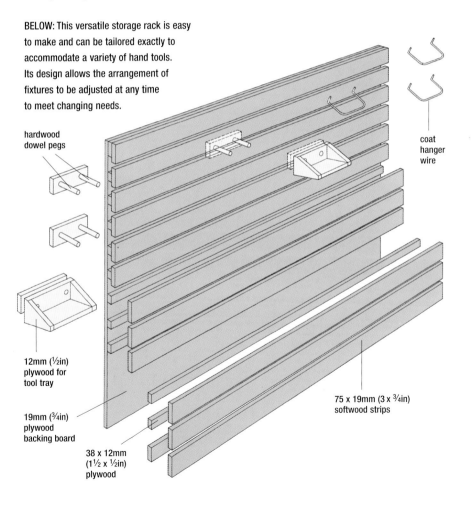

hardwood dowel pegs

coat hanger wire

12mm (½in) plywood for tool tray

19mm (¾in) plywood backing board

38 x 12mm (1½ x ½in) plywood

75 x 19mm (3 x ¾in) softwood strips

# MAKING A GARAGE STORAGE WALL

The garage is a favourite place to store all manner of things, including tools and materials for do-it-yourself, gardening and car maintenance tasks. Unless these are kept under control, they will spill over until there is no room for the car. The solution is to build a shallow full-height storage unit along either the side or the end wall of the garage, tailor-made to suit whatever will be stored there.

The design concept of the storage wall is quite simple. The structure is based on ladder frames fixed to the wall to support shelves, drawers and

BELOW: This simple storage wall unit is the ideal home for all the various tools, equipment and do-it-yourself materials that are likely to find a home in your garage, keeping the floor area clear for your car. You can easily adapt its design to fit your own garage and particular needs.

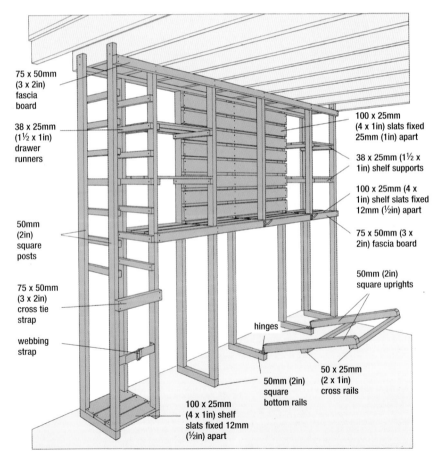

75 x 50mm (3 x 2in) fascia board

38 x 25mm (1½ x 1in) drawer runners

50mm (2in) square posts

75 x 50mm (3 x 2in) cross tie strap

webbing strap

100 x 25mm (4 x 1in) slats fixed 25mm (1in) apart

38 x 25mm (1½ x 1in) shelf supports

100 x 25mm (4 x 1in) shelf slats fixed 12mm (½in) apart

75 x 50mm (3 x 2in) fascia board

50mm (2in) square uprights

50 x 25mm (2 x 1in) cross rails

hinges

50mm (2in) square bottom rails

100 x 25mm (4 x 1in) shelf slats fixed 12mm (½in) apart

whatever else is required. The frame is made mainly from 50mm (2in) square sawn softwood, with 75 x 25mm (3 x 1in) wood for the shelves and the slatted hanging rack. The hinged section drops down to allow sheets of plywood and the like to be placed on edge behind it, and is held shut with a simple hasp and staple at each side. The wall-mounted rack allows heavy items to be hung out of the way, yet be readily to hand, on metal S-hooks.

1 Start by securing the uprights to the garage wall to form the various bays. Check that each is vertical before fixing it in place.

2 Set sole plates on something damp-proof (here sheet vinyl flooring has been used), and screw them down into expanding wall plugs in holes drilled in the garage floor.

3 Simply nail the components together as required to form the frames that make up each bay. Add horizontals to support wooden shelves or plastic bowl drawers.

4 To make the drop-down flap for the sheet materials storage bay, hinge the two front uprights to their baseplates and add a cross rail.

5 To make the wall rack, nail on the slats, using an offcut (scrap) as a spacer. Make the shelves in the same way.

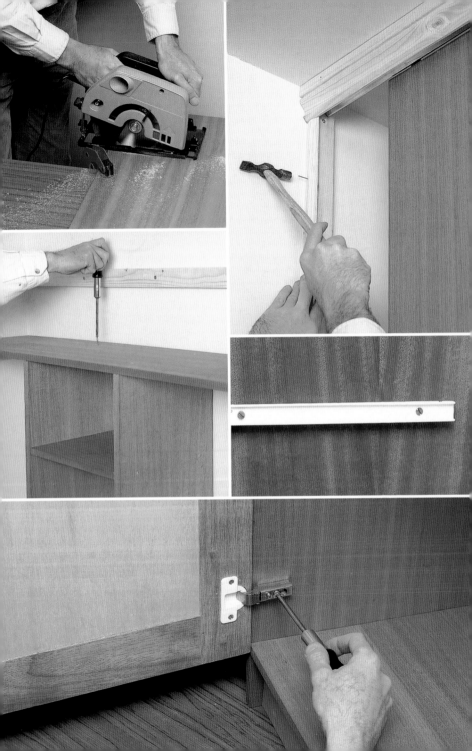

# CABINETS & WARDROBES

Cabinet-making is a skilled craft, but the ready availability of man-made boards faced with veneer or melamine and ready-made doors in a variety of styles has made it possible for any competent do-it-yourselfer to create attractive, functional cabinets for any room of the home. Panels can be joined by simple glued butt joints reinforced with nails, screws or wooden dowels, while doors can be hung with flush or concealed hinges. Even drawers can be added, using kits of plastic parts. Wardrobe space is invariably in short supply in the bedroom, but it is relatively simple to add doors, shelves and hanging rails to an alcove, or even across the entire end wall of a room.

# MAKING CABINETS

Freestanding storage units consist simply of a basic box, fitted out internally as required. For example, this can include one or more shelves, vertical dividers, hanging rails, drawers and doors. All this applies to units as diverse in scale as a small hi-fi cabinet and a large double wardrobe. A pair of boxes can be placed under a counter top to create a desk or dressing table.

Units will probably be made from manufactured boards. It is difficult to get natural wood wider than about 225mm (9in), which rather restricts its scope; it is also more expensive. The most popular material for making box furniture is chipboard (particle board), especially the veneered and melamine-faced varieties. It is sold in planks and boards of various sizes with the long edges (and sometimes the ends) already veneered or faced. Its main disadvantage is that it will sag under its own weight across spans of more than about 900mm (3ft).

Stronger alternatives are plywood, MDF (medium-density fiberboard) and blockboard. Blockboard is the strongest and can be used unsupported over spans twice as great as for chipboard. Sheets of blockboard sold as door blanks usually have the long edges faced.

Plywood offers the best of both worlds – it is almost as strong as blockboard, and has edges that can be neatly finished. It is also available in thicknesses from 4mm (just over ⅛in) to 19mm (¾in), so there should be a perfect match for any application.

MDF is a popular choice for box furniture as well as shelves, since it cuts beautifully without the need for finishing sawn edges. It is a medium-strength material and its very smooth surface finish can be painted, varnished or stained. Available in 2440 x 1220mm (8 x 4ft) sheets and in thicknesses

## MAKING BUTT JOINTS

**1** To make a box, take measurements and start by cutting the components to size. Use a circular saw or a jigsaw (saber saw).

**4** Reinforce a glued joint with nails driven in so that they pass into the centre of the panel underneath. Use a damp cloth to remove any excess adhesive.

ranging from 6 to 25mm ($\frac{1}{4}$ to 1in), MDF falls into the medium price range.

Those who are inexperienced in using power tools to make rebates (rabbets) and housing joints will be making boxes using glued butt joints, nailed or screwed for extra strength. These are adequate for small items, but will need reinforcing on larger pieces. The ideal way of doing this is with hardwood dowels. It is advisable to use dowels for chipboard, in which nails and even screws will not hold well. Alternatives, for light loads only, are special chipboard screws, or ordinary screws set in glued-in fibre wall plugs.

2 Label each piece in pencil and mark both halves of each joint with matching letters to avoid mix-ups during assembly.

3 To make a glued butt joint, spread adhesive along the edge of one component. Assemble the joint and clamp it to keep it square.

5 Screwed joints are stronger than nailed ones. Place the edge component against the face component and mark its position on the latter. Mark the screw positions carefully.

6 Drill clearance holes through the face component, then pilot holes in the edge component. Countersink the clearance holes and drive in chipboard (particle board) screws.

# USING DOWELS

**H**ardwood dowels are an effective means of reinforcing butt joints between panels, and you can buy them in various sizes. Since they are glued into blind holes, it is essential to allow glue to escape as they are pushed home. This can be achieved by sanding a "flat" along the length of the dowel or by using ready-grooved dowels.

Careful marking out and drilling is essential to ensure correct alignment of the dowel holes in adjacent panels. Various devices are available to make this possible. The simplest is the dowel pin. This is fitted into the dowel hole in one panel, which is pushed against the adjoining panel; a sharp point on the pin effectively marks the centre of the dowel hole in that panel, ensuring perfect alignment. Another method is a dowelling jig, which fits over the edges of the panels to align the holes.

**1** Draw a pencil line along the centre of the joint position, then align the two components carefully and mark corresponding dowel hole positions on both pieces.

**2** Drill the dowel holes in the face component, using a depth stop to avoid drilling too deep and breaking through the panel. Use a dowelling jig to drill holes in board edges.

**3** Insert glued dowels in the holes in the edge component, then glue this to the face component. Add more glue along the joint line to provide extra strength.

**4** A back panel will give any box extra strength, and also helps to resist skewing. Cut the panel fractionally undersize, then nail it in place, making sure the assembly is square first.

# FITTING FLUSH HINGES

Adding doors and drawers to a basic storage box will turn it into a cabinet or a chest. Doors can be hung on any one of the many types of hinge available, but two of the most versatile are the flush hinge and the concealed hinge. The former has one leaf fitting into a cut-out in the other, and so can be surface-mounted to the door edge and the frame, without the need to cut recesses.

These hinges have countersunk mounting screw holes in their leaves, so it is essential to buy screws that have heads that fit the countersinks exactly. If the heads are too big, they will prevent the screws from sitting flush with the faces of the hinge leaves and will stop the doors from closing.

1 Mark the hinge position on the door edge, then make pilot holes and screw the smaller flap to the door. Check that the hinge knuckle faces the right way.

2 Hold the door in position against the cabinet carcass, and mark the hinge position on it. Mark the screw holes too, then drill pilot holes for the screws.

3 Reposition the door and attach the larger hinge leaf to the carcass. Check the door alignment carefully, then attach the other hinge in the same way.

# FITTING CONCEALED HINGES

The concealed hinge is a little more complex to fit – the hinge body sits in a round hole bored in the rear face of the door, while the hinge arm is attached to a baseplate fitted to the side of the cabinet carcass – but it can be adjusted after fitting to ensure perfect alignment on multi-door installations.

Make in-out adjustments to the door by loosening the mounting screw and repositioning the door. Make side-to-side adjustments with the smaller screw.

1 Mark the centre line of the hinge baseplate on the side of the cabinet, then lay the door flat against the carcass and extend the line on to it.

2 Use a power drill fitted with an end mill, held in a drill stand, to bore the recess for the hinge body to the required depth in the rear face of the cabinet door.

3 Press the hinge body into the recess, check that the arm is at right angles to the door edge and make pilot holes for the fixing screws. Drive these in.

4 Next, attach the baseplate to the side of the cabinet, centred on the guideline drawn earlier. Check that it is fitted correctly.

5 Hold the door against the cabinet, slot the hinge arm over the screw on the baseplate and tighten the screw to lock the hinge arm in place.

# MAKING UP DRAWER KITS

When it comes to adding drawers to your cabinets, the simplest solution is to use plastic drawer kits. These consist of moulded sections that interlock to form the sides and back of the drawer, special corner blocks to allow a drawer front of any chosen material to be attached, and a base (usually a piece of enamelled hardboard). The drawer sides are grooved to fit over plastic runners that are screwed to the cabinet sides. The sides, back and base can be cut down to size if necessary.

1 Cut the sides and back to size if necessary, then stick the side and back sections together, using the clips and adhesive provided in the kit.

2 Cut the base down in size too if the drawer size was altered. Then slide the panel into place in the grooves in the side and back sections.

3 Screw the two corner joint blocks to the inner face of the drawer front, stick on the drawer base support channel, and glue the front to the ends of the side sections.

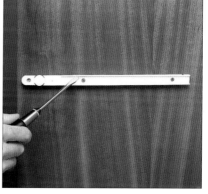

4 Hold the drawer within the cabinet to mark the positions of its side grooves on the side walls. Then attach the plastic drawer runners with the screws provided.

# FITTING BUILT-IN WARDROBES

The walls of a room can be used to create larger storage spaces. These can range from filling in an alcove, through a unit in the corner of a room, to one running right across the room to the opposite wall. If the room has a central chimney breast (fireplace projection) with an alcove at each side, both alcoves can be used for storage and the chimney breast can be concealed with dummy doors.

In each case, the most important part is a frame to support the doors; these can be hinged conventionally or suspended from ceiling-mounted track. Remember that hinged doors allow unlimited access, but need floor space in front of them so they can be opened easily. Sliding doors do not need this floor space, but they do have the minor disadvantage that access to the interior is sometimes restricted – when one door is open, it blocks access to the next section.

Such a flexible structure affords an opportunity to meet storage needs precisely. Start by selecting the depth needed for clothes to hang freely on hanging rails, then work out what width should be given to hanging space and what to shelving, drawers or basket space for storing other items of clothing. Shoe racks can be added at floor level.

Doors can be made into a feature of the room, or painted or covered to blend unobtrusively with the room's colour scheme. Large flat-surfaced doors become almost invisible if decorated with a wallcovering.

1 Screw a track support strip to the ceiling joists, levelling it with packing, then add the top track. Leave a gap at the wall for the side upright.

4 Use a spirit (carpenter's) level to check that the upright is vertical, mark its position on the wall and drill the clearance and fixing holes.

7 Hang each door by engaging the hanger wheels on the track as shown and lowering the door to the vertical position. Finally, fit the floor guides provided.

2 Hold the lengths of wood that will form the side frame uprights against the wall, and mark on them the profile of the skirting (baseboard).

3 Use a coping saw or power jigsaw (saber saw) to cut away the waste wood from the foot of the upright, then test fit against the wall.

5 Realign the upright with the positioning marks made earlier and screw it to the wall. Repeat the process at the other side of the opening.

6 Cut the doors to size if necessary, allowing for clearances or overlaps as required in the door gear instructions, then fit the door hangers.

8 Conceal the track and door hangers by pinning (tacking) a decorative moulding to the track support batten. Some tracks come complete with a metal pelmet strip.

9 Finish off the installation by pinning slim wooden mouldings to the front edges of the side uprights. These hide any slight gaps when the doors are closed.

# FITTING CLOTHES ORGANIZERS

In both freestanding and built-in wardrobes, best use of the interior space can be made by creating tailor-made hanging and shelving sections. Clothes organizers of this kind can be professionally made to measure, but in fact they can be constructed from the simplest of materials, at a great saving in cost. A wardrobe up to 2400mm (8ft) wide can be "organized" with just four standard lengths of veneered or plastic-coated chipboard (particle board), a length of clothes pole and some 75 x 25mm (3 x 1in) wood to act as shelf supports.

Start by marking and cutting out the components. All are 300mm (12in) wide. There are two uprights 1930mm (6 ft 4in) long, two shelves long enough to span the wardrobe or alcove, and six small shelves 300mm (12in) square. Sand all the cut edges.

Next, cut two sets of shelf supports to fit the back and side walls of the wardrobe or alcove. Nail or screw the first supports in place so that their top edges are 2140mm (7ft) above the floor. Add the second set 1930mm (6ft 4in) above the floor. Then make up the central shelf unit, using the two uprights and the six small shelves, spacing these to suit the storage requirements. Notch the top rear corners of the unit so that they will fit around the lower shelf support, and stand it in place. Add the lower shelf first, then the upper one, and complete the unit by adding upper (and, if desired, lower) hanging rails at each side of the central unit.

1 Fix the upper set of shelf supports to the sides and back of the wardrobe or alcove, with their top edges 2140mm (7ft) above floor level.

4 Mark the height of the uprights and the length of the shelves required on the components. Square cutting lines across them, using a try square.

7 Stand the unit against the back of the wardrobe or alcove. Mark the position of the lower shelf support on the uprights. Cut notches to fit around the support.

2 Add the lower set of shelf supports with their top edges 1930mm (6ft 4in) above floor level. Check that they are all horizontal.

3 Next, cut the components to width, using a circular saw with a fence or a guide strip clamped across it to keep the cuts straight.

5 Cut the shelves and uprights to the lengths required with the circular saw. Then cut the six small squares for the central shelf unit.

6 Make the central shelf unit by gluing and nailing or screwing the shelves between the uprights. Space the shelves as required.

8 Reposition the central shelf unit, then lay the lower shelf on its supports. Drill pilot holes, then nail or screw down through it into the supports and the shelf unit.

9 Fit hangers to support the clothes rail beneath the lower shelf. Add a second lower rail if wished. Complete the unit by fixing the top shelf to its supports.

# STORAGE PROJECTS

Although storage units are functional, they can often be attractive too. On the following pages you will find three simple storage projects that are just that. A magazine rack is a must for any home, providing a place for newspapers and magazines that have yet to be read. The rack shown has a large capacity, but can be folded up and stored when not needed. A small double-shelf wall unit will have many uses around the home, for books, ornaments and the like. It is made from board and trimmed with decorative moulding. Finally, there is an unusual sloping CD rack, which can be made from wood left over from other projects.

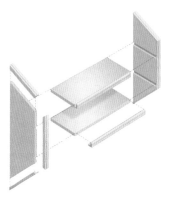

# MAGAZINE RACK

This folding rack takes little time to construct and uses a few basic techniques. There are no joints to make, and no expensive tools are required; all you need are the basics of accurate marking out, cutting and fitting together. The interlocking design allows the rack to be opened up or folded flat and stowed away, with no need for clips or catches.

The rack consists of two separate assemblies that form the sides. One slides inside the other and is attached with the two bolts that form the pivot mechanism. It can be made to any convenient size, but if you follow the diagrams, you will not have to calculate the dimensions and angles required for

## Materials

- 2.7m (9ft) of 50 x 25mm (2 x 1in) planed (dressed) softwood for the legs
- 4.2m (14ft) of 75 x 12mm (3 x ½in) planed (dressed) softwood for the slats
- 6mm (¼in) MDF (medium-density fiberboard) for the template
- 16 25mm (1in) brass woodscrews
- 2 50mm (2in) brass woodscrews
- Panel pin (brad)
- 2 65mm (2½in) coachbolts (carriage bolts), nuts and washers
- Thin cord

the legs. Draw it out full size on plywood or MDF (medium-density fiberboard) to create a template for marking out.

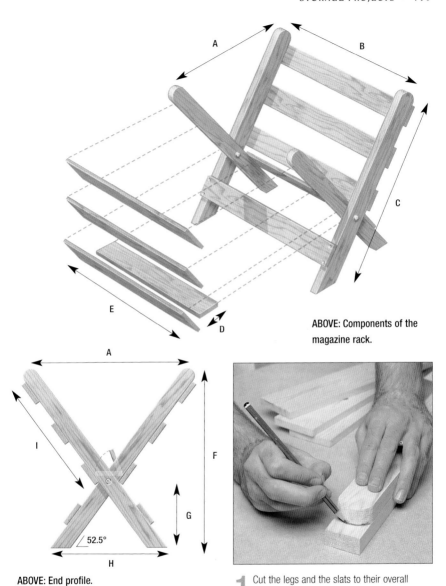

A

B

C

D

E

ABOVE: Components of the magazine rack.

A

I

F

G

52.5°

H

ABOVE: End profile.

KEY

| | | | |
|---|---|---|---|
| A | 510mm (20in) | E | 435mm (17⅛in) |
| B | 490mm (19¼in) | F | 520mm (20½in) |
| C | 660mm (26in) | G | 190mm (7½in) |
| D | 75mm (3in) | H | 345mm (13½in) |
| | | I | 400mm (16in) |

**1** Cut the legs and the slats to their overall length. The slats for the inner frame are 55mm (2⅛in) shorter than those used for the outer frame, allowing them to slide easily within the latter. Cut a rounded profile at the top of each leg if wished, using the first as a pattern for the others so that they will be uniform. ▶

**2** Lay each pair of legs in turn over the template drawn on a sheet of MDF (medium-density fiberboard) and mark the positions of the slats and pivot point. Support the upper leg with an offcut (scrap) of wood to keep it level. Drill a pilot hole through the pivot point of each leg at this stage.

**3** Assemble the inner frame. Insert one screw at each end of the top slat, then use a try square to adjust the assembly before you proceed. It is essential that the frames are absolutely square. Make sure the ends of the slats do not protrude over the sides of the frame.

**6** Use two small offcuts of 12mm (½in) thick wood at each side to support the outer legs at the correct level. Screw the top and third slats in place on the outer legs, checking that they are square as before. All four legs of the rack should be parallel with each other to allow the assembly to open and close freely without any binding. If necessary, make adjustments.

**7** Turn the assembly over to fit the bottom slat. At this stage, the two frames should enclose each other, but they can still be slid apart if required. Now is a good time to clean up any rough edges with medium-grade abrasive paper, wrapped around a cork sanding block, before proceeding. You could also apply a coat of clear sealer or varnish at this stage.

4 Add the third slat, then turn the frame over to attach the bottom slat. The final assembly will be easier if you omit the second slat at this stage; it can be added when the rack is bolted together. Three slats are sufficient at this stage to keep the assembly square.

5 Use the inner frame as a building jig for the outer frame. Position the components carefully, making sure that the pivot holes are in line. Insert a small panel pin (brad) to keep the legs aligned as you work. Note how the angled ends of the legs face in opposite directions.

8 Drill through the legs for the coachbolts (carriage bolts), using the pilot holes to guide the drill bit. Fit a coachbolt to each side, inserting a large washer between the moving parts to reduce the amount of friction. Fit the nuts on the inside, but do not over-tighten them or you will distort the framework. Note how the bottom slat on the outer frame will act as a stop to hold the rack open.

9 Insert the bottom piece, which acts as a floor for the rack. Cut it to fit between the legs of the inner frame and attach with two long brass screws. It should pivot easily, allowing the rack to be folded flat for storage. Add the remaining two slats. Fix a couple of lengths of thin cord between the bottom slats as a final touch to secure the legs in their open position.

# BOOKSHELF

**M**anufactured boards with veneered faces, sometimes called decorative boards, can make quick work of any project. However, the exposed edges of veneered plywood and MDF (medium-density fiberboard) are vulnerable to damage and not at all attractive. To overcome this drawback, you can buy solid wood trim to match most common types of veneer, or you can make your own if you have the right tools. This bookshelf was made from boards veneered with American white oak, edged with darker oak trim.

The dimensions of this small shelf unit are provided as a guide only. You can alter them to suit your own books

### Materials

- 760 x 610mm (30 x 24in) of 12mm (½in) veneered plywood or MDF (medium-density fiberboard)
- 2.7m (9ft) of 19mm (¾in) angled moulding for edge trim
- PVA (white) wood glue
- Panel pins (brads)

or any other items you may wish to display. A suitable height for most paperbacks is 205–255mm (8–10in). Bear in mind that 12mm (½in) boards will sag under heavy loads if you make the shelves too wide. Restrict unsupported widths to 600m (24in).

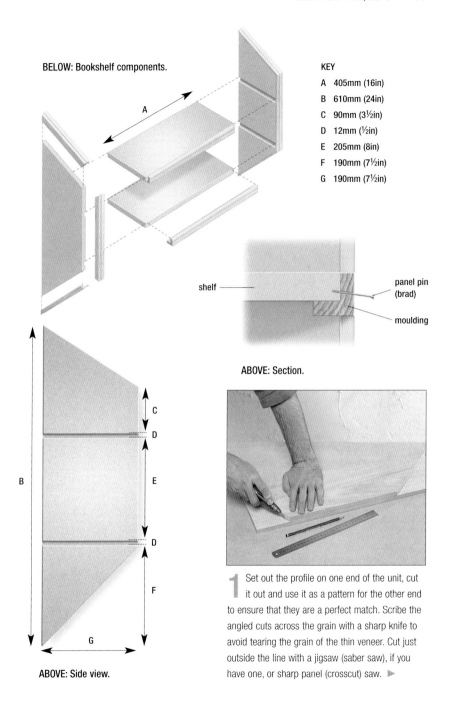

BELOW: Bookshelf components.

KEY

A   405mm (16in)
B   610mm (24in)
C   90mm (3½in)
D   12mm (½in)
E   205mm (8in)
F   190mm (7½in)
G   190mm (7½in)

shelf

panel pin (brad)

moulding

ABOVE: Section.

ABOVE: Side view.

Set out the profile on one end of the unit, cut it out and use it as a pattern for the other end to ensure that they are a perfect match. Scribe the angled cuts across the grain with a sharp knife to avoid tearing the grain of the thin veneer. Cut just outside the line with a jigsaw (saber saw), if you have one, or sharp panel (crosscut) saw. ▶

**2** Clamp the angled ends in a vice so that they are horizontal, then plane them down to the scribed lines with a block plane. Work with the grain angled away from you to avoid damaging the veneer. The block plane, with a finely set, sharp blade, is the ideal tool for working this material.

**3** Form the housings for the shelves with a router, running it along a straightedge pinned (tacked) to the inner face. To ensure accuracy, clamp the two ends together and cut the grooves in one operation. Pin a strip of scrap wood to the board edge to prevent breakout at the end of the groove.

**6** Sash clamps are ideal for holding the assembly steady while pinning the shelves in place. Small panel pins (brads) are sufficient for a small unit such as this. Check that all corners are square – measuring the diagonals is the easiest way of doing this; they should be equal – and leave overnight for the glue to set. Note the small scraps of wood inserted beneath the clamp heads to protect the veneer.

**7** Cut two lengths of decorative angled moulding to trim the front edges of the shelves. The moulding shown has a small shadow line, or "quirk", running along its length. This is designed to help conceal the heads of the panel pins after they have been punched down with a nail punch. When buying mouldings for this purpose, always check that their design provides a means of concealing the fixings.

4 The boards can vary in thickness depending on the type of veneer. It is not always possible to match the size of board exactly to the diameter of the router cutter. If necessary, plane small rebates (rabbets) on the underside of each shelf until it fits the grooves perfectly.

5 Apply glue to the housings and slot the unit together. It is good practice to use the glue sparingly. Any excess will have to be removed completely to prevent discoloration of the veneer at the finishing stage. Wipe off with a slightly damp cloth, and avoid rubbing glue into the grain.

8 The same moulding is used to trim the end panels. Mitre the ends at the corners with a tenon saw or adjustable mitre saw. To determine the angle for the mitred corners, place a short section of moulding in position and use it to mark pencil lines on the end panel, parallel to the front edges. Draw a line from the corner to the point of intersection to bisect the angle exactly. Use this as a guide for setting an adjustable bevel gauge.

9 Apply PVA (white) wood glue to the front edges of the end panels and pin (tack) the mouldings in place. Notice how the minimum of glue has been used. This is to prevent any excess from being squeezed on to the veneer surface when the pins are punched in with the nail punch. When the glue has dried, apply coloured stopping to each pinhole before sanding smooth all over, ready for finishing.

# CD RACK

The idea for this compact disc storage system came about because a piece of cherry wood, with distinctive figure in the grain, and a short offcut (scrap) of waney-edged yew with an interesting shape was left over in the workshop. You can use any type of wood, of course, possibly something left over from another job. With a little imagination, you can turn short lengths of wood into all manner of items.

The design is simplicity itself – it uses the cantilever principle to support the weight of the CDs. A width of 255mm (10in) will allow two columns to be stacked side by side. The rack can be any height you like, provided the base is wide enough to make it stable.

## Materials

- 760mm (30in) of 125 x 25mm (5 x 1in) hardwood for the rack
- 760mm (30in) of 25 x 12mm (1 x ½in) hardwood for the sides
- 280mm (11in) of 150 x 19mm (6 x ¾in) hardwood for the base
- PVA (white) wood glue
- Brass panel pins (brads)

As a guide, ensure that the top of the rack, inclined at 10 degrees, is vertically above the back edge of the base. The diagram shows how to set out the ingenious dovetailed housing joint that holds the unit together.

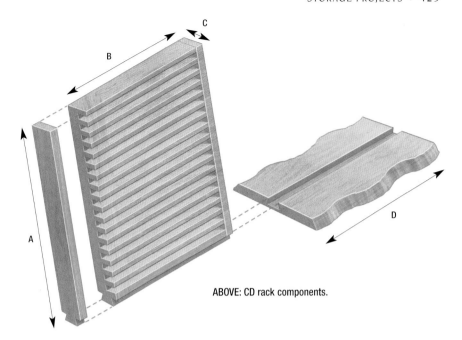

ABOVE: CD rack components.

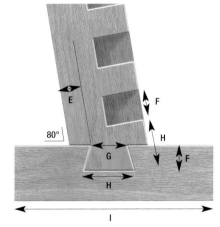

ABOVE: Section.

80°

**KEY**

| | |
|---|---|
| A | 370mm (14½in) |
| B | 255mm (10in) |
| C | 25mm (1in) |
| D | 280mm (11in) |
| E | 6mm (¼in) |
| F | 9mm (⅜in) |
| G | 12mm (½in) |
| H | 19mm (¾in) |
| I | 150mm (6in) |

1 Cut the 125 x 25mm (5 x 1in) hardwood into two pieces 370mm (14½in) long for the main portion of the rack. Plane the edges square, glue and clamp them together. Simple butt joints are sufficient in this case. To make sure that the board remains absolutely flat, clamp a stout batten over the top of the assembly before finally tightening the sash clamps. ▶

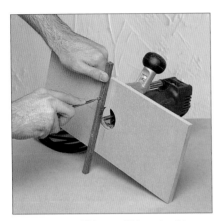

**2** Use a 9mm (⅜in) router bit to rout a slot 19mm (¾in) up from the bottom edge. Make a routing jig for the other slots by fixing a 9mm (⅜in) strip of hardwood to the router base, 9mm (⅜in) from the cutter's edge.

**3** It is a simple matter to run the hardwood strip along each slot to position the next groove correctly. Continue in this way to the end of the board. Make sure the work is clamped firmly to the bench when doing this, or use a bench stop.

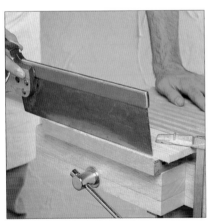

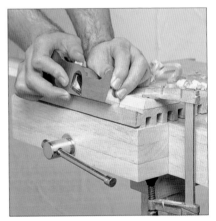

**6** Use the same template to mark out the bottom edge of the main upright. Scribe the shoulders along its length with a marking gauge, and clamp a straightedge along the shoulder line to guide the tenon saw. Keep the saw blade perfectly level to ensure the shoulders are straight and parallel.

**7** To form the tail on the upright, plane the required angle on a scrap piece of wood to make an accurate guide for a small shoulder plane. Use a paring chisel to remove the waste from the corners. The angles are different on each face because of the sloping profile and should match those on the two side pieces.

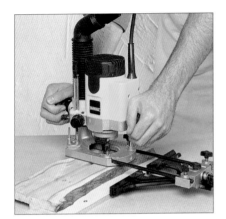

4 Use a dovetail cutter to rout the housing groove in the base. To deal with a waney edge, pin a straight-edged piece of plywood to the underside and run the router fence along it. Screw it down to the work surface so that it cannot move.

5 Cut the tails on the two side pieces with a fine dovetail saw. Use a bevel gauge to set the shoulders at an angle of 10 degrees. Then make a small template to mark the shape of the tails to suit the profile of the dovetail groove.

8 Plane the bottom edge of the tail to the required angle to complete the joint, paring it down until the tail achieves a good sliding fit in the housing. Before fitting the side pieces, you should clean up each groove with a small sanding block. Make this from a thin strip of wood and wrap it with abrasive paper.

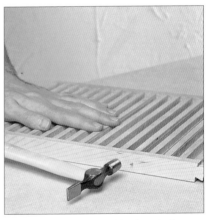

9 Pin (tack) and glue the side pieces to the upright, using small brass panel pins (brads). Align the dovetails accurately and position the pins so that they avoid the slots. Apply glue to the dovetailed housing in the base and slide the rack into place. Wipe off excess glue with a damp cloth. When the glue is dry, apply the desired finish.

# HOME
# REPAIRS

- Repairing walls & ceilings
- Repairing windows & doors
- Repairing floors & stairs

# INTRODUCTION

**W**here your home is concerned, prevention is often better, and certainly less expensive, than cure. A regular programme of inspection and maintenance will prevent small problems from becoming large and costly ones. From time to time, however, repairs will be necessary, and their successful completion depends on having all the relevant tools and equipment to hand, and understanding how to use them.

The following pages will guide you through a wide range of common repairs that may be needed to walls, ceilings, doors, windows, floors and stairs, showing you a variety of simple techniques for achieving professional results. By following its advice, and applying a little forethought, care and patience, you will not only save money, but will also have the satisfaction of knowing that you have done the jobs yourself. Moreover, the basic skills you learn will provide a core of knowledge that should give you the confidence to tackle more ambitious do-it-yourself projects.

**PREPARATION**

When beginning a repair job, be sure that everything is to hand; it is no use beginning to repair a wall, then finding that you are too short to reach the top and that you need to go looking for a trestle or a pair of steps. All your

LEFT: A beautiful home will stay that way only if it is well looked after. Sooner or later, however, repairs will be necessary; the various tasks shown on the following pages will help you to keep your home looking pristine.

RIGHT: The secret of success for any do-it-yourself job is preparation and planning. Before you start your repair job, lay out all the materials and equipment that you will be using, and try to keep your workplace tidy.

tools and equipment should be well prepared and in position. It is also important to keep your workplace tidy, and do not allow children or pets into areas where power tools or strong solvents are being used.

## PROTECTIVE CLOTHING

When doing repair jobs around the home, wear old clothes or overalls, and knee pads if you are laying, stripping or varnishing floors. If removing glass from windows, always wear a pair of industrial gloves, and a dust mask is essential when sawing and sanding wood.

## FIRST AID

It is inevitable that minor cuts and abrasions will occur at some point, so a basic first aid kit is an essential for the home or workshop. Keep your kit in a prominent position ready for use. If any of the contents are used, replace them immediately.

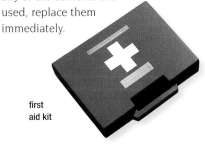

first aid kit

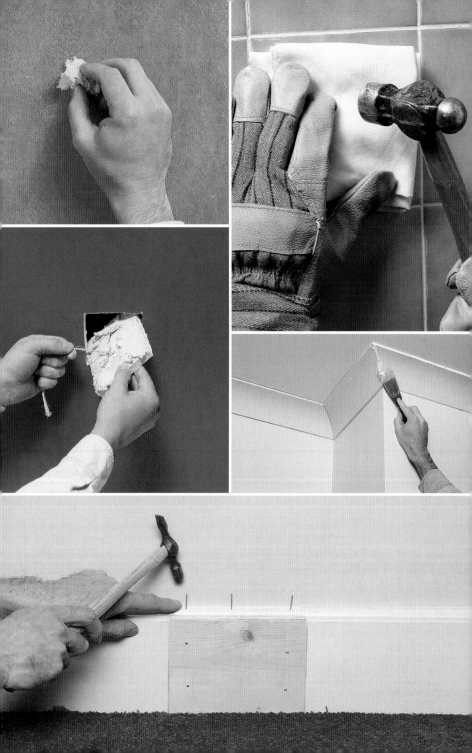

# REPAIRING WALLS & CEILINGS

Most walls and ceilings have some form of plaster surface, whether it be plaster on a backing of wooden laths or plasterboard (gypsum board) on a wooden framework. This rigid material may suffer from cracking and damage due to building settlement or accidental impact. Fortunately, this is relatively easy to repair, either with a filler material or a plasterboard patch. Walls also feature wooden skirtings (baseboards) and decorative architraves (trims) around door openings. These, too, can become damaged and may need repairing or replacing. The following pages show you how to do a range of wall and ceiling repair jobs, as well as how to use coving (crown molding) to hide ceiling-to-wall joints.

# PREPARATION AND MINOR REPAIRS

Walls and ceilings need to be prepared carefully so that the surfaces are in as good a condition as possible. The better the surface, the better the new finish.

If the room was papered originally, the first job is to remove all the old wallcovering. With vinyl, it should be possible to peel off the outer layer to leave the backing behind. If this is in good condition, you can paper over it again, but if you wish to paint the walls, it should be removed too.

Painted surfaces can be painted over, but make sure that any loose or flaking paint is removed first. Then you can begin to repair any cracks or other damage in the surfaces.

A general-purpose filler can be used for the majority of cracks in ceilings and walls. This comes ready-mixed in tubs or as a powder for mixing with water. Simply apply the filler with a filling or putty knife, pressing it into the cracks and smoothing it flush with the surface. Some cracks need enlarging slightly to give the filler something to grip; fine cracks can be filled with special hairline-crack filler.

Normal fillers are quite adequate if you are papering the ceiling or wall, but for paint, a fine surface filler is better. Most fillers take a short while to dry, after which they can be sanded flush with the surrounding surface.

1 Strip wallcoverings by soaking them with water or by using a steam stripper, then remove with scrapers. Peel off the top layer of vinyl types to leave the backing behind.

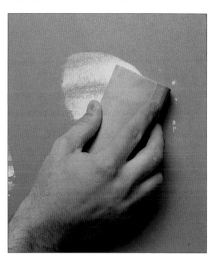

4 When dry, sand the filled area smooth with fine abrasive paper. On flat surfaces, wrap the abrasive paper around a sanding block. You may need to add more filler to fill any remaining defects.

2 Remove flaking paint with a scraper. Take care not to dig the blade into soft surfaces. Feather the edges of the sound paint by sanding lightly. This will disguise them under the new finish.

3 Fill any cracks and gaps in plasterwork with all-purpose filler. Press the filler firmly into the gap and finish off by leaving it slightly proud of the surrounding surface.

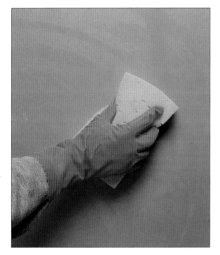

5 Give the walls a thorough wash with a solution of sugar soap (all-purpose cleaner). This will remove all dust and grease. Allow the liquid to dry completely before decorating the wall.

6 Using a squeegee mop to clean ceilings will allow you to work at ground level. Make sure you spread dust sheets (drop cloths) on the floor to protect it from drips.

# FILLING HOLES IN PLASTER

Small holes, especially those left by screws, can be filled in the same way as cracks. Cut off any protruding wall plugs or, better still, remove them altogether so that you can obtain a smooth finish.

Larger holes are more of a problem. The kind of hole left by removing a waste pipe from a wall can be made good with do-it-yourself repair plaster, which can usually be applied in layers up to 50mm (2in) thick. Smaller recesses up to 20mm (¾in) deep can be treated with a special deep-gap filler, while really deep cavities can be filled with an expanding foam filler. Once set, this can be cut and sanded smooth, then painted or papered over. If an area of plaster has fallen off the wall, use a repair plaster, levelling it with the surrounding sound plaster with a straight length of wood.

For larger areas, nail wooden battens to the wall. These should be equal in depth to the surrounding original plaster. By running a long wooden straightedge up the battens, using a sawing action, you will be able to level off the fresh plaster to the correct depth. When the plaster has set partially, the battens can be prised from the wall and the resulting gaps in the plaster filled.

You may need to divide a really large area of wall into workable "bays" using this technique.

ABOVE: Use a paintbrush to remove dust from holes and deep cracks prior to filling, then rinse and work the damp bristles into the hole. This will prevent moisture from being sucked from the filler, which would cause it to dry too quickly, weakening it and leading to poor adhesion.

ABOVE: Use a repair plaster for a deep hole, applied with a plasterer's trowel. Work the plaster well into the hole and smooth it off flush with the surrounding surface. Allow to dry slightly, then polish smooth with a wet trowel.

# REPAIRING LATH-AND-PLASTER

Holes in lath-and-plaster ceilings and walls can be repaired in the same way as holes in normal plastered surfaces, provided the laths are intact.

First brush the laths with diluted PVA (white) glue to reduce absorbency, then repair with general-purpose filler, deep-gap filler or repair plaster.

If the laths have broken, cut back the plaster until you expose the vertical studs. Cut a piece of plasterboard (gypsum board) to size and nail it in place before filling the hole.

If the damage covers a large area, it may be necessary to nail battens between the studs or joists to support the long edges of the patch. Nail them in place so that the nails project halfway into the opening.

This sort of repair can also be made using expanded aluminium mesh to support the repair plaster.

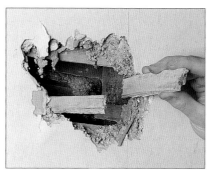

**1** If the wood laths are split or broken, pull them away from the surface. Remove any loose sections of plaster.

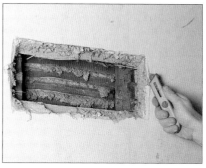

**2** Continue cutting back the old plaster and the laths behind it to expose the studs or ceiling joists at each side of the hole. Square off the edges.

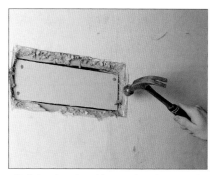

**3** Cut a plasterboard (gypsum board) patch to fit the hole, and nail it in place. Add two support strips if the panel is large.

**4** Complete the repair by plastering over the patch after filling and taping the cut edges all around. Polish the repair with a steel float.

# REPAIRING PLASTERBOARD

Surface damage and small holes in plasterboard (gypsum board) can be repaired in the same way as cracks and holes in solid plaster, but if a large hole has been punched in the material – by a door handle, for example – a different solution is required. In this case, a patch must be placed behind the hole to provide support for a layer of filler.

First, use a padsaw to open out the hole, squaring the sides. Then cut a section of fresh plasterboard to a length slightly less than the diagonal dimension of the hole. This will allow you to pass it through the hole at an angle. Drill a tiny hole in the middle of the plasterboard patch and pass a piece of knotted string through it before adding filler or coving (crown molding) adhesive to the edges on the grey side of the plasterboard. This will secure it firmly to the back of the existing plasterboard panel.

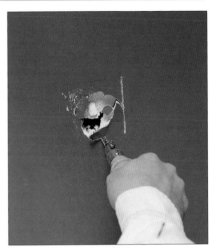

**1** Use a padsaw to square up a hole in damaged plasterboard (gypsum board). Keep the size of the hole to the minimum necessary to accommodate the damaged plasterboard.

Pass the patch through the hole and pull it back against the edges. Hold the string taut while adding filler to the hole, then leave this to set. Cut off the projecting string and make good with a final smooth coat of general-purpose filler or finish plaster, ensuring the surface is level.

If the area of damage in a plasterboard wall or ceiling is substantial, it is much more sensible to work back to the nearest studs or joists, using a padsaw to cut the cladding flush with the wood. Then nail 50mm (2in) square noggings between the studs or joists so that they project halfway into the opening. Nail 50 x 25mm (2 x 1in) battens to the studs or joists, flush with the faces of the noggings.

Cut a patch of plasterboard to fill the opening and nail this to the noggings and battens, using galvanized plasterboard nails.

Apply a layer of filler around the edges of the patch, bedding jointing tape into it as you go. Feather the edges with a damp sponge and apply another layer when it has dried to leave a perfect surface.

**2** Attach a piece of string to the patch, knotting it at the back so that it cannot be pulled through the hole. It may help to insert a galvanized nail through the knot for extra security.

**3** Butter the back of the patch with a layer of filler or coving (crown molding) adhesive, making sure the edges are covered and keeping the free end of the string out of the way.

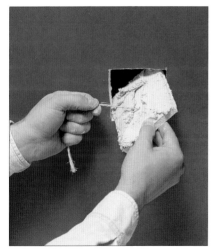

**4** Pass the plasterboard patch through the hole while holding the free end of the string. Use the string to pull the patch firmly against the back of the existing plasterboard surface.

**5** Add more filler or repair plaster to the hole while holding the patch tightly in place with the string. Leave the filler just below the surface of the wall and add a final thin layer when it has set.

# REPLACING SKIRTINGS

Skirtings (baseboards) protect wall surfaces at floor level from accidental damage. They can be plain or ornate, and can be painted, stained or varnished. They may need replacing if they are damaged or simply look unfashionable.

Skirtings are often fixed directly to masonry walls with large cut nails in older homes, or with masonry nails in more recent ones. Alternatively, they may be nailed to rough timber fixing blocks or grounds (furrings), which are themselves nailed to the masonry. Boards fixed to blocks are much easier to remove than those nailed directly to the wall, since both cut and masonry nails can have a ferocious grip. In the latter situation, it is often easier to punch the nails through the boards and into the walls than to try to prise them out. Boards on wood-framed walls are simply nailed to the frame and are easy to remove.

Provided the correct profile is available, small lengths of skirting can be replaced by levering the damaged section from the wall with a crowbar (wrecking bar), holding it clear of the wall with wooden wedges and sawing down through the moulding at each side of the damage with a tenon saw. For best results, the cuts should be made at 45 degrees with the aid of a mitre box, and the ends of the new piece cut in the same manner so that they overlap. Nails should be driven through the overlaps into wooden supporting blocks behind.

1 To replace a small area of damaged skirting (baseboard), prise it away from the wall slightly, wedge it and use a tenon saw and mitre box to cut out a section.

4 Nail the replacement board to the support blocks. If using plain wood, pin (tack) on decorative mouldings to build up a close match to the existing board.

2 Nail small support blocks behind the cut ends of the board, using masonry nails in brick and block walls, and then nail the cut ends to the support blocks.

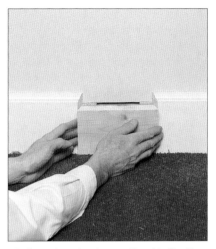

3 Cut a piece of replacement board to fit, with its ends mitred to match the cut ends of the original board. Use plain wood if the skirting profile cannot be matched.

5 When replacing whole lengths, use mitre joints at external corners. Fix the first length, then mark the inside of the mitre on the back of the next board.

6 Cut the mitre joints with a power saw. At internal corners, fit the first length right into the corner. Then scribe its profile on to the second board; cut this with a coping saw, and fit it.

# REPLACING ARCHITRAVES

Architraves (trims) are used around door and window openings to frame the opening and disguise the joint between the frame and the wall surface. Like skirtings (baseboards), they may need replacing if they are damaged or unfashionable.

Architraves are pinned (tacked) in place to the edges of the door or window frame. It is an easy job to prise the trims away with a bolster (stonecutter's chisel) without causing undue damage to the frame or the surrounding wall surface.

Once the old architrave has been removed, the edges of the wooden lining of the opening should be tidied up by scraping off ridges of old paint and filler.

Take careful measurements when cutting the new architrave, bearing in mind that mitred joints are normally used where the uprights meet the horizontal section above the opening.

If the new moulding is particularly ornate, it could be difficult to obtain neat joints, and you may prefer to add decorative corner blocks instead. These could also be fitted at the bottoms of the uprights if they are narrower than the originals and will not meet the skirtings.

Fit the new sections of architrave 6mm ($\frac{1}{4}$in) back from the edges of the lining of the opening.

1 Prise off the old mouldings. They should come away easily. If necessary, lever against a wooden block to avoid damaging the wall.

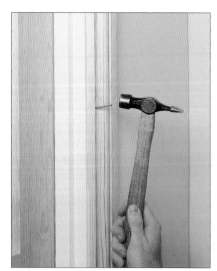

4 Fix the uprights to the frame by driving in nails at 300mm (12in) intervals. Recess the heads with a nail punch and fill the holes later.

2 Hold an upright against the frame so that the inside of the mitre joint can be marked on it. Repeat for the other upright.

3 Cut the end of the moulding, using a mitre block or box. Alternatively, mark the line across the moulding with a protractor or combination square.

5 Hold the top piece above the two uprights to mark the position for the mitre cut at each end. Make the cuts as before and test the piece for fit.

6 Nail the top piece to the frame, checking that the mitre joints are aligned accurately. Then drive a nail through each corner to secure the joint.

# HIDING CEILING-TO-WALL JOINTS

Coving (crown molding), a quadrant-shaped moulding made from polystyrene, plaster or wood can be fitted between the walls and ceiling of a room. It has two functions: to be decorative and to conceal unsightly joints between the walls and ceiling. An ornate coving may be referred to as a cornice; old plaster cornices may be clogged with several layers of paint and need cleaning to reveal the detail.

Coving normally comes in long lengths and you will find it easier to fit if you have someone on hand to help place it in position. Where lengths meet at corners, the ends should be mitred for neat joints. The manufacturer may provide a cutting template; if not, use a large mitre box.

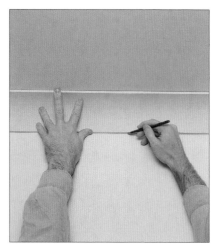

1 Mark guidelines on the ceiling and wall, using the dimensions given by the manufacturer. Alternatively, use a length of coving as a guide, but take care always to hold it at the same angle.

## PREPARING LENGTHS OF COVING

1 Measure the coving (crown molding) required for each run and cut it to length with a fine-toothed saw. Mitre the ends, using a large mitre box, where they will meet at internal and external corners.

2 Mix enough adhesive for one length of coving at a time, otherwise it may become unusable. Butter the back edges of the coving with a liberal amount of adhesive.

2 Using the point of a trowel, score the surface of the ceiling and wall between the parallel lines. This will provide a key (scuffed surface) for the adhesive, ensuring a good grip.

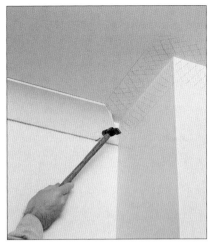

3 Press the coving into place, aligning it carefully with the guidelines. Support the coving with nails driven partially into the wall below its bottom edge; remove them when the adhesive has set.

4 Continue the coving on the adjacent wall, carefully aligning the mitred ends of the two lengths. Any slight gaps between them can be filled later.

5 Complete the external corner with another length of coving, butting the ends together. Fill any gaps at external and internal angles with cellulose filler and sand down once dry.

# REPAIRING WINDOWS & DOORS

Because of their design and purpose, windows and doors can be subject to considerable wear and tear. Most are made of wood, which can become distorted with age and/or exposure to damp conditions. The latter can cause extensive damage to external doors and windows if they are not well maintained. Windows, and sometimes doors, also have the added weakness of glass. Being very brittle, this is easily broken, and knowing how to replace panels of glass yourself can save you a lot of money. Hinges can be a source of trouble in both windows and doors. Their screws can loosen, preventing the window or door from opening freely, and they can cause squeaks, rattles and binding. All of these problems are easily fixed.

# REMOVING WINDOW GLASS

Removing broken window glass is a common do-it-yourself job, and something that is worth learning how to do properly.

Make sure you wear thick gloves that cover your wrists. Lay newspapers on the ground on both sides of the window. Collect the glass in newspaper or a cardboard box and dispose of it safely; your glass supplier may accept the broken pieces for recycling.

An old chisel can be used to chop out the old putty – do not use a good one, as its blade will be damaged by the sprigs (or clips in a metal frame) that hold the glass in place. Pull out the sprigs or clips and remove all the putty from the recess.

> **TIP**
>
> When removing broken glass from a window, apply a criss-cross pattern of adhesive tape to the pane to prevent the glass from flying around. For extra safety, grip the broken slivers of glass with a pair of pincers or pliers and pull them from the frame. Don't knock them out with a hammer.

1 Remove the broken glass, wearing gloves to prevent cuts.

2 Use an old chisel to remove the putty from the edges of the rebate (rabbet).

3 Pull out the glazing sprigs with pincers. Then remove the remnants of glass and putty.

# REPLACING LEADED LIGHTS

Replacing the glass in a leaded-light window is a little trickier than working with normal window panes. That said, it is a task well within the scope of anyone with patience and a practical frame of mind.

Many leaded-light windows will have one or more panes of coloured glass, so these will need to be replaced.

The best place to look for authentic coloured replacements is in an architectural salvage yard. A glass merchant can cut a piece of old glass down to size for you.

You will also need a really sharp trimming knife to cut through the lead cames at the corners, and a soldering iron to fuse the lead together.

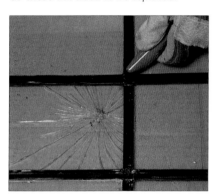

1 Use a sharp trimming knife to cut through the cames at the corners at 45 degrees.

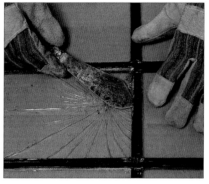

2 Lever up and fold back the cames all around the pane to remove the old glass.

3 With the new glass in place, press the cames back into place with a seam roller.

4 Fuse the lead together at the corners using a small electric soldering iron.

# REPLACING WINDOW PANES

The first stage in replacing a window pane is to measure the size of the glass needed and then buy the new pane. Your supplier will be able to cut the glass to fit.

## MEASURING UP

Take measurements of the width and height of the recess in several places. The size of glass you need is 3mm (⅛in) less than the size of the recess. If in doubt, cut a cardboard template to fit and take this with you to the glass supplier. Reckon on buying some new glazing sprigs or clips to hold the glass in place, and buy the correct putty for either wooden or metal windows.

## PUTTING IN THE NEW GLASS

Take a small amount of putty and work it in your hands until it is pliable; if it sticks to your fingers, roll it out on newspaper to remove some of the oil. When it is workable, begin pressing a layer into the window recess, squeezing it out of the palm of your hand between thumb and forefinger rather like toothpaste.

Put the glass in place, resting it on a couple of wooden matches, and press it gently into the opening until putty is squeezed out at the back – press against the sides of the glass, not the centre. Then fit the glazing sprigs to hold the glass, sliding the head of the hammer across the surface of the glass,

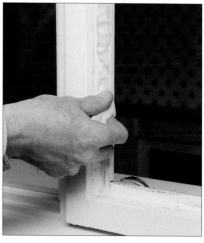

**1** Knead the putty in your hands until it becomes workable. Then squeeze a thin layer into the rebate (rabbet) of the frame, feeding it from your palm between finger and thumb.

or refit the clips. Remove putty that has been squeezed out on the inside of the window.

Add more putty to the outside of the window, using the same thumb-and-forefinger technique, until you have a good bead all the way around the glass. Take a putty knife and smooth off this bead at an angle of 45 degrees, pushing the putty into the edges of the frame. If the knife sticks, wet it with water.

Leave the putty for about 14 days before painting over it to disguise and seal the joints, allowing the paint to overlap on to the glass to prevent moisture from seeping down into the frame.

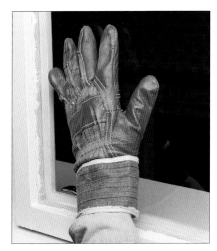

2 Support the bottom edge of the pane on a couple of wooden matches and press it into the putty, applying pressure to the sides rather than the centre.

3 Tap in the glazing sprigs at 300mm (12in) intervals. Hold the hammer so that its head slides across the face of the glass; that way, you will avoid breaking the glass.

4 Add more putty to the rebate and use the putty knife to strike it off to a 45-degree bevel. Make sure that the putty seals against the glass all round and that the sprigs are covered.

5 Trim the excess putty on the inside and outside of the frame to leave a neat finish. Allow the putty to harden before painting. Clean smears from the glass with methylated spirit.

# REPAIRING WINDOWS

The most obvious signs that there is something wrong with a window are when it starts to rattle in the wind or to stick, making it difficult to open and close. Rattling is most likely to be caused by worn hinges or wear of the window itself; sticking by swelling of the wood, build-up of paint or movement of the frame joints.

## REPAIRING HINGES

Loose or worn hinges are often a cause of window problems. To start with, try tightening the screws or replacing them with slightly longer screws of the same gauge. If that does not work, replace the hinges with new ones of the same size and type plus new screws. Remember that steel hinges will rust quickly, so apply suitable primer immediately, then repaint to match the window when this has dried.

Check the opening and closing of the window. If the window is sticking on the far edge, it may be necessary to deepen the recess for one or both hinges; if it binds on the closing edge, one or both recesses will be too deep and may need packing out with card. A rattling window can often be cured by fitting draught-excluder strip.

## WORN WINDOWS

Sash windows are particularly prone to wear. The best answer is to remove the windows and fit brush-pile draught excluder inside the sash channel. A new catch to hold the windows together may also be necessary.

Fit a new inner staff bead (window stop) around the window so that it fits more closely against the inner sash.

## WARPED WINDOWS

Wooden hinged windows can sometimes warp so that they meet the frame only at the top or at the bottom. The best way to cure this is to fit some mortise window locks, which fit into holes cut in the casement, with the bolts shooting into more holes in the frame. These allow the window to be held in the correct position (get someone to push from the outside while you lock it) so that the warp will self-correct.

## STICKING WINDOWS

Over time, a build-up of paint may cause windows to stick, especially when the weather is damp and the wood begins to swell. Use a plane to cut down the offending areas (this is much easier if you remove the window from its frame), then repaint before refitting the window.

Make sure that all bare wood is covered with paint, as this will prevent water from getting in, which causes the wood to swell. Also, check that the putty is in good condition.

### TIP

When replacing painted steel hinges with brass versions, always use brass screws to match the new hinges.

ABOVE: A binding window may be cured simply by tightening the hinge screws or replacing them with longer ones.

ABOVE: If a window is binding on the far side, it may be that the hinge recesses need to be deepened with a chisel.

ABOVE: A sticking window may be swollen or have too much paint on it. Plane down the leading edge of the window.

ABOVE: A loose window joint can be re-glued with fresh adhesive. Clamp it up while the adhesive dries.

# REHANGING DOORS

There may be occasions when the way in which a door opens is not the most convenient. Switching the hinges from one side to the other may provide a more attractive view of the room as the door is opened or allow better use of the wall space. Alternatively, making the door open outward may create more useful space. However, for safety, never have a door opening outward on to a stairway.

## SWITCHING THE HINGED SIDE

When switching the hinged edge of a door from one side to the other, you will need to cut a new mortise for the latch and drill new holes for the door handle spindles. The old latch mortise and spindle holes can be filled by gluing in small blocks of wood and lengths of dowel. Leave the blocks and dowels slightly proud of the surface, then plane and sand them flush when the glue has dried. If you reverse the door, you will be able to use the old latch and door handle spindle holes, but the latch itself will need to be turned around.

You will need to cut a new slot for the striker and striking plate (keeper) on the other side of the frame, and fill the old recess with a thin block of wood stuck in place. Again, make this oversize, planing and sanding it flush once the adhesive has dried.

## FILLING HINGE RECESSES

**1** When switching the hinged side of a door, you will need to fill the old hinge recesses. Cut slivers of wood to the correct length and width, but slightly thicker than the recess depth.

## REVERSING DOORS

When rehanging a door, it can reduce the amount of work required if you reverse the door – that is, turn it so that the side which faced inward now faces outward. This is the case when changing the hinges from left to right or the other way round. There are, however, two problems with doing this. The first is that the two sides of the door may be painted in different colours, which will mean a complete repainting job.

The second is that the door may not fit properly the other way round. Both doors and frames can move slightly over time, and while the door will operate perfectly well fitted one way,

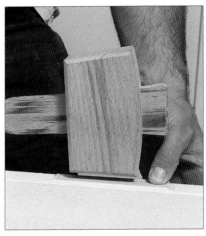

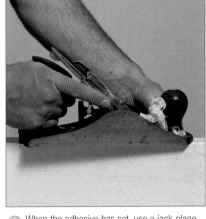

**2** Apply adhesive to each sliver of wood and tap it down into its recess. Wipe off excess adhesive with a damp cloth. Set the door aside for the adhesive to dry.

**3** When the adhesive has set, use a jack plane to remove the wood that projects above the surface of the door edge. If necessary, fill any gaps around the slivers with wood filler.

it may bind or catch when fitted the other way.

You will also need to chisel out new recesses for the hinges in both the door and the frame; if the door is reversed, you may be able to use part of the old hinge recesses in the door and need only fill the unused portions. Fill the old hinge recesses with thin blocks of wood glued into place and sanded flush.

If the door has rising butts or some other form of handed hinges, these will need to be replaced.

After rehanging the door, the light switch may be in the wrong place if it is in the room the door opens into. There are two choices here: reposition it on the other side of the door (which means running a new cable) or move it to the other side of the wall so that it is outside the room, but more or less in the same place (little or no new cable, but possible problems in securing the switch mounting box).

---

### TIP

Modern honeycomb-cored internal doors are quite light in weight, but traditional panelled doors can be very heavy. If you are rehanging such a door, make sure you have someone on hand to help lift it in and out of the opening.

## CHANGING THE LATCH POSITION

1 Remove the existing door handle and latch from the door, along with the operating spindle. Cut a block of wood to fill the latch recess and glue it in place, wiping off excess glue with a damp cloth.

2 Plug the spindle hole on each side of the door by tapping in lengths of glued dowel. Fill all the screw holes with wood filler. When the glue and filler has dried, sand everything smooth.

### OPENING IN TO OPENING OUT

When making a door open outward, you will be able to use the same latch and handle positions if the door is hung from the same side of the frame. You will have to reverse the latch, but will be able to make use of parts of the hinge recesses in the door. However, you will need to reposition the striking plate (keeper) and make new hinge recesses in the frame.

The one extra job will be to move the door stop, unless this is positioned centrally in the frame. Moving the door stop needs care to avoid splitting it – slide a chisel in behind the stop and lever it out. Remove the sides before the top, starting in the middle.

When repositioning the door stop, hang the door first, so that you can be sure that the stop fits snugly.

If you change the side of the frame from which the door is hung (as well as changing it from in to out), you can retain the existing door hinge, latch and door handle positions, although new recesses must still be cut in the frame for the hinges and striking plate.

---

**TIP**

To prevent the paint from chipping when you remove a door stop, run a trimming knife blade along the joint between door stop and frame to cut through the paint.

**3** On the other side of the door, cut a recess in the edge for the latch and drill a hole for the spindle. You may need to drill another hole for a key if the latch is lockable.

**4** Fit the latch and the operating spindle. Then add the handles. Fit hinges to the other side of the door and cut recesses in the frame for the hinges and striking plate (keeper).

## REPOSITIONING THE DOOR STOP

**1** After cutting through the paint film, carefully slide a chisel under the door stop and gently prise it from the frame. Remove the old nails.

**2** Drill new nail clearance holes in the stop and nail it to the door frame in its new position. Fill all the nail holes before repainting.

# REPAIRING DOORS

**D**oors can develop all sorts of problems, from simple squeaks and rattles to suddenly refusing to open and shut properly. Fortunately, most of the problems are easy to solve, although for most repairs you will need to remove the door from the frame.

## SQUEAKS

A door normally squeaks simply because the hinges need oiling. Often you can dribble sufficient oil on to the hinges with the door in place, but if they are caked in dirt and paint, it is best to remove the door and work the hinges back and forth with oil.

A door may also squeak if the hinges are binding, usually because the recesses have been cut too deep into the door and/or frame. To cure this problem, unscrew each half of each hinge in turn, place a piece of cardboard behind the hinge, then refit the screws.

## RATTLES

The simplest way to stop any door rattling is to fit a draught excluder. With an internal door, you could also try moving the door stop; with all types of door, you could try moving the latch striking plate (keeper), although this is not easy – drilling out and filling the old screw holes with glued-in dowels helps.

ABOVE: You can fix a squeaking hinge by unscrewing each half of the hinge in turn and packing the recess with cardboard.

## WARPED DOORS

If a door has become warped, you can straighten it with pairs of clamps, stout lengths of wood and packing blocks. Mount the door between the timbers, say lengths of 50 x 100mm (2 x 4in), and position the packing blocks to force the door in the opposite direction to the warp. Force it beyond straight by tightening up the clamps and leave for as long as you can. When the clamps are removed, the door should be straight.

## BINDING

External doors often bind during cold, damp weather, becoming free again when the weather is dry and warm. This is a sign that the bottom of the door was not sealed when the door was painted, allowing moisture to get in.

Binding doors can also be caused by a build-up of paint on the leading (non-hinge) edge. The cure is to remove the door and plane down the leading edge, repainting it once the door has been fitted. Add primer to the bottom of the door to prevent more moisture from getting in.

If a door binds at the bottom, it may be because the hinges have worked loose. Try tightening the screws, fitting larger or longer screws if necessary. If this does not work, remove the door and plane down the part that is rubbing.

A door can bind seriously when you have fitted a new floor covering. In this case, remove the door and cut a strip off the bottom with a door trimming saw.

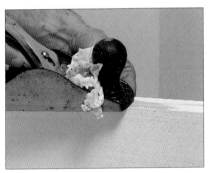

ABOVE: Take the door off its hinges and plane the leading (non-hinge) edge if it is binding.

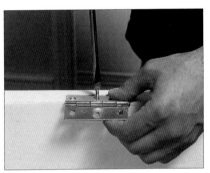

ABOVE: Fit longer screws to a hinge if the old ones have lost their grip.

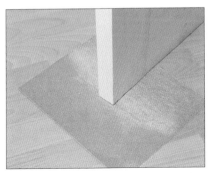

ABOVE: Running the base of a door over abrasive paper may be enough to cure binding.

ABOVE: You can hire a door trimming saw to adjust the height after fitting a new carpet.

# REPAIRING FLOORS & STAIRS

Of all the surfaces in your home, the floors take the most punishment. The continual passage of people to and fro, plus the scraping of furniture can cause substantial damage over time. In addition to day-to-day wear, wooden floors can also be attacked by rot and insects, with damage extending to the supporting structure of joists below. Older wooden floors invariably have individual boards that may warp, crack and shrink, opening up gaps that lead to draughts. Solid floors may develop cracks or be uneven, while floor coverings such as tiles and carpet can suffer from a variety of ills. Stairs are subject to heavy wear, too, as a result of which their joints can become loose and their treads broken.

# LIFTING FLOORBOARDS

The majority of floors in older homes will have individual floorboards nailed to supporting joists. In modern homes, sheets of flooring-grade chipboard (particle board) will be nailed or screwed to the joists. If a new floor covering is to be laid, it is essential that the floor is in good condition. If floorboards are to be exposed, they must be in even better condition, as any defects will be visible.

To inspect the underfloor space or fit new floorboards, you will need to lift existing floorboards. You may find some that have been cut and lifted in the past to provide access to pipes or cables. These should be easy to lever up with a bolster (stonecutter's chisel) – do not use a screwdriver as you will damage the floorboard.

To lift boards that have not been cut, check first that they are not tongued-and-grooved – a tongue along one edge of each board fitting into a groove along the adjacent edge of its neighbour. If they are, use a floorboard saw or a circular saw with its cutting depth set to 20mm (¾in) to cut through the tongues.

Lever up the floorboard with your bolster, and use a floorboard saw to make a right-angled cut across it. Make the cut exactly over a joist so that the two parts of the board will be supported when they are replaced.

Chipboard sheets are easy to unscrew, but you may need to cut through tongues in the same manner as for traditional floorboards to be able to lift them.

**1** If the board is tongued-and-grooved, cut through the tongue with a circular saw. Lift the end of the floorboard by levering with a bolster (stonecutter's chisel).

**2** Use wooden wedges to keep the end of the board raised. Check that there are no pipes or cables underneath and cut through it above the centre of a joist with a floorboard saw.

# JOIST PROBLEMS

Most of the problems associated with floor joists are due to dampness, which may occur if airbricks (vents) have become blocked or if there are not enough airbricks to ensure adequate ventilation of the underfloor space.

Lift a few floorboards and inspect the joists with a torch and a mirror, prodding any suspect areas with a bradawl (awl). If sections of joist are damaged, you should be able to cut and lift floorboards or chipboard (particle board) sheets over the damage and bolt on a new section of joist of the same size, making sure that it is fixed to solid wood. Do not bother to remove the old joist unless it is actually rotten. If you do find signs of dry rot (typically white strands), all damaged wood must be removed by a firm of professionals. If you find signs of woodworm attack, treat the affected areas with a recommended woodworm eradicator or call in a professional firm.

If you want to strengthen a floor so that it will support a partition wall running directly above a joist, you can sandwich the existing joist between two reinforcing joists. These should be supported at each end by metal joist hangers screwed to the wallplate or masonry and butted up to the existing joist. Cut the new joists to length, drop them into the hangers and drill holes through all three joists at 900mm (3ft) intervals. Pass 12mm (½in) bolts through the holes and tighten.

1 Cut the new joist section to length and clamp it in place while you drill holes through it and through the old joist. A right-angled drill attachment makes this easy.

2 Fit washers beneath the bolt heads, pass them through the holes and add another washer beneath each nut before tightening them with an adjustable spanner.

# REPAIRING WOOD FLOORS

**A** wood floor should have a sound and smooth surface. Even if the wood is covered by carpet or tiles, any faults not rectified will eventually show through any floor covering and may damage it. It is therefore essential that you fill holes, cracks and gaps, as well as make the surface level and smooth.

### FILLING HOLES

Nail and screw holes can easily be plugged using a flexible wood filler applied with a filling or putty knife. If the floorboards are to be left exposed and treated with a clear sealer, try to match the wood filler, or stopping, to the colour of the surrounding floorboards – so carry out the filling after any sanding.

Larger recesses can also be filled with flexible filler, but if a knot has fallen out, leaving a large round hole, plug this by gluing in a short length of dowel and planing it smooth when the glue has dried. Select a dowel that matches the colour of the floor or stain it once planed down.

### FILLING CRACKS

You will find two main kinds of crack in wood floors: splits in the ends of the floorboards and gaps between the boards.

A split can often be cured by skew (toe) nailing – i.e. driving two nails through the end of the board at an angle toward the centre and down into the joist. As the nails are driven in, they should close up the split.

Gaps between floorboards are more difficult to deal with. If they are narrow, flexible wood filler will work, but for wider gaps, you must cut slivers of wood and glue them into place in the gaps. Once the glue has dried, plane or sand the slivers flush with the surrounding floor and stain to match.

If there are lots of wide gaps between floorboards, a better solution is to lift all the floorboards one by one, starting at one side of the room and working toward the other, and re-lay them tightly against one another. Floorboard clamps will help you do this, as they force a board against its neighbour while you nail or screw it down.

### LEVELLING A WOOD FLOOR

Individual rough patches on a wood floor can be sanded down by hand, but where floorboards have become cupped or are heavily encrusted with old paint, grease and polish, the best move is to hire an industrial-type sanding machine and re-sand the floor. Begin with coarse abrasive and progress through to the fine grades, working across the floorboards at an angle. Finish off by working along the boards with fine abrasive. Hire an edging sander as well, unless you own a belt sander, because the floor sander will not sand right up to the skirtings (baseboards).

## FILLING GAPS BETWEEN FLOORBOARDS

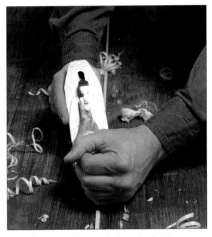

**1** Drive glued slivers of wood between floorboards to fill large gaps. Leave them just proud of the surrounding boards, wipe off excess glue with a damp cloth and allow the glue to dry.

**2** Plane down the wood slivers flush with the floor when the glue has dried. If the floorboards are to be left exposed, stain the slivers so that they match the colour of the boards.

## FILLING HOLES AND SPLITS

**ABOVE:** Use flexible wood filler to cover the holes made by nail heads and screws.

**ABOVE:** With a split board, glue the split, then drive in nails at an angle to close it up.

# FITTING NEW FLOORBOARDS

Over a period of time, floorboards can develop a number of faults. The natural flexing of the wood as it is walked on can begin to loosen nails, leading to squeaks and creaks. If sections are lifted regularly, they can be damaged, or the wood may simply warp and split with age.

## LOOSE FLOORBOARDS

If floorboards are loose, the best answer is to replace the nails holding them down with screws. Do not put a screw in the middle of a board – there could be a pipe underneath. If nail heads are protruding, use a hammer and nail punch to set them below the surface of the floorboards. This is essential before attempting to use a sanding machine or laying carpet or sheet vinyl.

## DAMAGED FLOORBOARDS

If floorboards are split or broken, the damaged section, at least, will need to be replaced. The most likely problem is that old floorboards will have become "cupped", or turned up at the edges. You can overcome this by hiring a floor sanding machine.

You do not need to replace a whole floorboard if only part of it is damaged; simply lift the board and cut out the damaged section, making the cuts over the centres of joists.

## FITTING FLOORBOARDS

ABOVE: Plane down a floorboard if it is too wide to fill the gap.

If a replacement floorboard is too wide, plane it down to fit the gap – do not fit a narrower replacement floorboard, as this will result in draughts. If the board is slightly thicker, chisel slots out of it where it fits over the joists; if it is thinner, use packing

## FIXING FLOORBOARDS

ABOVE: Drill pilot holes for floorboard nails to avoid splitting the wood.

ABOVE: Use card or plywood packing pieces over the joists if the board is too shallow.

ABOVE: Use a chisel to cut slots to fit over joists if the board is too thick.

pieces of cardboard or plywood between the joists and the board. Secure each floorboard with two floorboard nails at each joist, positioning them about 25mm (1in) from the edge of the board and exactly in the middle of the joist. It is a good idea to drill pilot holes in the board first.

### TIP

When laying new floorboards, make sure that you can still gain access to pipes and cables underneath. If necessary, cut removable inspection hatches in both the floor and any new floor coverings.

ABOVE: Hammer down protruding nails to prevent them from damaging the floor covering.

ABOVE: Secure loose floorboards by replacing the nails with screws.

# REPAIRING SOLID FLOORS

Provided a solid floor is basically sound and dry, you should be able to fill cracks and holes using a quick-set repair mortar. All loose material should be removed and the cracks enlarged if necessary to give the mortar something to grip.

The surface of the crack or hole should be brushed with a solution of one part PVA (white) glue and five parts water to reduce absorbency and help the mortar adhere to the floor. Use the same PVA glue and water solution to make up the mortar, then trowel it into place, building up two or more layers in a deep hole. Level the surface with a plasterer's trowel.

## DEALING WITH DAMP

Concrete floors should incorporate a damp-proof membrane to prevent moisture from rising up from the ground below. However, it is possible that this may have broken down, or not have been incorporated at all. To check for rising damp, lay a piece of polythene (polyethylene) sheet on the floor and seal its edges with tape. After a couple of days, moisture should be visible on the underside of the sheet if the condition exists. To protect against rising damp, paint the floor with two or three coats of a waterproofing compound. When it has dried, floor coverings can be laid on top, or a self-levelling compound added.

**1** After opening out a crack in a solid floor and brushing out all debris and dust, brush the surfaces with a solution of PVA (white) glue to help the new mortar bond to it.

**2** Mix a small amount of quick-set repair mortar, again using PVA solution, and work it into the crack with a small trowel. Smooth the mortar flush with the surrounding floor and leave to harden.

# LEVELLING SOLID FLOORS

Little skill is required to produce a smooth, flat, solid floor surface, as a self-levelling floor compound will do the job for you.

Before you start, clear the room, removing all skirtings (baseboards) and doors; nail battens across thresholds to prevent the compound from spreading. Fill any cracks or holes more than 6mm (¼in) deep and brush the floor with PVA (white) glue/water solution. Mix the floor levelling compound in a bucket and tip it out on to the floor, spreading it with a plasterer's trowel or a float. Leave it to settle. Once the compound has dried, you can refit the skirtings and doors, but check that the latter will clear the higher floor when opened.

1 If the floor is excessively porous, seal it by brushing on a coat of diluted PVA (white) glue. Then mix up the self-levelling floor compound according to the manufacturer's instructions.

2 Starting from the corner farthest from the door, pour the compound on to the floor. Do not pour too much on to the floor at any one time, otherwise you will not be able to reach across it.

3 Using a plasterer's trowel, smooth the compound to a thickness of approximately 3mm (⅛in). Allow at least 24 hours for the compound to dry before walking on it.

# REPAIRING FLOOR TILES

**O**f all the types of floor covering, tiled finishes can be the easiest to repair, since individual tiles can often be lifted and replaced. The way you do it depends on whether the tile is hard or soft and on how it has been secured to the floor. Even damaged carpet can be patched effectively, but care needs to be taken to avoid further damage to surrounding areas.

Ceramic and quarry tiles are among the most difficult tiles to replace, as first you will have to chip out the old tile. Drill a few holes in the tile with the biggest masonry drill you own, then use a club (spalling) hammer and small bolster (stonecutter's chisel)

to chip out the tile, making sure you do not damage the surrounding tiles. Chip out all old adhesive or mortar and grout from the hole.

Lay some new tile adhesive (for ceramic tiles) or mortar (for quarry tiles) and push the replacement tile gently into place. If it is not flush with its neighbours, lift it quickly and add or remove adhesive or mortar as necessary. Clean any excess mortar or adhesive off the face of the tile and leave to set before making good the gaps around the tile with grout (ceramic tiles) or more mortar (quarry tiles). If re-laying several tiles, it helps if you make up some small spacers.

**1** Remove any cracked quarry or ceramic tiles with a club (spalling) hammer and small bolster (stonecutter's chisel). Wear gloves to protect your hands, and safety goggles to shield your eyes.

**2** Bed a new quarry tile on mortar, but use the recommended adhesive for a ceramic tile. Level the tile with its neighbours using a strip of wood; wipe off excess mortar or adhesive.

# REPAIRING WOODEN MOSAIC TILES

There are two ways to replace wooden mosaic tiles. One is to lift the whole tile, which consists of four groups of timber strips, and replace it with a new one. First drill or chisel out one strip, then lever the rest of the tile from the floor. The second method is to remove just the damaged strip or strips and glue in replacements taken from a spare tile, pressing them into place with a block of wood.

If the new strip sits a little proud of its neighbours, it should be sanded down, using abrasive paper and a sanding block, until it lies flush. Then sand the entire tile and revarnish it. If the tiles are pre-finished, you will have to sand the back of the strip before gluing it.

**1** First drill a sequence of closely spaced holes through the damaged mosaic strip, stopping each when you just break through the wood. Take care not to allow the drill to wander.

**2** Carefully cut away the strip, working outward from the holes with a narrow-bladed chisel held bevel down. Do not let the chisel slip when you approach the edges of adjoining strips.

**3** Apply a little adhesive to the new mosaic strip and place it carefully in position, taking care not to get adhesive on the adjoining strips. Using a block of wood and a hammer, tap it down.

# REPLACING SOFT FLOOR TILES

Most soft floor tiles – vinyl, cork, lino and rubber – are replaced in the same way. First you have to soften the adhesive holding the tile in place, which is best done with a hot-air gun, starting at one corner and gradually peeling the tile back. This becomes easier once you can direct the hot-air gun beneath the tile. An old chisel can be used to remove any remaining adhesive. Check that the replacement tile is an exact fit.

Some soft tiles are self-adhesive, requiring only the removal of backing paper, while others require a separate adhesive. Always add the adhesive to the back of a replacement tile to avoid staining the other tiles.

With the adhesive in place, or the backing paper removed, hold the tile against the edge of one of the surrounding tiles and lower it into place. You may only get one attempt at this, so take care to get it right.

## TIP

If you do not have any spare tiles and are unable to obtain a matching colour or pattern for the existing flooring, consider replacing the damaged tile with one of a contrasting colour or pattern. To disguise the repair, replace a few of the undamaged tiles with similar contrasting tiles, setting them out in a regular or random pattern. If you cannot find tiles of the correct size, buy larger ones and carefully cut them down to fit.

**1** Remove a vinyl or cork tile using a hot-air gun to soften the adhesive. Work a scraper under the edge and gradually prise the tile from the floor.

**2** Apply adhesive to the back of the replacement vinyl or cork tile, set one edge in place against its neighbour and lower it in place.

# PATCHING CARPET

Provided you have a matching piece, you can patch most types of carpet, but it may be worth cleaning the carpet first, since the patch could be a brighter colour. First decide how large the patch should be – if the carpet is patterned, you may want to join along a pattern line – cut the patch about 25mm (1in) larger than this all round, with the same part of any pattern. Lay the patch over the carpet, lining up the pattern exactly, and secure it with adhesive tape.

Using a trimming knife fitted with a new blade and a metal straightedge, make a single cut down through both thicknesses of carpet along each edge of the patch. Remove the tape and lift both pieces of carpet – the patch should fit exactly into the hole in the carpet with the pattern matching.

With foam-backed carpet, lay double-sided tape on the floor around the edges of the hole so that each strip overlaps the joint between the old carpet and the patch. Brush the edges

of the patch and the hole with latex adhesive to prevent fraying, then press the carpet patch on to the tape. Remove excess adhesive with a damp cloth.

With fabric-backed carpet, use non-adhesive carpet repair tape and latex adhesive on the back and edges of the patch and the hole. Press the patch down into the hole with a wallpaper seam roller and wipe off any excess adhesive with a damp cloth.

1 Use a trimming knife and straightedge to cut through both the patch and the existing carpet to ensure an exact fit.

2 Press the carpet patch on to double-sided adhesive tape. Brush the edges with latex adhesive to prevent fraying.

3 The finished patch of carpet should fit exactly into the hole and the seams should be invisible in long-pile carpet.

# CURING STAIRCASE PROBLEMS

A timber staircase consists of a series of evenly spaced horizontal treads that form the flight. Most staircases also have vertical risers, which fill the space between the rear edge of one tread and the front edge of the tread above; these may be nailed in place, or may have tongued edges that slot into grooves in the treads.

The treads are supported at each side by two parallel beams called strings. A closed-string staircase has the treads and risers set into grooves cut in the inner faces of the strings, while an open-string staircase has the outer string cut in a zigzag fashion so the treads can rest on the cutouts. The inner string – the one against the wall of the stairwell – is always a closed string.

At the open side of a conventional flight, a guard is fitted to run between the top and bottom newel posts – main uprights supporting flight. This usually consists of a series of closely-spaced balusters, which are fixed between the top edge of the outer string and the underside of a handrail, but it may be a solid panelled barrier. There may also be a wall-mounted handrail at the other side of the flight; freestanding flights must obviously have a balustrade at each side.

Stairs creak because one of the components has become loose; a footfall then causes the loose part to move against an adjacent component of the flight. A cure is simple if the underside of the flight is accessible, but less straightforward if it is not.

**1** If there is no access to the underside of the flight, secure loose or squeaking treads by fixing metal repair brackets to tread and riser. If the underside can be reached, check that the wedges securing the treads and risers to the strings are in place. Hammer them in firmly if they are loose.

**4** Insert a crowbar (wrecking bar) between the string and the tread, and prise it up and out to free it from the risers above and below it. Mark out and cut a replacement. Plane the nosing to shape, and cut notches in one end for the balusters.

2 Glue back any of the support blocks beneath the fronts of the treads if they have fallen off. Fit extra blocks beneath troublesome treads. Drill clearance holes up through the rear edge of each tread, then drive screws up into the bottom edge of the riser above to lock the tread to it.

3 If the tread is found to be split, it must be replaced. Start by prising off the side moulding, then tap the balusters out with a mallet. Insert a knife into the joint along the back of the tread to check if it has been nailed or screwed. If it has, use a hacksaw blade to cut the fixings.

5 Glue and clamp support blocks to the rear face of the riser below, and nail another block to the closed string to provide extra support for the replacement tread.

6 Fit the new tread in place and secure it to the support blocks and to the cut-out in the open string with screws rather than nails. With the tread securely fixed in position, replace the balusters in their notches and nail the side moulding back on.

# HOME INSULATION

- Insulation materials

- Insulation & draughtproofing

- Ventilation

- Overcoming damp conditions

# INTRODUCTION

Insulation is a means of preventing heat from escaping from a house. Heat loss can occur through roofs, walls, floors, doors and windows, and each of these can be insulated in different ways – with loose-fill or blanket insulation, or by installing double glazing, to name a few.

Related to insulation is draughtproofing, which is also a method of reducing heat loss, particularly under doors, through letter plate openings and keyholes, and through gaps in windows.

Insulating and sealing a house totally is not the answer, however, as there always needs to be some air ventilation to prevent condensation, which can lead to mould and structural damage. So a combination of insulation, draughtproofing and ventilation is required.

This chapter shows how to insulate, draughtproof and ventilate the main areas of the home where heat loss can be a problem. Doing this will save energy and money, and will also cut down on unnecessary wastage of fossil fuels, which in turn causes the widespread environmental problems associated with the release of carbon dioxide into the atmosphere.

## CAUSES OF HEAT LOSS

The primary areas of heat loss are through the roof, walls and floors – around 25 per cent of heat is lost through the roof and pipework, 35 per cent through the walls, and 15 per cent through the floors – so these are the first areas to work on.

Doors and windows are the next most likely places where heat is lost, due to draughts coming through gaps and cracks. About 15 per cent of heat loss is attributed to poor draughtproofing.

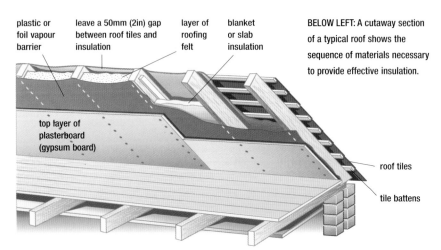

plastic or foil vapour barrier

leave a 50mm (2in) gap between roof tiles and insulation

layer of roofing felt

blanket or slab insulation

top layer of plasterboard (gypsum board)

roof tiles

tile battens

BELOW LEFT: A cutaway section of a typical roof shows the sequence of materials necessary to provide effective insulation.

ABOVE: Draughts can enter your home through the smallest of gaps. You can easily prevent draughts through keyholes by installing keyhole covers.

## CAUSES OF CONDENSATION

Condensation can be caused by a lack of ventilation and over-insulation in properties not designed for it, both inside the rooms and within the building's structure. When water vapour condenses, the water runs down windows and walls, and causes mould, health problems, and even damage to the structure of the home.

People themselves are a major source of the moisture in the air inside a building. Breath is moist and sweat evaporates; one person gives off 250ml ($\frac{1}{2}$ pint) of water during eight hours of sleep, and three times as much during an active day.

Domestic activities create even more moisture. Cooking, washing up, bathing, washing and drying clothes can create as much as a further 10 to 12 litres (about 3 gallons) of water a day, and every litre of fuel burnt in a flueless oil or paraffin (kerosene) heater gives off roughly another litre of water vapour.

The air in the house is expected to soak up all this extra moisture invisibly. It may not be able to manage unaided. However, a combination of improved insulation and controlled ventilation will help eliminate condensation. An electric dehumidifier can also help in soaking up excess moisture.

ABOVE: A significant cause of condensation in the kitchen is cooking. Steam rises from pans and the vapour then condenses, forming droplets on walls and ceilings.

ABOVE: Constant condensation ruins paintwork and will eventually cause wooden window frames and sills to rot, unless action is taken to increase ventilation.

### PROVIDING GOOD INSULATION

Good insulation reduces the rate at which expensive domestic heat escapes through the fabric of your home and helps to protect vulnerable plumbing systems from damage during cold weather. The different parts of your home can be insulated by various methods, and most jobs can be handled by a competent person.

### ROOFS AND PIPEWORK

The roof is a good place to start your insulation project. This is where pipework is at greatest risk of freezing, so pipes must be tackled as well. The main options for roof insulation are loose-fill, blanket and slab insulation, and pipes are best insulated with foam taped around them.

### WALLS

The best solution for cavity walls is a job that must be left to the professionals. Despite the extra outlay, the work is very cost-effective, and you can expect to see a return on your investment after a few years. The usual procedure is to pump foam, pellets or mineral fibres into the cavity through holes drilled in the outer leaf of the wall. Make sure that the work is carried out by an approved contractor.

Applying insulation to the inner faces of walls is well within the scope of most people. One possibility is to use thermal plasterboard (gypsum board) to dry-line external walls. Another is to add a framework of wood strips to the wall, infill with slab or blanket insulation and face it with plasterboard. To prevent condensation, plastic sheeting should be stapled to the insulating material.

### FLOORS, DOORS AND WINDOWS

Suspended floors can be insulated by fixing sheets of rigid polystyrene (plastic foam) between the joists, and solid floors can be lined with a vapour

ABOVE: Installing cavity wall insulation is a specialist job that can take up to three days.

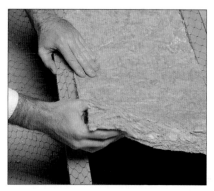

ABOVE: You can insulate a suspended floor by laying loft (attic) or wall insulation batts between the joists.

ABOVE: Glass is an extremely poor insulator, and double glazing can cut down on heat loss. It can also help to reduce noise penetration from outside and will give added security against burglars.

ABOVE: To control ventilation in steamy rooms, such as kitchens and bathrooms, extractor fans can be fitted. The types linked to humidity detectors are ideal, as they activate automatically.

barrier of heavy-duty plastic sheeting, topped with a floating floor of tongued-and-grooved chipboard (particle board) panels. Draughty floorboards can easily be repaired by applying silicone sealant (caulking) to small cracks, or by tapping slivers of wood into larger gaps.

Doors and windows are the two main sources of draughts in the home, and many products have been designed to deal with the problem. For example, gaps under doors and around windows can be sealed with draught excluder strips. Some are self-adhesive and easy to apply, while others can be fixed with screws. Make sure you choose the correct size for your doors and windows.

Windows can also be insulated by installing double glazing, either as a thin film stuck to each window frame or by fitting sliding units on to separate tracks within the window frames.

### PROVIDING GOOD VENTILATION

A free flow of fresh air, ventilation is essential in a home, not only for humans to breathe, but also to prevent condensation occurring. There are many types of extractor fan that will help air to circulate. These can be fitted to ceilings, windows and walls, and can be installed by any competent do-it-yourselfer. For underfloor ventilation, airbricks are a good solution: ideally there should be an airbrick every 2m (6ft) along an external wall.

### OVERCOMING DAMP

The best way of dealing with damp is to install a damp-proof course, but seek professional guidance before carrying out this work yourself. Other solutions include waterproofing exterior walls, installing ventilation fans and buying an electric dehumidifier.

# INSULATION MATERIALS

There are three basic aspects involved in saving energy in your home: insulation to prevent heat from escaping; draughtproofing to prevent cold air from seeping into your home; and ventilation to prevent condensation from forming and causing problems. Various types of insulation material are made to cope with different situations; all are easy to use. Likewise, draughtproofing materials are easy to install, although ventilation devices require a bit more effort to fit. None of this work is beyond any competent do-it-yourselfer equipped with a relatively small collection of basic tools. As with all do-it-yourself work, due regard for your own safety, and that of others who may be nearby, is essential.

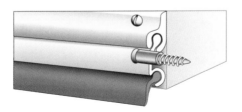

# TYPES OF INSULATION

**B**efore thinking about individual types of insulation, it is important to understand the concept of cost-effectiveness. Insulation costs money to install, and can bring benefits in two main ways.

It can reduce heating bills, since the home will waste less heat and the same internal temperatures can be maintained without burning so much fuel. The annual saving on the heating bill will therefore "pay back" the cost of the extra insulation. Also, when replacing a heating system, having better standards of insulation allows a less powerful, and less expensive, boiler to be used – an indirect saving, but valuable none the less.

**ESSENTIAL BUYS**

Good insulation need not mean great expenditure. The most effective items are relatively cheap and could save you a great deal in the long term. Any water storage tanks in the roof must be insulated to protect them from freezing. Padded jackets are available for the purpose. Likewise, any exposed pipework in the roof should be fitted with insulating sleeves.

ABOVE: Fix reflective foil between rafters to act as a vapour barrier over insulation.

ABOVE: Split foam pipe insulation comes in sizes to match standard pipe diameters.

ABOVE: Secure an insulation blanket to a hot water cylinder.

ABOVE: Insulate a cold water cistern with a purpose-made jacket.

## LAYING LOOSE-FILL INSULATION

Lay loose-fill insulation by pouring the material between the joists. Spread it out so that it is level with the tops of the joists to ensure a thick and effective layer.

## LAYING BLANKET INSULATION

If the roof of the house is pitched (sloping), blanket insulation can be laid over the loft (attic) floor. This is one of the most cost-effective forms of insulation.

### LOOSE-FILL INSULATION
This is sold by the bag and is simply poured between the joists and levelled off with their top surfaces. The dustier varieties, such as vermiculite, can be unpleasant to work with.

### BLANKET INSULATION
This consists of rolls of glass fibre, mineral fibre or rock fibre, in standard widths to unroll between the joists. A typical roll length would be 6–8m (20–26ft), but short lengths are also available, known as batts. Always wear a face mask, gloves and protective clothing when laying the insulation.

### SLAB INSULATION
These products are light and easy to handle, but as with the blanket versions some types may cause skin irritation. The slab widths match common joist spacings.

## PAY-BACK PERIODS

Hot water cylinder jacket *****
   *Pay-back period: less than 1 year.*
Loft (attic) insulation ****
   *Pay-back period: 1–2 years.*
Reflective radiator foil ****
   *Pay-back period: 1–2 years.*
Draught excluders ***
   *Pay-back period: 2–3 years.*
Flat roof insulation **(*)
   *Pay-back period: 2–4 years.*
Floor insulation **
   *Pay-back period: 3–5 years.*
Cavity wall insulation **
   *Pay-back period: around 5 years.*
Double glazing **(*)
   *Pay-back period: 5 years or more.*
Solid wall insulation *
   *Pay-back period: over 10 years.*

* Star rating indicates cost-effectiveness.

# DRAUGHT EXCLUDERS

**D**raught excluder strips are an inexpensive method of sealing gaps around windows and doors. The strips are self-adhesive and easy to apply, although foam strips offer variable levels of success. Avoid the cheapest varieties, as they may soon become compressed and will not do the job properly. Look for products that are guaranteed for between two and five years. These will be easy to remove and replace if you wish to upgrade the draughtproofing system.

Rubber strips, commonly with E- or P-shaped profiles, are dearer, but are better in terms of performance and longevity. Normally, casement windows are easier to draughtproof than the sash variety.

The most effective way of keeping draughts out at the sides of sashes is to fix nylon-pile brush strips to the window frame. The top and bottom do not need special treatment, as any of the products recommended for casement windows can be used.

The gap between the bottom of a door and the threshold (saddle) can be draughtproofed by attaching a solid blade or brush strip to the bottom edge of the door, so that it meets the floor or sill, or by fixing a special strip across the threshold so that it is in contact with the underside of the door.

Unused chimneys can be sealed, or a temporary solution is to block off the flue with a "balloon" device which can be removed when a fire is needed.

**V-strip metal draughtproofing strip with brush**

ABOVE: A metal draughtproofing strip can be fixed to a door frame, such as the example shown here, a V-strip type. The insert shows where the brush strip should be fixed.

ABOVE: A brush-type strip fitted at the base of the door works well on uneven surfaces.

ABOVE: A flexible rubber blade held in a plastic or aluminium extrusion, secured by screws.

# EXTRACTOR FANS AND AIRBRICKS

There are several options for ensuring a constant circulation of air in the home. Each works by providing ventilation, thus preventing condensation and its associated problems.

Extractor fans can be fitted in ceilings, windows or walls. Ceiling fans are particularly effective in bathrooms and kitchens, where warm water vapour rises. Window fans need care when installing; you can either cut a hole in a single-glazed window or order a new pane with the hole already cut by a glass supplier. Wall extractor fans are fixed to an outside wall. Always check for pipes before cutting into brickwork.

Airbricks are installed into external walls to ventilate the space below suspended wooden floors.

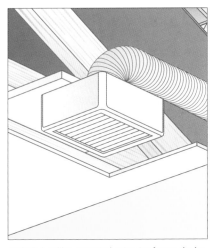

ABOVE: A ceiling-mounted extractor fan works by extracting the moist air that tends to collect just below the ceiling. A fan like this extracts this air to an outlet.

ABOVE: It is best to install a wall extractor fan as high as possible, where rising steam collects. Employ an electrician if you are unsure about how to install the wiring.

ABOVE: An airbrick contains perforated openings that allow ventilation in rooms and under wooden floors. It is important to keep them clear of earth, leaves and other debris, so clean them regularly.

# INSULATION & DRAUGHTPROOFING

Heat rises, so the most important area of your home to insulate is the roof. Fortunately, this is very easy to do, although working in a small roof space can be difficult. Keeping the heat below the ceiling may have unforeseen consequences, however, in that any pipes and water tanks in the roof may freeze, so these too must be wrapped in insulating material. Once you have dealt with the roof, turn your attention to the walls and floors, since both can be insulated to provide a real bonus in energy saving. Floors not only act as heat sinks, but if boarded, they can allow in cold draughts. Sealing the gaps between boards will make your rooms feel cosy, as will draughtproofing the doors and windows. For extra comfort, opt for double glazing.

# INSULATING ROOFS

In a building with a pitched (sloping) roof, where the loft (attic) space is used only for storage, it is usual to insulate the loft floor. To do this, use either blankets of glass fibre or mineral wool, sold by the roll, or else use loose-fill material (vermiculite, a lightweight expanded mineral, is the most widely used). Some kinds of loose-fill insulation, usually mineral wool or fireproofed cellulose fibres, can be blown into the loft by specialist professional contractors.

Blanket materials are generally easier to handle than loose-fill types unless the loft is awkwardly shaped, contains a lot of obstructions or has irregular joist spacings. The rolls are generally 600mm (24in) wide to match standard joist spacing, and common thicknesses are 100mm (4in) and 150mm (6in).

Choose the latter unless there is already thin sonic loft insulation, and ensure that it is laid with eaves baffles to allow adequate ventilation of the loft, otherwise condensation may form and lead to rotting of the wood. It is essential to wear protective clothing when handling glass fibre insulation. Wear a face mask, gloves and cover any exposed skin with suitable clothing.

Apart from being awkward to handle, loose-fill materials have another drawback. To be as effective as blanket types, they need laying to a greater depth – usually at least an extra 25mm (1in). With few ceiling joists being deeper than about 150mm (6in), there is nothing to contain the insulation and allow for maintenance access, unless strips of wood are fixed along the top edge of every joist.

## LAYING LOOSE-FILL INSULATION

**1** Lay loose-fill insulation by pouring the material between the joists. Prevent it from running out at the eaves by fixing lengths of wood between the joists.

**2** Level it off with a spreader, which you can make from chipboard (particle board). You may need to add strips of wood to the joists to obtain the required depth of insulation.

## LAYING BLANKET ROOF INSULATION

1 Clear all stored items from the loft (attic) area, then put down a sturdy kneeling board and use a heavy-duty vacuum cleaner to remove dust and debris.

2 Always put on gloves and a face mask, and wear long sleeves, to handle the insulation. Unroll it between the joists, leaving the eaves clear for ventilation.

3 Butt-join the ends of successive lengths of blanket. To cut the material to length, either use long-bladed scissors or simply tear it.

4 While working across the loft, make sure that any electrical cables are lifted clear of the insulation so they cannot overheat.

5 Insulate the upper surface of the loft hatch by wrapping a piece of blanket in plastic sheeting and stapling this to the hatch door.

6 Do not insulate under water tanks. If the tank has a lid, blanket insulation can also be wrapped around the tank and tied in place.

# INSULATING PIPEWORK

When the loft (attic) floor is completely insulated, remember to insulate any water tanks and pipework within the loft, since they are now at risk of freezing. For this reason, do not lay insulation under water tanks.

### FOAM PIPE INSULATION

Exposed pipework in the loft can easily be protected by covering it with proprietary foam pipe insulation. Basically, this comprises lengths of foam tubing, which have been split along the length and which come with inside diameters to match common domestic pipe sizes. All that is necessary is to open the split to allow the foam to be fitted over the pipe.

### PIPE BANDAGE INSULATION

An alternative method is to use pipe bandage, but this is more labour intensive, since it must be wrapped around the pipe, although the fibrous material is useful for pipes with awkward bends. To secure it, tie each end firmly with a short length of string.

### JACKETS FOR TANKS

Tanks can be insulated with proprietary jackets, or you can tie lengths of blanket insulation around them, or tape on thick rigid foam sheets. Alternatively, you can build a plywood box around the tank and fill the gap between it and the tank with loose-fill insulation material.

### INSULATING PIPES WITH BANDAGE

**1** Pipe bandage can be used instead of foam insulation. Wrap it around the pipe in a spiral, with successive turns just overlapping. Don't leave any pipework exposed.

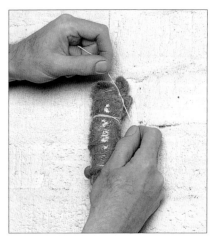

**2** Tie the insulation bandage in place at the end of each length, or where the pipe passes through a wall. Simply tear the material to length as necessary.

## INSULATING PIPES WITH FOAM

1 The quickest and easiest way of insulating pipework is to slip on lengths of foam pipe insulation, which is slit lengthways. Join the lengths with PVC (vinyl) tape.

2 To make neat joins in the insulation at corners, cut the ends at 45 degrees, using a mitre box and a carving knife or hacksaw blade. Tape the corner joint.

3 Make a V-shaped cut-out in the insulation at a tee joint, then cut an arrow shape to match it on the end of the insulation which will cover the branch pipe.

4 As with butt and corner joints, use PVC tape to secure the sections of insulation together and prevent them from slipping out of position. In time, you may need to renew this.

# BOXING-IN PIPES

Some people regard visible pipes in the home as an eyesore. Moreover, where the pipes are in rooms that are unheated, or where they run against external walls, there is a possibility that they may freeze during a severe winter. Fortunately, with a little time and minimal woodworking skills, exposed pipes can be hidden successfully from view and protected from freezing at the same time, by building boxing around them and filling it with loose-fill insulation. If the boxing is decorated to match the room, the pipes can be concealed completely. Be sure to allow for the boxwork to be easily removed in situations where it may be necessary to gain access.

### ACCESSIBILITY
Bear in mind that stopcocks, drain taps, pumps, hand-operated valves and the like will need to be readily accessible and require some form of removable box system. For this reason, the boxing around them should be assembled with screws rather than nails. If a panel needs to be regularly or quickly removed, turn buttons or magnetic catches are a good idea.

### BOXING BASICS
Steel anchor plates and screws can be used to secure the sides of boxing to walls, and these will be easy to remove when necessary. Battens (furring strips), either 50 x 25mm (2 x 1in) or 25 x 25mm (1 x 1in), can be used to fix boards at skirting (baseboard) level.

Disguise the boxing by decorating it to match the rest of the room. If pipework is running along a panelled or boarded wall, construct the boxing so that it follows the general theme, using similar materials and staining and varnishing the boxes accordingly.

### WALL PIPES
Measure the distance the pipes project from the wall, taking account of any joints and brackets. Cut the side panels from 25mm (1in) board slightly over this measurement and to their correct length. Fix small anchor plates flush with the back edge of each panel and spaced at about 600mm (24in) intervals.

If using plywood, you may need to drill pilot holes. Hold the panels against the wall and mark the positions of the screw holes on the wall. Drill the holes and fix the panels to the wall with rawl plugs and screws.

Cut the front panel to size from 6mm (¼in) plywood. Drill evenly spaced screw holes in the front panel and fix it in position with 19mm (¾in) No. 6 screws. Use cup washers underneath the screw heads to protect the panel if it is likely to be removed often. Trim the edges flush with a block plane.

With horizontal pipes, arrange the boxing so that you can remove the top panel to make filling with loose-fill insulation easy. For vertical pipes, leave a small access panel at the top of the box and pour the insulation through this, tapping the boxing to make sure that it fills the void completely.

## BOXING-IN WALL PIPES

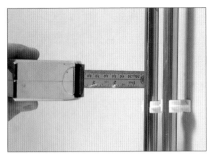

1 Measure how far the pipes protrude from the face of the wall.

2 With a pencil, mark the positions for the side batten fixings.

3 Attach the side battens, screwing them firmly into position.

4 Cut the front panel of the box to size with a jigsaw (saber saw). Use 6mm (¼in) plywood.

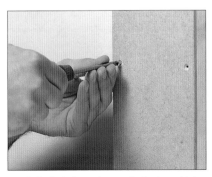

5 Drill pilot holes and screw the front panel into position, using 19mm (¾in) No. 6 screws.

6 Trim the edges of the front panel with a block plane. Add loose-fill insulation from the top.

# INSULATING SOLID WALLS

**H**ouse walls are the most extensive part of the whole building and absorb a lot of heat, which is why a house takes so long to warm up once it has become cold. Some of the lost heat can be retained by insulating the walls.

For solid walls, the most economical solution is to dry-line them on the inside with insulating plasterboard (gypsum board), fixed directly to the wall with panel adhesive or nailed to a supporting framework of treated wood strips. Alternatively, ordinary plasterboard sheets can be used, with insulation blanket or boards placed between the support strips and covered with a plastic vapour barrier.

## INSULATING CAVITY WALLS

The cavity wall consists of two "leaves" of masonry with a gap, usually of 50mm (2in), between them. Their insulation performance can be improved by filling the cavity with insulating material. This is done by specialist installers who pump treated fibres, pellets or insulating foam into the cavity through holes drilled in the wall's outer leaf.

For wood-framed walls, the best alternative is to remove the interior finish, install insulation batts and cover these with a vapour barrier, such as plastic sheeting. Then add a new inner skin of plasterboard.

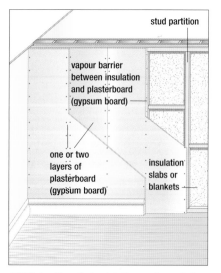

ABOVE: A wall can be insulated by erecting a stud partition wall in front of it, the void being filled with blanket or slab insulation, while two layers of plasterboard (gypsum board) are added to the framework.

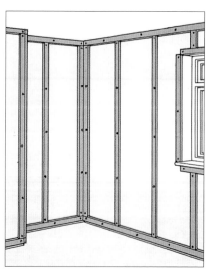

ABOVE: Fix a framework of 50 x 25mm (2 x 1in) softwood strips to the walls with masonry nails to support the edges and centres of the insulating boards.

## ADDING THE DRY-LINING

**1** Mark cutting lines on the board surface in pencil, then cut along the line with the insulation facing downwards, using a fine-toothed saw.

**2** Use a simple lever and fulcrum to raise the boards to touch the room ceiling as they are fixed. A skirting (baseboard) will cover the gap.

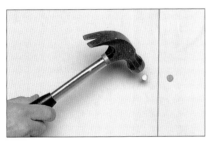

**3** Fix the boards by positioning them against the supporting framework so that adjacent boards meet over a strip, and nail them in place. The nail heads should just "dimple" the surface.

**4** At external corners, remove a strip of the polystyrene (plastic foam) insulation as wide as the board thickness so the edges of the plasterboard (gypsum board) can meet in a butt joint.

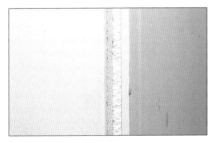

**5** Arrange the boards at external corners so that a paper-covered board edge conceals one that has its plaster core exposed. Finish off all joints with plasterboard tape and filler.

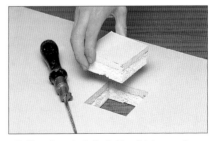

**6** To make cutouts for light switch boxes, plug sockets and similar obstacles, mark their positions on the boards and cut them out with a padsaw.

# INSULATING SUSPENDED FLOORS

**F**ew people think of ground floors when considering insulation, yet a surprisingly large amount of heat can be lost through both solid and suspended wood floors. Insulating a suspended floor will involve disruptive work, since the floorboards will need lifting. However, if you are prepared to do this, the methods are very similar to laying roof insulation.

## INSULATION METHODS

With suspended wood floors insulation can be fixed between the joists after lifting the floorboards. One method is to cut strips of rigid expanded polystyrene (plastic foam) and rest them on nails driven into the sides of the joists, or on battens nailed to the sides of the joists. Bear in mind that the material is very light and may be dislodged by severe draughts caused by windy weather; a few nails driven into the joists to "pinch" the edges of the insulation will help.

Another method of treating a suspended floor is to fill the gaps between joists with lengths of insulation blanket, supported on nylon garden netting stapled to the joists. Pull up the netting tightly before

## LIFTING FLOORBOARDS

Unless you have a basement that allows you to reach the underside of a suspended floor, to insulate it you will have to lift all of the floorboards.

To lift a board, tap the blade of a bolster (stonecutter's) chisel into the gap between two boards, close to the end of the board you want to lift, and lever the board upward; repeat for the other side.

Continue levering until the end of the board is clear of the floor and you can insert the claw of a hammer beneath it.

Use the hammer to lever the end high enough to insert a length of wood beneath the board to hold the end clear of the floor. Continue in this way along the board until you can lift it completely.

nailing down the boards so that the blanket does not sag and let cold air through. The insulation is then covered with a vapour barrier.

## USING INSULATION BLANKET

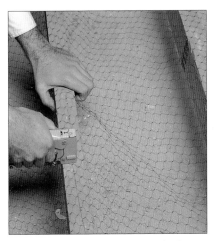

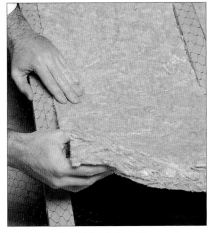

1 To insulate the void beneath a wooden floor, lift all the floorboards. Then drape lengths of garden netting loosely over the joists and staple them in place.

2 Lay lengths of loft (attic) insulation blanket or wall insulation batts in the "hammocks" between the joists. If the netting sags, pull it up a little and staple it again.

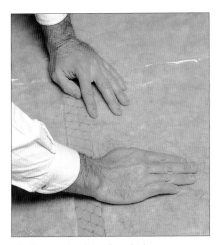

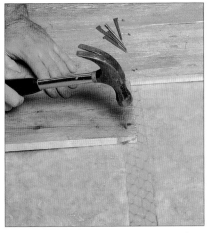

3 To prevent moisture from the house condensing within the insulation, cover the insulation with a vapour barrier of heavy-duty plastic sheeting.

4 Re-lay the floorboards by nailing them to the joists. Take this opportunity to close up any joints between the boards for a neat finish and to cut down draughts.

# INSULATING SOLID FLOORS

With direct-to-ground concrete floors (slab on grade), the commonest method of insulation involves lining the floor with a vapour barrier of heavy-duty plastic sheeting, and installing a floating floor of tongued-and-grooved chipboard (particle board) panels. If additional insulation is required, place rigid polystyrene (plastic foam) insulation boards directly on top of the vapour barrier, then lay the new flooring on top of them.

Treat damp floors with one or two coats of a proprietary damp-proofing liquid and allow to dry before laying the vapour barrier. A gap of 9mm (⅜in) should be left between the chipboard and the wall to allow for expansion. This gap will not be noticeable once a new skirting (baseboard) is installed. The layer of trapped air under the floating floor will help keep the area warm.

Since the new floor will be at a raised level, any doors will need to be removed and planed down to a smaller size. Also, the flooring will either have to be cut to fit around architraves (door trim), or the architraves will have to be shortened so that the flooring fits beneath them.

## LAYING A FLOATING FLOOR

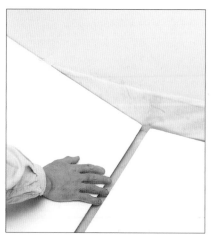

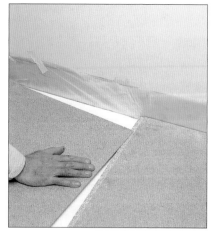

**1** Remove the skirtings (baseboards) and put down heavy-duty plastic sheets. Tape the sheets to the walls; they will be hidden behind the skirting later. Then butt-joint 25mm (1in) polystyrene (plastic foam) insulation boards over the floor, staggering the joints in adjacent rows.

**2** Cover the polystyrene insulation board with tongued-and-grooved flooring-grade boards. Use cut pieces as necessary at the ends of rows, and add a tapered threshold (saddle) strip at the door. When finished, replace the skirtings with hammer and nails.

# DRAUGHTPROOFING FLOORS

Gaps between the boards of a suspended wooden floor can allow cold draughts to enter a room. There are various methods for coping with this problem, depending on the size of the gaps and whether you want the boards exposed as a decorative feature, or are happy to conceal them beneath a floorcovering.

## EXPOSED FLOORBOARDS

Large gaps in floorboards can be filled with strips of wood, carefully cut to fit tightly. Spread adhesive on the sides of each strip and tap it into the gap. Allow the glue to set, then plane down the strip so that it is flush with the surrounding floor. The strips can then be stained to match the colour of the other floorboards.

In severe cases, and if you want the boards to be exposed, you may have no option but to lift all of the boards and re-lay them, butting them tightly together as you do so. You can hire special flooring clamps for this purpose, which attach to the joists and allow you to push the boards tightly together before you nail them down. ▶

### TIP

A papier-mâché mix made from pieces of newspaper and a thick solution of wallpaper paste can be used to repair small holes in floorboards. Add woodstain to match the surrounding boards, then sand the repair smooth when dry.

ABOVE: Tap slivers of wood in place to cure draughts through large gaps. Leave the repair slightly proud of the surface. Once the glue has set, sand down the raised area to a smooth finish with a power sander or planer.

ABOVE: Stop draughts at skirting (baseboard) level by filling any gaps with silicone sealant (caulking) and covering with quadrant (quarter-round) moulding. Secure the quadrant moulding with pins.

## COVERED FLOORS

Where there are large gaps between floorboards, and especially if the boards themselves are in poor condition, you can cover the floor with sheets of hardboard to provide a sound surface for carpeting or some other form of floorcovering. At the same time, this sub-floor will eliminate draughts.

Before laying, condition the hardboard by spraying the textured side of each sheet with 450ml (¾ pint) of water. Stack the sheets back-to-back and flat, separated by strips of wood, on the floor of the room where they are to be laid. Leave them for 48 hours, until they are completely dry.

Begin laying the hardboard sheets in the corner of the room farthest from the door, fixing each sheet in place with 19mm (¾in) annular (spiral) flooring nails. Start to nail 12mm (½in) from the skirting (baseboard) edge. To ensure the boards lie flat, work across the surface in a pyramid sequence, spacing the nails 150mm (6in) apart along the edges and 230mm (9in) apart in the middle.

Butt boards edge to edge to complete the first row, nailing the meeting edges first. Use the offcut (scrap) from the first row to start the next row, and continue in this way, staggering the joins between rows.

If boards are in really poor condition, you may be better off replacing them completely with tongued-and-grooved chipboard (particle board) panels, which will eliminate draughts.

ABOVE: Nail across a hardboard sheet in a pyramid sequence to avoid creating bulges. Nails should be 150mm (6in) apart along the edges and 230mm (9in) apart in the middle.

## LAYING A HARDBOARD SUB-FLOOR

1 Condition the hardboard sheets by brushing or spraying them with water, and leave them for 48 hours before laying.

## CARPET

If the gaps between boards are narrow, and you don't want the boards to be exposed, the easiest method of coping with a draughty floor is to lay fitted carpet with a good underlay.

Put down the underlay and cover with double-sided adhesive tape. Unroll the carpet and butt the edges up against the walls of the room and ensure that the carpet is lying flat. Trim the edges against the skirtings (baseboards) and tape them down.

Laying carpet will effectively block the passage of air through the floor. For added protection, you can repair any major gaps between the boards with a silicone sealant (caulking).

### LAYING CARPET

**When the gaps between floorboards are relatively narrow, simply laying a good-quality, thick underlay beneath the carpet will prevent draughts from being a problem.**

**2** To ensure a secure fixing, use annular (spiral) flooring nails. A piece of wood cut to size will allow you to space nails correctly and rapidly.

**3** Use the offcut (scrap) from each row to start the next so that joins are staggered.

# DRAUGHTPROOFING DOORS

Ill-fitting doors are a major source of heat loss, as well as causing cold draughts. Fitting efficient draught stripping around them will reduce the losses and cut down the draughts, and is a simple job to carry out.

Doors are best draughtproofed with pin-on (tack-on) plastic or sprung metal strips or types containing a compressible rubber seal. Special draught excluders are available for door thresholds (saddles), and can be fitted to the door bottom or across the threshold. There are even excluders designed to fit over letter plate openings.

## REMEMBER VENTILATION

Don't forget that draughtproofing a home will close off many "unofficial"

sources of ventilation, turning it into a well-sealed box. Fuel-burning appliances such as boilers and room heaters must have an adequate source of fresh air to burn safely, so it is wise to ask a fuel supplier to check that there is adequate ventilation in rooms containing such appliances. Often a ventilator in a window pane will solve the problem. However, you may need to take more drastic steps, such as fitting an airbrick into a wall with a vent cover that can be opened and closed.

Efficient draughtproofing may also increase condensation, especially in kitchens and bathrooms. This can be prevented by providing controlled ventilation in these rooms with an extractor fan.

**ABOVE:** Letter plate openings can be draught-proofed in a variety of ways. You can fit a hinged plate to the inside to provide extra protection. Alternatively, rubber and brush seals are available that will also do the job.

**ABOVE:** Draughts may not only pass around doors, but also through them. The problem is quite easy to solve. Keyhole covers are inexpensive. Many locks intended for external doors are provided with them as standard.

**1** The simplest type of door-bottom draught excluder is a brush seal mounted in a wood or plastic strip. Simply cut it to length and screw it on to the foot of the door.

**2** Alternatively, fit a threshold (saddle) strip. Cut the metal bar to length and screw it to the sill, then fit the compressible rubber sealing strip in the channel.

**3** Draughtproof a letter plate opening by screwing on a special brush seal. Check beforehand that it does not foul the letter plate flap if this opens inwards.

**4** Draughtproof the sides and top of the door frame by pinning (tacking) on lengths of plastic or sprung metal sealing strip. Pin the edge farthest from the door stop bead.

**5** Alternatively, stick lengths of self-adhesive foam excluder to the stop bead against which the door closes. At the hinge side, stick the foam to the frame.

**6** A third option is to use lengths of self-adhesive brush strip excluder. These three types can also be used for draughtproofing hinged casement windows.

# DRAUGHTPROOFING WINDOPING

Windows are a major source of draughts in the home and are responsible for about ten per cent of heat loss. Many products have been designed to deal with these problems, but they vary in cost-effectiveness. The simplest are draught excluder strips, similar to those used for doors, while the most expensive remedy is to replace single-glazed units with double glazing. The latter will provide a considerable degree of comfort, as well as reducing sound transmission, but it may take up to 20 years to recoup your investment in terms of energy savings.

## SEALING THE GAPS

You can choose from a variety of draught stripping products for windows, but some are more effective on certain types of window than others. For example, modern self-adhesive foams are much more efficient and longer lasting than older types, and are ideal for hinged casement windows. Simply stick strips around the rebate (rabbet) of the frame so that the opening casement compresses them when closed.

Sash windows, however, are not so easy to treat. The best solution is to use the same type of plastic or sprung metal strips that are suitable for doors. These can be pinned (tacked) around the frame to provide a seal against the sliding sashes. The job can be completed by attaching strips of self-adhesive foam to the top edge of the upper sash and bottom edge of the lower sash, so that these seal against the frame.

## SASH WINDOWS

1 To fit a sprung metal strip excluder to a sliding sash window, first prise off the staff bead (window stop) that holds the inner sash in position, and swing it out.

4 Use the special wheeled springing tool provided with the draught excluder to make a small groove in the strip, causing it to spring outwards to press against the sash.

**2** Measure the length of strip needed to fit the height of the window, and cut it to length with a pair of scissors. Beware of the sharp edges of the metal.

**3** Pin (tack) the strip to the side of the frame so it will press against the edge of the sliding sash. Drive the pin through the edge facing towards the room.

**5** Pin a length of the strip along the inner face of the top sash meeting rail (mullion), and "spring" it so it presses against the outer face of the bottom sash rail.

**6** You can draughtproof the bottom edge of the lower sash and the top edge of the upper one by sticking on lengths of self-adhesive foam draught excluder.

# DOUBLE GLAZING

The glass in windows is the least efficient part of the house at keeping heat in, and the only way of cutting this heat loss while still being able to see out is to add another layer of glass. Double glazing can be done in two ways: existing single panes of glass can be replaced with special double-glazed panes called sealed units, or a second pane can be installed inside the existing one – so-called secondary glazing.

### SECONDARY GLAZING

This is the only practical form of double glazing for the do-it-yourselfer, and it is relatively inexpensive. There are dozens of types available, providing hinged and sliding inner panes that blend in well with most types of window; similar systems are also available from professional installers. The panes are either fixed directly to the window frame, or fitted within the window reveal on special tracks.

### SLIDING UNITS

Do-it-yourself secondary glazing systems come in kit form and are easy to install. The kits provide enough materials to cover a range of window sizes; all you need do is cut the lengths of special track to fit within the window reveal and screw them in place. You do have to provide your own glass, however, and careful measurements must be taken so that you can order this from your local glass supplier. Then all you need do is fit the glazing gaskets and insert the panes in the tracks.

### FITTING SLIDING UNITS

**1** Measure the height and width of the window reveal at each side. If the figures differ, work from the smaller measurements for height and width. Cut the track sections to size.

**4** When positioning the bottom track on the windowsill, use a straightedge and a spirit (carpenter's) level to check that it is perfectly aligned with the top track.

**2** Offer up the side track sections and screw them to the window reveal. Use thin packing pieces to get them truly vertical if the walls are out of square.

**3** Next, secure the top track section in place. Screw it directly to a wooden lintel or pre-drill holes in a concrete beam and insert plastic wall plugs first.

**5** Measure up for the glass as directed in the kit manufacturer's instructions, and order the glass. Fit cut lengths of glazing gasket to the edges of each pane.

**6** Fit the first pane into the track by inserting its top edge in the top channel, and then lowering its bottom edge. Repeat the procedure for the other pane.

## CLEAR FILM

There is a particularly cheap form of secondary glazing that involves attaching a clear PVC (vinyl) film to the inside of the window with double-sided adhesive tape. This can be discarded during the summer months and fresh film applied for the winter.

A sturdier option is acrylic sheet. If you opt for this method, make sure that at least one window is easy to open in case of an emergency.

## DON'T FORGET THE DOORS

Heat is lost through external doors too, and solid doors are best. If you prefer a glazed door, however, opt for a modern replacement fitted with a sealed double-glazing unit. You can reduce heat loss still further with an enclosed porch.

## FITTING THIN-FILM SECONDARY GLAZING

**1** Start by sticking lengths of double-sided adhesive tape to the window frame, about 12mm (½in) in from the surrounding masonry.

**2** Press the film on to the tape, pulling it as taut as possible. Then play hot air from a hairdrier over it to tighten it up and pull out any wrinkles.

**3** When the film is even and wrinkle-free, trim off the excess all the way around the window with a sharp knife.

# APPLYING SEALANTS

Silicone sealants (caulking) are good for filling large or irregularly shaped gaps around windows and doors. They come in white, brown and clear versions. Use a caulking gun for ease of application, although products that do not require a gun are also available.

To make a repair with silicone sealant, clean the frame rebate (rabbet) and apply the sealant to the fixed frame. Brush soapy water on to the closing edge of the window or door. Close and immediately open the door. The soapy water acts as a release agent, preventing the door or window from sticking to the sealant.

Because silicone sealants are flexible, they will absorb movement in the structure of your home that otherwise would produce cracking. For particularly large gaps around frames, you can use an expanding foam filler.

## TIP

For good adhesion, always clean and dry window and door frames thoroughly before applying self-adhesive sealant.

ABOVE: Fill cracks between the window frame and plasterwork with silicone sealant (caulking).

ABOVE: You can also use silicone sealant outdoors to seal gaps between frames and masonry where a rigid filler might crack.

ABOVE: Coloured silicone sealants can be used to blend in with their surroundings – or you can paint over them when a skin has formed.

# VENTILATION

You can go too far in draughtproofing your home; if you seal up all the sources of outside air, you will prevent moist air from being carried away. This will cause condensation to form on any cold surfaces, such as windows, tiles and exterior walls. In severe cases, this can result in mould growth and even damage to the structure of your home. Moreover, a lack of airflow can cause problems with certain types of heater. The ideal is to keep out the cold draughts, but provide a sufficient flow of air to prevent condensation and ensure the efficient operation of heaters. The judicious use of manual vents, airbricks and electric extractor fans will provide all the ventilation you need without making you feel chilly.

# FITTING A CEILING EXTRACTOR FAN

An extractor fan provides positive ventilation where it is needed, in a kitchen or bathroom, removing stale or moist air before it can cause a problem. There are three places you can fit an extractor fan: in a window, in a wall or in the ceiling, where ducts carry the stale air to the outside. In a kitchen, an extracting cooker hood can serve the same function, provided it is ducted to the outside; a recirculating cooker hood only filters the air.

It is important that an extractor fan is positioned so that the replacement air, which normally will come through and around the door leading to the remainder of the house, is drawn through the room and across the problem area. In a kitchen, the problem areas are the cooker and the sink; in a bathroom, they are the lavatory and shower unit.

Ceiling-mounted extractor fans are particularly efficient in bathrooms and kitchens, since the warm moist air will tend to collect just below the ceiling. Moreover, fitting the fan in the ceiling often makes for an easier installation, since all you need do is cut a circular hole in the ceiling with a padsaw, taking care to avoid the ceiling joists. From the fan, plastic ducting needs to be taken to an outside wall or to the eaves, where it is connected to an outlet. On no account allow it to discharge into the roof.

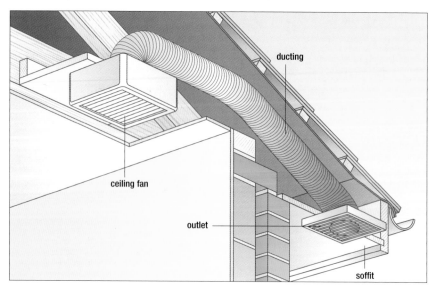

ducting

ceiling fan

outlet

soffit

ABOVE: Fit an extractor fan in the ceiling so that it discharges via a duct to a hole with an outlet at the soffit.

# FITTING A WINDOW EXTRACTOR FAN

If a simple window ventilator already exists in a fixed window, you may be able to replace it with an extractor fan. If not, you will have to cut a hole in one of the window panes. However, this will not be possible if the glass is toughened or laminated. The same applies to double-glazed units; they must be ordered with the hole pre-cut.

The only window you can cut a hole in is one made from normal glass in a single-glazed frame, and even here you may prefer to order a new pane from a glass supplier with the hole already cut. That way, the only work you will have to do is to take out the old pane and fit the new one.

Fit the extractor fan near the top of the window, since warm, moist air rises and it will do the most good at high level. Also, this will keep the fan away

from inquisitive children, who may be tempted to push things into it.

To cut the hole in the glass yourself, you will need a beam circle cutter as well as a normal glass cutter. Use the beam cutter to score two circles: one the correct size for the extractor fan, and one slightly smaller inside it. Then use the normal glass cutter to make cross-hatched lines inside the inner circle, and single radial lines between the two circles. Tap out the glass from the inner circle, then use the glass breaker rack on the glass cutter to snap off the remaining margin of glass. Smooth the edge with fine abrasive paper wrapped around a circular tool handle or piece of thick dowelling rod. Once you have a hole of the correct size, fitting a window fan is simply a matter of following the instructions.

ABOVE: If the window was fitted originally with a simple ventilator unit such as this one, you may be able to remove it and fit an extractor fan in the existing hole.

ABOVE: If no ventilator is fitted, you will need to cut a hole in the glass to fit an extractor fan. For this, you will need a special tool known as a beam circle cutter.

# FITTING A WALL EXTRACTOR FAN

Most designs of extractor fan will require a circular hole to be cut through the house wall. The best tool to use for this is a heavy-duty electric drill fitted with a core drill bit, both of which you can hire. These will cut a hole of exactly the right size. Make holes in both leaves of a cavity wall and fit the sleeve supplied with the extractor fan. Some fans require a rectangular hole to be cut, which may mean removing one or more whole bricks. Take care when doing this; cut through the mortar joints around the bricks with a cold chisel and club (spalling) hammer, and try to ease the bricks out in one piece. Keep as much debris as possible out of the wall cavity, since this could bridge the cavity and lead to damp problems. Once the sleeve for the fan is in place, make good the brickwork and plaster.

Fitting the fan is easy – simply drill holes for wall plugs to take the fan on the inside wall, and fit the outlet on the outer wall.

## WIRING

An extractor fan needs to be wired up via a fused connection unit to the nearest power supply circuit. If you are not sure how to do this, employ a qualified electrician to do the job. In a bathroom or shower room, with no opening window, a fan is a compulsory requirement and it must be wired via the light switch so that it comes on with the light and remains on for 15 minutes afterwards.

**1** The first step when fitting a wall-mounted extractor fan is to mark the exact position of the wall sleeve. Place the fan near the top of the wall for the best performance.

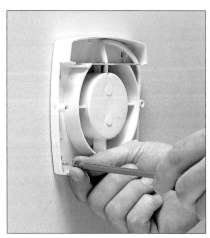

**4** Offer up the extractor and mark its fixing-hole positions on the wall. Drill these and fit them with wall plugs so that you can screw the extractor to the wall surface.

2 Use a core drill bit, fitted to a heavy-duty electric drill, to cut a hole of the correct size through both leaves of the wall (if it is of the cavity type).

3 Check the fit of the sleeve in the hole and push it through the wall. Mark it off for length, then remove it and cut it down with a hacksaw. Replace it.

5 Wiring comes next (get help with this if necessary). Make a check that the extractor functions correctly, after which the cover of the unit can be put on.

6 Finally, fit the outlet on the outside wall. Sometimes this simply pushes into the end of the sleeve. In other cases, you may need to screw it to the wall.

# FITTING EXTRA AIRBRICKS

In other rooms, fitting small "trickle" ventilators at the top of window frames and putting in extra airbricks will often supply enough ventilation to allow the moist air to disperse before condensation becomes a problem.

### UNDERFLOOR VENTILATION

A suspended wooden floor consists of floorboards or sheets of flooring-grade chipboard (particle board) supported on joists. To keep the joists and the flooring dry, some kind of underfloor ventilation is essential. This takes the form of airbricks in the outer walls.

The first thing to check is that all the existing airbricks are free of debris and have not been blocked up in the mistaken belief that this will save money on heating. Next, check that there are enough airbricks – there should be one airbrick for every 2m (6ft) of wall length. Inserting a new airbrick is not difficult, as most match the size of standard bricks.

Decide where you want to put it, drill out the mortar around the existing brick and remove it. With a cavity wall, you will have to continue the hole through the inner wall and fit a terracotta liner to maintain the airflow. Use the corners of the hole in the outer wall to line up and drill four holes in the inner wall, then chip out the hole with a bolster (stonecutter's) chisel and club (spalling) hammer, working from the inside. You will need to lift floorboards to do this.

Fit the airbrick from the outside, applying mortar to the bottom of the hole and the top of the brick, pushing mortar in the sides. Point the mortar joints to the same profile as the surrounding joints. Mortar the liner in place from inside the house.

### VENTILATING ROOF SPACES

If your house has a gable end wall, the roof space can be ventilated by fitting airbricks in the gable. If the house is semi-detached, ask your neighbour to do the same, and fit another airbrick in the party wall to allow air to circulate.

### SAFE VENTILATION

There are two very important points to remember concerning ventilation. Firstly, many fuel-burning appliances need an adequate supply of fresh air to work efficiently and safely, so rooms where they are sited must contain provision for this if they are well sealed against natural draughts. Secondly, disused flues must be ventilated at top and bottom; if they are not, condensation can occur within the flue, which may show up as damp patches on the internal chimney walls.

### TIP

You may need to install more airbricks in a room where there is a solid concrete hearth (from an old cooking range, say). This can create "dead" areas which may need extra ventilation to prevent rot.

1 Airbricks are the same size as one, two or three bricks. To fit one, start by drilling a series of closely-spaced holes through the joint around a brick.

2 Then use the club (spalling) hammer and a wide bolster (stonecutter's) chisel to cut out the brickwork. With solid walls, drill holes right through and work from inside too.

3 Fit a cavity liner through to the inner wall if the wall is of cavity construction, then trowel a bed of fairly wet mortar on to the bottom of the opening.

4 Butter mortar on to the top of the airbrick and slide in place. Push more mortar into the gaps at the sides. Inside, make good the wall with plaster and cover the opening with a ventilator grille.

5 As an alternative to the traditional terracotta airbrick, fit a two-part plastic version. The sleeves interlock to line the hole as the two parts are pushed together.

6 Slide the outer section into place, and point around it. Slide the inner section into place from the inside of the house. Make good the plaster and fit its cover grille.

# OVERCOMING DAMP CONDITIONS

Damp conditions can cause serious problems if allowed to persist in the home, even leading to structural decay, so it is essential to deal with damp as soon as it becomes obvious. The first task is to recognize the type of damp you are faced with: it could be condensation, caused by moisture inside the home, or penetrating or rising damp from outside. In some cases, finding a remedy is relatively straightforward; in others, solving the problem can be complex and costly, and may require the involvement of professionals. If damp conditions are not corrected, they may lead to wet rot or dry rot in structural wooden framing. Both can be a major problem if not tackled quickly, since they weaken the wood with potentially disastrous consequences.

# DAMP

This can ruin decorations, destroy floorcoverings, damage walls and plaster, and cause woodwork to rot, so it is important not only to treat the symptoms, but also to track down the causes. These might be rain coming in through the roof or walls, condensation, moisture being absorbed from the ground, or a combination of any of these.

## PENETRATING DAMP

This is caused by moisture getting in from the outside, often because of wear and tear to the structure of your home, but it may also affect solid walls that are subjected to strong driving rain. The first sign of penetrating damp appears after a heavy downpour and can occur almost anywhere, although it may be some distance from the actual leak; mould often forms directly behind where the problem lies. Pay particular attention to rainwater systems, which are common causes of penetrating damp.

## RISING DAMP

This is caused by water soaking up through floors and walls, and is usually confined to a 1m (3ft) band above ground level. It is a constant problem, even during dry spells.

The main areas to check for rising damp are the damp-proof course (DPC) around the foot of walls, and damp-proof membrane (DPM) in the ground floor. Older properties were often built without either, which can lead to widespread rising damp. If existing

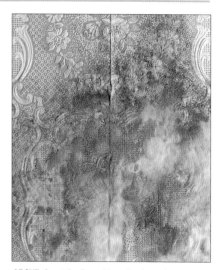

ABOVE: A patch of mould on the inner face of an external wall is usually the first sign of penetrating damp.

ABOVE: Gaps between masonry and woodwork around windows will let in rain, causing patches of damp to occur.

materials have broken down or structural movement has caused defects, there may be isolated, but spreading, patches of damp where water is penetrating. A DPC that is less than 150mm (6in) above ground level will allow rain to splash above it and penetrate the wall, which may cause damp patches at skirting (baseboard) level. If a DPC has been bridged, there will be evidence of damp just above skirting level. A wall cavity filled with rubble may also allow damp to penetrate.

## DEALING WITH DAMP

Once the cause of penetrating damp has been traced and repaired, the problem will be eradicated. When the damp patches have dried out, it may be necessary to replaster those areas and make good any decorations.

Dealing with a DPC that has been bridged is quite straightforward. If the ground level is the cause, digging a 150mm (6in) trench along the house wall, then filling it with gravel will allow rainwater to drain away rapidly. When you suspect that debris in the cavity is the cause, removing a few bricks will give access to remove it.

The remedy for rising damp caused by a non-existent or defective DPC or DPM is not so easy; the only solution is to install a replacement or make repairs.

## DAMP-PROOFING METHODS

Laying a new damp-proof membrane involves digging up and re-laying the floor slab, which is the most effective method of damp-proofing a concrete floor. However, a floor can also be damp-proofed by applying several coats of moisture-curing urethane, but it is essential that any leaky patches are sealed first with a hydraulic cement.

A third option is to apply two coats of rubberized bitumen emulsion to the old surface, then cover this with a cement/sand screed, which will raise the level of the floor by about 50mm (2in).

Whichever method you choose, the DPM material should be taken up the adjoining walls to meet the DPC, if there is one. The problem of damp floors caused by rising ground-water levels, which typically affects basements, is more serious and requires structural waterproofing or "tanking". This is certainly a job for the professionals.

ABOVE: A damp-proof course should be clear of soil, debris or plants growing up walls, otherwise moisture can bypass it.

# INSTALLING A DAMP-PROOF COURSE

There are many ways of installing a damp-proof course, ranging from physical DPCs that are cut into the brickwork to chemical slurries, which are pumped into a series of drilled holes.

In theory, it is possible to do the job yourself, but dealing with rising damp is rarely simple; it is worth seeking the advice of professionals. If there is a mortgage on your home, the lender may require a guarantee of workmanship, which rules out tackling the job yourself. The standard of workmanship is as important as the system used, so choosing a reputable company that offers an insurance-backed guarantee is essential, and often compulsory.

If you do choose to go ahead yourself, you should be able to hire the necessary equipment to install a chemical DPC, and the same company may supply the chemical too.

After installing a DPC, walls and floors can take up to a month for each 25mm (1in) to dry out, while old plaster may be heavily contaminated with salts from rising damp, which will continue to absorb moisture from the air. Delay replastering for as long as possible to allow the walls to dry out.

**1** A chemical damp-proof course is injected into a line of holes drilled in the wall about 115mm (4½in) apart.

**2** Once injected into the drilled holes, the chemicals overlap to form a continuous impermeable barrier.

**3** When the fluid is dry, the drilled holes are filled with mortar and then a rendered surface can be painted.

# WATERPROOFING WALLS

The external walls of modern brick houses are built with a cavity between the inner and outer leaves of the wall that effectively prevents damp from reaching the inner leaf. Unless the cavity becomes bridged in some way, there should be no problems with penetrating damp. However, older properties are likely to have been built with solid walls and it is possible that, over time, the masonry may become porous, allowing damp to penetrate to the inside.

Penetrating damp in solid walls is difficult to cure, and one solution, albeit rather drastic, is to build false walls inside, complete with vapour barriers, effectively creating cavity walls. However, this solution is expensive, and it will reduce the size of rooms considerably.

Less expensive is to treat the outer faces of the walls with a water-repellent coating. This will prevent rainwater from soaking into the walls and reaching the interior.

The first job is to clean the walls and make good any structural defects. Wash them down and treat them with a fungicide to kill off any mould. Check the condition of the mortar joints and repoint any that are soft and crumbling; fill cracks in the joints or bricks with mortar or an exterior-grade filler.

When the walls have dried, brush on the water-repellent liquid, following the manufacturer's instructions; you may need to apply more than one coat.

**1** Brush, clean, and remove any fungal growth from the wall. Fill any surface cracks so that the surface is sound.

**2** Apply the water seal by brush, working from the bottom up, coating the whole wall. If necessary, apply a second coat.

# CONDENSATION

When warm, moist air reaches a cold surface, such as a wall exposed to icy winter winds or ceramic tiles, the result is condensation. It is most likely to occur in bathrooms and kitchens where the main activities are bathing, washing and cooking.

Controlling condensation requires a fine balance between good ventilation and adequate heating, but while the modern home is warm, it is also well insulated and draughtproofed, so the level of ventilation is often poor. The key to success is to provide sufficient ventilation, without allowing expensive heat to escape.

Ventilation can be provided by a variety of passive and active means. Passive ventilation may be achieved by opening windows and/or fitting airbricks and simple vents. Active ventilation relies on powered extractor fans.

### CONDENSATION OR DAMP?

If you are not sure if a moisture problem is due to condensation or damp, lay a piece of aluminium foil over the patch, seal the edges with adhesive tape and leave it for 48 hours. Condensation will cause beads of moisture to appear on the surface of the foil; penetrating or rising damp will produce beads of moisture underneath the foil.

ABOVE: Water vapour from everyday activities, such as cooking, can cause condensation.

ABOVE: Poor ventilation will make condensation problems worse.

## COPING WITH CONDENSATION

Steam from cooking can be removed by a fully vented cooker hood, but where a great deal of steam is produced, when you take a shower for example, the best way to remove it from the room is with an extractor fan.

To be quick and efficient, the fan must be sited properly and it should be the correct size for the room. In a kitchen, a fan must be capable of ten to 15 air changes per hour, and in bathrooms six to eight air changes per hour, which should be increased to 15 to 20 air changes for a power shower. Simply multiply the volume of the room by the number of air changes required and look for a fan that offers the same cubic metre/foot capacity per hour ($m^3/hr$ or $ft^3/hr$).

An extractor fan should be installed as high as possible on the wall, and as far as possible from the main source

of ventilation; usually diagonally opposite the main door is ideal.

More widespread condensation can be alleviated with an electric dehumidifier, which draws air from the room, passes it over cold coils to condense it, then collects the drips of water. The dry air is then drawn over heated coils and released back into the room as heat.

RIGHT: A cooker hood removes steam from cooking at source. Beware, however, since some cooker hoods merely recirculate the air, filtering out the particles from cooking, but not the moisture. For this, you must have an extractor hood. Remember, too, that kettles produce steam, as do other forms of cooking that may not be in range of a cooker hood. Consequently, it may be worth adding a window vent or even an additional extractor fan.

# DRY ROT

The fungus that causes dry rot loves moist, humid conditions and has a taste for resins and silicones in untreated wood. However, the grey strands are fine enough to penetrate masonry, which means that it can spread rapidly from room to room.

Untreated dry rot will destroy floors, doors and skirtings (baseboards), and infect plaster and ceilings. Initially, it manifests itself as a brownish-red dust, but within days the spores will have developed into a fungus that looks like a mushroom growing upside-down, and it also gives off a distinctive musty smell. This is the final stage of germination, by which time the fungus will be producing millions of spores to infect surrounding areas.

Dealing with dry rot is a job that should be entrusted to a specialist, as it may recur if not treated properly. Make sure you choose a reputable company that offers an insurance-backed guarantee.

### PREVENTATIVE ACTION

• Make sure that a damp-proof course (DPC) has not been bridged, by looking for tell-tale signs of damp on walls above skirtings (baseboards).

• Dry rot will not flourish in well-ventilated areas, so make sure there is good ventilation in roofs and under suspended wooden floors. If necessary, fit air vents or extractor fans in soffits and gable end walls.

ABOVE: An example of severe dry rot on a destroyed wooden floor.

ABOVE: A sporophore, or dry rot fungus, on a structural roof timber. Immediate action is necessary as soon as the fungus is spotted to minimize its spread through wooden structures.

ABOVE: Inspect your loft (attic) space and check for the first signs of dry rot. Ensure there is good ventilation in the loft and under the floors to help prevent the conditions in which dry rot can flourish.

# WET ROT

This thrives on wet wood and frequently appears where wood is close to the ground or near leaking plumbing, and in woodwork where the protective paint coating has broken down. Skirtings (baseboards) may also be affected where a damp-proof course is defective.

Wet rot can be due to a number of species of fungus, but the most common consist of brown or black strands that appear on the surface, causing the wood to crack and eventually disintegrate. Affected wood tends to look darker than healthy wood and feels spongy.

Once the cause of the damp conditions that have led to the problem is eliminated, wet rot fungus will die. Treat small areas, such as window frames, with proprietary wood hardener solution and insert preservative tablets into holes drilled into the wood to stop any recurrence. Where damage is extensive, the wood should be cut out and replaced.

## REPAIRING WET ROT

**1** Chisel out all the rotten wood, making sure only sound wood is left.

**2** Brush the sound wood with hardener and leave to dry as recommended.

**3** To fit wood preservative sticks, drill holes of the correct size in the sound wood. Push the preservative sticks into the drilled holes and below the surface.

**4** Fill the damaged area with exterior wood filler. Leave to dry before sanding. Then apply a good paint finish.

# OUTDOOR PROJECTS

- Outdoor materials
- Paving, decking & beds
- Walls, fences & garden structures
- Rock & water gardens

# INTRODUCTION

**E**very gardener knows that there is a lot more to producing a beautiful garden than planting the right species in the right places. Before you can begin to grow plants, shrubs and trees, the ground must be shaped – worked into the right form. Boundaries must be marked, easy access routes to all parts of the garden laid, levels changed and provision made for the future enjoyment of your labours. As a gardener, you need more than just green fingers; you need to be part surveyor, part landscaper, part architect, part carpenter and part builder.

You will need some of the skills of all those professions to create your garden, and since you are unlikely to be able to employ such a variety of

ABOVE: Paving provides much-needed access in the garden, and its harsh edges can be softened with planting.

professionals, you will have no option but to learn the skills yourself. That's not to say that building a garden is a complicated business – it can be, of course, but it doesn't have to be, provided you don't attempt projects that are completely beyond your abilities.

In the process of building a garden, you will have to learn, among many other things, how to mix and lay concrete, how to build walls, how to lay paving, erect fencing, construct a variety of structures from wood, and possibly even create a pond. It is true that some of these jobs require a considerable degree of skill; others, however, are quite simple, and if you are determined to learn and prepared to practise (and accept the occasional failure), you will succeed.

LEFT: Wooden decking provides a durable, practical and easy-to-care-for surface. Ready-made wooden tiles make laying simple.

Although the construction aspect of a garden may seem less attractive to you than the planting, it can be satisfying in its own right. To look at a wall and know that you have built it, or a deck and know that you have designed and constructed it can be very rewarding.

In the following pages, you will find a variety of projects that will help you build your garden, from simple gravel paving, through fencing, decking and trellis structures, to rock gardens and water features. You can follow them closely or adapt them to suit your own needs.

Don't be afraid to try new skills, or to try again if things don't go quite as you planned first time around. Practice does – nearly – make perfect, and the results will be well worth the effort.

ABOVE: Fences and walls provide an ideal means of supporting climbing plants, or you can train fruit trees along them.

BELOW: Even a small pool can make an eye-catching feature in the garden; when teamed with a rockery, which offers the opportunity of incorporating a cascade, the effect is wonderful.

# OUTDOOR MATERIALS

Garden projects can involve dealing with a variety of materials. Fortunately, most of the jobs you are likely to encounter are fairly straightforward and rarely require many special tools. Apart from normal gardening tools, you will probably need a few woodworking and masonry tools. Any materials you choose must be rugged enough to withstand weathering. This is particularly true of fixings like nails and screws. Concrete and mortar are commonly found outdoors, too, so an understanding of these materials is essential. Safety is a major consideration when working outdoors, particularly if working from a ladder. If you intend using electric tools, you must take steps to prevent electrocution.

# PAVING, DECKING AND BEDS

Hard surfaces are important in your garden, allowing easy access to its various parts and providing a firm "floor" for enjoying the outdoors. They can work in conjunction with raised beds to give the garden form and structure.

## PAVING

There is an incredibly wide range of materials suitable for garden paving. Which you choose is largely a matter of personal preference, although each type does have its own advantages and disadvantages. Try to choose a paving material that is sympathetic to the overall design and to the style of your house. Selecting materials that are already used elsewhere in the garden will help create a co-ordinated effect. Regularly shaped paving works well in a formal setting, whereas paving that consists of smaller units or a range of paving sizes is often a better choice if you are trying to create a more relaxed feel. If you are combining different materials, make sure they are the same thickness to make laying easier.

## GRAVEL

One of the big advantages of gravel is that it makes a noise when you walk on it and provides a significant deterrent to potential intruders. It is also good for drives, as it can soak up oil drips from cars without showing permanent stains. However, gravelled surfaces can become weedy and the pieces may blow about. Gravel may also be trodden into the house and develop thin patches.

BELOW: The top row shows (from left to right) natural stone sett, clay paver, brick, artificial sett. The centre row shows a range of the different shapes of concrete paving blocks available. The bottom row shows some of the colours and sizes of concrete paving slabs available..

ABOVE: Gravels naturally vary considerably in colour and size.

## DECKING PATTERNS

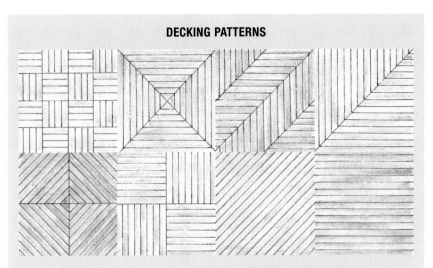

Wooden decking can be laid in a number of decorative patterns. Each style will give your garden a subtly different effect, so consider the pattern carefully before you start. If in doubt, ask a professional designer for help.

### DECKING

Decking can be made from hardwood, pressure-treated (tanalized) softwood or plain softwood. Hardwood decks made from white oak or western red cedar are durable and practically maintenance free, but they cost a lot more to construct. Decking made from pressure-treated softwood is less expensive and reasonably durable, but requires seasonal maintenance, while plain softwood decking needs regular maintenance and is prone to rotting, so it is not very durable. Clad the deck with non-slip grooved planks spaced about 6mm (¼in) apart to allow for expansion and to allow water to drain away freely.

### BEDS

Traditional permanent raised beds made from bricks or blocks are built in much the same way as solid brick retaining walls.

Raised beds can also be constructed from wood. Old railway sleepers (railroad ties) were traditionally recommended, but designer mini-sleepers are more readily available from garden centres.

**ABOVE:**
Railway sleepers
(railroad ties) can be used
to make traditional raised beds.

# WALL AND FENCE MATERIALS

Mark the boundary of your garden with walls or fencing, which can also define areas within the garden.

## WALLS

These can be made from a wide range of materials so can be constructed to suit any style. Substantial or prominent walls, such as those used along the boundary, will fit in more easily with the rest of the garden if they are constructed of the same material used for the house.

BELOW: Bricks come in many colours and finishes, and these are just a small selection of the many available.

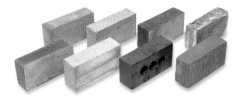

ABOVE: Fencing constructed from ready-made panels is popular, and easy and quick to erect. There is a wide choice of styles and panel sizes.

## FENCES

The most popular type of fence is the ready-made panel, which comes in various forms, including horizontal lap, vertical lap and interwoven. They are also available in several heights including 1.2m (4ft), 1.5m (5ft) and 1.8m (6ft). Fencing panels are very cheap and easy to put up between regularly spaced, well-anchored posts.

## BRICK BONDING

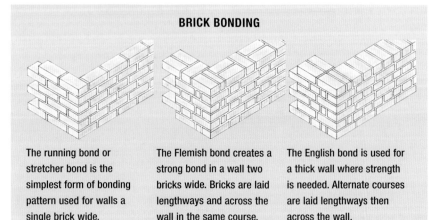

The running bond or stretcher bond is the simplest form of bonding pattern used for walls a single brick wide.

The Flemish bond creates a strong bond in a wall two bricks wide. Bricks are laid lengthways and across the wall in the same course.

The English bond is used for a thick wall where strength is needed. Alternate courses are laid lengthways then across the wall.

## POSTS

With all types of fence, the posts should be durable. For preference choose a naturally rot-resistant hardwood, but pressure-treated (tanalized) softwood is more commonly available. With panel fencing the posts are set 1.8m (6ft) apart to accommodate the panel width, but with close-board fencing they are usually spaced more widely – 2.4–3m (8–10ft). Either buy posts that are long enough for the bottom section to be buried into the ground and held firm with concrete, or buy posts the same height as the fence and secure them with fence spikes.

## RUSTIC POLES

In an informal or country-style garden, structures made from rustic poles blend naturally into their surroundings. These can be bought as ready-made structures from fencing suppliers or made from fresh-cut wood. Rustic poles are usually roughly jointed and held together with galvanized nails. Rustic structures are not usually as strong as other types and often require more cross-members to improve their rigidity and strength.

If you are using sawn timber for arches and pergolas, choose timber that has been pressure-treated with preservative to prevent it rotting.

## SUPPORTS FOR CLIMBING PLANTS

There are several types of support to choose from, but it is important to provide one that matches the size and vigour of the climber it is to support. Against a wall or fence you have the choice of fixing trellis panels, expanding trellis or plastic mesh to the surface or attaching parallel wires.

ABOVE: Rustic poles are ideal in an informal, country-style garden to make open-frame structures such as pergolas and trellises.

ABOVE: Traditional trelliswork made from narrow battens makes a good support for climbing plants against walls or as screening between posts.

# ROCK AND WATER MATERIALS

When you build a rock garden, aim as far as possible to create a natural-looking outcrop, otherwise it will take on the appearance of a rock-encrusted heap of soil. The most important ingredient is the rocks, which are more likely to "gel" as a rocky outcrop if they are of the same natural stone. Choose a type of rock that has clear strata lines running through it and an attractive texture and colour. Limestone and sandstone are among the best rock types.

You will need a range of sizes of rock – anything from 15kg (33lb) to 100kg (220lb) – so make sure you have help on hand to manoeuvre the larger stones. If you live near a quarry, use this as your source, otherwise suppliers can be found in local directories; a limited selection of rocks will be offered at some garden centres.

## LINING A POND

A pond can be made with a rigid, pre-formed liner or with a special flexible liner. Rigid liners are usually made from plastic or fibreglass, and they come in a range of shapes and sizes to suit most styles of garden. Rigid liners tend to be on the small side, with little space for marginal plants, and are more work to install. A flexible liner, made from PVC, butyl rubber or heavy-duty

ABOVE: White marble cobbles.

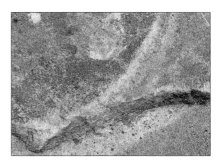

ABOVE: York stone.

ABOVE: Snowdonian slate.

ABOVE: Welsh green granite.

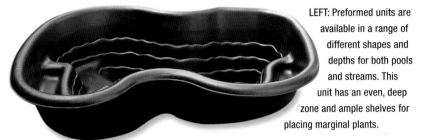

LEFT: Preformed units are available in a range of different shapes and depths for both pools and streams. This unit has an even, deep zone and ample shelves for placing marginal plants.

polythene (polyethylene), gives you a lot more control over the design of your pond. It can be pleated at the corners to fit a rectangular pond, and it is particularly suitable for an informal pond because it can be folded to fit any shape you want. It does, however, require some skill to create a convincingly shaped pond, and the liner can be easily damaged, especially on stony soil.

Although a beginner to water gardening may find a preformed unit tempting because it seems easier to install, such a pond is, in fact, more expensive than a pool of the same size made with the best of the flexible pool liners. In addition, although the units seem huge when they are seen displayed on their sides in a retail centre, they can be disappointingly small when they are dug into the ground.

ABOVE: Flexible pond liners are available in a variety of materials, thicknesses and colours, and are offered with varying guarantees according to quality. Cheaper types can deteriorate when exposed to direct sunlight. An underlay may be necessary on stony ground. From left to right: 1–2 Butyl liner; 3 Low-density polythene (polyethylene); 4 Low-density polythene; 5–9 PVC in different grades; 10 Underlay.

# CONCRETE AND MORTAR

Concrete is used to provide a solid and rigid surface as a floor, as paving or as a base for a garage or outbuilding. Mortar is the "glue" that holds the bricks together in a wall. The basis for both concrete and mortar is cement and sand (fine aggregate); concrete also contains stones (coarse aggregate). When mixed with water, the cement sets to bind the aggregates solidly together.

## CEMENT

Most cement used in the home is OPC (Ordinary Portland Cement). This is air-setting (that is, moisture in the air will cause it to harden unless bags are kept sealed and in the dry).

## BUYING CONCRETE AND MORTAR

There are three ways of buying concrete and mortar: as individual ingredients, as wet ready-mixed and as dry pre-mixed. Buying cement, sand and coarse aggregate separately for concrete is the cheapest option, but you do have to ensure dry storage for the cement. For big jobs, having wet ready-mixed concrete delivered is convenient, provided sufficient manpower is available to transport it from the truck to the site and to level it before it sets. You also need to calculate the quantity needed accurately. For small jobs, bags of dry pre-mix are a good choice: the ingredients are in the correct proportions, and all you do is add water.

## CONCRETE AND MORTAR MIXES

| CONCRETE | mix | cement | sand | aggregate | yield* | area** |
|---|---|---|---|---|---|---|
| General-purpose | 1:2:3 | 50kg | 100kg | 200kg | 0.15 | 1.5 |
| | | (110lb) | (220lb) | (440lb) | (5.3) | (16) |
| Foundation | 1:2½:3½ | 50kg | 130kg | 200kg | 0.18 | 1.8 |
| | | (110lb) | (290lb) | (440lb) | (6.4) | (19.4) |
| Paving | 1:1½:2½ | 50kg | 75kg | 150kg | 0.12 | 1.2 |
| | | (110lb) | (165lb) | (330lb) | (4.2) | (13) |

| MORTAR | mix | cement | sand | lime*** | yield* | bricks laid |
|---|---|---|---|---|---|---|
| Normal | 1:5 | 50kg | 200kg | 50kg | 0.25 | 850 |
| | | (110lb) | (440lb) | (110lb) | (8.8) | |
| Strong | 1:4 | 50kg | 150kg | 15kg | 0.19 | 650 |
| | | (110lb) | (330lb) | (33lb) | (6.7) | |

\* cubic metres (cubic feet) per 50kg (110lb) of cement
\*\* area in square metres (square feet) of concrete 100mm (4in) thick
\*\*\* or plasticizer are optional - they can be added to the standard mix to improve workability

## MIXING CONCRETE

1 Start by measuring out the dry ingredients in the right proportions.

2 Mix the dry ingredients thoroughly until you have a consistent colour.

3 Make a small well in the centre of the pile and add a small amount of water.

4 Work from the edges of the pile, mixing the ingredients and adding more water.

5 Work the material with the edge of your spade to get the right consistency.

6 When the concrete is mixed, transfer it to a bucket or wheelbarrow.

# PAVING, DECKING & BEDS

Hard surfaces are an integral part of practically every garden; in the form of paths, they allow easy, all-weather access to all the important parts of the plot; as patios and terraces, they provide somewhere to entertain outdoors or simply to sit and enjoy the sights and scents of the garden. Common hard-surface materials include paving slabs, bricks, pavers and gravel. Which you choose depends on the overall garden style and your pocket. For a less harsh appearance, wooden decking is perfect, providing a firm, practical surface that is inexpensive and easy to construct. Many hard surfaces help divide the garden into specific areas; raised beds can do this too, and they bring plants closer to hand.

# LAYING PATIOS

A patio provides a smooth, level, hard surface on which to sit and relax and entertain. For these reasons patios are usually best sited in a spot that is not overlooked by neighbours and that is in a convenient position near to the house. If you want to use your patio for sunbathing, it will need to catch the sun for much of the day, and if you want it for entertaining, a site close to the kitchen would be best.

In a north-facing garden, the best place to site a patio may be at the bottom of the garden to catch the maximum amount of sun. It may be more convenient to have two smaller areas of paving: one for sunbathing and one near to the house for entertaining. Wherever you decide to site your patio, make sure that the outlook is pleasing and that it is well screened; the privacy will create a relaxing atmosphere.

## DECIDING ON A SIZE

The size of the patio should also be determined by what you want to use it for. To accommodate a standard patio set of table and four chairs, you would need a paved area at least 3 x 3m (10 x 10ft), but preferably larger, about 4 x 4m (13 x 13ft), so that there is room to walk around the furniture while it is in use. However, in a small garden, the patio can dominate the space and create an unbalanced effect in the overall design. In this case, you may be better off paving the whole garden and using planting pockets, raised beds and containers to provide visual interest.

**1** Excavate to a depth that will allow for about 5cm (2in) of compacted hardcore (rubble) topped with 2.5–5cm (1–2in) of mixed aggregate, plus the thickness of the paving and mortar.

**4** Use a spirit (carpenter's) level placed over more than one slab to ensure that the slab is level. Use a small wedge of wood under one end of the level to create a slight slope over the whole area if necessary. Tap the slab down further, or raise it by lifting and packing in more mortar.

**2** On top of the layers of hardcore and aggregate, put five blobs of mortar where the slab is to be placed – one at each corner, and the other in the middle.

**3** Position the slab carefully, bedding it down firmly on the mortar. Over a large area of paving, create a slight slope in one direction to allow rainwater to run off freely.

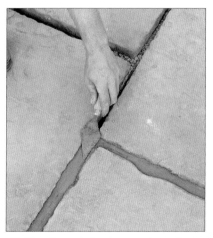

**5** Use spacers of an even thickness, such as scraps of wood, to ensure regular spacing between the paving slabs. Remove these later, before the joints are filled with mortar. When you have completed laying the slabs, leave the paving for a day or two for the mortar to set.

**6** When the mortar is set, go over the paving again to fill in the joints. Use a small pointing trowel and a dryish mortar mix. Finish off with a smooth stroke that leaves the mortar slightly recessed. This produces an attractive, crisp look. Brush any surplus mortar off the slabs before it dries.

# LAYING BRICK AND BLOCK PATHS

Paths exert a strong influence on the design and sense of movement in a garden, so consider the effect during the planning process.

A path's design should reflect the overall theme of the garden. In a formal setting, straight paths with clean lines will reinforce the formality of the design, whereas in an informal garden gently meandering paths will be more appropriate. Calm the feeling of movement by adding changes in direction along the path, and create a sense of mystery by allowing the path to disappear from view – behind a garden structure or border, for example.

## LAYING PAVERS

1 Excavate the area and prepare a sub-base of about 5cm (2in) of compacted hardcore (rubble) or sand-and-gravel mix. Set an edging along one end and side first. Check that it is level, then lay the pavers on a bed of mortar.

2 Once the edging is set, lay a 5cm (2in) bed of sharp sand over the area. Use a straight-edged piece of wood to level the surface. Position the pavers, butting them tightly to the edging and to each other.

3 Brush loose sand into the joints of the pavers with a broom. Hire a flat-plate vibrator to consolidate the sand or tamp the pavers down with a club hammer used over a piece of wood.

4 Brush in more sand and repeat the vibrating process. To avoid damage do not go too close to an unsupported edge with the vibrator. The path should be ready to use straight away.

# LAYING GRAVEL PATHS

**G**ravel paths are simple to construct on firmed soil with an underlay of membrane. They can be made any shape, including complicated curves. Little maintenance is required apart from removing the odd weed and raking occasionally to keep it looking neat. Unfortunately, the gravel tends to be kicked into nearby borders and may be walked into the house.

## NEAT EDGING

For a period garden, Victorian-style rope edging looks appropriate. You can use it either to retain a gravel path or as an edging to a paved path. Alternatively, waving edgings can be used in a modern setting to create a formal effect.

**1** Excavate the area to a depth of about 15cm (6in), and ram the base firm. Provide a stout edge to retain the gravel. For a straight path, securing boards by pegs about 1m (3ft) apart is an easy and inexpensive method.

**2** Spread out a layer of compacted hardcore (rubble). Then add a mixture of sand and coarse gravel (sold as combined aggregate). Rake level and tamp or roll until firm.

**3** Top up to within 2.5cm (1in) of the edge or boards with the final grade of gravel. In small gardens, the size often known as pea gravel looks good and is easy to walk on. Rake the gravel level.

# LAYING A PEBBLE PATIO FEATURE

Create an outdoor "fireside rug" from pebbles, broken garden pots and old china ginger-jar tops. Choose a simple design that is not difficult to achieve; you can always add to it as your confidence grows. The "rug" will make an appealing, witty motif in any paved patio or terrace.

## PREPARATION

The bed on which the "rug" is to be set should be prepared to a depth of about 10cm (4in), allowing a 5cm (2in) clearance below the level of the rest of the paving. Dig out the area to the dimensions of the panel and to a depth of 15cm (6in). Mix equal parts of fine aggregate and cement. Then, using a watering can, dribble in water a little at a time until you have a dry, crumbly mix. Use this mix to fill the area, leaving a 5cm (2in) clearance. Level and allow the mix to dry. Gather together plenty of materials for the design and lay them out for size on the dry bed before you begin. Using tile nippers, cut off the bottoms of at least six terracotta pots and snip off the rims in sections. Choose pebbles and slates that are long enough to be wedged in at least 2.5cm (1in) below the surface of the "rug".

You can use a variety of other materials for this kind of decorative feature, such as clay tiles, glass marbles, shells – in fact, anything that is hard and durable. Just use your imagination. Lay out the items "dry" first to determine the best arrangement.

**1** Prepare the mortar bedding by mixing equal quantities of sharp sand and cement. Add mortar colour and mix in well. The design is worked while the mortar mix is dry, to enable you to change it if necessary. But the whole design must be completed in a day because moisture from the atmosphere will begin to set the mortar.

**4** Brush mortar over the worked areas to make sure that any gaps are filled. To build up the border design, continue working towards the centre, carefully tapping in the pebbles and pieces of slate and terracotta. In this case, china pot lids were added to provide splashes of colour in the four corners.

2 Pour the dry mixture on to the flat bed and, using a straight edge, smooth it out until it is level with the rest of the paving. Then remove a small quantity of the mix from the centre so that it does not overflow as you work. This extracted mix can be put back at a later stage as required, when the design begins to take shape.

3 Plan the edge design by arranging pebbles, pieces of slate and rim sections from terracotta pots around the outside edge of the "rug" until you have achieved a level, decorative border design. Working in towards the centre, gently tap the pieces down into the mortar mix with a hammer.

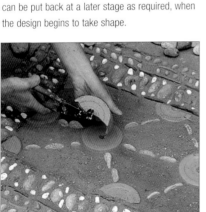

5 Plan the design of the central portion of the "rug" using the bases of terracotta plant pots, pebbles and pieces of slate. Make sure the central area of mortar is level before you begin inserting the pieces. Using tile nippers, cut the sections of terracotta to size, then gently tap everything into position.

6 When the pattern is complete, carefully brush the mortar around the decorative pieces so that there are no gaps between them and the mix. Then use a watering can fitted with a fine rose just to dampen the surface. As the mortar mix absorbs the moisture, it will set hard, fixing the pattern permanently.

# LAYING DECKING

Garden decking is a popular choice these days and in many situations is often the best option. It can be cheaper and easier to construct than paving, especially on a sloping site, and provides a hard, flat surface that is functional and looks good too.

Different designs can be achieved by fixing planks in different ways, but on the whole, it is best to keep any pattern fairly simple. In some countries there are building codes that may have to be met. If in doubt, seek professional help with the design, even if you intend to construct it yourself.

## CHOOSING A DECK

The easiest way to create a deck is to use ready-made decking tiles that can be laid straight on to a firm, flat surface, such as an old patio, roof terrace or firmed hardcore (rubble). For a better result, lay the tiles on top of a framework of pressure-treated (tanalized) timber and treat any cut ends or joints with wood preservative. You can also buy decks in kit form, and these are very easy to put together and a good choice where the deck isn't fitted into a particular space, such as an island deck part-way down the garden.

Custom-made decking, supplied and fitted by a specialist company, is the most convenient but most expensive option. Such suppliers will take on the whole process, from planning, checking local planning (zoning) regulations and getting the permissions necessary to constructing the deck.

1 Level the area, then use bricks or building blocks to support your decking. Calculate the position of each row. Each timber bearer should be supported in the middle as well as the ends. Excavate the soil and position the blocks.

4 Use wood preservative on the bearers if necessary. Space out the bearers on the block supports. Add extra bearers near the ends and sides of the decking, where the decking will need extra support.

**2** Position each block so that about half of it sits in the soil – it is important that air circulates beneath the bearers. Tap down each block to ensure it is level and bedded firmly, adding or removing soil if necessary.

**3** Use a spirit (carpenter's) level to ensure that the blocks are level. If the ground is unstable, set the bricks or blocks on pads of concrete. Making sure that they are level is essential, otherwise the final decking will not be stable.

**5** Your bearers may not be long enough to stretch the whole length of the deck, in which case make sure joints are made above a block. Use a damp-proofing strip between each block and bearer to prevent water seeping up.

**6** Add a plastic sheet to suppress weeds, then saw the decking planks to size and treat with a preservative. Fix in position with galvanized nails leaving gaps of about 6mm (¼in) between planks to allow for expansion.

# MAKING GRAVEL BEDS

Sometimes an existing garden can be transformed into a low-maintenance one simply by replacing the lawn. This is especially worth considering if the physical effort of mowing is a problem or if it is too time-consuming.

Not everyone wants to be involved in a major redesign in order to reduce the amount of time and effort spent on the garden. It may be possible to change a few labour-intensive features, and the lawn is often a priority in this respect. For example, you could leave existing beds where they are, lift the grass and replace it with gravel. Even though weeding and dead-heading would still be demanding at times, the chore of mowing the lawn would be eliminated. To prevent gravel spreading on to the surrounding beds, you would need to add an edging to keep it in place.

### IN REVERSE

If you consider that a garden simply isn't a proper garden without a lawn, but are not too concerned about lots of flowerbeds to look after, you could keep the grass and fill the beds or borders with gravel instead. This will also suppress weeds in the beds. To reduce the amount of grass that needs mowing, it may be worth cutting some new beds into the lawn.

1 Start by marking out the shape and size of the bed with a length of rope, garden hose or sand sprinkled where the outline should be. Make adjustments until you are happy with the look. Oval-shaped beds are ideal for small gardens.

4 If you want to plant through the gravel, loosen the soil in the bed and fork in a generous quantity of well rotted manure or garden compost (soil mix), together with a slow-release fertilizer. Rake the soil level.

2 Cut the outline of the new gravel bed in the turf, working along the hose, rope or sand trail. Ideally, use a half-moon edger, as shown, but if you don't have an edging tool, you can achieve the same result with a spade.

3 Lift the turf from within the outline, digging down to a depth of about 10cm (4in), using a spade. This allows you to add about 8cm (3in) of gravel, well below lawn level so that the chippings do not spread on to the grass.

5 Allow the compost to settle before adding the gravel or firm it by treading it down. Then spread a 5–8cm (2–3in) layer of your chosen gravel evenly over the firmed surface, and level it carefully with a rake.

6 Gravel beds are best planted sparsely, allowing plenty of space between the plants. Try adding a few stones or pebbles here and there to enhance the effect. The result is attractive and easy to care for.

# MAKING RAISED BEDS

Although they are time-consuming and expensive to build, raised beds can solve a range of gardening problems, such as poor soil or bad drainage. They are also useful for adding interest to flat plots or for providing level ground in sloping gardens.

### DESIGNING WITH RAISED BEDS

Raised beds can be made from bricks mortared together, with "weep holes" (vertical joints free of mortar) every metre (yard) along the base of each wall to allow water to drain out, or they can be constructed from wood such as mini-sleepers (railroad ties). In small gardens they can be combined with paving to produce an intimate courtyard garden. A raised bed can be a functional square or rectangle, or designed to fit a corner in the garden.

### CHOOSING THE RIGHT SOIL

Raised beds hold a lot more soil than containers, so they are much easier to look after and you can grow much bigger plants. They also offer the opportunity to grow plants in your garden that otherwise would fail to thrive. For example, if your soil is poor or badly drained, raised beds can be filled with good quality imported loam. Indeed, if you fancy growing plants that

## MAKING A RAISED BED USING BRICKS

**1** Mark out the shape of the bed using short pointed stakes and string. Use a builders' set square (triangle) to ensure the correct angles. Define the lines with a thin stream of fine sand or use line-marker paint.

**4** Clean up the mortar joints while still wet, using a pointing trowel to produce a neat finish. Leave the mortar to harden.

like a specific type of soil, such as acid-loving rhododendrons, raised beds filled with ericaceous compost (soil mix) will provide that opportunity even if your garden soil is not suitable.

The soil in raised beds warms up more quickly than garden soil, so you can start off new plants earlier in spring. Moreover, for anyone who finds bending difficult, raised beds are particularly welcome.

2 Dig out along the markings to a depth of 30cm (12in) and width of 15cm (6in). Fill with concrete to within 5cm (2in) of the top. Firm down, level and leave for 24 hours to set. For concrete, use 1 part cement to 4 parts combined aggregate.

3 Mix some mortar and build up four or five courses of bricks, checking frequently with a spirit (carpenter's) level that the courses are level and the walls of the bed vertical. Check, too, that the sides meet at right angles.

5 Before filling the raised bed with soil, coat the inside of the walls with waterproof paint to prevent moisture from damaging the bricks.

6 Put in a layer of hardcore (rubble) topped with gravel for drainage. Fill with topsoil and stir in a layer of a good potting medium.

7 Make sure the soil is 2.5–5cm (1–2in) below the top of the walls. Then plant up the raised bed in the usual manner, watering in well.

8 The completed bed. In this case, it has been planted with a selection of culinary herbs and wild strawberries.

## MAKING A RAISED BED USING WOOD

1 Set the log edging in position and tap it into place. Check with a spirit (carpenter's) level. If you are using flexible edging, drive in stakes to which you can nail the edging.

2 Where the bed has a rectangular shape, as here, you can simply fix the wooden panels together at the corners, using galvanized nails. Drill pilot holes first to avoid splitting the wood.

3 Fill with soil, ensuring that you create the correct conditions for the types of plant you are intending to grow. In this example heathers will be planted; they will need an acid soil.

4 Plant up the raised bed and water in the plants well. Mulch the soil with a thick layer of shredded bark or gravel to retain moisture and discourage weed growth.

# MAKING A HERB WHEEL

**H**erb wheels are charming and popular features that display herbs to their best advantage. They are sometimes made out of old cart or wagon wheels, but these are not easy to obtain. It's far easier to adapt the concept and make a brick "wheel".

The larger the "wheel", the more "spokes" you can introduce. Allocate a contrasting colour, scent or leaf shape to each bed within the spokes to give definition to the wheel. Because most herbs are low growing, the walls of the wheel need not be very high.

**1** Use string and canes to mark a circle, then measure off equal points on the circumference for the spokes. Sink a length of earthenware sewage pipe in the centre. Trace over the whole design with fine sand or line-marker paint.

**2** Prepare the footings for the walls of the wheel by digging trenches that follow the outline marked on the ground. Fill these with a dry concrete mix. This will provide a firm base for the brickwork.

**3** Build the rim and spokes of the wheel with one or two courses of bricks. Set them out dry first to determine whether or not you will need to cut bricks to fit. If you do, use a bolster (mason's chisel) and club hammer, placing the brick on a bed of sand first. Remember to maintain a bonding pattern in the brickwork.

**4** Fill in the sections of the wheel and the earthenware pipe with rubble and gravel to provide drainage. Then add topsoil. Plant up the herb wheel with a selection of culinary herbs, such as sage, thyme, rosemary and lemon verbena. Water in well and add an organic mulch. Continue to water until the herbs are established.

# WALLS, FENCES & GARDEN STRUCTURES

Walls and fences perform a valuable role in the garden: not only are they useful for marking the boundary of your property and providing essential security, but they can also be used to create positive divisions between specific parts of the garden. While the construction of tall walls requires some skill, low walls can be tackled by the proficient do-it-yourselfer. Fences, on the other hand, require much less skill to erect, particularly if ready-made panels are used. These come in various styles and sizes. Other garden structures you will find useful include pergolas and arches, open-frame constructions that are ideal for supporting climbing plants. You can make them yourself or buy them in kit form.

# BUILDING BRICK WALLS

Although walls are mainly thought of as structures to provide security and privacy along the boundary, they are also useful within a garden for building terracing on a sloping plot as well as a range of other features, including raised beds, barbecues, garden screens, seats and plinths for containers and ornaments.

## RETAINING WALLS

Solid retaining walls are made from bricks or blocks mortared together. The wall will have to be strong enough to hold back the weight of the soil behind it. For this reason, always use the double-brick construction method, but this time lay the foundations and build the wall so that it slopes back slightly. Leave weep-holes (vertical joints free of mortar) every metre (yard) or so along the base of the wall to allow water to drain out from the soil. Pack in rubble behind the weep-holes and cover with coarse gravel to prevent soil washing out and to stop the weep-holes from becoming blocked with soil.

Dry-stone walls also make good retaining walls up to 1m (3ft) high. Again, the wall needs to be built so that it leans back slightly. The blocks should be selected so that they interlock as much as possible, leaving few gaps. Pack rubble behind the wall as you go to help secure each layer. Large crevices can be filled with suitable plants.

Retaining walls provide an excellent opportunity to experiment with climbers and wall shrubs.

1 All walls require a footing. For a low wall this is one brick wide; for larger, thicker walls the dimensions are increased. Dig a trench 30cm (12in) deep and put 13cm (5in) of rammed hardcore (rubble) in the bottom. Drive pegs in so that the tops are at the final height of the foundation. Use a spirit (carpenter's) level to check they are level.

4 For subsequent courses, lay a ribbon of mortar on top of the previous row, then "butter" one end of the brick to be laid.

2 To form the foundations, fill the trench with a concrete mix of 2 parts cement, 5 parts sharp sand and 7 parts 2cm (¾in) aggregate, and level it off with the top of the pegs. Use a straight-edged board to tamp the concrete down and remove any air pockets. Leave the concrete foundation to harden for a few days.

3 Lay the bricks on a bed of mortar, adding a wedge of mortar at one end of each brick as you lay them for the vertical joints. For a single brick wall with supporting piers, the piers should be positioned at each end and at 1.8–2.4m (6–8ft) intervals, and can be made by laying two bricks crossways.

5 Tap level, checking constantly with a spirit level to make sure that the wall remains level and vertical as it grows.

6 The top of the wall is best finished off with a coping of suitable bricks or with special coping stones sold for the purpose.

# ERECTING PANEL FENCES

One of the most popular choices for marking boundaries, fences offer instant privacy and security. They are less expensive to construct than walls and need less maintenance than hedges.

## DESIGNING WITH FENCES

There is a huge selection of fencing styles in a range of different materials, including various woods, metals and plastic, so you should have no problem finding a style that will enhance your garden. In the front garden, fences with a more open structure are often used. Examples include picket or post-and-rail fences, ranch-style fences and post-and-chain fences. They do not provide privacy or much security, but they are an attractive way of marking the boundary.

In most back gardens, a boundary fence should recede from view, so choose something robust enough to support climbers and wall shrubs that will help disguise it. However, in certain circumstances you might want to make a feature of a fence. Painting with a wood stain used elsewhere in the garden or to co-ordinate with a planting scheme will emphasize its presence.

### PLANNING PERMISSION

Check with your local planning (zoning) authority before erecting a new wall or fence. Normally, you require planning consent for any fence more than 1.8m (6ft) high and for a fence more than 1m (3ft) high that abuts a highway.

1 Post spikes are an easier option than excavating holes and concreting posts in position. Use a special tool to protect the spike top, then drive it in with a sledge-hammer. Check with a spirit (carpenter's) level to ensure it is vertical.

4 Lift the panel into place, supporting its free end with a scrap of wood, and fix it in position by driving galvanized nails through the holes in the brackets. Insert the post at the other end, add more clips and nail the panel to it.

2 Insert the post in the spike, checking that it is vertical again, then lay the panel in position on the ground and mark the position of the next post. Drive in the next spike so that it abuts the panel, testing for the vertical again.

3 There are various ways to fix the panels to the posts, but panel brackets are the simplest. Simply nail a pair of these galvanized U-shaped brackets to each post, either aligning them with one edge or the centre.

5 Always check that each panel is level before making the final fixings, using a spirit level. Check too that the tops of the panels are in line, unless you are working on a sloping site and are stepping them.

6 Finish off by nailing a cap to the top of each post. This will keep water out of the end grain of the timber and extend its life. Wooden and plastic caps are available, some incorporating decorative finials.

# ERECTING RANCH-STYLE FENCES

anch-style fences consist of broad horizontal rails fixed to stout upright posts. They are usually quite low, and frequently consist of just two or three rails. White-painted wood is a popular material, but wipe-down plastic equivalents are very convincing and easy to maintain. For a small garden they provide a clear boundary without becoming a visual obstruction. Also, rain and sun shadows are not created in the way that occurs with solid fences.

1 The posts of a ranch-style fence must be well secured in the ground. Use 10cm (4in) square posts, set at 2m (6ft) intervals. For additional strength, add 8cm (3in) square intermediate posts. Make sure the posts go at least 45cm (18in) into the ground. Concrete the posts into position, then fill in with soil.

2 Screw or nail the boards in place, making sure that the fixings are galvanized to protect them against rust. Use a spirit (carpenter's) level to check that the boards are horizontal. Butt-join them in the centre of a post, but try to stagger the joints on each row so that there is not a weak point in the fence.

3 Fit a post cap to improve the appearance and also protect the posts. Paint with a good quality paint recommended for outdoor use. Choose the colour of the paint carefully; you will need to keep white paint clean if the fence is to remain looking good.

ABOVE: Low ranch-style fences are ideal as less obtrusive boundary markers where the security of a tall solid fence is not required. When weathered, they can merge into the background, helping to delineate the landscape without overwhelming it.

# CONSTRUCTING TRELLIS ARBOURS

Trellises can be used to divide the garden into separate "rooms" and add a strong vertical dimension to an otherwise flat garden scheme. If you are looking for a more subtle application, a trellis can provide a secluded corner for a garden seat, creating a peaceful sitting area or arbour.

The upright trellis arbour shown here can be adapted if you want to erect an overhead trellis. For a 200cm (6ft) long arbour, you will need the following panels of lattice (diagonal) trellis: three panels, 200 x 60cm (6 x 2ft); two panels, 200 x 30cm (6 x 1ft); one concave panel, 200 x 45cm (6 x 1½ft); and one panel, 200 x 90cm (6 x 3ft). You will require six wooden posts, 8 x 8cm (3 x 3in), each 2.2m (7ft) long, and six post spikes.

1 The 200 x 60cm (6 x 2ft) panels are for the sides and top. The two narrow panels and concave panel are for the front, and the remaining panel is used horizontally across the top of the back. Trim the posts to length, making each of them 200cm (6ft) plus the depth of the socket in the post spikes.

2 Start with each back panel. Mark the post positions 200cm (6ft) apart and drive in post spikes. Insert a post into each spike socket. Using 5cm (2in) nails, temporarily fix the top of the trellis to the tops of the posts. Drill clearance holes for 5cm (2in) No.10 rust-proof screws down each side of the trellis. Drive in the screws.

3 In the same way, position the front outside posts and fix the side panels, then the inside front posts and front panels. Fix the concave panel into the panels on each side of it. Finally, fix the roof in position, screwing it into the posts. Paint the arbour with exterior decorative wood stain and leave to dry.

# ASSEMBLING ARCHES

Arches are not only quick and easy to construct, but also, if correctly positioned, can effectively transform the appearance of a garden. Flatpack kits are now available in a variety of materials and styles to suit both traditional and contemporary gardens.

## DESIGNING WITH ARCHES

Arches can perform several functions in the garden. They look lovely when positioned over a path and festooned with colourful climbing plants. Ideally, the structure should frame a distant object, such as an ornament, or focus the eye on the path as it leads tantalizingly out of sight into the next area of the garden. Arches can also be used to link borders on each side of the garden to give the overall design a feeling of coherence.

Although an arch will stand quite effectively on its own as a decorative feature in its own right, you can also incorporate one into a fence or open-frame screen (such as trellis or rustic poles) that acts as a divider between one part of the garden and another, adding greater interest to the access point. Another possibility is to erect a series of arches along a path to create an airy tunnel effect, which would create interesting patterns of shade and light and be particularly effective if fragrant climbing plants were allowed to clamber over them.

Many kit arches are made from trellis panels, which are simply nailed together, and a typical example is shown here.

**1** The simplest way to make an arch is to use a kit, which only needs assembling. First, establish the post positions, allowing a gap between the edge of the path and each post, so that plants do not obstruct the path.

**4** The next stage is to construct the overhead beams of the arch. Lay both halves on a large flat surface and carefully screw the joint together at the correct angle. Use rust-proof scews to prevent them becoming weakened by corrosion.

2 Dig four 60cm (2ft) deep holes to hold the posts. Alternatively, choose a kit with shorter posts for use with fence spikes. Drive the spikes in with a special tool, using a spirit (carpenter's) level to ensure they are vertical.

3 Position the legs of the arch in the holes. Backfill with the excavated earth and compact with your heel. Check that the legs are vertical using a spirit level. If using spikes, insert the legs and then tighten any securing bolts or screws.

5 Fit the overhead panels for the arch to the posts. In this example, they simply slot into the tops of the posts and are nailed in place. Use galvanized nails, which will resist corrosion when exposed to the elements.

**ABOVE:** The completed arch provides an interesting focal point in the garden. It can be left like this to stand on its own or be used to support a climbing plant – preferably one that produces fragrant blooms.

# MAKING PERGOLAS

A pergola is simply an open-frame structure, often placed over a patio adjacent to the house to create an intimate area for outdoor entertaining. It can be clad in shading materials, or a more natural covering of climbers. Pergolas also can be used away from the house, as a covered walkway along the sunny side of the garden or a point of focus in the middle of the garden.

There are two main styles of wooden pergola: traditional and Oriental. The former has fewer, larger roofing timbers with square-cut ends, while the latter has bevelled ends.

You can also buy plastic-coated tubular metal pergolas. These are lightweight and easy to put up.

ABOVE: If you need to attach a horizontal pole to a vertical one, saw a notch of a suitable size in the top of the vertical one so that the horizontal piece will fit snugly on top.

ABOVE: Use a halving joint where two poles cross. Mark the position of the joint on each pole and make two saw cuts halfway through the pole, then remove the waste wood carefully with a chisel. Fix the two poles together with galvanized nails or screws.

ABOVE: Bird's-mouth joints are useful for connecting horizontal or diagonal pieces to uprights. Cut out a V-shaped notch about 2.5cm (1in) deep and saw the other piece of timber to match the shape. You may need to use a chisel to achieve a good fit.

ABOVE: To join two horizontal pieces of wood, saw two opposing and matching notches so that one sits over the other. Secure the two pieces with galvanized nails or screws.

ABOVE: To fix cross-pieces to horizontals or uprights, remove a V-shaped notch, using a chisel if necessary to achieve a snug fit, then fix in place with galvanized nails.

ABOVE: Try out the assembly on the ground, then insert the uprights in prepared holes and make sure these are secure before adding any further pieces. Most pieces can be nailed together, but screw any sections subject to stress. Use rust-proof screws and nails.

ABOVE: In contrast to traditional rustic poles, this Oriental-style pergola has been made from sawn timbers. Make sure that the timbers are strong enough to take the weight of any climbers and rambling plants that you plan to grow on the pergola.

# ERECTING POSTS AND WIRES

The simplest form of support for fruiting canes consists of stout posts at 3m (10ft) intervals along the row with horizontal fencing wire strung between the posts and held taut with tensioning bolts. Only two wires are needed, one running about 60cm (2ft) from the ground, and the second at a height of about 1.2m (4ft). It is important to ensure that the posts are set firmly in the ground, since they must resist the pull of the wire when it is taut. For this reason, the end posts must be reinforced with diagonal braces.

1 Knock a stout post well into the ground at the end of the row of cane fruit. It may be easier to dig a hole and insert the post before backfilling and ramming down the earth. You can hire an auger to keep the hole size to a minimum.

2 Knock in another post at an angle of 45 degrees to the vertical to act as a support to the upright post. Nail firmly using galvanized nails so that the upright post is rigid and will support the tension of tight wires.

3 Fasten the wires around one end post and pull tight along the row, stapling it to each vertical post. Keep the wire as taut as possible. If necessary, use eye bolts on the end posts to tension the wire.

4 Fasten the canes – in this case raspberry canes – to the wires with string or plant ties. Space the canes out evenly along the wires so that the maximum amount of light can reach the leaves to ensure good growth.

# ERECTING PILLARS

**M**any climbers are suitable for training up single posts, often called pillars, although it is probably best to avoid very vigorous climbers. If space permits, a series of pillars can be erected along a path, linked garland-fashion by chunky rope along which climbers can grow. Climbers also look effective trained up tripods or, alternatively, you can make your own supports from canes.

Whichever freestanding support you choose, it is essential that it is anchored securely into the ground. This means digging a deep hole and ramming down the infill around the post. It may even be necessary to concrete the support into the ground. Check that it remains vertical while you do this.

1 Dig a hole at least 60cm (2ft) deep. Put in the post and check that it is upright. Backfill with earth, ramming it firmly down as you work. In exposed gardens a more solid pillar can be created by filling the hole with concrete.

2 Plants can be tied directly to the post, but a more natural support can be created by securing wire netting to the post. Self-clinging climbers such as clematis will then be able to climb by themselves with little attention required.

3 Plant the climber a little way from the pole. Lead the stems to the netting and tie them in. Self-clingers will take over, but plants such as roses will need to be tied in as they grow. Twining plants can be grown up the pole without wire.

# FIXING TRELLISES TO WALLS

**C**limbing and rambling plants can provide an interesting vertical element to the garden and are useful for disguising or concealing less attractive features. There are many different types to choose from, and lots of them produce beautiful, often fragrant, blooms; others are evergreen, offering year-round pleasure.

When choosing a support for a climbing plant, it is important to take into consideration the method by which it climbs. Some climbers, such as ivy, can be grown on a bare brick wall, but most will need a trellis to support them as they grow. For example, climbers such as climbing and rambler roses are not self-clinging and need to be tied in to their supports.

**1** The trellis should be sturdy and in good condition. Ensure it has been treated with wood preservative. Take the trellis panel to the wall and mark its position. The bottom of the trellis should be about 30cm (12in) from the ground. Drill holes for fixing the spacers and insert plastic or wooden plugs.

**2** Drill matching holes in a wooden batten and secure it to the wall, checking with a spirit (carpenter's) level that it is horizontal. Use wood that will hold the trellis at least 2.5cm (1in) from the wall. Fix another batten at the base, and one halfway up for trellis more than 1.2m (4ft) high.

**3** Drill and screw the trellis to the battens, first fixing the top and then working downwards. Check that the trellis is straight using a spirit level. The finished trellis should be secure, so that the weight of the climber and any wind that blows on it will not pull it away from its fixings.

# WIRES TO SUPPORT CLIMBERS

**W**here plants are to be trained up walls or solid fences, stretching horizontal wires across the surface can provide an effective means of supporting them, particularly if they need to be tied in to the supports. On a fence, the wires can be secured with galvanized staples driven into the posts, provided the plant is not a vigorous grower likely to produce heavy stems, which might pull them out.

To support trees against walls, use wires held by vine eyes. Depending on the type of vine eye, either knock them into the wall or drill and plug before screwing them in. Pass heavy-duty galvanized wire through the holes in the eyes and fasten to the end ones, keeping the wire as tight as possible.

**1** Drill holes in the wall and insert vine eyes to support the wires. If you use vine eyes with a screw fixing, insert wall plugs first. Vine eyes are available in several lengths, the long ones being necessary for vigorous climbers, such as wisteria, that need wires further from the wall.

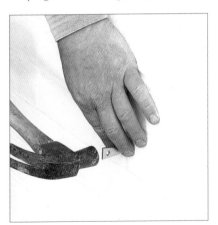

**2** The simplest vine eyes are wedge-shaped. Hammer them directly into the masonry and then feed the wire through holes. Although wedge-shaped eyes are suitable for brick and stone walls, the screw type are better for wooden fences and posts.

**3** Thread galvanized wire through the hole in the vine eye and wrap it around itself to form a firm fixing. Thread the other end through the intermediate eyes, set at no more than 2m (6ft) intervals and preferably closer, and fasten the wire around the end eye, keeping it as taut as possible.

# ROCK & WATER GARDENS

Among the many decorative aspects you can add to your garden, rock gardens and water features can make wonderful, eye-catching displays. Neither needs to be particularly large, so even the smallest garden can take advantage of what they have to offer, and each provides the opportunity of growing something different. With the former, you can choose delicate, colourful alpine plants; with the latter, lush water lilies or statuesque marginal plants. Moreover, a water feature will allow you to add movement and the relaxing sound of dappling water if you incorporate a pump to operate a fountain or cascade. Even a simple pebble fountain will bring the benefits of moving water to a patio corner.

# BUILDING ROCK GARDENS

Rock gardens benefit from an open site. If planned well, they can each enhance the other. In a level garden the soil excavated during pond installation can be used to form the base.

## DESIGNING A ROCK GARDEN

On sloping ground you can build a natural-looking outcrop or a series of terraces, or a combination of the two for a very large rockery. On a level site a more acute outcrop, with strata lines at a 45-degree angle, can work well, or choose a series of flattish stones to create a pavement effect with horizontal strata lines.

Careful planning is essential. Mark out the site using string and improve drainage if necessary – if you have heavy soil this may mean digging a hole 30cm (12in) deep, half-filling it with rubble and covering it with a layer of sharp sand before topping with good, free-draining topsoil.

## BUILDING A ROCKERY ON A SLOPE

If practicable, start at the bottom of the slope and build in layers. Choose the best-looking stone to start building your rockery and position it in the middle so that the strata lines angle gently back into the ground. About one-third of each stone will be underground, so you will have to scoop out a hole to accommodate it. Then add stones on each side so that the strata lines fall away at exactly the same angle. Add subsequent layers in the same manner.

1 The base of the rock garden is a good place to dispose of rubble and subsoil excavated during the creation of a pond. On heavy soil, take steps to improve the drainage within the outline of the rock garden.

4 Repeat the process for the next row of rocks, levering them into position. Using rollers and levers is the best way to move heavy rocks around – do not try to lift them. Make sure you have someone on hand to help too.

2 Use a special soil mixture for the top 15–23cm (6–9in), especially if soil excavated from a pond is used. Mix equal parts of soil, coarse grit and peat (or peat substitute) and spread evenly over the mound.

3 Lay the first rocks at the base, making sure that the strata run in the same direction, and add more soil mixture around them. Make sure each stone is set firm before positioning the next by ramming soil around it.

5 As each layer is built up, add more of the soil mixture and consolidate it around each of the rocks in turn. Take care to prevent the creation of voids between the rocks, which could lead to subsidence later on.

6 Make sure that the sides slope inwards and make the top reasonably flat rather than building it into a pinnacle. Position the plants, then cover the exposed soil with a layer of stone chippings to give the appearance of scree.

# PONDS WITH FLEXIBLE LINERS

After deciding on the best position for a pond in your garden, you need to consider its style and dimensions as well as the construction materials.

## PLANNING A POND

A self-sustaining pond that does not require constant maintenance should be as big as possible. Whatever the shape, it should have at least 5 square metres (54 square feet) of surface area, and so that it doesn't heat up too quickly in summer or get too cold in winter, it also needs to be at least 60cm (2ft) deep over much of that area. A marginal shelf 23cm (9in) wide and about 15cm (6in) below the surface of the water around the edge is needed to accommodate plants that like their roots in water, but their shoots and leaves in the air. Before excavating, check that there are no underground obstructions, such as pipes and cables.

**1** Mark out the shape of the pond with garden hose or rope for curves, and pegs and string for straight edges. Then remove any turf and start to excavate the pond. Redistribute the topsoil to other parts of the garden.

### WHAT SIZE FLEXIBLE LINER?

Flexible liners are available in a range of standard sizes. To calculate the size you will need for your proposed pond, use the following formula:

Length = 2 x maximum depth + maximum length of the pond

Width = 2 x maximum depth + maximum width of the pond

For example, a pond that is 3 x 2m (10 x 6ft) with a maximum depth of 50cm (20in) will require a flexible liner that is at least 4 x 3m (13 x 10ft).

**4** On stony soil, you may need to line the hole further with insulation material or special pond liner underlay. Trim the liner underlay so that it fits neatly into the hole to form a continuous layer without any gaps or voids.

2 Dig the whole area to about 23cm (9in) deep, then mark the positions of the marginal shelves. Each should be about 23cm (9in) wide. Dig the deeper areas to 50–60cm (20–24in) deep. Angle all the sides so they slope slightly inwards.

3 Check the level as you work. Correct discrepancies using sieved garden soil. Make sure there are no sharp stones on the base and sides that might damage the liner, then line the hole with builders' sand.

5 Place the liner into position without stretching it unduly. Choose a warm day as this will make it more flexible. Weigh down the edges with stones, then fill the pond slowly. Ease the liner over the contours as the pond fills.

6 Once the pond is full, trim back the excess liner to leave an overlap of at least 15cm (6in) around the edge. Cover the overlapping liner with paving or other edging. To disguise the liner, overlap the water's edge by 2.5cm (1in).

# INSTALLING PREFORMED PONDS

If you would like to have a small, formal pool with a symmetrical shape, a preformed pool unit is ideal. Such a pool is relatively easy to install and you will not have to deal with the bulky folds in tight corners that can be a problem with some of the thicker flexible liners. The stronger preformed units are useful for raised or partially raised pools because the walls are strong enough to support the internal water pressure; a decorative outer wall can be built to disguise the unit.

There are two main types of preformed unit: rigid and semi-rigid. Rigid units are made of fibreglass or thick reinforced plastic; semi-rigid units are thinner and made from a cheaper plastic. Both types are better when they are moulded into simple shapes rather than being too fussy, with narrow outlines and several different levels. The regular shapes make it easier to pave around the edges and to disguise the plastic with a slight overhang of the edge of the paving.

Do not be tempted to skimp on the preparation of the hole, and make sure that the sides and base are evenly supported. The larger units are extremely heavy when full of water and are subject to enormous strain if they are not properly supported. This can result in hairline cracks forming in even the thicker fibreglass units. Greater care is necessary with the plastic preformed units because their sides are less rigid and can bend in any uneven pressure of water and soil.

1 Place the rigid liner in the desired position. Transfer its shape on to the ground by inserting canes around the edge of the unit. Use a garden hose, rope or sand to mark the outline on the ground.

4 Remove any large stones protruding from the bottom and sides. Place the liner in the hole, then add or remove soil as necessary to ensure a good fit so that the liner is well supported. Check with a spirit level that it is level.

**2** Remove the unit and canes, and excavate the hole to approximately the required depth, following the profile of the shelves as accurately as possible. Make frequent checks with a measuring tape, or trial-fit the liner.

**3** Use a spirit (carpenter's) level and straight-edged board, laid across the rim of the hole, to check that it is level. Measure down from the board to ensure that it is the required depth. Make any necessary adjustments.

**5** Remove the pond and line the hole with damp sand if the soil is stony. With the pond in position and levels checked again, backfill with sand or fine soil, being careful not to push the pond out of level.

**6** Fill with fresh water and backfill further if necessary as the water level rises, checking the level frequently to make sure the liner has not moved. Allow to stand for a few days before stocking with plants.

# BUILDING RAISED POOLS

Raised pools are easier to empty than sunken pools, and they suffer from fewer problems, such as leaves and other plant debris blowing in. They require very little excavation and are an ideal solution on sloping sites. A substantial surround, such as twin walls, is necessary when a raised pool is made with a flexible liner so that it can withstand the internal water pressure, and this makes them more costly to build than sunken pools; if they are built with brick or walling stone, some degree of bricklaying skill will be necessary.

A simple raised pool can be made by installing a rigid preformed unit and surrounding it with a raised edge of several courses of old railway sleepers (railroad ties), secured with brackets. Alternatively, a rigid unit can be raised above the ground according to the height and type of rock edging.

## INITIAL PREPARATION

Mark the outline of the shape that the raised wall of sleepers will occupy. Check that the preformed unit will fit inside the outline. Clear the turf and other plants from the ground beneath the position of the pool and rake the soil level. Spread a layer of gravel, 5cm (2in) deep, over the marked-out area. This will prevent the bottom course of sleepers from sitting on wet soil, which could lead to rotting.

**1** After marking out and preparing a level site, lay the first course of sleepers (railroad ties) to the shape required. For a rectangle, which will hold a variety of preformed shapes, you will need to cut down half of the sleepers to form the two shorter sides and use a builders' set square (triangle) to check that a true right angle is formed by the sleepers on the short side. A square surround will save considerable cutting. Where possible, butt a cut edge to the inside of a neighbouring sleeper so that it is not exposed.

**2** As each course is placed on top of the one before, arrange the sleepers in a bonding pattern so that the joints in one course are overlapped by the sleepers above. This method will provide extra rigidity and strength in the construction. Continue adding courses of sleepers until the correct level for the preformed liner is reached. If the height of the liner is not equal to a whole number of sleepers, add another course so that the surrounding wall is slightly higher than the pool.

**3** When sufficient height is reached, spread a 5cm (2in) layer of sand inside the surround to act as a base for the liner. This will make any final levelling of the rigid unit much easier.

**4** Make the structure more rigid by screwing galvanized steel angle brackets inside the corners of the surround to connect each sleeper to its neighbour.

**5** Extra rigidity will be given by driving in galvanized nails, 15cm (6in) long, from one course of sleepers to the next. Knock the nails in at an angle on the inside edge of the surround so that they are not seen later.

**6** Line the inside of the raised bed with cheap polythene (polyethylene) secured to the sleepers by nails. This helps to prevent small mammals like mice from creeping inside the gaps between the sleepers and nesting in the sand.

**7** Enlist help to lift the pool inside the sleepers and check that the sides are level. Keep the sides of the pool just lower than the top of the sleeper wall.

**8** Add sieved soil between the pool rim and the sleepers. Firm this with a sawn-off broom handle, then level it around the rim. Add small rocks and alpine plants, top-dressed with fine grit.

# MAKING A PEBBLE FOUNTAIN

The easiest way to create a small water feature with moving water is to sink a reservoir into the ground so that it is about 5cm (2in) below the surrounding soil. Then create a catchment area for the feature by sloping the soil around the hole towards the reservoir, so that when it is lined with heavy-duty polythene (polyethylene) or a flexible pond liner, water will drain back into the reservoir. Position the pump in the reservoir and cover with heavy-duty steel mesh and smaller mesh to prevent small pebbles from falling through. Arrange cobbles and pebbles on the mesh to hide the reservoir and the catchment area to create a pebble fountain.

You can change the display by adding a millstone or another focal point, or by connecting different types of fountain jet to the outlet pipe of the submerged pump to create all manner of display fountains.

## WHAT SIZE PUMP?

The size of pump you require will depend on the amount of water needed to produce the effect you want. A small water feature will require a pump with a flow rate of about 450 litres (about 120 gallons) per hour, while a large fountain will need one that can supply 650 litres (about 170 gallons). If you want to combine features or have a watercourse you will need a much larger pump (see product packaging for details).

1 Mark out the diameter of the reservoir on the ground and dig a hole that is slightly wider and deeper than its dimensions. Place a shallow layer of sand at the bottom of the hole. Ensure the reservoir rim is slightly below the level of the surrounding soil.

4 Replace the plastic sheet over the reservoir, with the fountain pipe protruding through the hole and fit the fountain spout. Check the operation of the pump, adjusting as necessary.

2 Backfill the gap between the reservoir and the sides of the hole with soil. Firm in. Create a catchment area by sloping the surrounding soil slightly towards the rim of the reservoir. Place two bricks at the bottom to act as a plinth for the pump. Then position the pump.

3 Ensure the pipe used for the fountain spout will be 5–8cm (2–3in) higher than the sides of the reservoir. Line the catchment area with a plastic sheet and either cut it so the plastic drapes into the reservoir, or cut a hole in the centre for the fountain pipe. Fill with water.

5 Place galvanized mesh on top to support the weight of large cobbles. If you are using small stones, place a smaller mesh on top of the larger one to prevent them falling through.

6 Cover the area around the pump with a layer of cobbles. Check that the height of the spout is satisfactory. When you are happy with the fountain, finish arranging the cobbles.

# OUTDOOR REPAIRS

- Repairing drains, gutters & roofs

- Repairing fences & walls

- Repairing paths, drives & patios

# INTRODUCTION

Even in the most temperate of climates, the weather can take an incredible toll on the structure of your home. The sun can crack and blister paintwork and the coverings of flat roofs; rain can soak into woodwork, causing it to rot, or seep into brickwork or behind flashings, penetrating the walls; a moist atmosphere causes fixings to rust and fail, leading to unsightly staining of walls, sagging gutters, missing roof tiles and broken

ABOVE: Carry out the majority of outdoor maintenance work during the summer months. The dry, warm conditions will make the tasks much less arduous.

fences; the wind can carry away or wreck all manner of structures; while the action of frost and snow can cause masonry and concrete to crumble. If you are to protect your home and its surroundings from the elements, you must be prepared to carry out regular outdoor maintenance and repairs.

The secret to keeping the outside of your home looking good is not letting things get out of hand. Don't delay

ABOVE: Guttering and downpipes are essential to carry away rainwater, preventing it from running down the walls and causing damage. They must be in good condition.

### TIP

If you decide to make concrete yourself, consider buying a second-hand concrete mixer, and selling it again when the job is complete – it should save you money on buying or hiring costs.

when you see a problem; tackle it as soon as possible. Once a surface or finish outdoors begins to break down, the weather will quickly get in and speed up the process, turning a simple repair into a major project in no time. Fortunately, most outdoor maintenance and repair tasks require fairly basic skills, and they are not beyond the average do-it-yourselfer; structures tend to be of a rugged nature, requiring only a limited degree of finesse when it comes to finishing off.

Don't be over-confident, however. The weatherproofing and structural integrity of your home may depend on some tasks being done correctly, and some work may need to be carried out in fairly hazardous situations (on a roof for example). If you are in any doubt about completing a task successfully and safely, call in the experts.

ABOVE: The front door is often the first impression callers get of your home, so it pays to make sure that it is kept in good condition; that goes for the path, too.

RIGHT: Your home is a valuable investment, but it is under constant attack from the elements. You must carry out regular maintenance and repairs to prevent its fabric from deteriorating; once the weather gets in, it can cause untold damage. Fortunately, you don't need a lot of skill to carry out many outdoor tasks.

# REPAIRING DRAINS, GUTTERS & ROOFS

Making sure that the drains, downpipes and guttering around your home are well maintained is essential to ensure that rainwater and waste water from indoors are carried away without having an opportunity to damage the structure. From time to time, however, pipes or gutters may become blocked, leading to an overflow. When that happens, you must be able to deal with the situation immediately, otherwise the results could be disastrous. Roofs are exposed to the full force of the weather and may, in time, become damaged: tiles may become dislodged, felt coverings may crack or blister, and flashings may deteriorate. Fortunately, all can be fixed with relative ease.

# CLEARING DRAINS AND PIPES

A large auger can be used to clear blocked underground drains. It should be passed down through an open gully and along the drain until you reach the blockage.

The main soil pipe will run vertically either inside or outside the house. If it is blocked, your best chance of clearing it will be to unscrew an inspection hatch and then to use either an auger or drain rods to dislodge the blockage.

## USING DRAIN RODS

These are used for clearing drains when there is a blockage between one (full) inspection chamber and the next (empty) one. When you discover the empty chamber, go back to the last full one and rod from there. Drain rod sets come with a choice of heads – plungers to push the blockage along the pipe, scrapers to pull it back and wormscrews or cleaning wheels to dislodge it.

Start with a wormscrew connected to two rods, lowering it to the bottom of the chamber. Feel for the half-round channel at the bottom of the chamber and push the wormscrew along this until it enters the drain at the end.

## INSPECTING A SOIL PIPE

**1** If you suspect that the blockage is in the vertical soil pipe, or at its base, begin by unscrewing an inspection hatch. Wear gloves and protective clothing.

Push it along the drain, adding more rods to the free end, and only turn the rods clockwise, otherwise they may become unscrewed. Keep working at the obstruction until water flows into the empty chamber, then use the scraper and plunger to clear the underground drain section.

wormscrew    cleaning wheel    scraper    plunger

2 Then remove the inner cover – make sure you are standing well out of the way, as the contents of the pipe will be discharged through the opening.

3 Use an auger or drain rods to clear the blockage before replacing the cover. Make sure it is tight, then flush the system through by turning on taps and flushing lavatory cisterns.

ABOVE: Use drain rods in an inspection chamber to remove a blockage. You can hire a set from a local tool-hire company; they will come with all the necessary fittings.

ABOVE: Use an auger in a waste gully at the foot of a drainpipe to clear a blockage. Alternatively, you may be able to shift it with the aid of a bent wire coat hanger.

# CLEARING GUTTERS

The gutters and downpipes of your home are essential to remove rainwater. Nevertheless, they are exposed to the elements and are likely to become blocked, so regular maintenance is necessary to keep them clear and also to keep them in good condition.

Autumn is the ideal time to clear out gutters, removing leaves, birds' nests and general dirt and debris so that the winter rains can drain away freely. Use a garden trowel or gutter clearing tool to scoop out blockages from the gutters into a bucket, which should be secured to your ladder.

If there is a blockage near to the top of a downpipe, use something like a bent metal coat hanger to pull it out. Blockages farther down can be removed by using drain rods fitted with a wormscrew head.

LEFT: You can use a garden trowel to clean sediment and the remains of dead leaves from gutters. Protect downpipes temporarily with balls of screwed-up newspaper.

ABOVE: Alternatively, use a gutter cleaning tool specially designed for the job. You could even make your own from a length of broom handle with a piece of plywood screwed to the end. Cut the plywood so that it approximates the shape of the gutter profile and will clear the overhang of the roof covering.

# REPAIRING GUTTERS

If a gutter is sagging, the most likely cause is failure of the screws that hold a bracket in place. First, remove the section of gutter above the offending bracket.

If the screws have worked loose, it may be possible to retighten them, perhaps replacing them with longer or larger screws; if the holes have become too large, move the bracket slightly to one side, making new holes in the fascia board for the bracket screws. Make sure it aligns with its neighbour. A rise-and-fall bracket is adjustable in height and so corrects sagging gutters without the need to remove them.

## CAST-IRON GUTTERS

Traditional cast-iron gutters may look attractive, but they can give no end of trouble. To start with, they rust, so need regular painting to keep them looking good.

## UNBLOCKING DOWNPIPES

You could fit a wire balloon into the top of a downpipe to prevent birds from nesting and to keep leaves and other debris out. If a downpipe gets blocked, clear it with drain rods fitted with a wormscrew.

## PAINTING CAST-IRON GUTTERS

ABOVE: Prior to painting a cast-iron gutter, clear it out using a wire brush.

ABOVE: Treat cast-iron guttering with black bituminous paint to seal leaks.

## REPAIRING CAST-IRON GUTTERS

ABOVE: If a cast-iron gutter bolt has rusted in place, you will not be able to unscrew it. Remove it by cutting through the bolt with a hacksaw.

ABOVE: Wearing gloves, use glass fibre to repair a crack in a cast-iron gutter. Remove the gutter from the brackets to make it easier.

A more serious problem, however, is that the putty used to seal the joints can dry out, causing leaks.

You may be able to overcome minor joint leaks by cleaning the gutter out and brushing the inside with bituminous paint, but a proper repair will mean unscrewing the joint and replacing the old putty with non-setting mastic (caulking). Use a hacksaw to cut through the securing bolt if it has rusted in place. Then remove the screws holding the gutter to the fascia board and lift it clear. It will be very heavy – do not drop it, as it will shatter. Clean the joint faces, apply a layer of mastic and replace the gutter, using a new nut and bolt to connect the sections.

A crack or hole in a cast-iron gutter can be repaired with a glass fibre repair kit sold for use on car bodywork. Clean the damaged area thoroughly, then apply the glass fibre sheets over the damage and fill to the level of the surrounding metal with the resin filler provided with the kit. Glass fibre bandage can also be used in the same way for repairing cast-iron downpipes. Once it has cured, you can paint it as normal.

### PLASTIC GUTTERS

Plastic guttering has largely replaced cast iron and is easier to repair. It is also much easier to replace because it is much lighter in weight and the joints simply clip together.

Leaks at the joints between lengths of plastic gutter are prevented by rubber seals, and if these fail it is usually quite easy to replace them. Take the old seal to the shop as a guide when buying a replacement. Otherwise, try cleaning them with some liquid soap to make them more efficient. If an end stop is leaking, replace the rubber seal in this in the same way.

The alternative is to use a gutter repair sealant, available in a cartridge for use with a caulking gun, forcing this into the joint to make a seal. Self-adhesive gutter repair tape is also available for sealing splits in plastic gutters and for covering small holes in gutters and downpipes.

When separating and reconnecting lengths of plastic guttering, note that some types simply snap into their securing brackets, while others have notches cut near the ends to take the clips. When fitting a new length, you will have to cut the notches with a hacksaw.

### REPAIRING END STOPS

Rubber seals in the end stop of plastic guttering can be replaced if they fail.

## REPAIRING PLASTIC GUTTERS

ABOVE: Gutter repair sealant can be used to fix a leaking joint between gutters.

ABOVE: Repair a crack in a gutter with gutter repair tape applied to the inside.

# REPLACING ROOF SLATES

Slates that cover a pitched house roof can sometimes fail and work loose; you can repair small areas of damage yourself, but large-scale repairs may mean wholesale replacement of the roof covering, which should be entrusted to a professional roof contractor. Never walk directly on a roof covering; use a proper ladder that hooks over the ridge.

The most common cause of roof slates slipping is "nail sickness", that is one or both of the nails holding a slate has rusted through and snapped. The slate itself may be undamaged and still be on the roof somewhere.

If only one nail has failed, use a slate ripper to cut through the other one. This tool is slid under the slate, hooked around the nail and given a sharp tug to break the nail off or wrench it free of the batten (furring strip).

With the slate removed, you will be able to see, between the two exposed slates, one of the wooden battens to which the slates are attached. Cut a strip of zinc or lead sheet, about 150 x 25mm (6 x 1in), and nail one end of it to the exposed batten so that the strip runs down the roof.

Slide the slate back into its original position and secure it by bending the end of the zinc or lead strip over the bottom edge. Note that slates at the edges of the roof have mortar fillets beneath them to prevent the wind from blowing debris into the roof space. The mortar also prevents the edges from lifting in strong winds.

**1** Use a slate ripper to cut through a slate nail that is still holding the slate.

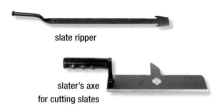

slate ripper

slater's axe
for cutting slates

## REPLACING A DISLODGED TILE

Most concrete and many clay tiles are held in place by hooks, or nibs, on the top edge, which fit over the roof battens. If these are still intact, a dislodged tile can simply be replaced by gently lifting the surrounding tiles, supporting them on wooden wedges and slipping the tile back into position. If the nibs have broken off, the tile can be replaced in the same way as a slate. Edge tiles also have a fillet of mortar beneath them.

2 Slide out the damaged slate by lifting it with the blade of a trowel, taking care not to let it fall to the ground. Look for the batten (furring strip) between the exposed slates.

3 Fit a narrow strip of lead or zinc sheet in place by nailing one end of it to the batten under the slates. Use a galvanized nail and leave the strip running down the roof.

4 Slide the old (or replacement) slate into place over the lead or zinc strip. It may help to lift the slates in the course above by inserting wooden wedges beneath them.

5 Align the bottom edge of the slate with its neighbours, then bend the end of the strip over the bottom edge of the slate to hold it securely in place.

# RIDGE TILES AND VALLEYS

On a pitched roof, ridge tiles and valleys seal the junctions between the faces of the roof.

### RIDGE TILES

The curved tiles that run along the top of a tile or slate roof are mortared into place. With age and weathering, one or two may have become loose.

To replace ridge tiles, you need a roof ladder with hooks that fit over the ridge and wheels that allow you to run it up the roof from the top of a conventional ladder.

Once you have reached the ridge, remove the loose tiles, then use a small trowel to scrape away crumbling mortar until you reach sound mortar. Dampen the tiles and trowel on a bed of fresh mortar. Place each ridge tile gently into position, tapping it down with the handle of the trowel. Add mortar to the ends of each ridge tile to fill the joints with its neighbours.

### VALLEYS

If you have a dual-pitch roof – different parts of the roof pointing in different directions – there will be a lead-lined valley between them to allow rainwater to escape and provide a junction between the tiles.

A severely damaged roof valley will need to be replaced completely – a job for professionals. But simple cracks can be repaired with self-adhesive flashing tape. Once the area around the crack has been cleaned, the tape is applied and rolled out flat using a seam roller.

### REPLACING RIDGE TILES

**1** If a ridge tile is loose, carefully lever it free and place it safely to one side. Clean away debris and apply a fresh bed of mortar.

### REPAIRING VALLEYS

**1** Clear out any leaves and debris from a leaking roof valley using a stiff brush. Wash off the lead and allow to dry completely.

2 Soak the old (or replacement) ridge tile in water, then place it in position, pushing it firmly down into the mortar.

3 With the ridge tile firmly in place and level with its neighbours, fill the joints with mortar and trowel them off to a neat finish.

2 Roll out self-adhesive flashing tape to repair the roof valley. In some cases, you may need to apply a special primer first.

ABOVE: Lead flashing is used to seal between a pitched roof and a parapet wall. It should be secured in a mortar joint.

# REPAIRING FELTED FLAT ROOFS

U nless expensive materials have been used, the average life of a felted flat roof is about 10 to 15 years. If a felted flat roof fails, it is not worth trying to repair it and you should re-cover it. However, there are things you can do to repair minor faults and to extend the roof's life.

## REPAIRING CRACKS AND BLISTERS

You will need bituminous mastic (caulking) to repair a crack or blister in a felted flat roof. Although quite messy, the job is straightforward.

First remove any loose chippings from around the damaged area with a brush. Using a hot-air gun, soften the felt first if necessary, and brush or scrape away dirt, moss and any other debris. With a crack or split in the roofing felt, pull back the edges; with a blister, make a cross-shaped pattern of cuts in the centre of the blister and peel back the four sections. If any seams are lifting, clean the area below them.

When the underlying surface has dried out, apply mastic to the exposed area and press down the edges of the crack, blister or lifted seam, using a wallpaper seam roller. If a crack cannot be closed up, use polyester reinforcing tape or flashing tape to strengthen the repair.

Some emergency roof repair compounds can be used to seal a leaking roof even if it is wet or under water. Instant repair aerosols can be used on damp roofs; check the manufacturer's instructions.

## PATCHING A BLISTER

**1** When tackling a damaged flat roof, brush all solar-reflective chippings, and dirt and debris away from the area to be repaired. This will show the extent of the damage.

### SOLAR SEAL

A solar-reflective roof seal will absorb less heat and will remain more flexible, preventing the formation of blisters.

2 If necessary, use a hot-air gun to soften the damaged roofing felt before lifting the edges with a scraper. Clean the area beneath the damage and allow to dry out.

3 If the roofing felt has formed a blister, cut a cross shape in it with a sharp knife. Carefully fold back the triangular flaps of felt to expose the structure below.

4 When the damaged area is dry, apply the repair mastic (caulking) with a small brush, working it under the flaps of felt. Be generous to ensure a waterproof seal.

5 Self-adhesive flashing tape can be applied to cover up a crack that will not close up. Make sure it is pressed down firmly, particularly around the edges.

# REPROOFING FELTED FLAT ROOFS

If a felted flat roof has several cracks or blisters, or is in bad condition generally, it is possible to waterproof it with either a bituminous emulsion or a longer-lasting elastomeric liquid rubber.

The whole roof should be swept clean before treating the surface with fungicide to kill any mould. Carry out any local repairs, then apply emulsion or liquid rubber.

Some bituminous emulsions require a priming coat before applying the main coat; all liquid rubber compounds are one-coat treatments.

When the emulsion or liquid rubber has dried, reapply stone chippings. Use new chippings if the old ones are dirty or have lost their shine – their purpose on a flat roof is to keep it cool by reflecting sunlight.

1 Sweep the whole roof clear and treat the surface with fungicide. Slit open blisters, allow the interior to dry and stick the flaps down with a layer of mastic (caulking).

2 Apply liquid rubber compound over the entire roof surface, spreading it evenly with a soft brush or broom.

3 Clean up splashes before they dry, and re-cover the roof with a good layer of loose stone chippings once the rubber compound has dried.

# REPAIRING ROOF JUNCTIONS

The junction between a flat roof and the house wall is particularly prone to damage, allowing water to seep through. The correct way to seal this joint is with lead flashing, inserted into one of the mortar courses of the wall.

If a mortar fillet has been used to seal the junction, or if lead flashing has split, the simplest way to effect a repair is with self-adhesive flashing tape.

Clean the surfaces that are to be covered and apply any necessary primer before removing the backing paper and pressing down the flashing tape, first with your fingers, then a seam roller. Wear heavy gloves when doing this. The tape can be cut with scissors if required. Make good the mortar joints where any lead flashing meets the house wall, using fresh mortar.

1 You can use self-adhesive flashing tape to seal porous felt or metal flashings. In some cases, you may need to brush on a coat of special primer first.

2 Unroll the flashing tape, peel off the release paper and press the tape into position. Try to keep it as smooth and straight as possible.

3 Run a wallpaper seam roller firmly along both edges of the flashing tape to ensure that it bonds well.

# PAINTING PIPES AND GUTTERS

New plastic pipes and gutters do not generally need to be painted. Older systems may be discoloured, however, in which case a coat of paint will rejuvenate them.

Clear away any rubbish that has built up and pour one or two buckets of water into the gutter to clean the system. Modern plastic gutters should require little additional preparation, but older cast-iron systems are prone to rusting, which can leave ugly deposits on brickwork and render. Remove the rust with a wire brush, clean the surface with turpentine, then lightly sand and remove all dust. Metal pipes and gutters should be primed, then a suitable undercoat and top coat applied. Begin at the top of the work area and work downward.

If the pipework and guttering have an existing bituminous paint finish, you will need to apply an aluminium primer before over-painting to prevent the old finish from bleeding through. When it comes to repainting the walls, any rust stains should be treated with a metal primer, otherwise they will show through the new finish. When the primer has dried, apply your decorative finish.

## PAINTING PIPES

1 Start painting pipework from the top and work downward. This will prevent any dust or dirt you may disturb from dropping on to the newly painted surface and spoiling it.

2 Use card to protect the wall behind when painting downpipes. This will also prevent the brush from picking up bits of dust from the wall, which would mar the finish.

# PAINTING BARGEBOARDS

A wealth of products has been developed for painting exterior woodwork. Never try to economize by using interior gloss paints outside; they will not cope with temperature extremes and will soon flake and split. Do not be afraid to experiment with bright colours on woodwork, but choose a finish that complements, rather than clashes with, other houses in the neighbourhood.

Choose a dry, calm day to paint and avoid working in direct sunlight, as the glare will prevent you from obtaining good, even coverage. Furthermore, if you are using a water-based (latex) paint, it will dry too rapidly, leaving hard edges.

Start by priming any bare areas, then apply an undercoat and finally one or two coats of gloss. With a standard gloss paint, begin by applying the paint vertically, and then use sideways strokes to blend it well. Work in the direction of the grain, blending in the wet edges for a uniform finish. If you are using a one-coat paint, apply the finish quite thickly in close, parallel strips and do not over-brush, as this will leave noticeable marks.

LEFT: Paint bargeboards early on in your work schedule. By starting from the top and working down you ensure that any dislodged dirt or paint droplets only fall on unpainted surfaces.

# REPAIRING FENCES & WALLS

Making sure the fences and walls around your property are kept in good condition is essential. Not only do they provide a physical marker of the boundary, but also they prevent your children or pets from straying, ensure privacy and help keep out the uninvited. Most fences are made completely of wood, which can suffer considerably when exposed to the elements. A regular programme of maintenance and repair is essential if a wooden fence is to do its job properly. Even a masonry wall can deteriorate through the effects of weathering: bricks and mortar joints can crumble, while ground movement can lead to serious damage.

# REPAIRING FENCE POSTS

A fence relies on its posts to provide much of its strength and to keep it upright – but because the posts are set in the ground and can get wet, they are prone to rotting, leading to the collapse of the fence.

The most vulnerable part of a fence post is the portion underground. Either this will be completely rotten, making the post unstable, or the post will have snapped off at ground level. In both cases, there are ways to effect a repair using the remaining sound piece of post.

If the fence post is still standing or is attached to a closeboard fence – overlapping vertical boards nailed to triangular-section horizontal (arris) rails – the best way to repair it is with a fence-post spur. This is a short concrete post that you set into the ground next to the broken post. Then you bolt the two together. Start by digging a hole roughly 30cm (1ft) square and 50cm (20in) deep in front of the broken post, that is on your side of the fence; you may need a long cold chisel and a club (spalling) hammer if you encounter concrete.

Place the spur in the hole so that it lines up with the post, then insert coach bolts in the holes in the spur, giving them a tap with a hammer to transfer their positions to the post. Drill holes in the post to take the bolts. Secure the spur to the fence post with the coach bolts

and fill the hole around it, first with a layer of hardcore (rubble), ramming it down well so that there are no voids, then with a concrete collar. Trowel this off neatly. If necessary, prop the main post upright while the concrete sets.

With a panel fence, release the adjacent panels from the post and saw through it at ground level. Then hammer a repair spike – a shorter version of the normal fence-post spike – over the rotten wood in the ground. Fit the sound portion of the post into the socket of the spike and secure it with galvanized nails or rustproof screws. Finally, refit the fence panels to the posts.

## POST LEVELS

A post level is a useful tool that can be strapped to a fence post to ensure that it is vertical in both directions when it is being installed.

## FITTING A FENCE SPUR

**1** With the fence still standing, dig a large hole – around 30cm (1ft) square – alongside the damaged post. Dig the hole to a depth of about 50cm (20in).

**2** Place the concrete fence spur in the hole, setting it up against the post so that you can mark the positions of the coach-bolt holes ready for drilling.

**3** Drill the holes in the damaged fence post, insert the coach bolts from the other side and secure the spur. Fit washers and nuts, and tighten the bolts with a spanner (wrench).

**4** Fill the large hole first with hardcore (rubble) and then with concrete. Smooth down the surface and leave to set completely, supporting the post temporarily while it does so.

## FITTING A REPAIR SPIKE

1 Remove the fence panels on each side of the damaged post. Then use a large saw, such as a bow saw or cross-cut saw, to cut off the post stump at ground level.

2 Position the repair spike carefully so that it is aligned with the remains of the old post. Using the spike driver and a sledgehammer, hammer in the repair spike over the rotten post.

### POST SPIKES

3 Insert the end of the new post into the spike socket, check that it is upright and secure it with galvanized nails or rustproof screws. Replace the fence panels.

Four different types of post spike. From the left: a normal post spike for new posts; a repair spike for rotten posts; a spike for mounting in fresh concrete; a spike for bolting down to a hard surface.

# REPLACING FENCE PANELS

A panel fence has posts regularly spaced at 1.83m (6ft) intervals. The panels come in a variety of designs – interwoven, overlapping and imitation closeboard are the most popular. They are all fixed between the posts in the same way: with either U-shaped metal clips or nails holding the panels to the posts.

If clips have been used, replacing a broken panel with a new one will be easy, since the panel is usually secured to the clips with screws. If the panel has been nailed in place, you may destroy it as you lever it out.

The new fence panel should fit exactly between the posts and can be secured in the same way. If the new panel is a tight fit at any point, use a planer-file or rasp to trim it; if it is loose, trim a section of the timber from the old panel to fill the gap.

1 To remove a fencing panel, start by levering out the nails holding it in place.

2 You may need to use a crowbar (wrecking bar) to lever out the panel.

3 If using clips to secure the new fence panel, nail these in place before sliding the panel through.

4 If using nails, drive them through the end section of the panel into the supporting post.

# REPAIRING CLOSEBOARD FENCES

Timber fences are constantly exposed to the effects of rain, sun and wind. Sooner or later, parts of a fence will rot, split, break or simply fall off. Regular treatment with preservative or stain will prolong the life of a fence, but when repairs are necessary, do not delay, otherwise the fence will no longer do its job.

## CLOSEBOARD FENCES

A closeboard fence consists of two or three horizontal triangular (arris) rails fitted between posts and supporting overlapping vertical lengths of tapered (feather-edge) boarding (pales). The result is an extremely durable and strong fence. Even so, arris rails can split and sag, while individual boards can become damaged. A horizontal gravel board will run along the bottom of the fence to protect the end grain of the vertical boards from ground moisture. Normally, this is easy to replace, as it is held with just a couple of nails or screws.

Usually, a single broken board can be levered off with a claw hammer and the nails securing it prised out. If they will not budge, hammer them into the arris rail with a nail punch. Cut the replacement board to the same length and slide its thin edge under the thick edge of the adjacent board, having levered this clear of the arris rails slightly and removed the nails from it. Then nail through both boards – each nail holds two boards. If you are

replacing several boards, use a short piece of wood as a gauge to ensure even overlapping.

Make sure you treat the end grain at the foot of any new boards with preservative before they are nailed in place, as this will be very difficult to do once they are in position. You may want to treat the overlapping edges of the boards, too, as you won't be able to reach these either. Finish the job when the boards have been fitted.

Ideally, a closeboard fence should have capping strips nailed along the top to protect the end grain at the top of the boards from the weather. This is worth doing if your existing fence does not have them. Make sure the posts have caps that will shed water, too.

## REPAIRING ARRIS RAILS

If an arris rail has split in the middle, you can buy a galvanized repair bracket that simply fits over the rail and is screwed or nailed in place. If necessary, have a helper lever the fence up, using a crowbar (wrecking bar) over a block of wood, while you fit the repair bracket.

A repair bracket that is similar, but with a flanged end, is available for reconnecting an arris rail that has broken where it is fixed to the fence post. This is screwed or nailed to both the rail and the post. You can use two of these brackets to replace a complete length of arris rail after sawing through the old rail at the ends and levering it from the fence.

## REPAIRING CLOSEBOARD FENCING

1 Use an old chisel to lever out a damaged board in a closeboard fence. Prise out any nails that pull through the board, or drive them down into the arris rails.

2 Slide the replacement board into place, fitting its narrow edge beneath the adjacent board. Make sure the overlap is even, then nail the board to the horizontal arris rails.

3 You can reinforce a broken arris rail by nailing a galvanized steel repair bracket over the broken section. Use galvanized nails, as these will resist rusting.

4 Arris rails are tapered at their ends to fit slots cut in the posts, but this can weaken a rail. If an end breaks, nail a flanged galvanized repair bracket between the rail and the post.

# REPAIRING GATES

If a wooden gate is sagging and dragging on the ground, check first that the posts are upright, using a level and paying particular attention to the hinged side. If a post has rotted, replace it with a new one.

If it is leaning slightly, it may be possible to force it back, with the gate removed, and ram some hardcore (rubble) or more concrete into the ground to hold it in place.

Wooden gates may also sag if the joints have become loose. You can fit a variety of metal brackets to support the framework of a wooden gate: flat L-shaped or T-shaped brackets at the corners where the vertical stiles meet the cross-rails or the diagonal brace, a right-angled bracket on the inside of the frame between stile and cross-rail,

and straight flat brackets to repair simple splits. All will look better if they are recessed into the wood. Alternatively, you could try replacing the main diagonal support brace or fitting longer hinges.

## REPAIRING METAL GATES

First, check that the posts are vertical, then that you can move the adjusting nuts – often these will be rusted or clogged with paint. If this is the case, wire brush off the worst of the rust and paint, and apply a silicone spray or penetrating oil until you can turn the nuts freely. Finally, adjust the hinges so that the gate no longer rubs on the ground and swings freely, but closes properly.

## REPAIRING A SAGGING GATE

ABOVE: Fit a replacement diagonal brace to support a wooden gate.

ABOVE: Using longer hinges is one way to secure a sagging wooden gate.

# REPAIRING GARDEN WALLS

A common problem with garden walls is that bricks suffer from spalling, that is the surface breaks up. This results from water getting into the brick and expanding as it freezes.

Depending on how well the wall has been built, it may be possible to

### REMOVING A DAMAGED BRICK

1 Remove the mortar around the old brick by drilling and chiselling it out.

remove the damaged brick and turn it around, using a masonry drill and a thin-bladed plugging chisel to remove the mortar from the joints. However, it is likely that mortar on the back of the brick will prevent its removal. Therefore, the only solution will be to break it up with a bolster (stonecutter's) chisel and club (spalling) hammer, then insert a new brick. Remove all the old mortar from the hole, then lay a bed of fresh mortar on the bottom of the hole. Add mortar to the top and sides of the new brick and push it into place, forcing more mortar into the gaps. Finally, finish off the joints to the same profile as the remainder of the wall.

A garden wall can crack along mortar lines, and this often indicates a problem with the foundations. There is little alternative to demolishing at least the split section, investigating the problem and making good the foundations before rebuilding it.

2 Insert a new mortared brick, pushing it in until it is flush with its neighbours.

3 Repoint the mortar around the replaced brick to the correct profile.

# REPOINTING BRICKWORK

Failed mortar joints between bricks are not only unsightly, but they also allow water into the wall, damaging the bricks when it freezes. The solution is to repoint the joints with fresh mortar.

First, use a thin-bladed plugging chisel to remove all the loose mortar until you reach sound material. Brush all the dust from the joints and dampen them with a paintbrush dipped in water or a hand-held garden sprayer.

Use a pointing trowel to push fresh mortar into the joints, working on the verticals first, then the horizontals. To do this, put a batch of mortar on a hawk – a flat metal plate or wooden board on a handle – then hold this against the wall directly beneath the joint you want to fill. Use the pointing trowel to slice off a thin strip of mortar and press it into the joint.

When you have used one batch of mortar, go back over all the joints, shaping the surface of the mortar to the required profile:

- Weatherstruck – using the edge of the pointing trowel to create a sloping profile that sheds rainwater from the wall. Start with the vertical joints and slope them all in the same direction.
- Recessed – using a square-shaped stick, or special tool.
- Flush – using sacking to rub the surface and expose the sand aggregate in the mortar.
- Concave (or rubbed) – using a rounded stick or a piece of hosepipe to make the profile.

A weatherstruck profile is often used on house walls for its rain-shedding properties, while recessed joints are only appropriate to wall surfaces inside. A concave profile is a good choice for garden walls.

ABOVE: The causes of cracked pointing should be investigated immediately and repaired. In some cases, it may be an indicator of serious problems with the foundations of the wall.

## TIPS

- The secret of good repointing is to keep the mortar off the face of the brickwork. Take great care when forcing mortar into the joints, removing any excess immediately before it dries; clean off small splashes with a stiff brush.
- Let the joints harden a little before you give them a profile.
- Clean all bricklaying tools immediately after use with clean water. They will be much more difficult to clean if the mortar is allowed to dry.

1 Use a thin-bladed plugging chisel, or a small cold chisel, with a club (spalling) hammer to chop out all the loose mortar from the joints. Take care not to damage the edges of the bricks.

2 Brush any dust and debris from the joints and dampen the existing mortar with water. This will prevent the new mortar from drying too quickly, which would weaken it.

3 Load the hawk with a small amount of mortar and hold it tightly against the wall. Push narrow strips of mortar into the joints using a small pointing trowel.

4 Allow the mortar to "go off" slightly, then shape the pointing to the profile you want; in this case a concave profile is being obtained with a length of hosepipe.

# PAINTING EXTERIOR WALLS

The best time to tackle exterior decorating is in early summer or autumn, when the weather is fine, but not too hot. Remember that this work will be on a much larger scale than an interior decorating project, so allow plenty of time to complete it. You may have to spread it over several weekends or perhaps take a week or two off work.

There is a wide range of paints available for painting exterior walls. Choose from cement paints, supplied as a dry powder for mixing with water, rough- and smooth-textured masonry paints, exterior-grade emulsion (latex) paints and exterior-grade oil-based paints for weatherboarding (siding). Masonry paints can typically be used straight from the can, but if you are painting a porous surface with a water-based product, it is advisable to dilute the first coat. Use a ratio of four parts paint to one part water.

Exterior paints come in a wide choice of colours, but exercise caution with some of the more flamboyant shades. White, cream, yellow, blue, green, soft pink and terracotta finishes, which are easy on the eye and blend into the background, are generally favoured by house buyers.

ABOVE: A typical example of pebbledash rendering. A coat of masonry paint can greatly improve its appearance. Use a brush with long bristles to get into all the cavities.

ABOVE: Avoid painting brickwork, if possible. Simply protect the face of the wall with a clear waterproofer. This will seal the surface and prevent water penetration.

## PAINTING TECHNIQUES

ABOVE: Apply smooth masonry paint using a brush with coarse bristles.

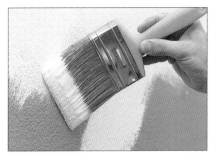

ABOVE: You should apply textured masonry paint in the same way.

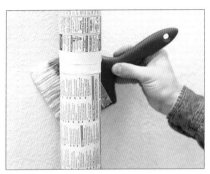

ABOVE: To protect downpipes from paint splashes, tape newspaper around them.

ABOVE: Use a banister brush to paint coarse exterior wall finishes such as pebbledash.

ABOVE: Choose a deep-pile roller for coarse surfaces and a medium one for others.

ABOVE: For speed, use a spray gun. Mask off surfaces you do not want painting.

# PAINTING EXTERIOR WOODWORK

Exterior painted woodwork includes features such as fascias, soffits and bargeboards, as well as entire surfaces such as weatherboarding (siding). New woodwork should be sanded lightly, working with the grain. Remove any dust, then wipe with a cloth moistened with white spirit (paint thinner). Seal any knots with knotting solution (shellac), and fill holes or cracks. Existing paintwork should be washed down with a solution of sugar soap (all-purpose cleaner) and water, sanded and wiped off with a cloth moistened in white spirit. Scrape off flaking paint; any bare areas should be primed and undercoated in the normal way.

## WINDOWS AND DOORS

Exterior windows and doors can be treated in much the same manner as other outdoor wood. Start by filling and

## PAINTING A DOOR

1 Remove flaking paintwork, then smooth the surface with a palm sander.

2 Apply a suitable primer and allow to dry completely before over-painting.

3 Apply one or two undercoats and lightly rub down with abrasive paper between coats.

4 Apply topcoat to mouldings and panelled areas first, then move on to cross rails.

sanding any cracks or holes in the wood. Bare wood should be primed and undercoated, while old or defective paintwork will need sanding before over-painting. If the existing paintwork is badly cracked or blistered, it should be stripped off completely and a new primer, undercoat and top coat applied.

## FENCES

For fences and outbuildings, there is a wide selection of exterior wood stains and paints in all shades. Many are water-based and plant-friendly, while being tough enough to withstand the rigours of quite harsh climates. Special paints and stains have also been developed for decking with a greater resistance to scuffing and cracking.

The best time to paint fencing is on a dry day in the late autumn, when many plants will have died back, making access easier. Brush off dirt and dust, and scrape soil away from the foot.

## PAINTING A FENCE

ABOVE: Fences and gates can be painted in all shades of bright colours.

## WEATHERBOARDS

For weatherboard (siding) surfaces, wash down with a solution of sugar soap. Leave to dry for a week. Replace any severely damaged sections and fill smaller cracks with a sealant (caulking). Punch in any protruding nails and cover with metal primer. Then prepare as for other woodwork.

## PAINTING WEATHERBOARDS

1 It is easy to miss sections of weatherboarding (siding), so paint the undersides first.

2 Paint the facing boards next, and finish off with the end grain.

# REPAIRING PATHS, DRIVES & PATIOS

The hard surfaces around your home – paths, a drive and perhaps a patio – may be paved in a variety of materials, but the most common are concrete, slabs of stone or concrete, concrete blocks and asphalt (tarmacadam). Again, the weather and the simple wear and tear of being walked on can cause damage. This must be repaired immediately, not only because it is likely to spread, particularly if water gets in and freezes during the winter, but also because a damaged surface is a danger to walk on.

Making repairs to concrete is quite easy, while any form of slab or block paving can be fixed simply by lifting and replacing the damaged sections. An asphalt surface can be made good with a cold-cure repair pack.

# REPAIRING CONCRETE PATHS

There are many materials that can be used for surfacing paths, patios and drives, and in time most will need some form of repair or maintenance.

Concrete is a popular choice for paving because it is relatively cheap and easy to lay. Nevertheless, it can crack, develop holes and crumble at exposed edges.

Before carrying out any repairs to concrete paving, it is a good idea to clean it thoroughly, and the best way of doing this is to use a pressure washer, which directs a high-velocity jet of water at the surface, removing all algae, slime, dirt and debris. Chip out any damaged areas until you have a solid surface to work on.

Minor holes and cracks can be repaired with exterior filler, quick-setting cement or mortar made with fine sharp sand rather than soft builder's sand. However, you should chip out holes to a depth of about 20mm (¾in) and enlarge cracks to allow the repair compound to grip properly. Any repairs involving edges will require the use of timber shuttering to contain the repair compound while it dries. Fitting shuttering is fairly simple, using stout timber boards. Solid timber pegs are driven into the ground so that the boards fit tightly against the edge of the existing concrete.

Spread the repair compound over the damaged area – some PVA adhesive (white glue) brushed over the surface will help it stick – and smooth it out with a trowel.

1 Sweep the path clear of dead leaves and debris. Then clean the damaged area with a pressure washer to remove all ingrained dirt and algal growth.

Before the repair compound sets completely, lightly roughen the surface with a stiff brush, as smooth concrete surfaces are dangerous to walk on when wet.

Finally, remove the shuttering and smooth off any rough areas with the trowel and a piece of sacking.

### TIP

Apart from brushing, there are several ways you can make a concrete surface more attractive and less slippery. Embedding small stones in the surface is one method, or you could provide surface texture with a plasterer's trowel or by rolling a heavy pipe over the concrete.

2 Fit a length of wood along the edge of the path and drive pegs into the ground to hold it in position. This will act as shuttering to retain the repair compound while it sets.

3 Mix up the concrete repair compound in a bucket with a small amount of water. Adding a little PVA (white) glue will improve adhesion. Soak the damaged area with water.

4 Use a plasterer's trowel to press the concrete into the damaged area. Smooth it off level with the top of the shuttering and the surrounding path. Roughen the surface lightly.

5 Allow the repair one or two days to dry, then remove the shuttering and pegs. It should come away easily, but if not, tap the wood gently with a hammer to jar it loose.

# REPAIRING CONCRETE STEPS

Solid concrete steps are very prone to damage, especially at the edges. You need only a minimum of tools to carry out the necessary work, but make sure you have the right safety wear (gloves and safety shoes) and do not work in very cold weather.

Minor damage in a concrete step, such as small cracks and holes, can be repaired in much the same way as repairing cracks and holes in plaster walls, except that you use an exterior-grade filler, quick-setting cement or mortar made from three parts fine sharp sand to one part cement.

Brushing the damaged area with PVA adhesive (white glue) will help the repair compound to stick. Smooth off the surface of the repair compound with a trowel before it has finally set, as you will not be able to rub it down afterwards. Any repair involving a broken corner or edge, however, will require shuttering to contain the repair compound while it sets.

For small repairs to the edge of a step, you need only a block of wood propped in place; more extensive repairs need complete shuttering. Exterior-grade plywood is the best material for this. Use three pieces to make a three-sided mould of the correct height. Secure them at the back with timber anchor blocks screwed to wall plugs inserted in the wall alongside the step. For

**1** Use a wire brush to remove loose and damaged concrete around the step. You may need to clean up the damaged area with a cold chisel and club (spalling) hammer.

freestanding garden steps, secure the shuttering in place with sash clamps.

Before fitting the shuttering, use a wire brush to remove any loose concrete and plant matter from the step. Hack off any split pieces of concrete and then brush the surface with PVA adhesive.

With the shuttering in place, trowel in the repair compound and smooth it off, using the top of the shuttering as a guide. As it begins to dry, when moisture has disappeared from the surface, roughen the surface with a stiff broom or hand brush. Then use a small pointing trowel to round off the edges where they meet the shuttering. Remove the shuttering when the filler, cement or mortar has set.

2 Apply a coat of PVA adhesive (white glue) to the surface to help the repair compound stick. Add a little to the water when mixing the repair concrete.

3 Fit a length of wooden shuttering to the step edge to retain the new concrete while it sets. This can be held in place by means of wooden props or pegs, or even screwed to the step.

4 Using a small trowel, fill the damaged area in the step edge with repair concrete and smooth it out. Make sure it is level with the top of the wooden shuttering.

5 Once the concrete has dried a little, give it a non-slip finish to match the surrounding surface and trowel off the sharp corner. Allow to dry completely, then remove the shuttering.

# REPAIRING ASPHALT PATHS

Asphalt (tarmacadam) is an economical and hardwearing paving material. Provided it has been laid properly, an asphalt path or drive can last a long time.

However, many domestic asphalt paths and drives may have been laid badly and may start to crumble. If weeds begin to break through the surface, it is a sign that an insufficient thickness of asphalt has been laid, and the only sensible answer is to have a second layer professionally installed on top of the existing one. Laying a complete asphalt drive, which needs to be done with hot asphalt, is not a job for the amateur. However, small holes can be readily mended without professional assistance.

The first step is to sweep the existing drive thoroughly, paying particular attention to the area around the intended repair. If the surface adjacent to the damage has become distorted, you may be able to reshape it by heating the surface with a hot-air gun and tamping the asphalt down with a piece of wood.

Cold-lay asphalt repair compounds are normally laid after the application of a coat of bitumen emulsion.

Compact the repair compound into the hole or depression, using a stout piece of wood or a garden roller for a large area. Spray the roller with water to prevent the repair compound from sticking to it. If you want, scatter stone chippings over the asphalt and roll them in.

**1** Sweep the damaged area of the path or drive to remove all dirt, dead leaves and loose particles of asphalt (tarmacadam). You must have a clean working area.

Really deep holes should be filled partially with concrete before adding the final layer of cold-fill compound.

### GOOD DRAINAGE

If there are puddles forming on your paving or if rainwater does not clear away, it is a sign that the paving has not been laid to the correct slope (fall).

This does not need to be huge, and around 1 in 100 is recommended, that is 1cm per metre ($\frac{1}{2}$in per 3ft). The fall can be checked using a straight wooden batten set on edge with a small block of wood under its lower end and a spirit (carpenter's) level on top. The thickness of the wood block depends on the length of the batten; for a 3m (10ft) batten, you need a 30mm (1$\frac{1}{4}$in) block.

2 Apply asphalt repair compound and press it into the damaged area with a spade or trowel. You may need to treat the area of the repair with a bitumen emulsion first.

3 Tamp down the filled area with a stout piece of wood or use a garden roller to flatten it. If necessary, add extra asphalt to bring the level of the repair up to the surrounding surface.

4 Large areas of asphalt often have contrasting stone chippings bedded in the surface to break up the expanse of single colour. These can be sprinkled on the repair and rolled in.

## SAFETY FIRST

• Many paving materials, especially paving slabs, are heavy and have rough edges. So it is important that you wear the correct safety gear to avoid injuries to your hands and feet – stout gloves and safety shoes are a minimum. Gloves will also provide some protection for your hands when using heavy hammers.

• If you are not strong enough, do not attempt to lift paving slabs by yourself as you could damage your back. When lifting, always bend your knees and keep your back straight.

• Take care, too, when using tools such as angle grinders for cutting paving slabs to fit in corners and other awkward areas.

# REPAIRING CONCRETE SLAB PAVING

**C**oncrete paving slabs are a common choice of surfacing for patios. The same slabs can also be used for paths, but for drives, stronger and thicker, hydraulically pressed slabs must be laid on a much stronger base. Normally, paving slabs are set on dabs of mortar on a sand base, but they may also be laid on a solid bed of mortar, a method that is always used when laying heavy-duty slabs for a drive.

A slab may have broken because something too heavy has been placed on it or as a result of something hitting it. Sometimes, individual slabs may become loose or may sink, in which case they will need to be lifted and re-laid.

If the joints around the slab have been filled with mortar, the first job will be to chip this out.

If possible, remove a broken slab from the centre, working outward; you can use a bolster (stonecutter's) chisel or a garden spade to lever up sections or whole slabs. Clean out the bottom of the hole and level it using builder's sand tamped down with a stout piece of wood – allow about 10mm (⅜in) for the mortar. Mix up a batch of mortar and put down five dabs, one in the centre and one near each corner. Also lay a fillet of mortar along each edge.

Lower the new slab, or the old slab if it is undamaged, into position and tap it down with the handle of a club (spalling) hammer. Check that the slab is level with its neighbours by placing a spirit (carpenter's) level across them. Fill the joints with more mortar.

**1** Use a narrow-bladed masonry chisel and club (spalling) hammer to chip out the mortar around a damaged paving slab. Be careful not to chip the edges of neighbouring slabs.

**4** Lower the replacement paving slab into position, making sure that it lines up with the surrounding slabs and that there is an even gap all around.

2 Lift out the broken pieces, or lever them up with a bolster (stonecutter's) chisel or spade, but protect the edges of adjoining slabs with pieces of wood.

3 Clean out the hole, removing all the old mortar. Add more sand, tamping it down well, then trowel in five blobs of mortar and apply a thin strip of mortar around the edges.

5 Use the handle of your club hammer to tap the slab down until it is exactly level. Check by laying a long spirit (carpenter's) level or a straightedge across the slabs.

6 Add some more mortar to finish the joints, smoothing it down level with the paving. Brush off the excess immediately, otherwise it will stain the surface of the paving.

# REPAIRING CONCRETE BLOCK PAVING

oncrete blocks are commonly used for paving: the individual blocks are bedded in a layer of sand and held tightly against one another by edging blocks or restraints set in mortar. Fine sand is brushed into the joints between the blocks.

Because the blocks will be packed so tightly together, a damaged block will have to be broken up to remove it.

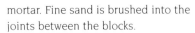

**1** Use the largest masonry bit you possess to make a hole with a hammer drill in a damaged paving block. Several holes would be even better.

**2** Use the hole as a starting point for chipping out the block with a cold chisel and club (spalling) hammer. Wear eye protection.

**3** Clean up the hole, then add a little more sand to the bottom. Level it off with the edge of a short length of wood.

**4** Push the new block into place. Tamp it down until it is level with the surrounding blocks, using a length of wood to protect it.

# REPAIRING CRAZY PAVING

This form of paving employs pieces of real stone or broken slabs (whole slabs of real stone are prohibitively expensive) and is popular for paths, although larger areas may also be paved in this manner. It can be laid in one of two ways: on a bed of sand or a bed of concrete. Like full-size paving slabs, individual pieces may break, sink or work loose.

When repairing crazy paving, you may need to re-lay quite large areas. As when laying new crazy paving, work from the sides toward the centre, using the biggest pieces with the straightest edges along the sides, then filling in with smaller pieces.

Whichever way you lay crazy paving, the joints should always be well mortared, and the mortar finished flush or shaped with a pointing trowel to give V-shaped grooves around the slab.

If an individual block becomes damaged, the main problem will be getting it out to replace it. Drill holes in it with the largest masonry drill you own, then break it up with a cold chisel and club (spalling) hammer. In this way, you will reduce the risk of damaging the surrounding blocks. Loosen the sand at the base of the hole and add a little more so that the new block sits proud of the surface by around 10mm (⅜in). Tap it down with the handle of the club hammer, then force it into its final position by hitting a stout piece of wood laid over the block with the head of the hammer. Brush fine sand into the joints.

## CLEANING PAVING

A pressure washer is the most effective way of cleaning paving, but you need to be careful not to splash yourself (wear protective clothing in any case) and not to wash earth out of flowerbeds. Never point the spray directly at the house walls.

ABOVE: Crazy paving paths can be both functional and attractive. You may need to re-lay large areas when laying new slabs.

# INDEX

ACKNOWLEDGEMENTS
The publisher would like to thank
the following for supplying pictures:
**The Amtico Company** 279t;
**Axminster** 48bl, 598 (cut-outs);
**Black and Decker** 38t; **Crossley**
276tr, 280t; **D.I.Y. Photo Library**
478bl, 522t, br, 606bl, 631bl; **Forbo
Nairn Ltd** 275t, 279bl; **Heuga**
281t; **HSS Hire Tools** 518b, 522bl;
**Hunter Plastics** 588b, 589b;
**Junckers Ltd** 272ml, br, 276b,
283t, b; **Kosset** 275b, 280b; **Peter
McHoy** 550–1; 578–9; **Rentokil**
518tl, 526t, bl, br; **Simon J. Gilham**
521, 525; **Thompson's (Ronseal
Ltd)** 518tr, 523bl, br; **Mr Tomkinson**
282t; **Wicanders** 276tl, 282b.

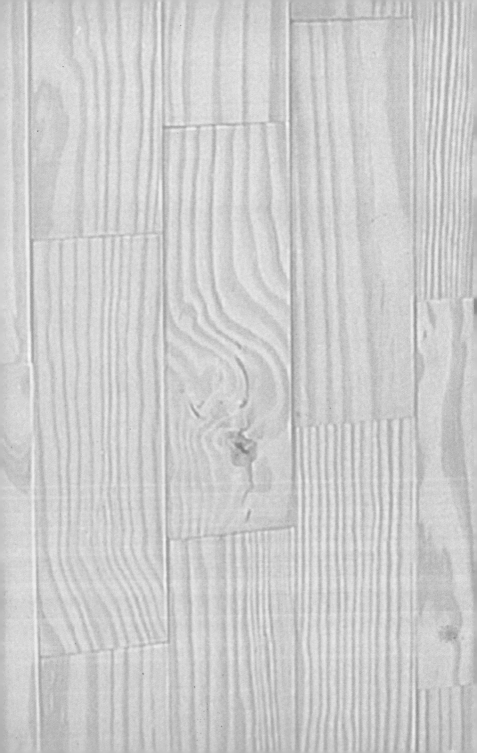